ECONOMIC THOUGHT AND THE IRISH QUESTION 1817–1870

ECONOMIC THOUGHT AND THE IRISH QUESTION
1817-1870

BY

R. D. COLLISON BLACK

Senior Lecturer in Economics
The Queen's University of
Belfast

CAMBRIDGE
AT THE UNIVERSITY PRESS
1960

PUBLISHED BY
THE SYNDICS OF THE CAMBRIDGE UNIVERSITY PRESS

Bentley House, 200 Euston Road, London, N.W. 1
American Branch: 32 East 57th Street, New York 22, N.Y.

©

CAMBRIDGE UNIVERSITY PRESS
1960

Printed in Great Britain at the University Press, Cambridge
(Brooke Crutchley, University Printer)

FOREWORD

It seems apparent to me that a wide variety of scholars will find matter of interest and value to them in Dr Black's study of *Economic Thought And The Irish Question, 1817–1870*, among them those concerned with the history of doctrine with respect to the economic role of the State, with the political and economic history of Ireland, and with the theories of 'colonialism', 'economic imperialism', and 'economic development'. To the economic theorist, however, its major importance lies in its investigation of the interaction of theory and of policy, of the economist and the statesman in a problem-case of unusually sharp and well-defined pattern, where the economist had beyond any doubt real influence, but was not master, and, moreover, was not strongly enough convinced that his standard economic doctrines suited the special circumstances, to be himself an unqualified advocate of their application to Ireland.

The 'Irish problem' had many facets, but for the economist it was primarily the problem of Irish poverty. England, of course, also at the time had a poverty problem of its own. But there was no doubt that the distress of the masses of the Irish population was without close English parallel in degree or in proportion of the total population involved. In England, moreover, there was visible, or was believed to be visible, a strong tendency towards improvement. This was less apparent for the lowest-income class than for those higher in the social scale. But the middle classes, the improvement in whose economic status was apparent to all, were, unlike the case in Ireland, growing absolutely and relatively in number and were enlarging their ranks to an appreciable extent from below as well as by their own natural increase in numbers. The future of the English working classes did not appear grim enough nor were the English poor, on the whole, discontented, despairing, and threatening enough, to disturb seriously the two-centuries-old complacency of the English ruling classes with respect to the problem of domestic poverty. A corresponding degree of complacency about the problem of the Irish poor it was, however, impossible to maintain.

The period dealt with by Dr Black was, for England, characterised by a greater degree of dominance of *laissez-faire* as doctrine and as practice than in any other period in England's history. In England, however, *laissez-faire* was tempered, as far as the poor were concerned, by the Poor Law and by private charity. Ireland had at first no Poor Law, and too small a proportion of middle- and upper-class population for its charity to make much of an impression, even had it been extraordinarily generous, on the great mass of distress below. Another difference between English and Irish poverty, moreover, was in the fact that the proportion of the population dependent on agriculture was much greater in Ireland than in England, and that Irish landlordism was to a large extent a rack-rent, absentee, and alien landlordism, without anything like the same degree of concern for agricultural improvement or of paternalistic interest in the well-being of its tenants, sub-tenants, and labourers as was displayed by the land-owning aristocracy of England.

It was not true in England, as it was in Ireland, that for the ordinary man labouring on the soil there was no prospect of betterment from working harder, or more skilfully, or with the aid of better tools, and that the only escape at all available to him from his plight was through migration to join the lowest ranks of the English working class, or through emigration to even stranger and more distant lands overseas.

No one who was at all confident at the time that he saw a remedy for Irish poverty could find the remedy within the limits of strict adherence to *laissez-faire*. As Dr Black shows, the major remedies proposed were the extension of the English Poor Law, or some variety of it, to Ireland, reform of the Irish system of land-tenure, and public investment, especially in railroads. All of these faced formidable obstacles, of doctrinal opposition, of resistance by vested interests, and of inability to attain strong conviction that the proposed remedies would prove effective.

Since England had had a system of public poor relief financed by taxation since Elizabethan times, and showed no signs of planning to abandon it, the remedy having the least mental and doctrinal hazards associated with it would seem to be extension of the Poor Law to Ireland. But to be effective and productive of revenue in Ireland, where there was no large number of prosperous tenant-farmers or of rateable merchants, it would have presumably been necessary to impose the poor-rates directly on the Irish landlords, rather than, as in England, as a charge based on the annual value of lands and tenements and levied on the occupier. Given the larger proportion of poor in Ireland, the direct tax burden on the Irish landlords would probably have had to be several times greater on the average than the corresponding indirect burden on English landlords. The Irish landlord had enough ties of friendship among the influential in England and enough direct political influence to delay any such action until 1838. I think there is evidence also in the contemporary English literature of fear that, given the extreme poverty of the Irish masses, and given the wide impression in the upper-class English circles that they were feckless and shiftless and lazy, almost any level of poor relief available as a right would be high enough to seem a more attractive means of sustenance for many of the Irish poor than working the land of a rack-rent landlord.

The English were aware that, aside from legal differences, the relations of landlord and tenant were radically different in England and Ireland.

But English landlords could not contemplate radical tampering by legislation with Irish landed institutions without foreboding that there would thus be undermined also the foundations of their own sacred rights of property.

Investment of national public funds in productive enterprise had never been common in England. Except for the Post Office and the Mint, such investment was in the middle years of the nineteenth century left to local government or to private enterprise or, as in the case of education, permitted to go by default. For an English Parliament to make appropriations for such expenditure in Ireland would, time of famine excepted, have been a greater breach of precedent than was tolerable.

In addition to all this, there was the widespread belief that the fundamental cause of Irish poverty was excess population in Ireland, that the remedies proposed would still further foster growth of population rather than restrain it, and that without restriction of population there could be no real and lasting cure of Irish poverty. If, as I gather, the problem of extreme poverty has been largely solved in Ireland, political independence and land reform have, no doubt, made large contributions. But an unplanned reduction of population, without parallel anywhere else in the western world, or perhaps in the world at large, and attained by a combination of famine, of wholesale emigration, and of the practice of Malthusian 'moral restraint' to a degree far exceeding Malthus' most optimistic expectations, seems to have been largely responsible. Aware as I am of how grievously astray modern experts, equipped with a full set of newly invented forecasting techniques, have gone in predicting modern population trends, I find it difficult to criticise the statesmen and economists of the mid-nineteenth century for failing to foresee what Providence had in store for Ireland. It would be a nice problem to set before modern experts on economic development, with the advantage of all the information made available to them in this book and elsewhere, to design a model reform programme for the Ireland of the 1840's and 1850's which the statesmen of the time could conceivably have adopted, and which would have worked successfully for the Ireland of the next century.

It is the amalgam of solid dogmas, powerful vested interests resistant to change, and statesmen and economists nevertheless persuaded that some action was necessary, which makes the story Dr Black relates so fascinating to read and so puzzling to appraise. Dr Black believes that there was too rigid adherence to dogmas and too abject yielding to vested interests for Ireland's, and I presume, also for England's, good. I have no doubt that he is right. I am struck by the fact that the nineteenth-century history of Ireland seems to offer a striking illustration of the possibility that a greater prevalence of uncalculating compassion and sympathy with suffering may at times be a better instrument of reform than the most carefully reasoned weighing of prudential pros and cons in deciding whether immediately-helpful expedients would in the long run do more good than harm.

It is interesting, nevertheless, to observe how all along the line, for the economists, as for the statesmen, dogmas *were* modified and vested interests *were* resisted or even made concessions on their own initiative. Even Joseph Hume voted in the affirmative on a Bill providing for the construction of railways in Ireland out of public funds. Even Richard Cobden conceded that 'It is difficult to deal with *Irish* questions on *English* grounds'.

In the case of John Stuart Mill, of course, his adherence to *laissez-faire* was always a conditional one, and he was by temperament and on principle always ready to consider afresh any economic or social principle wherever he recognised that the circumstances there prevailing were in any important respects substantially different from those of the England of his time, which provided the milieu for his general system of social thought. He demonstrated this readiness in practical and concrete ways where India was concerned, as well as where Ireland was concerned. But even Bentham would, in principle, adapt his rules of policy to the circumstances of time and place. As for the rule of governmental non-intervention, he would adhere to it only where the capacities and resources and motivation of the people were such that they could be relied upon, or could be induced, to do for themselves and by themselves all that needed urgently to be done. 'In Russia, under Peter the Great, the list of *sponte acta* being a blank, that of *agenda* was proportionally abundant.' It is even conceivable that Jeremy would not have protested overmuch if one of his many editors had changed the 'Russia' in this passage to Ireland, and the 'Peter the Great' to Parliament in London.

In any case, this study has few rivals in the light it throws on how the standard English doctrines as to the economic role of Government fared when they were tested by a concrete and major issue which urgently demanded consideration. It is only as such studies are multiplied that we will attain an adequate understanding of the actual role of ideas and doctrines in the political and economic history of nineteenth-century England.

JACOB VINER

PRINCETON UNIVERSITY

TO
MY MOTHER

CONTENTS

PREFACE   *page* xiii

I INTRODUCTION   1
1 Purpose of the Study, *p.* 1
2 The Irish Economy, 1817–1870, *p.* 3
3 Theory and Policy: Methods of Study, *p.* 12

II THE LAND SYSTEM   15
1 Thought and Policy on the Land Question, 1817–1845, *p.* 15
2 Thought and Policy on the Land Question, 1845–1852, *p.* 28
3 Thought and Policy on the Land Question, 1852–1866, *p.* 44
4 Thought and Policy on the Land Question, 1866–1870, *p.* 51

III THE ABSENTEE LANDLORD   72
1 Nature of the Problem, *p.* 72
2 Absenteeism and Economic Theory, *p.* 73
3 Absenteeism as a Social Problem, *p.* 82
4 Summing-up of the Debate, *p.* 84

IV THE POOR LAW   86
1 The Classical Economists' View of the Question of Irish Economic Development, *p.* 86
2 Discussion of an Irish Poor Law: The Economists' Contribution, *p.* 89
3 Discussion of an Irish Poor Law: The Politicians' Contribution, *p.* 99
4 The Course of Policy—to 1845, *p.* 105
5 The Course of Policy—1845–1849, *p.* 112
6 Thought and Policy on Irish Poor Laws, 1850–1870, *p.* 131

V PRIVATE ENTERPRISE AND FREE TRADE   134
1 The Development of Investment in Ireland—English and Irish Opinions, *p.* 134
2 Government Policy towards the promotion of Private Investment in Ireland, *p.* 144
3 The Actual Development of Private Investment over the period, *p.* 155

VI PUBLIC WORKS   159
1 Contemporary Theories of Public Works and their application to Ireland, *p.* 159
2 The System of Administration of Public Works in Ireland and its growth over the period, *p.* 168
3 Special Schemes of Public Works: (i) Drainage and Land Reclamation, *p.* 178
4 Special Schemes of Public Works: (ii) Railways, *p.* 189
5 Survey of Public Works Policy, *p.* 201

CONTENTS

VII EMIGRATION   *page* 203
    1 Thought and Policy on Irish Emigration, 1817–1830, *p.* 203
    2 Thought and Policy on Irish Emigration, 1830–1846, *p.* 215
    3 Thought and Policy on Irish Emigration, 1846–1850, *p.* 226
    4 Thought and Policy on Irish Emigration, 1850–1870, *p.* 235

VIII CONCLUSION   239
    1 The Economists and Ireland, *p.* 239
    2 The Policy pursued, and its relation to Economic Theory,
       p. 243
    3 The Facts and the Possibilities, *p.* 245

BIBLIOGRAPHY   249

INDEX   293

PREFACE

This book is intended as a case-study of the relations between economic theory and economic policy, which have more often been the subject of broad generalisations than of detailed examination. Any such study must be more microscopic than macroscopic in form, but the absence of reliable secondary sources to which the reader can be referred for many aspects of Irish history in the nineteenth century has often compelled me to include a fuller account of the circumstances surrounding the making of economic policy than might be thought necessary in other cases.

Partly because of the large volume of material which had to be examined in its preparation, and partly because it has often had to take second place to other work, this book has been over eight years in the making. In that time I have accumulated more than the usual amount of indebtedness to friends and colleagues for help and advice, which I can only inadequately acknowledge here. The greatest debt should be put first, and that I certainly owe to Professor Jacob Viner. The groundwork for this book was laid while I was working under his supervision at Princeton University: I profited immensely by the example of his meticulous scholarship, and from the stimulating experience of personal discussions with him, which never failed to provide me with new insights into classical economic thought and new ideas on my subject. At a later stage Professor Viner read the entire manuscript of the book and suggested many corrections and improvements.

I also had the benefit of discussions with Professors F. W. Fetter and W. L. Burn, both of whom read and commented on parts of the manuscript, as did Professor K. S. Isles, Dr Will E. Mason, Dr E. R. R. Green and Dr A. W. Coats. I am grateful to the staffs of many libraries for much help, but especially to Professor Arthur H. Cole, of the Kress Library of Business and Economics at Harvard University, and Mr T. P. O'Neill, of the National Library of Ireland. I need hardly add that I am alone responsible for those errors and imperfections which still remain.

Much of the material for this book was collected while I was in the United States during the academic year 1950–1, and I am indebted to the Trustees of the Rockefeller Foundation for the award of a Social Science Fellowship, and to the Senate of the Queen's University of Belfast for the grant of a year's leave of absence, which made that visit possible. I am also indebted to the Senate of Queen's University for grants from the Research Fund to enable me to examine manuscript materials in London and elsewhere, and for a further generous grant towards the cost of publication of this book.

For permission to make use of manuscript material in their custody, my thanks are due to the Marquess of Anglesey, the Earl of Clarendon, and the Keeper of Western Manuscripts at the Bodleian Library, Oxford; the Keeper of Manuscripts at the British Museum; the Deputy Keepers of the Public Records at London, Belfast and Dublin; the Librarian of University College, London; the Director and Trustees of the National Library of Ireland; the Curator of Manuscripts, Princeton University, the Head of Special Collections, Columbia University, the Head of the Manuscript Division and Archives, Baker Library, Harvard University, and the Library Committee of Yale University. Extracts from unpublished Crown Copyright material in the Public Record Office are reproduced by permission of the Controller of Her Majesty's Stationery Office.

R. D. COLLISON BLACK

QUEEN'S UNIVERSITY
BELFAST

8 January 1960

CHAPTER I

INTRODUCTION

I

OF recent years, the growing importance of economists as advisers of governments has led to an increased interest in the relationship between economic theory and economic policy, and there has been considerable discussion as to the possibility and content of a 'theory of economic policy'.[1]

At first glance, all this appears to be of purely contemporary interest and, in fact, in marked contrast to the position of the classical economists whose beliefs and environment would have precluded them from saying or doing much in the line of policy advising. But such a view is obviously superficial; it has long been commonplace to point out that the classical economists drew the line between theories and precepts much less sharply than their successors have come to do, while such writers as the late Professor D. H. Macgregor[2] have amply shown that classical acceptance of *laissez-faire* never implied undiscriminating belief in a do-nothing policy for the State. Professor Lionel Robbins has recently elaborated and supplemented this view in the course of his account of *The Theory of Economic Policy in English Classical Political Economy*.[3] Professor Robbins has there shown that the classical economists considered themselves as possessing 'a systematic body of scientific knowledge' on which policy prescriptions, essentially of a reformist character, could be based, and he provides a number of examples of this 'theory of economic policy' in action.[4]

Yet so far no detailed account has been given of the inter-relation between classical economic thought and actual economic policy over any considerable period, although, as Sir Alexander Gray has said, 'the relationship between academic discussion and the debates in Hansard furnishes a problem with many curious facets'.[5] The present work undertakes to examine the influence of classical economic thought on the policy pursued in Irish affairs by successive governments between 1817–70, and,

[1] See, for example: E. R. Walker, *From Economic Theory to Policy* (Chicago, 1943); H. G. Johnson, 'The Taxonomic Approach to Economic Policy', *Econ. J.* vol. LXI, no. 244 (December 1951); J. Tinbergen, *On the Theory of Economic Policy* (Amsterdam, 1952); H. Tyszynski, 'Economic Theory as a Guide to Policy', *Econ. J.* vol. LXV, no. 258 (June 1955).
[2] In his *Economic Thought and Policy* (London, 1949), especially chapter 3.
[3] (London, 1952).
[4] Robbins, especially pp. 169–76.
[5] Review of Macgregor's *Economic Thought and Policy*, *Econ. J.* vol. LX, no. 238 (June, 1950), p. 355.

in turn, the effect of Irish conditions on the thought of professional economists of the time.

The period from 1817 to 1870 is in some sense an entity both in the development of economic doctrine, and in Irish history. It begins with the publication of Ricardo's *Principles* and ends with the appearance of Jevons's *Theory of Political Economy*; but 1817 was also the year in which the British and Irish Exchequers were amalgamated, while 1870 saw the passing of Gladstone's First Irish Land Act.

To say that the two events mentioned in the field of political economy mark out an epoch is hardly open to question; but the significance attaching to the two events cited in Irish history seems to call for further explanation.

It might seem more appropriate to select 1800 as a starting-point, because of the passage of the Act of Union in that year, but it is true that from then until 1817 the Union was 'legislatively complete, fiscally incomplete'.[1] Moreover, in that period the Napoleonic Wars at once subjected the Irish economy to very abnormal influences and placed the question of economic policy in Ireland very much in the background.

After the Napoleonic wars the political and economic difficulties of Ireland became increasingly evident, and the 'Irish question' came to occupy the attention of Government and the time of Parliament more and more. The 'Irish question' was not settled in 1870; but the Land Act of 1870 represents the first deliberate and comprehensive interference of Parliament with the rights of landed property in Ireland, and landed property formed the foundation of the Irish economic system. In this respect 1870 provides a landmark of considerable importance in the history of economic policy in Ireland.

The period in which the authority of classical political economy was at its height was then also a period in which conditions in Ireland presented a continuing problem with which successive Governments wrestled. Such a problem clearly provides an important case for the application of a theory of economic policy, and an examination in detail of the manner in which classical economic thought influenced, or was in turn influenced by, economic policy in Ireland is capable of yielding results of some general significance.

Thus, such an examination should throw fresh light on the much-debated question of the classical attitude towards the functions of the State in economic affairs. The Irish case is of particular interest in this respect; for while Great Britain and Ireland were legally one United Kingdom throughout this period, the former presented all the features of a rapidly advancing industrial society, the latter those of a backward agricultural community—in fact, in modern terms, 'an under-developed

[1] Lord Dunraven, *The Finances of Ireland before the Union and After* (London, 1912), p. 64.

area'. Two important questions arise from this: first, how far did the theorists and the practitioners of economic policy consciously realise that the Union had created a very special problem by integrating two very different economies at widely divergent levels of development? Second, were the economists generally prepared to admit that the appropriate spheres of public and private enterprise might be different in the less-developed economy? In this connection there is special interest in the comparison of Great Britain, Ireland, and other countries such as India. The classical economists were generally insistent on the virtue of individualism, but there is some evidence that they were prepared to contemplate collective action or paternal government in cases of the Indian type, where the mass of the population could not be led to a perception of their own interests.[1] What, then, would have been the classical attitude to Ireland, economically backward, yet possessed of the institutions of representative, or semi-representative government?

Consideration of this problem in turn raises the more general question of 'economic relativity'—were the doctrines of nineteenth-century political economy regarded by their originators and popularisers as having general application, irrespective of time or place, or as being true only in relation to a particular set of institutions and conditions? The Irish case would seem to provide a significant test on which to base an answer to this. In treating these questions, then, the first step must be to provide an outline of the main features of the Irish economy during the period, as the material on which the economists had to work.

II

From the general standpoint of economic history, the period chosen for this study is clearly separated into two parts by the Great Famine of 1846. The outstanding feature of that history before 1846 was the extraordinarily rapid growth of the Irish population;[2] after 1846 it was the surging tide of Irish emigration which drew the attention of the world.

The underlying causes of this sequence of events are to be found in the condition of Irish agriculture, for throughout the whole period the majority of the Irish people were dependent on agriculture for their livelihood. According to the Census of 1841, 66 per cent of all families in Ireland obtained their living from agriculture, but this figure would have been higher had it not been for the prevalence of domestic industry in Ulster; in most other areas the proportion of families dependent on farming was at least 75 per cent.[3]

[1] See Robbins, p. 183.
[2] See K. H. Connell, *The Population of Ireland 1780–1845* (Oxford, 1950), *passim*; J. R. Hicks, *The Social Framework* (Oxford, 1942), pp. 40–2; D. V. Glass (ed.), *Introduction to Malthus* (London, 1953), pp. 25–55.
[3] *Report of the Commissioners Appointed to take the Census of Ireland for the year 1841* (Dublin, 1843), p. xviii. See T. W. Freeman, *Pre-Famine Ireland* (Manchester, 1957), p. 75.

I-2

Numerous and varied reasons for this state of affairs were assigned by contemporaries and have been discussed by historians. Many Irishmen found the cause in the blow which Ireland's infant industries had suffered by the removal of protection after the Union; Daniel O'Connell was inclined to place part of the blame, at least, on the violence of workers' combinations, especially in Dublin;[1] the lack of capital in Ireland, or the lack of security for its investment, was also widely cited for the comparative absence of industrial development in the country. It seems true to say, however, that the fundamental factor was the lack of basic raw materials; once the age of coal and iron had dawned, Ireland was placed at an inevitable disadvantage as regards industrial development.

In spite of this, there was a certain amount of industrial growth in nineteenth-century Ireland. In the north-east, especially in the city of Belfast, all the main phases and features of the Industrial Revolution were experienced,[2] while in Dublin trades such as brewing and distilling were well established. Outside these districts, dependence on agriculture was almost complete.

The condition of the vast majority then depended on the condition of agriculture: yet here the evidence of contemporary witnesses is curiously contradictory. During the pre-Famine years, many of them testified to the fact that Irish agriculture showed numerous signs of improvement and progress; yet the whole weight of evidence showed that the condition of the peasantry was generally miserable in the extreme. This paradox was clearly stated by H. D. Inglis, one of the many nineteenth-century travellers in Ireland who set down his reflections in book form:

If by improvement, be meant more extended tillage, and improved modes of husbandry,—more commercial importance, evinced in larger exports,—better roads,—better modes of communication,—increase of buildings,—then Ireland is a highly improving country; but, up to the point at which I have arrived, I have found nothing to warrant the belief, that any improvement has taken place in the condition of the people.[3]

In this respect, as with industrial development, there were important regional differences. The more fertile eastern counties generally enjoyed a somewhat higher level of prosperity than the west, but the most striking distinction was between Ulster and the rest of the country. So great was the distress of the peasants in other provinces that the prosperity of Ulster was frequently exaggerated, but W. T. Thornton expressed the matter fairly in saying that 'in Ulster only is the English tourist occasionally reminded of the happiest parts of his own country, by the comparative

[1] See his speech on the motion for a Select Committee to inquire into the condition of the Glasgow cotton spinners: *Hansard*, 3rd ser. vol. XL, cols. 1087–90 (13 February 1838).

[2] See E. R. R. Green, *The Lagan Valley, 1800–50: a Local History of the Industrial Revolution* (London, 1949).

[3] H. D. Inglis, *Ireland in 1834: A Journey Throughout Ireland during the Spring, Summer and Autumn of 1834* (London, 1834), vol. I, p. 80.

neatness of the white-washed cottages, and by the appearance of the comparatively well-dressed and well-fed inmates'.[1]

This state of affairs was the result of the system of property relations under which agriculture operated; in Ulster that system was such as to afford a reasonable incentive to improving cultivation; in the rest of the country no such incentive existed. Outwardly in Ireland the law and practice of landed property was the same as in England. The land was held in the form of substantial estates by a comparatively small number of landlords;[2] and by them leased to tenants for cultivation in return for a money rent. But that this outward similarity concealed major inward differences was amply shown by the contrast between the rural economies of England and Ireland—the one normally prosperous and certainly stable, the other decaying, slovenly, and restless.

One basic difference, from which many others followed, was that in England improvements and investments in the land—such as drainage, fencing and erection of buildings—were normally carried out by the landlord, whereas in Ireland the landlords leased the bare soil, and improvements were the responsibility of the tenant. The law, based on English usage, afforded no right of compensation to the tenant for such investments, which became the property of the landlord at the conclusion of the tenancy.

Clearly this placed a penalty on improvement. But its evil results might not have been so marked had the occupier been afforded a reasonable security of tenure, which the great majority did not possess. In the early years of the nineteenth century many Irish landlords, especially those who were absentees, let their lands on long leases at comparatively moderate rents, to individual tenants. But these head-tenants, or 'middlemen' as they were usually called, were merely speculators who sought a profit from sub-letting the estate. The pressure of population, and the lack of alternative occupations, so increased the demand for land that sub-division was universal, and two or three under-tenants might intervene between the actual cultivator and his landlord. The cultivator's rent per acre might be several times greater than that of the middleman, and his status was that of a mere tenant-at-will. Moreover, the state of the law made it possible for the landlord to distrain against any of the tenants, so that a cultivator who had punctually paid his rent to the middleman might find

---

[1] W. T. Thornton, *A Plea for Peasant Proprietors; with the Outlines of a Plan for their Establishment in Ireland* (London, 1848), p. 201.

[2] Although the classification of occupations began in Ireland with the Census of 1841, the category 'landed proprietor' was not introduced until 1861. 8412 persons were then recorded as coming into this category, but this was recognised as being an under-estimate; the 1876 *Return of Owners of Land (Ireland)* recorded 13,369 proprietors of 100 acres or more. Since the Incumbered Estates Act served to increase the number of proprietors somewhat, a reasonable estimate for the pre-Famine period would be about 10,000 land-owners in a population of 8,000,000. Cf. *Census of Ireland* (1861), part IV, p. 62; 1863 [3204–III], vol. LX, *Owners of Land (Ireland)*, (1876 (412) vol. LXXX), p. 178.

INTRODUCTION

himself subject to distress or eviction through the middleman defaulting.[1] Nor was even the middleman's tenure secure, being usually based on a lease for lives, with a covenant for renewal on payment of a fine. The right to renewal under such a lease was often the subject of litigation, and might well be challenged successfully and the tenancy ended.[2]

The practice of a lessee sub-letting a property was prohibited in 1826,[3] but even before that date landlords were beginning to attempt to end the middleman system and consolidate small holdings into larger farms—a process which necessarily involved the eviction of many tenants of the poorest class. Thereafter most tenants held directly from the landlord, who managed the property through an agent, but their security in general became no greater. Few landlords gave leases, and even if they were willing to do so, many of their smaller tenants could not afford the legal costs involved. Apart from this the competition for land was such that most prospective tenants were willing to offer rents far greater than the land could reasonably produce under any system of cultivation.[4] In consequence they quickly fell into arrears with their payments and continued in occupation under the constant threat of ejectment.

It was this state of affairs which gave rise to the many secret societies of a terrorist character which existed in rural Ireland, such as the 'Whiteboys' and 'Ribbonmen', and produced a long and repulsive record of agrarian crime. Finding no protection in the law, the peasants sought to establish their right to the occupation of land by such means as maiming the cattle and burning the ricks, or the houses, of those who went into occupation of holdings from which the previous tenant had been evicted. Murder of such 'usurping' tenants, or of particularly harsh agents, was not unknown; by universal custom, no one could be found to give evidence against those who performed such crimes, just as no one could be found to bid at auctions where goods seized for non-payment of rent or tithes were put up for sale.[5]

Only in Ulster did tenants generally enjoy some security of tenure, because of the recognition there of the custom of 'tenant-right'—'a practice or usage by which a tenant in occupation of a farm, paying or willing to pay a fair rent to his landlord, should not be evicted without being paid by the incoming tenant or by the landlord himself the full

[1] See the evidence of John Howley, Serjeant-at-Law, before the Devon Commission, *Law and Practice in Respect to the Occupation of Land in Ireland, Royal Commission, Minutes of Evidence* (1845 [606], vol. XIX), p. 5.
[2] *Law and Practice in Respect to the Occupation of Land in Ireland, Royal Commission Report* (1845 [605], vol. XIX), p. 14.
[3] By 7 Geo. IV, c. 28, 'The Sub-Letting Act'. On the actual extent of consolidation effected, see below, pp. 20–1.
[4] See the evidence of John D. Balfe before the Devon Commission: *Minutes of Evidence*, (1845 [606], vol. XIX), p. 278.
[5] See [Rev. Mortimer O'Sullivan], *Captain Rock Detected* (London, 1824), *passim*; G. C. Lewis, *On Local Disturbances in Ireland; and on the Irish Church Question* (London, 1836), esp. chs. II and III.

6

marketable price of his interest in the farm, this interest being the value of his own improvements and those inherited from his ancestors'.[1] Contemporary witnesses stressed that the purchase of tenant-right was often as much a 'goodwill' payment by the incoming tenant for the quiet enjoyment of the holding as compensation for improvements made by the occupant, so that in fact the latter was combined with a provision for security of tenure. They were unanimous in concluding that its existence largely accounted for the greater prosperity and tranquillity of Ulster. The custom had no legal basis before 1870, but was always accepted as 'one of the sacred rights of the country, which cannot be touched with impunity'.[2] Outside Ulster, most tenants could only envy their fortunate countrymen in the north, and attempt to enforce by outrage those rights which neither law nor custom accorded them.[3]

The general absence of security of land tenure, and of employment opportunities outside agriculture, combined with a rapid growth of population, produced a system of social and economic relations in Ireland widely differing from that known in Great Britain. Landlord and tenant did not enter into contracts as equals in bargaining power; very rarely was the Irish tenant what the English tenant normally was, a man with a substantial capital who proposed to rent a farm and cultivate it for profit, paying out money wages to labourers to assist him, and able to move elsewhere if the landlord's terms did not satisfy him. In the first half of the nineteenth century Irish tenants could be divided into two types—small farmers and cottier-labourers. The small farmer held his land either from a middleman or from the proprietor and paid a money rent for it, but generally he either possessed little capital, or thought it prudent to conceal what he possessed for fear of having his rent increased.[4] Many such farmers employed no labour outside their own families, but those who did usually did not pay their labourers money wages. Instead they gave their labourers a cabin and a plot of ground on which to grow potatoes, and allowed them to work out the rent in labour. Some contemporary writers recognised this as being a variant of the truck system— with wages paid in potatoes.[5] It provided the farmer with labour without

---

[1] Brian A. Kennedy, 'Tenant Right before 1870', *Ulster since 1800* (London, 1954), p. 40.
[2] Evidence of John Hancock before the Devon Commission, *Minutes of Evidence* (1845 [606], vol. xix), pp. 483–4.
[3] Tenant-right was recognised on some estates in other provinces, notably Lord Lansdowne's in Co. Kerry. See the evidence of W. S. Trench before the Select Committee of the House of Lords on the Tenure (Ireland) Bill, 2 July 1867 (H.L. Rep. 1867 (518), vol. xiv), p. 8. In many areas some payment to an outgoing tenant by his successor or his landlord was not unknown, but there was a great difference between such practices and the wellestablished custom of Ulster; see *Relations between Landlord and Tenant in Respect of Improvements in Farms, Poor Law Inspectors' Reports*, 1870 [C. 31], xiv.
[4] See below, p. 135, and references there cited.
[5] Lord Clements, *Present Poverty of Ireland* (London, 1838), *passim*; J. Wiggins, *Monster Misery of Ireland* (London, 1844), pp. 122–3; J. W. Rogers, *The Potato-Truck System of Ireland* (London, 1847), *passim*; J. Pim, *Condition and Prospects of Ireland* (Dublin, 1848), p. 124.

need for working capital, and the labourer with the security of subsistence at least for himself and his family—so long as the potato crop was good.

Poor as such a man might be, the cottier-labourer who was allowed potato ground by his employer was much more secure than a labourer who had no more than a cabin and had to take land under what was known as the 'conacre' system to secure food. Conacre, or the eleven-months system, amounted to a letting for a single crop, the land being generally manured and prepared for seed by the lessor, and the lessee paying a money rent for it. These rents were usually relatively high and, since agricultural wages were low and the demand for labour in rural areas small and fluctuating, a labourer who leased potato ground in conacre was always in a precarious position. During the summer months, when their store of potatoes was exhausted and the new crop not ready to harvest, many such cottiers from the western counties tramped eastwards in search of work, travelling to England or Scotland if need be to earn money to pay their rents; often their families had to support themselves by begging until the autumn, when the men returned and the potatoes were dug. The cottier-labourers followed this system because it gave them access to the land, and possession of a patch of land was the only way in which they could guarantee a supply of food for themselves and their families; money wages were too low and too rarely paid for any rural labourer to rely on buying his provisions in the market. The fatal defect in the system was that the food supply was never guaranteed; if the crop failed 'beggary or at least the greatest distress must necessarily ensue to many of the labourers' and their landlord had no hope of recovering his rent.[1]

With the continuing pressure of population in the years from 1817 to 1846, the distinction between the small farmers and the cottiers tended to become increasingly blurred. Sub-division had reduced many farmers' holdings to such a size that the sale of the whole produce would scarcely pay the rent, and the farmer and his family were reduced to depending on the universal subsistence crop, the potato. While such men struggled to hold their land and avoid being reduced to the status of labourers, the labourers in turn sought to escape from the conacre system by bidding for land and setting themselves up as farmers.[2] In this situation the rents which were offered came to be out of all proportion to the productivity of the land, for 'the only protection against want, the only means by which a man could procure food for his family, was by getting and retaining possession of a portion of land'.[3] In consequence, no farmer

[1] *Report of the Commission of Inquiry into the Condition of the Poorer Classes in Ireland* (1836 [38], vol. xxxiii), Appendix F, p. 16. For another, shorter, account of the conacre system, see Devon Commission Report (1845 [605], vol. xix), pp. 34–5; also Green, 'Agriculture', in Edwards and Williams, *The Great Famine*, pp. 93–5.

[2] See evidence of Rev. R. Ryan before the Lords' Select Committee on Collection and Payment of Tithes in Ireland (1831–2 (271), vol. xxii), p. 161.

[3] *Report of Geo. Nicholls, Esq., on Poor Laws, Ireland* (1837 [69], vol. li), p. 8.

with any capital behind him would compete for a tillage farm, since he could never obtain one at a rent which would leave him a fair return on his capital. Such large farmers as there were invested in cattle and took grazing lands—where good profits could be made, but very little employment was given to agricultural labourers. So, at the other end of the scale, those who were unsuccessful in the competition for land usually drifted to the nearest town in search of work, but even in the country towns the normal demand for labour never approached the supply. Though many found their way to Dublin or Belfast and the English industrial cities, there was usually a reserve of labourers in most Irish towns, willing but unable to find work at any wage, even though the current average was sixpence a day.[1]

Socially, the effect of this situation was to produce a class structure composed of the landlords and their agents, the small farmers and the cottiers. There was virtually no class of substantial tenantry, and only a very small urban middle class, to which the agents sometimes belonged, since many landlords employed solicitors in this capacity.[2] Between these classes in Ireland, the normal relation was one of antagonism rather than co-operation and mutual respect. 'There exists to the most frightful extent a mutual and violent hatred between the Proprietors and the Peasantry', wrote the Lord-Lieutenant, Anglesey, to Lord Grey in 1831,[3] and fifteen years later his successor, the Earl of Bessborough, still testified that there was 'no congeniality of feeling between those of any class'.[4] The economic situation of landlord and tenant made this inevitable, but the position was aggravated, outside Ulster, by the fact that generally the landlords were Protestants and the tenants Roman Catholics, who, up to 1838, had to pay tithes for the support of the Established Church of Ireland while their own clergy depended entirely on voluntary contributions.

Economically, the operation of the land system created a situation which was a curious hybrid—neither a pure subsistence nor a fully developed money economy, but a mixture of the two. The landlords received their rents in money from the small farmer, who obtained it from the sale of crops or livestock, sometimes supplemented from outside sources such as labour on public works or elsewhere, fishing, or the profits of an illicit still. But the rent payment was almost the only money transaction in which many small tenants were involved from year to year, since it absorbed most of their cash resources. The prevalence of very small

[1] See speech of William Roche, M.P. for Limerick; *Hansard*, 3rd ser. vol. XVII, col. 912, (3 May 1833).
[2] 'The traveller in Ireland meets only magnificent castles or miserable hovels, but no edifice holding a middle rank between the palace of the great and the cabins of the lowly; there are only the rich and the poor' (de Beaumont: *Ireland, Social, Political and Religious* (trans. W. Cooke Taylor, London, 1839), vol. I, p. 262).
[3] Anglesey to Grey, 15 April 1831, Anglesey Papers (Public Records Office, Northern Ireland [hereafter P.R.O., N.I.], T. 1068/4).
[4] Bessborough to Russell, 22 December 1846 (Russell Papers, P.R.O. 30/22/5).

9

holdings tended to reduce the regular demand for labour, while the use of the potato-truck system—itself a symptom of the poverty of the farmers—ensured that much of the employment that was given was not paid for in ready money. In general, only the landed proprietors were in a position to give steady employment to labour, but many did not do so to any great extent. Often the wealthier proprietors were absentees, and many others were struggling with properties so encumbered by debts and settlements that they could do little for their tenants.[1]

Such was the system which produced the results that puzzled travellers —increasing produce accompanied by increasing distress; the landlords indifferent or powerless, the tenants indolent and improvident. This ramshackle economy was ill-equipped to withstand any shock to its agricultural foundations; bad seasons inevitably reduced many of its members from poverty to destitution. In 1817 and again in 1822 crop failures brought much distress, met primarily by the organisation of voluntary relief.[2] When the potato blight reached Ireland in 1845, however, it was no longer a question of distress, but of disaster. The potato-truck system broke down—tenants and cottiers were left without the essentials of life and without money to pay for any substitute for the potato. Thus it was of no avail simply to import corn and meal, and in 1846 the Government had to undertake a programme of public works on an unprecedented scale in order to employ the able-bodied and give them the means of earning money to buy food. But in many rural areas there was no mechanism of wholesale or retail trade in existence, while the people tended to crowd to the relief works and neglect the cultivation of the land, so that eventually the authorities were compelled to provide direct relief in kind through the medium of soup kitchens. Inevitably jobbery and corruption went side by side with fever and starvation.[3] When Ireland emerged from the crisis, in 1848 and 1849, landlords and tenants alike were ruined. The landlords had been unable to collect their rents, and the steadily rising poor-rates were beyond the capacity of many of them to pay. Many of the tenants had been evicted, or had given up their holdings in order to obtain poor relief,[4]

---

[1] Cf. Devon Commission Report (1845 [605], vol. xix), p. 12.

[2] There was then no general system of poor relief in Ireland, but in 1817 the Government advanced £30,000 to supplement private subscriptions for relief, and in 1822 advanced £50,000 for public works, mainly road-making. Cf. Parker, *Sir Robert Peel* (London, 1891), vol. I, pp. 244–5; *Hansard*, 2nd ser. vol. VII, cols. 1124–5; Goulburn to Wellesley, 29 March 1822 (B.M. Add. MSS. 37298); and below, chapter VI, p. 171.

[3] Most contemporary, and many subsequent, accounts of the Famine are strongly biased. C. E. Trevelyan, *The Irish Crisis* (London, 1848; reprinted from vol. LXXXVII of the *Edinburgh Rev.*), gives an account of official policy from the standpoint of one of its framers. Much information is contained in the *Transactions of the Central Relief Committee of the Society of Friends During the Famine in Ireland in 1846 and 1847* (Dublin, 1852). The standard historical treatment is now Edwards and Williams (eds.), *The Great Famine; Studies in Irish History, 1845–52* (Dublin, 1956).

[4] One of the most widely criticised features of famine relief policy was the so-called 'quarter-acre' clause in the Poor Relief (Ireland) Act, 1847, which made it unlawful for any

and many who remained were unwilling to risk relying on potato cultivation again.

The Government solved the problem of the insolvent landlords through the passage of the Incumbered Estates Act of 1849, which provided for the rapid disposal of such properties through a special tribunal, the purchaser receiving a clear guaranteed title. The peasants solved their own problem through the medium of voluntary emigration, those who went first financing the passages of their relatives by remittances home. The scale of this movement was unprecedented, and between 1851 and 1860 1,163,000 people left Ireland, mostly for the United States.[1]

For some ten or fifteen years these developments seemed to provide a solution to the Irish problem. Agricultural production recovered quickly, and the countryside had an appearance of greater prosperity. The bankrupt landlords were replaced by more substantial proprietors, with a sounder knowledge of business and estate management. Reduction in the pressure of population made possible the introduction of larger farms and their cultivation by more substantial tenants.

In fact, as events later proved, these changes only touched the surface of the problem. Many of the new landowners were mere land speculators, often the creditors of the old proprietors, but less inclined to be lenient about arrears since they looked on the land solely as a source of profit. The substantial tenants whom they encouraged, because of the shift in world price trends, mostly went in for livestock rather than grain or root crops, and gave comparatively little employment. So the condition of the mass of the rural population was not improved, and emigration remained their only prospect of advancement. That the problem had not been solved was clearly revealed when a series of bad harvests in the early 1860's brought renewed distress. The events of the Fenian rising in 1865–7 startled public opinion and convinced Gladstone that prompt and far-reaching measures were essential to eliminate the discontent on which revolution could be founded.[2] Thus originated the Irish Church Disestablishment Act of 1869 and the Irish Land Act of 1870, measures which for the first time showed clear recognition of the difference between the English and Irish economies, and placed the tenure of land in Ireland on a new footing.

Board of Guardians to grant either indoor or outdoor relief to any person in occupation of more than that extent of land. See O'Neill, 'The Organisation and Administration of Relief, 1845–52', in Edwards and Williams, *The Great Famine*, p. 253.

[1] See S. C. Johnson, *A History of Emigration from the United Kingdom to North America, 1763–1912* (London, 1913), App. I, p. 350.

[2] See E. L. Woodward, *The Age of Reform, 1815–1870* (Oxford, 1938), p. 346.

III

Such, in very brief outline, was the nature and course of the Irish problem in the period of this study. To the successive Tory and Whig administrations to whom the task of governing Ireland fell it was persistent and intractable—the problem of a country which was politically disaffected and economically backward. In tackling the situation, the political and religious alignments of the time, both English and Irish, forced an uneasy vacillation between a policy of coercion and one of conciliation. Disturbances were put down with a strong hand, frequently not merely with the ordinary powers of civil law, but with special powers as well; much of the time which Parliament spent on Irish affairs was used in suspending the Habeas Corpus Act and debating bills which empowered the executive government to search for and seize arms, and to proclaim certain districts as 'disturbed' and coming under martial law.[1]

But the temporary suspension of the ordinary constitutional rights of the citizen was no solution of the problem; however often it was done, it always seemed necessary to repeat the process. Most of the Lord-Lieutenants and the Chief Secretaries of Ireland recognised the need for more positive measures, and many of their Cabinet colleagues concurred with them. Select Committees and Royal Commissions were appointed frequently, and their reports and evidence constitute perhaps the most fruitful source of information about the condition of Ireland in the nineteenth century. Many proposals for improving legislation came from them and from other sources, were debated in Parliament and sometimes found their way on to the Statute Book. Poor Laws were introduced, after extended investigations; railways and public works were authorised and much public money granted or loaned to help them. Plans for aiding emigration or cultivating waste land were amongst the 'hardy perennials' for discussion, though not action. Yet the extent of legislation on the basic problem of land tenure up to 1870 is conspicuously slight. Irish members might, and often did, introduce the question, but the landed interest was still too strong in Parliament to allow of any far-reaching measure being passed.

What part did political economy, and political economists, play in all this? What advice, if any, did the leading economists give in regard to the formulation of policy for Ireland, and to what extent was it followed? If they had no specific advice to give, how far were the policy makers influenced by the general principles which the economists had developed? These are the main questions to be examined here, but it does not seem possible to limit the inquiry to finding strictly factual answers to them

---

[1] Between 1817 and 1870 thirty-seven 'Coercion Acts' for Ireland were passed. (G. L. T. Locker-Lampson, *A Consideration of the State of Ireland in the Nineteenth Century* (London, 1907), App. LXXVIII, p. 637.)

alone. Some value judgments appear inevitable, and it is preferable that they should be openly made. So the question of whether the advice which classical political economy provided was good or bad, a help or hindrance in the framing of successful policy, will be specifically included here. The period from 1817 to 1870 appears now sufficiently, yet not unduly, remote, so that a reasonably objective judgment as to the ends of policy and the appropriateness of the means employed to achieve them should be possible.

In connection with this, it must again be stressed that the interaction of theory and policy is mutual in form. So the economists of the time will have had their own judgments to make on policy, and it will be important to consider what lessons they took from their experience of current policy in Ireland, and whether they were led by it to modify any of their theories or to evolve any new constructions.

The statement of these questions at once prompts the asking of a more general one—how can the inter-relations of economic thought and policy be traced and assessed?

It is possible for an economist to influence policy in two main ways. First, he may give specific advice on a particular problem to those responsible for policy-making. It is a commonplace to say that this approach was used to a very small extent in the nineteenth century by comparison with the present day, but it should not be thought that it was never used at all. Ministers did on occasion call for expert opinions from their contemporaries in the field of academic political economy, and sometimes followed out the advice they received with remarkable faithfulness.[1] More often, however, the economist exercised his influence not through being officially retained in a professional capacity, but through friendships and personal contacts with members of the Government, which afforded the opportunity for an exchange of views on problems of policy.

Secondly, the economist may exercise an indirect influence through his writings, either on a specific topic or on general principles. Political economists of the classical era quite frequently sought to influence public opinion, and hence the Government of the day, by making contributions to newspapers and journals on issues of current concern.[2] But their more general and abstract writings were not without their effect in practical affairs. Some, at least, of the 'laws' and 'principles' which economists set up do find their way into the current stock of accepted ideas, and so serve to direct economic policy into particular channels. The classical economists were especially influential in this respect. Their ideas about the wages-fund, about international trade, and above all about the proper place of Government in economic life, were frequently invoked to impose

---

[1] For examples in the case of Ireland, see below, pp. 46 and 108.
[2] See, for example, J. S. Mill's leading articles in the *Morning Chronicle* in 1846–7; below, p. 30.

tabus on certain lines of legislative action, and to confer the stamp of respectability on others.

In a study of the relation of economic thought and policy, it is necessary to follow out and examine these different forms of influence as fully as possible. The first, where the economist acts directly, is the easiest to trace. Comparatively few contacts of any importance can have occurred in the period here under examination which did not leave some record in the documents, published and unpublished, of the time, and of those documents a high proportion still survives.

The second, or indirect, influence is of greater overall importance, but by its very nature more difficult to demonstrate and evaluate. Yet although the question of the relationship between political economy, public opinion, and official action is clearly a difficult one, it may still be reduced to manageable terms. It is well known that in this period influential public opinion was the opinion of certain classes, and it is well established what those classes were. Now it is possible to ascertain the basis on which the majority of people in those classes are likely to have formed their opinions —what newspapers they read, what weeklies and quarterlies circulated among them, to what societies and churches they belonged. It is still possible to see what economic ideas were put forward through such media, and in many cases to discover by whom they were put forward. Thus a very fair reconstruction of the process of propagation of economic ideas is possible, though it cannot be denied that an element of uncertainty must often remain. For example, the nineteenth century was still to a significant extent a period in which ideas and projects were advanced in pamphlet form. The true influence of most pamphlets is almost impossible to assess, because their circulation is unknown; yet it is certain that many ideas of considerable importance were first ventilated in this way. A reference to a pamphlet in a statesman's correspondence or in the columns of Hansard may give some clue to its effect, but no definite conclusion is normally justifiable. In the absence of definite evidence about the influence of pamphlet publications, caution dictates that it should be regarded as minimal.

It cannot, then, be pretended that it is possible to reconstruct every channel through which the ideas of economists may have acted on policy, and show the precise importance of each. Nevertheless, in the case of Ireland in the nineteenth century there is a sufficient volume of evidence available to make it reasonable to attempt the task of answering the questions posed in the preceding sections.

CHAPTER II

THE LAND SYSTEM

I

THROUGHOUT the whole of the nineteenth century the dominant importance of agriculture in the Irish economy made the questions of tenure and cultivation of land central to any consideration of economic policy, and the wretched return which the Irish people seemed to obtain from comparatively good natural resources placed it beyond question that some positive economic policy was necessary. Whatever that policy might be, whether or not it contemplated any direct interference with the land system, its form was bound to be conditioned by the view which its formulators took of that system.

In order to examine how, in turn, those views were linked with contemporary economic theorising, the place of land and agriculture in the classical system may first be reviewed, and then set alongside actual conditions in the Irish economy. This must not be taken to mean that a static comparison of theory and fact is possible—both were in a continual process of development. An examination of their interaction can properly begin with a consideration of the Ricardian doctrine and its relation to Irish conditions in the post-Napoleonic period.

In certain respects, land plays an important part in the Ricardian system, not simply in the construction of the famous theory of rent, but also in the application of the concept of diminishing returns to the division of the social product between land, labour and capital in the course of economic progress. On the other hand Ricardo constructed his model of 'the distribution of the produce of the earth between three classes of the community' almost completely without explanation of the institutional background which he assumed, so that there is no explicit reference in his *Principles* to forms of land tenure or modes of cultivation. Ricardo was in fact interested in logical analysis, not in the comparative study of institutions[1] and it is evident from his analysis that the institutional framework which he postulated was simply that with which he was familiar— the England of his day.

Thus the existence of private property in land is assumed, and a landlord-tenant relationship in the form of a business contract as its natural corollary. Ricardo never paused to consider the foundations of this, but his friend and contemporary, Bentham, did, and virtually all the classical economists, when they considered the question of the justification for private property, found the answer in Bentham's Utilitarian philosophy.

[1] See J. A. Schumpeter, *History of Economic Analysis* (New York and London, 1954), p. 472.

Bentham held that the foundation of prosperity was not to be found in any 'natural right', but in considerations of utility or expediency—the expediency of securing to the labourer the fruits of his own industry. It is true, as later economists such as Mill and Cairnes were to point out,[1] that this affords only a limited justification for individual property in land, but to Bentham the paramount need for security in the social fabric indicated the desirability of maintaining the existing order undisturbed.[2]

The second implication of the Ricardian rent theory is that if the land-lord does not wish to cultivate the soil himself, he will have no difficulty in finding a person ready to pay him for the privilege of cultivating it—at least once all 'land of the first quality' has been brought into use. The principle of competition is thus assumed to operate in determining rent according to demand and supply—of 'corn' on the one hand, of land on the other. But if the price term of the contract is assumed to be settled by competition, it is also assumed, implicitly, that the two parties to the contract are of equal bargaining strength. Ricardo's rent analysis plainly refers to the cultivator advancing stock, the tenant 'with a capital of 1,000 pounds'[3] and makes it clear that he is to be thought of as a capitalist, employing labour. And if Ricardo and his disciples did not stress that land was a resource with many alternative uses, they certainly took it for granted that its cultivators were men to whom alternative employments were open, and who would readily move their capital out of agriculture if it did not there receive the common average return.

On the other hand, the distinction between contractual rent and eco-nomic rent made by every classical economist hinges primarily on the point that contractual rent includes an element of interest—which implies that the landlord himself may have a substantial capital invested in the soil. Economic rent then, as the distributive share accruing to landed property, is strictly confined to 'that compensation, which is paid to the owner of land for the use of its original and indestructible powers'.[4] The landlord can claim, and should obtain, no more than this from the total product, unless his investment entitles him to some part of the capitalist's share.

These, then, are the main assumptions and conclusions about land and its rent which can be taken out of the Ricardian model, and it need hardly be stressed that they differed widely from the facts of the situation in Ireland in 1817. Some of Ricardo's critics, with less taste for rigorous

[1] J. S. Mill, *Principles of Political Economy* (London, 1848), bk. II, ch. II, para. 6. J. E. Cairnes, 'Political Economy and Land', *Essays in Political Economy, Theoretical and Applied* (London, 1873), Essay VI, pp. 190–1.
[2] See R. Schlatter, *Private Property, the History of an Idea* (London, 1951), p. 247; E. Halévy, *Growth of Philosophic Radicalism*, trans. Morris (London, 1928), p. 46.
[3] Ricardo, *Principles of Political Economy and Taxation* (Sraffa's edition), ch. II, p. 71.
[4] *Ibid.* ch. II, p. 69.

analysis than he, seized on this discrepancy and used it as a basis for attack on the theory of rent. Thus Thomas Hopkins[1] quoted instances from Wakefield's *Account of Ireland* (1812) of Irish landlords arbitrarily increasing rents 'in the most harsh and odious form imaginable', but pointed out that—

If Mr Wakefield...would attend to Mr Ricardo and his followers on this point, he would learn from them that his indignation has been entirely thrown away, as rent cannot be more than the difference between the returns from the last dose of capital, and of all previous doses employed on these lands. That this difference is determined by the laws of nature, and that the arbitrary will or discretion of the proprietor has nothing at all to do with the matter....But this gentleman appears to have been too a great collector of facts, to be satisfied with a theory so much at variance with what he saw.

It was, however, not so much the theory of rent itself as the tendency of Ricardians to imply that it afforded an immutably correct guide in actual cases which stimulated Hopkins's irony. Other critics made much the same point with less vigour but more care, pointing out that while the Ricardian analysis might be correct on the basis of its assumptions, adjustment of those assumptions to accord with the Irish situation must necessarily lead to significant modification of its conclusions. One of the best examples of this is to be found in Wilmot Horton's little-known *Lectures on Statistics and Political Economy*,[2] where the Irish land situation is discussed in terms of the classical apparatus:

The application of the principle of *supply and demand* to the case of rent may be seen strikingly exemplified in the circumstances under which land is let in Ireland. In that country, from the deficiency of employment for the labouring population, and from the practice which has prevailed of letting land in minute portions, and sacrificing the permanent improvement of estates to the object of obtaining the greatest amount of present rent; the possession of land is sought, not by capitalists for the purpose of profit, but by mere labourers for the purpose of obtaining the bare means of subsistence. The number of those who have no other resources being excessive, in reference to the opportunities of obtaining land, an extreme degree of competition exists among them, and they eagerly offer any rent by which they may obtain their object. This is the reason why we so often hear of the extremely high rents at which land is let in Ireland. The tenant has not, like an English farmer, to calculate the amount of rent which the produce of his farm will enable him to pay, in addition to the ordinary rate of profit on his capital. He has no capital, he therefore requires no profit: he looks only for the means of subsistence, and his habits render a very small allowance sufficient to provide those means. He knows that many others, in the same condition with himself, are prepared to offer any rent which they have the slightest hope of being enabled to pay, in order to obtain possession of the land. Having but little to lose, the apprehension of his ultimately

---

[1] *On Rent of Land, and its Influence on Subsistence and Population* (London, 1828), especially p. 56.

[2] Sir Robert Wilmot Horton, *Lectures on Statistics and Political Economy, as Affecting the Condition of the Operative and Labouring Classes. Delivered at the London Mechanics' Institution, in 1830 and 1831* (London, 1832).

finding himself unable to fulfil his contract is not so powerful as the fear of being outbidden in the offer of rent, and thereby losing his only present resource. Under these circumstances, he offers a rent which, in many instances, he is utterly unable to pay.[1]

The point stressed by Wilmot Horton, that the Irish landlord dealt not with a capitalist tenant but with a labourer, and thus absorbed the share of profits as well as rent, was frequently made in this period, and some writers introduced as a corollary the argument that the landlord should either undertake the investment, of which the tenant was incapable, or else remit some part of the rent.[2] Such a corollary, however, could not be fitted into a strictly classical interpretation of the situation, such as was given by Torrens.[3] Torrens held that the only effect of lowering rents would be to stimulate a further increase of population. So, 'while similar causes continue to produce similar effects, the same improvident and reckless habits which now land the peasant on the verge of famine upon the inferior land which pays no rent, would also, if rents were wholly remitted, speedily land him on the verge of famine upon the fertile land which yields a surplus over and above the subsistence of the present cultivators'.[4]

Merivale, who became Drummond Professor at Oxford in 1837, on the other hand, dissented from this view and argued that under a cottier system such as existed in Ireland the landlords could depress the level of wages and so even trench upon the share of labour itself.[5]

Despite some such differences of emphasis, the orthodox economists of the early nineteenth century were virtually unanimous in interpreting the Irish land problems in the light of their available theoretical equipment. They knew that the Ricardian theory did not fit the facts as they found them; but it did not therefore follow that a reformulation of it was necessary. Rather, they recognised that the theory applied to a more advanced form of tenure and agriculture than the Irish cottier system, and a form of agriculture which yielded much higher real returns. And from this there followed readily a policy conclusion—the improvement of economic conditions in Ireland must depend on the cottier system being supplanted by capitalist farming, on the English model. There are few clearer statements of this than that given by Hutches Trower in a letter to Ricardo:[6]

It appears to me, that no permanent or substantial good can be done till all small farms and small tenancies, are got rid of. These are the curse of Ireland. They are

---

[1] Wilmot Horton, *Lectures*, Lecture VII, pp. 8 and 9.

[2] See *The South of Ireland and her Poor* (London, 1843), p. 72.

[3] R. Torrens, *A Letter to the Rt. Hon. Lord John Russell on the Ministerial Measure for Establishing Poor Laws in Ireland...* (London, 1837).

[4] Torrens, *Letter to Lord John Russell*, p. 46.

[5] H. Merivale, *Five Lectures on the Principles of a Legislative Provision for the Poor in Ireland* (London, 1838). See also Anon., *Commentaries on National Policy, and Ireland* (Dublin, 1831), p. 217.

[6] Trower to Ricardo, 10 January 1822 (*Works and Correspondence of David Ricardo*, Sraffa's ed., vol. IX, p. 145).

calculated to destroy that wholesome dependence of the lower upon the upper classes, which is one of the master links of society; and to encourage habits of idleness, which are the bane of all moral feeling. I am aware, there would be difficulty in carrying this measure into execution, but the object is most important. The two deficiencies in Ireland are *want of capital*, and *want of Industry*. By destroying small tenancies you would obtain both.

With this judgment Ricardo himself agreed in principle.

I think it desirable [he wrote in reply], that small farms, and small tenancies should be got rid of, but I do not look upon these, and many other things which might be advantageously corrected in Ireland, as the cause of the evils under which that unfortunate country groans, but as the effect of those evils. If Ireland had a good system of law—if property was secure—if an Englishman lending money to an Irishman could by some easy process oblige him to fulfil his contract, and not be set at defiance by the chicanery of sheriffs agents in Ireland, capital would flow into Ireland, and an accumulation of capital would lead to all the beneficial results which everywhere follows from it. The most economical processes would be adopted—small farms would be laid into large—there would be an abundant demand for labour, and thus would Ireland take her just rank among nations.[1]

Ricardo here stated a view widely held in, and after, his time, but one in no way contradictory of Trower's. For, as George Nicholls argued: 'Want of capital produces want of employment—want of employment, turbulence and misery,—turbulence and misery, insecurity—insecurity prevents the introduction or accumulation of capital, and so on.'[2]

Opinions might differ amongst the political economists as to the best means of administering the cure for the ills of Irish agriculture at this period, but there was virtual unanimity on the nature of the true cure:

The want of combined labour and capital on the land, is the cause of the low effective powers of agricultural industry in Ireland [wrote Torrens in emphatic italics]. When the cause of the poverty of Ireland is placed in the proper point of view, we see at once the nature of the remedies which ought to be applied, and the extent of the difficulties which are opposed to their application. Two objects must be accomplished. In the first place, farms must be consolidated, until the agricultural labour of Ireland can be performed by two-fifths of the labourers now employed in performing it; and in the second place, adequate provision must be made for maintaining the other three-fifths of the present agricultural population, which the consolidation of farms must displace from their small holdings.[3]

The extent of the difficulties involved in carrying out such a policy of agricultural resettlement was indeed very great, but for the moment that

---

[1] Ricardo to Trower, 25 January 1822, *Works*, vol. IX, p. 153.

[2] *Poor Laws—Ireland. Report of Geo. Nicholls, Esq., to His Majesty's Principal Secretary of State for the Home Department* (1837 [69], vol. LI), p. 7.

[3] Torrens, *Plan of an Association in Aid of the Irish Poor Law* (London, 1838), pp. 6 and 8. The same argument appears, partly reproduced verbatim in Torrens's other works, *The Colonisation of South Australia* (London, 1835) and *The Budget* (London, 1842), Letter v.

point may be set aside.[1] So far as agriculture and land tenure were concerned, in the pre-Famine period, the economists were in little doubt about either diagnosis or treatment. Irish agriculture was inefficient and backward, combining low productivity with high rents only through the reduction of the cultivator's standard of living to the lowest possible level. This primary evil of rack-renting, the result of the pressure of population, was further aggravated by the abuses of the tithe system.[2] By comparison, the English system of capitalist farming appeared economically efficient and socially stable. The need for a reform of the Irish system could not be denied; what more natural, then, than to suggest its replacement by that which the economists knew from experience to be a success? Whether institutions and methods which flourished in England could be implanted in Ireland and flourish there was a question simply not asked at this time.

In the circumstances of the first decade after the peace of 1815, the policy which the economists recommended was also that which the Irish landlords were disposed to put into operation. With the fall in prices following the end of the war many middlemen were ruined through the failure of their sub-tenants to meet the rents, and the landlords resumed possession. In other cases, leases merely fell in and were not renewed. Landlords in general now felt that their estates could be more profitable under a system of direct management—but the possibilities of profit could only be realised if uneconomically small holdings were consolidated into reasonably large farms, to be leased to solvent tenants.

The Sub-letting Act of 1826 and the withdrawal of the franchise from forty-shilling freeholders in 1829 provided further motives for consolidation, though contemporary opinion was that they served as only secondary stimuli to a movement already under way.[3]

Wherever consolidation was undertaken, eviction was its inevitable corollary, and this in turn led frequently through resentment to violence. Thus attempts at consolidation frequently received a disproportionate amount of unfavourable publicity, and a study of the many publications sympathetic to the tenant would create the impression that this was a period of wholesale clearances, harshly effected. Reliable evidence as to the true extent of consolidation between 1817 and 1846 is hard to obtain, but such as is available seems to point to the conclusion that it was not very great.[4] It seems beyond question that most landlords in

[1] These problems are considered below, in the chapters on Poor Laws, Public Works and Emigration.   [2] See 'Ireland', Encyclopaedia Britannica, 4th ed., suppl. p. 112.
[3] See Report of the Select Committee on the State of the Poor in Ireland, 1830 (589), vol. VII. The importance of the forty-shilling franchise as a cause of sub-division appears to have been much exaggerated by many later writers. See evidence of W. Blacker before the Lords Committee on Colonization from Ireland, Minutes of Evidence (1847 (737), vol. VI), p. 229.
[4] See K. H. Connell, The Population of Ireland, 1780–1845 (Oxford, 1950), pp. 175–81; Digest of Evidence taken before Her Majesty's Commissioners of Inquiry into the State of the Law and Practice in respect to the Occupation of Land in Ireland (Dublin, 1847), ch. XII.

this period were convinced of the necessity of ending sub-division, and desirous of making consolidations, but that they also found a considerable gulf to exist between what they thought desirable and what was possible.

Against the economic advantages of consolidation, so evident in theory, had to be set its social disadvantages, in the consequences for the evicted tenantry. Humanity prevented some landlords from attempting clearances, and fear of the consequences probably more, but there still remained those who were deterred by neither consideration and followed the course which self-interest indicated.[1]

Attempts at consolidation, and the fear of their extension, did nothing to improve the already embittered relations between landlord and tenant in most parts of Ireland. Since this policy of consolidation was one which economists advocated and supported, they naturally came to be linked in the minds of many Irishmen with the landlord class, and shared their unpopularity. Bryan, a Dublin barrister, was giving expression to a common view when he wrote in 1831:

> ...the disciples of Malthus conceive that the landowners, who are the legislators, *can do no wrong*. Their political economy was well defined by the late Mr Hazlitt, as the *divine right of landlords*. According to this school, there are to be no checks to inordinate power, no countervailing measures to arrest the evils produced by its exercise.[2]

This impression might well have been created by some of the balder theoretical statements of the advantages of consolidating small farms into large, but the comment was scarcely a fair one. Most classical economists were fully aware of the difficulties involved in the process of change, as the passage already quoted from Torrens shows.[3] But they differed in the weight which they attached to these difficulties, and while some argued that the process of consolidation must necessarily be accompanied by the introduction of a general Poor Law into Ireland, others, notably Nassau Senior, would have denied any right of relief to the displaced tenants, and placed their faith entirely in rapid emigration.[4]

Yet even the most unguarded generalisations of English economists about the Irish questions could scarcely be construed as apologies for the Irish landlord. It is one of the commonplaces of the history of economic thought that Ricardo and his contemporaries were unsympathetic towards the landed interest; the extent of this opposition has probably often been

---

[1] See the account of the eviction of Lord Stradbrook's tenants in 1823, and other cases quoted by G. C. Lewis, *On Local Disturbances in Ireland* (London, 1836), pp. 79–81.
[2] J. B. Bryan, *A Practical View of Ireland, from the Period of the Union* (Dublin, 1831), p. 118.
[3] Above, p. 19.
[4] Senior, *A Letter to Lord Howick on a Legal Provision for the Irish Poor* (London, 1831); and cf. Merivale, *Legislative Provision for the Poor in Ireland*.

exaggerated, but there can be no doubt that most of the classical writers reserved their harshest strictures for the Irish landlord:

An English landlord knows that it is not his interest to make his tenant a beggar by exacting the very hardest terms from him if he had the power of dictating the rent [wrote Ricardo], not so the Irish landlords—they not only do not see the benefits which would result to themselves from encouraging a spirit of industry and accumulation in their tenants, but appear to consider the people as beings of a different race who are habituated to all species of oppression: they will for the sake of a little present rent, divide and sub-divide their farms till they receive from each tenant the merest trifle of rent, altho' the aggregate is considerable.—They consider as nothing the severe means to which they are obliged to resort to collect these rents, nor to the individual suffering which it occasions. Ireland is an oppressed country— not oppressed by England, but by the aristocracy which rules with a rod of Iron within it.[1]

Although Ricardo here attacked the rapacity of the landlords in permitting sub-division where it increased their rent roll, his successors in later years were not slow to denounce the heartless behaviour of those who uprooted the cottiers they had thus permitted to settle on their lands; Poulett Scrope, for example, spoke vividly of the evicted cottier 'flung away to rot on the nearest dunghill'.[2] This feeling against the Irish landlord grew as the situation worsened; a very typical expression of it appeared in 1833 in the columns of the *Morning Chronicle*, then the daily spokesman of liberal political economy:

the resources of England are at the command of the Irish landholder, who could not exist for a moment without them....In plain English, the people of England are taxed to keep up a large army in Ireland to collect rents and tithes. When violation of law is spoken of, interference with the right of landlords to pillage their tenants is all that is meant.[3]

Such quotations could easily be multiplied, and would certainly absolve the economists from the charge of having heartlessly asserted the 'divine right of [Irish] landlords'; yet at the same time this raises a more subtle charge against them—that they were involved in a contradiction, by advocating an economic policy—the introduction of capitalist farming— and denouncing those who wished to put it into effect. At least one contemporary observer, Samuel Laing, saw this clearly:

with singular inconsistency, those Irish landlords who are taking the most vigorous and effective measures for introducing that system of large-scale occupancy on their estates, by ejecting and clearing their land of the small cottar tenants, are universally condemned, and held up to public reprobation, by those very persons, journalists and political economists, who approve and recommend the principle, and the introduction of large farm occupancy, as the only salvation of Ireland. This incon-

[1] Ricardo to Trower, 24 July 1823, *Works* (Sraffa's ed.), vol. IX, p. 314.
[2] G. P. Scrope, *Principles of Political Economy* (London, 1833), p. 130.
[3] *Morning Chronicle* (London), 28 February 1833.

sistency shows that there must be something wrong in a theory which is so universally condemned by the secret instinct of good sense and right feeling of the public mind, when the very first step is taken by an individual landlord in Ireland to bring the theory into practice on his estate.[1]

The line of policy which the classical economists at first advocated for the Irish land was in plain fact impracticable. It necessarily implied the simultaneous adoption of a coherent group of measures—if the new system of farming were to succeed, clearances must be accompanied by organised emigration, poor relief, or the provision of alternative employment, or a combination of all these. Since these measures were not carried through in any co-ordinated fashion, clearances alone could not be successful. Even had all the concomitant measures been put into effect in good time, however, the system of English farming could hardly have succeeded in Ireland, in face of the settled opposition of the tenants and cottiers to all that it implied. They did not wish to exchange the status of occupying cultivators for that of day labourers, however strong the logic of the proof that they might be more prosperous in the latter state— and they were prepared to go to virtually any lengths to prevent the change. As quite a few contemporary observers saw, agrarian outrages, when viewed in perspective, were not merely insensate outbursts of hatred: 'they appear', wrote John Revans, the Secretary of the Irish Poor Law Commission, 'rather as cool and deliberate punishments inflicted by a community upon those who had offended against the general laws of that community—laws enacted not by the legislature, but by a still more powerful lawgiver—public opinion'.[2]

That the basic purpose of these general laws ran directly counter to any policy of clearances was plain at least to Senior:

In rural districts the particular object has been, sometimes to lower rents, sometimes to abolish rates, sometimes to reduce the dues of the Catholic priests, sometimes to raise the price of labour, sometimes to prevent the employment of strangers —but always to prevent any diminution in the number of holdings.... the great evil of Ireland—the evil which creates or perpetuates all her other calamities—is the insecurity of person and property; arising from the detestation, by the mass of the people, of her existing institutions, and their attempts to substitute for them an insurrectionary law of their own.[3]

Here Senior had summed up the essence of the Irish land problem— that the institutions which classical theory assumed as fundamental were detested by the people of Ireland. Senior regarded this 'as a proof of the greatest IGNORANCE'[4] but the opposition of the peasantry was not

---

[1] S. Laing, *Observations on the Social and Political State of the European People in 1848 and 1849* (London, 1850), p. 29.
[2] J. Revans, *Evils of the State of Ireland* (London, 1835), pp. 21–2.
[3] [Senior], 'Ireland' in *Edinburgh Rev.* vol. LXXIX (January 1844), p. 189. Reprinted as 'Ireland in 1843' in *Journals, Conversations and Essays relating to Ireland*, vol. I (London, 1868), pp. 35 and 50.   [4] Senior, *Journals*, vol. I, p. 42. [Senior's capitals.]

merely ignorant, but based on a belief in an alternative system, the essence of which was clearly set out by a number of spokesmen. One of the earliest and most remarkable of these was William Conner,[1] himself an Irish landlord, who put the tenant's case before the public in a series of speeches and pamphlets, published between 1830 and 1850. The essence of it was summed up in a phrase which recurs many times in Conner's writings—'a valuation and a perpetuity'.[2] Rents should be fixed not by competition but by an independent valuation, and as long as the tenant paid the rent so set, he should be entitled to undisturbed occupation of the soil.

The excessive competition for land which was frequently remarked as so injurious to the Irish tenant figures largely in Conner's arguments, but he was inclined to view the problem in terms of inelasticity of supply rather than excess of demand, contrasting the increase of population with the non-increase of the soil, and denouncing 'the all-devouring monopoly of the landlords'. Unfortunately, there is more of invective than of analysis in Conner's writings, and he never considered the question in what sense the landlords could be said to act monopolistically; nor did he ever pause to work out the consequences of 'a valuation and a perpetuity' to any but the present occupiers of the soil. There is no trace in his work of any appreciation of the Malthusian arguments which could be brought against him, for example.

In other respects, the limitations of Conner's programme are very significant. He denounced the landlords for their abuse of the rights of property, but never the institution of property itself. In fact, in Utilitarian fashion, he was concerned to assert the right of 'the industrious class' to the property in their product (in this case the tenant's right to a fair return on his labour on the soil) and to secure it from confiscation by landlord rapacity.[3] This contains the essence of the Irish view on landlord-tenant relations in this period—the right of the landlord to his property was not called into question, nor his right to receive a fair return for its use: on the other hand, the tenant, by virtue of his cultivation of the soil, possessed a right to its undisturbed occupation which the landlord should not be entitled to challenge as long as he received his rent.[4]

[1] For some account of Conner's career and writings see G. O'Brien, 'William Conner', *Studies*, vol. xii (June 1923), pp. 279–89.

[2] See W. Conner, *The True Political Economy of Ireland: or, Rack-rent, the one Great Cause of all her Evils, with its Remedy* (Dublin, 1835); idem, *The Axe Laid to the Root of Irish Oppression: and a Sure and speedy Remedy for the Evils of Ireland* (Dublin, 1840). Conner's proposals are quoted by J. S. Mill, with whom he afterwards corresponded, in *Principles of Political Economy*, bk. ii, ch. x, para. 1. And see Elliot, *Letters of John Stuart Mill* (London, 1910), vol. i, pp. 147–9. [3] See O'Brien, *Studies*, pp. 281, 284.

[4] The work of James Fintan Lalor, the first Irish nationalist to link the land question with the issue of nationality, has sometimes been considered to constitute an exception to this. But Lalor held that, after national independence had been achieved, landlords who agreed to hold in fee from the Irish nation and grant security to their tenants were to be

This conception, which later gained the name of 'dual ownership', was not recognised by the existing law of real property, and was naturally regarded by the landlord class as revolutionary;[1] but it was an essentially conservative doctrine. The Irish peasant as a rule would have accepted it, for he believed firmly in the rights of property, but conceived that he possessed them as well as the landlord. That this was so is shown by the comparative lack of interest displayed by the rural population in any schemes of Utopian socialism.

Robert Owen had in fact attempted to introduce his system of co-operative communities into Ireland in 1823;[2] his attempts to obtain legislative support for it were unsuccessful, but a 'Hibernian Philanthropic Society' was founded to carry Owen's plan into effect; this achieved nothing substantial. One community on Owenite lines was founded in 1831 at Ralahine, Co. Clare, by a landowner, John Scott Vandeleur; it began hopefully, but was wound up after two years, not through its own failure, but because of Vandeleur having dissipated his estate in gambling and become bankrupt.[3]

Nevertheless, the support which Owen's plans received in Ireland came primarily from a comparatively small number of humanitarians in Dublin, and the mass of the people were never influenced by them, nor showed any desire to take them up. Such schemes were wholly alien to the nature and interest of the Irish peasant, as a clear-sighted French observer, Amédée Pichot, readily saw:

le paysan irlandais, avec toute son imagination, serait difficilement seduit par des utopistes régénérateurs, religieux ou humanitaires...il ne comprendait pas un partage babouvien, un État propriétaire unique, une république phalanstérienne; ni une hiérarchie saint-simonienne: le paysan irlandais ne demande généralement que la reconnaissance de son privilége héréditaire d'occupant, antérieur ou non a celui du landlord—privilége reconnu en effet, avons-nous déjà dit, dans plus d'un comté, mais non partout, même dans l'Ulster,—privilége plus ou moins étendu selon les localités, et qui, sous toutes les formes, exprimera l'antagonisme de land-lord et du tenancier jusqu'à la reforme radicale des lois sur la propriété.[4]

confirmed in their estates. Cf. T. P. O'Neill, 'The Economic and Political Ideas of James Fintan Lalor', *Irish Ecclesiastical Record*, vol. LXXIV (1950), pp. 398–409, but especially p. 404.
    [1] Conner was in fact prosecuted for sedition and sentenced to six months' imprisonment at Maryborough in 1842. See his *Prosecuted Speech Delivered in Proposing a Petition to Parliament in Favour of a Valuation and a Perpetuity of his Farm to the Tenant, with an Introductory Address on the Nature and Spirit of Toryism* (Dublin, 1842), and cf. O'Brien, *Studies*, p. 282.
    [2] See *Report of the Proceedings at the Several Public Meetings, Held in Dublin, by Robert Owen Esq.* (Dublin, 1823). Also, Owen's *Statements, Showing the Power that Ireland Possesses to Create Wealth Beyond the Most Ample Supply of the Wants of its Inhabitants* (London, 1823).
    [3] See E. T. Craig, *The Irish Land and Labour Question, Illustrated in the History of Ralahine, and Co-operative Farming* (London and Manchester, 1893).
    [4] A. Pichot, *L'Irlande et le Pays de Galles* (Paris, 1850), vol. II, p. 453.

It is necessary here to distinguish between two conceptions which were closely intermingled, and often confused in these discussions—the 'tenant-right of occupancy' and the 'tenant-right of compensation for improvements'.[1] It was the former which Conner sought to have recognised, and which later came to be referred to as 'fixity of tenure'. William Ford, the Town Clerk of Dublin, claimed to have originated this term, and thus defined it:

'By fixity of tenure I mean the abolition of all tenancies from year to year and tenancies at will...and in their stead that a fixed tenure in the land, for a given time, should be created by the statute law, so that the farmer should have his land for that period free from ejectment, save for non-payment of rent.' By this means only, Ford argued, could the tenants be protected from 'the whims and caprices of their landlords, when they are resident, who are carried away by the opinions of almost every political economist—at one period all for large farms, at another all for small farms'.[2]

The notion of fixity of tenure gained the support of Daniel O'Connell, and formed part of the programme of the Repeal Association in the eighteen-forties, though not a very prominent part. O'Connell was indeed shrewd enough to realise the eventual 'necessity of doing something substantial for the occupying tenants' but also knew 'how unpalatable such a system [as fixity of tenure] would be to the landlords, especially the absentees'.[3] In fact, however strong the conviction of the Irish tenants that they had a moral right of occupancy, it would have been impossible, in view of the strength of landlord representation in the parliaments of the eighteen-thirties and forties, to have secured any statutory recognition of such a right.

Although both forms of tenant-right were implicitly recognised in the 'Ulster custom', many writers interpreted it as amounting to a right of compensation for tenants' improvements only, and such a right was clearly consistent with a capitalist farming technique, if the investment were made mainly by the tenant. Since this was almost invariably the case in Ireland, it could be argued that a legal recognition of tenant-right in this sense would contribute to the establishment of that security so vital to the encouragement of capital investment in agriculture. The recognition of the tenants' right of compensation was in fact consistent with advocacy of either large- or small-scale farming, and offered at least the possibility of an acceptable compromise between landlords' views and tenants' claims.[4]

---

[1] This is the terminology adopted in W. D. Ferguson and A. Vance, *The Tenure and Improvement of Land in Ireland* (Dublin, 1851).
[2] Evidence of W. Ford before the Devon Commission: *Minutes of Evidence*, part III (1845 [657], vol. XXI), p. 871.
[3] Cf. W. J. O'Neill Daunt, *Personal Recollections of O'Connell* (London, 1850), vol. II, pp. 230–2.
[4] See W. L. Burn, 'Free Trade in Land: an Aspect of the Irish Question', *Trans. Royal Historical Soc.* 4th ser. vol. XXXI (1949), p. 62.

From 1835 onwards, the cause of tenant compensation found an untiring parliamentary advocate in the person of William Sharman Crawford, member for Dundalk, and later for Rochdale.[1] In 1835 and 1836 Crawford introduced Bills in the House of Commons designed to give evicted tenants a right to claim compensation for improvements effected by them. The very modest measure which Crawford put forward in 1836 was supported by Poulett Scrope, but attacked by other members as 'unprecedented and unjustifiable', 'a monstrous interference between landlord and tenant', and eventually thrown out.[2]

Sharman Crawford was out of Parliament from 1837 until 1841, but in 1843 he introduced another Bill to amend the law of Landlord and Tenant in Ireland; on this occasion he obtained a more favourable reception, Peel stating 'that the Government would be disposed to give a fair consideration to the subject' but adding that 'he must at the same time say that they would discountenance any expectation that they meant to recognize in any shape what was called fixity of tenure, or any alienation of the rights of the landlord'.[3]

In consideration of Peel's undertaking, Crawford withdrew his bill, and the Government pledge was shortly redeemed by the appointment of a Royal Commission 'to inquire into the State of the Law and Practice in respect to the Occupation of Land in Ireland', with the Earl of Devon as Chairman.

Peel at this time was much concerned to produce an alternative to Repeal which would be acceptable to moderate opinion in Ireland,[4] and was willing to contemplate legislation on the land question as a part of it, but the composition of the Devon Commission, whose five members were all landlords, gave little reason to expect an early recognition of the tenants' claims. Peel's Whig opponents judged that he was merely playing for time, and expected a futile report from the Commissioners: 'they will probably give an account of what is complained of, in each district, forbear to suggest any remedy, whitewash landlords a little, make a few recommendations and so leave the matter'.[5]

The Report, when it appeared in the spring of 1845, did not wholly justify such cynicism. In the collection of evidence alone the Commissioners did work of permanent value, and they did not hesitate to admit that 'the testimony given is unfortunately too uniform in representing the unimproved state of extensive districts, the want of employment, and the

---

[1] For a full biography, see B. A. Kennedy, *William Sharman Crawford, 1780–1861*, unpublished thesis for degree of D.Litt. (1953), in the Library of Queen's University, Belfast.
[2] *Hansard*, 3rd ser. vol. xxxii, cols. 183–9 (10 March 1836); and cf. Kennedy, *Crawford*, p. 78.　　[3] *Hansard*, 3rd ser. vol. lxxi, col. 419 (9 August 1843).
[4] See Peel Papers, B.M. Add. MSS. 40540, *passim*; and G. Shaw Lefevre (Lord Eversley), *Peel and O'Connell* (London, 1887), part iii, chap. i, especially pp. 214 and 243–8.
[5] Bessborough to Russell, 10 Jan. 1845 (Russell Papers, P.R.O. 30/22/4).

consequent poverty and hardships under which a large portion of the agricultural population continually labour'.

The Commissioners clearly recognised that this was mainly due to 'feelings of distrust and insecurity that too often prevail amongst the tenant class in Ireland' impeding improvement, and recommended the early introduction of a measure for tenant compensation. But the measure which they proposed would have taken account only of prospective improvements, duly notified to the landlord, and ignored existing investments altogether.[1]

After the publication of the Report, Lord Devon did not allow its recommendations to be neglected, and on 9 June 1845, Lord Stanley introduced into Parliament a tenant-compensation Bill which even went slightly beyond them; it provided for the appointment of Commissioners who were to inspect the land, authorise improvements contemplated by the tenant, and assess compensation in cases of eviction. Stanley's Bill was introduced in the Lords, and there met with such uncompromising opposition that the Government dropped it. Sharman Crawford then reintroduced his 1843 Bill in the Commons, but did not press it before the end of the session. Matters stood thus when, on 21 October, Peel found it necessary to send Professor Lindley and Dr Lyon Playfair to Ireland to investigate the causes of the newly appeared potato blight.

II

The Famine placed the Irish land question in an entirely new light. It realised all the worst forebodings of the critics of the old system, but at the same time it opened up a new range of possibilities. Radical reform had long seemed desirable, but now it seemed practicable and urgent as well. The Governments of the next few years could no longer postpone the problem, and in coping with it they had no lack of proffered advice from all sides, much of it coming from the leading economic thinkers of the day—thinkers of a new generation from that of Ricardo and McCulloch.

The preceding survey of the Irish land problem before the Famine has shown that there were three distinct lines of thought on the subject then existing. Perhaps the most widely canvassed, if not the most widely accepted, was the view that Ireland could only prosper through the introduction of medium- and large-scale farming carried on by capitalist tenants, and the conversion of the cottier population into hired labourers. Directly opposed to this was the doctrine which would give the tenants virtually complete security of tenure at rents fixed according to an independent valuation. The views of those who would have recognised the landlords' rights, but qualified them by granting the tenants' right to

---

[1] *Report of the Commissioners Appointed to Inquire into the Occupation of Land in Ireland* (1845 [605], vol. XIX), pp. 16 and 17. See Shaw Lefevre, *Peel and O'Connell*, pp. 237–40.

compensation for improvements effected by them, might be said to lie somewhere between the first two; where exactly depending very much on the individual stating the argument. As has been suggested, there was some tendency to confuse tenant compensation with fixity of tenure, and many advocates of the former wished to make it as close to the latter as possible.

Political economists had been the main exponents of the 'commercial' view of the question, as Seebohm later called it,[1] but in the eighteen-forties, the opposing doctrine of customary tenure was beginning to find some favour amongst their ranks. Irish writings seem to have had some effect in this, but observation of conditions in other European countries also played a part.

In Ireland such men as Conner had written vigorously in defence of the small tenant's right to live on the land; but theirs was a social and moral argument mainly, and the purely economic argument, that small-holdings were hopelessly inefficient and unproductive by comparison with large farms, did not seem to be affected by their reasoning. But there were also those who were prepared to defend the small farm on technical and economic, apart from merely social, grounds. One of the first, and most consistent, of these was William Blacker, the agent for the Earl of Gosforth's property in County Armagh. In a series of writings[2] Blacker opposed consolidation, holding that the land was the only permanent source of employment in Ireland, and that it could, and must, be made to yield an adequate livelihood for the people. Blacker's papers include many accounts of experiments in small-scale cultivation which he had carried out successfully on the Gosforth estates.

Sharman Crawford had also shown himself as a supporter of the small farm system, and attacked Torrens for his advocacy of consolidation and emigration in a series of letters to the *Northern Whig* in 1839.[3] Crawford argued 'that the object of political economy ought to be, to reduce, as far as possible, the proportion of the labouring class solely dependent on support from hired labour', but that this proportion would be increased by consolidation of farms, which would tend to increase class antagonism. His main economic argument against large farms was that Irish farmers had not the requisite capital or knowledge to maintain them, and that

[1] See F. Seebohm, 'The Land Question', *Fortnightly Rev.*, n.s. vol. VI (September 1869), p. 626.

[2] Blacker's principal publications were: *Prize Essay, Addressed to the Agricultural Committee of the Royal Dublin Society, on the Management of Landed Property in Ireland* (Dublin, 1837); *The Claims of the Landed Interests to Legislative Protection* (London, 1836); *An Essay on the Best Mode of Improving the Condition of the Labouring Classes of Ireland* (London, 1846).

[3] W. S. Crawford, *Defence of the Small Farmers of Ireland* [ten letters to the] *Northern Whig* (Belfast), 10 September to 1 October 1839, reprinted as a pamphlet (Belfast, 1839).

For a later, and more balanced, account of the same problem, see Sir Robert Kane, 'The Large or Small Farm Question Considered', *Agricultural and Industrial Journal* 1848 (Dublin, 1849), pp. 147-71.

even in England large farmers were only enabled to survive through the protection of the Corn Laws. Torrens remained unconvinced by Crawford's propositions,[1] but the example not only of Down and Armagh, but of Belgium, Switzerland and Prussia also, showed that small holdings could be as productive as large. Continental economists, such as Sismondi, had long asserted this, and the testimony of such travellers as Samuel Laing and H. D. Inglis[2] brought new evidence of its truth to English readers. Furthermore, when English translations of books of travels in Ireland written by such notable Europeans as Friedrich von Raumer and Gustave de Beaumont[3] became available, they were found to contain unhesitating advocacy of peasant proprietorship as the solution for the miseries of Ireland.

The weight of this evidence served to convince a number of English economists, amongst them G. Poulett Scrope, W. T. Thornton, and, most influential of all, John Stuart Mill. Scrope summed up the views of this group concisely when he asserted 'that the small farm system can in Ireland be made as conducive as it is in Belgium to the comfort of the population and the increase of production: but that the secret of this comfort and increased production,—in other words, of the industry by which both are created—*lies in the possession by the cultivator of a durable and certain interest in the results of his labour*'.[4]

Scrope was here writing in connection with the reclamation of waste lands, and both Thornton and Mill also based their proposals for the introduction of a peasant proprietary in Ireland on the notion of cultivation of waste. Thornton made his original suggestion along these lines in 1846 in his *Over-Population and its Remedy* and repeated it, somewhat modified, in *A Plea for Peasant Proprietors; with the Outlines of a Plan for their Establishment in Ireland*, published in 1848. Mill's proposals appeared in the leader pages of the *Morning Chronicle* during the winter of 1846–7, and were subsequently incorporated into his *Principles of Political Economy*.[5]

---

[1] See his reply to Crawford, *Northern Whig*, 12 October 1839. Torrens's views on the Irish land problem were repeated without alteration in his *The Budget*, Letter v (London, 1842). Torrens, however, was prepared to allow the possibility of some 'colonisation' of Irish waste lands. See p. 217 below.

[2] Cf. S. Laing, *Notes of a Traveller on the Social and Political State of France, Prussia, etc.* (London, 1842); D. Conway [H. D. Inglis], *Switzerland, the South of France, and the Pyrenees in 1830* (London, 1831).

[3] F. von Raumer, *England in 1835*, vol. III, trans. H. E. Lloyd (London, 1836), p. 199; de Beaumont, *Ireland, Social, Political and Religious*, vol. II, ed. W. Cooke Taylor (London, 1839), pp. 219–33.

[4] G. P. Scrope, *Extracts of Evidence Taken by the Late Commission of Inquiry into the Occupation of Land in Ireland, on the Subject of Waste Lands Reclamation; with a Prefatory Letter to the Right Honourable Lord John Russell* (London, 1847), preface, pp. xix–xx.

[5] First ed. (London, 1848), vol. I, pp. 381–400. The proposals were altered in subsequent editions, as the condition of Ireland changed. For an account of the *Morning Chronicle* articles, and their relation to the writing of the *Principles*, see M. Packe, *John Stuart Mill* (London, 1954), p. 296.

The ideas which Mill advanced at this time were strikingly at variance with orthodox classical ideas on the subject. He characterised the introduction of capitalist farming into Ireland generally as 'wholly impracticable': 'the people are there, and the problem is not how to improve the country, but how it can be improved by and for its present inhabitants'. Mill asserted firmly that the problem could only be solved by converting the cottiers into peasant proprietors, but neither he nor Thornton advocated the immediate introduction of a general system of occupying ownership, for they both saw that legislation on such lines was not a practical possibility for Ireland in 1848. In consequence, they proposed a gradual introduction of peasant proprietorship in schemes which differed in details but were similar in principle. Both involved the compulsory acquisition or purchase of waste lands from their owners, and the settlement of cottiers thereon; the cottiers, with the aid of some advance of materials and implements, were to reclaim the waste, and, on so doing, to become the owners of it, subject to a small fixed rent-charge to recoup the outlay made by the State.

The transfer of the cottiers on to the waste lands, it was hoped, would reduce the pressure of demand for land and raise the level of wages in the rest of the country, so that, in Mill's words, 'the introduction of English capital and farming over the remaining surface of Ireland would at once cease to be chimerical'. For the settlers on the waste, holdings of about eight acres were advocated, which Thornton felt should enable a man and his family (five persons in all) to obtain a reasonable subsistence without dependence on the potato.[1]

Thus it appears that this Thornton–Mill scheme differed considerably from later schemes of land purchase. It was in fact a project for 'home colonisation', with a proprietor status for the colonists, leaving the landlord-tenant relationship unaltered in the rest of the country, but freed from the aberrations which had brought it into disrepute.[2]

Although at this time 'the avowed dissenters from the established creed became numerous enough to constitute a sect',[3] the established creed still claimed the adherence of a majority, including powerful advocates amongst its numbers. While the *Morning Chronicle* advocated small farms and peasant proprietorship, the *Spectator* was equally vigorous in its support of consolidation of small holdings, aided by emigration. In this it had the backing of the *Edinburgh Review*, where Nassau Senior attacked the schemes of Mill and Thornton with all the weapons of orthodox doctrine. Senior was ready to admit the merits of occupying ownership

---

[1] W. T. Thornton, *A Plea for Peasant Proprietors* (London, 1848), chap. v, especially p. 233.

[2] For a further discussion of projects of waste-land reclamation, see below, chapters VI and VII.

[3] Thornton, *A Plea for Peasant Proprietors*, preface, p. vii.

and small farms, but not that they could be realised in Ireland. He argued that the cost of resettling pauper families on waste lands would be considerably greater than that of assisting them to emigrate, and that there could be no adequate safeguard against renewed sub-division of the small farms and excessive growth of population. Yet this was not the most cogent argument which Senior could produce: he was able to instance the views of William Blacker himself, given before the House of Lords Committee on Colonisation, in 1847. Blacker readily admitted that since the failure of the potato 'with five or six acres the farmer cannot now support himself upon his land', and Senior was not inclined to believe that the eight-acre man would be in any better plight.[1]

Indeed, to many at this time it seemed that the failure of the potato made the introduction of English farming into Ireland all the more necessary and inevitable. But it was clear that it could not be achieved by the existing landlords any more than by their existing tenants. Even before the Famine many Irish landlords had been proprietors in name only—holders of life interests in estates heavily encumbered by mortgages and family settlements. The Famine completed the ruin of many who had been staving off disaster for years, as rent rolls diminished and poor-rates increased. Such decayed gentry could never be converted into improving landlords capable of putting their lands into a state where substantial tenants would wish to rent them; yet even when they wished to sell their lands, it was difficult to complete a transfer, because of the numerous legal problems involved in proving a title.

Even in the years before the Famine, English opinion was beginning to label Irish landlords as improvident and extravagant, and during the Famine itself there was scant sympathy for them.[2] The view was widely expressed that Irish property must bear the cost of Irish poverty, and if the landlords could not shoulder the burden, they must be sold out to make way for others more capable of managing an estate efficiently.[3] Carlyle expressed this feeling with typical pungency when he wrote:

Unwisdom cannot be left to *laissez-faire*, or to the guidance of injustice and still deeper unwisdom. Foolish Irish peasants must have wise Irish landlords to command them. Unwise will do no longer; wise must be had, or death has come for us all.[4]

In the existing state of the law, however, unwise landlords could only be dislodged by slow and costly legal processes, and while these were in

[1] N. W. Senior, 'Relief of Irish Distress in 1847 and 1848', *Edinburgh Rev.* vol. LXXXIX (1849); reprinted in *Journals relating to Ireland*, vol. I, p. 257.
[2] This development was anticipated by Lord Monteagle in a letter to Peel, 24 October 1845, B.M. Add. MSS. 40576.
[3] See, for example, 'The Lords' Legislation for Ireland', *The Examiner*, 21 July 1849, p. 450.
[4] Thomas Carlyle, 'The Rakes of Mallow', unpublished MS., c. 1848, Yale University Library.

progress, the estate would usually fall under a receiver appointed by the Court of Chancery, whose management of it was only too likely to be worse than that of the landlord himself.[1] To the mass of the middle classes, just beginning to know the weight of their influence, the solution seemed abundantly evident—the laws of property must be amended or repealed, just as the Corn Laws had been:

Are we to have a free trade in the products of the land, and not in the land itself? Are the utmost facilities to be given to the sale and transfer of all other articles, and is land alone to be considered as requiring an exception in this respect? Let the principle of commercial freedom be fully and fairly carried out. Let it apply to land as well as to other property.[2]

This doctrine of 'Free Trade in Land' might be considered as a logical extension of the line of thought on Irish land questions which the majority of classical economists had developed in earlier years. Such indeed it was, but it was not the professional economists who made the extension: they did not generally concern themselves with the question of the proprietor's title, but only with his contract with the tenant. The idea that the land problem might be solved by making the sale of land as easy as the sale of furniture was primarily due to the 'Manchester men'. It was an idea espoused by Cobden and Bright[3] and it is notable that its chief advocates in Ireland were prosperous Quaker merchants like Jonathan Pim and Joseph Bewley, whose success had come through the channels of trade.[4]

Varying opinions were entertained by the advocates of free trade in land as to the effect which its introduction would have on the landlord-tenant relationship. Some, such as Pim, were prepared to trust entirely to the operation of free exchange, believing that it would produce a state of affairs in which 'large estates, with farms managed on the most scientific principles, and whose extent admits the profitable use of machinery, will co-exist with small properties, under garden cultivation by the spade, where persevering industry and economy may compensate for any disadvantage of size'.[5] Such authors would not have conferred on the tenant any legal right of compensation for improvements, believing that free sales of land would introduce solvent proprietors who could, and would, effect all necessary improvements themselves.

Others believed that it might be desirable to combine a tenant-compensation law with measures facilitating transfer of ownership. Amongst

---

[1] For some account of the difficulties of selling property and proving title in the Courts of Equity before 1849, see 'Incumbered Estates Court', *Dublin University Magazine*, vol. xxxvi (September 1850), pp. 311–28.

[2] Jonathan Pim, *Condition of Ireland*, p. 236.

[3] See John, 1st Viscount Morley, *Life of Cobden* (London, 1881), vol. ii, p. 51; G. M. Trevelyan, *Life of John Bright* (London, 1913), p. 163.

[4] The Central Relief Committee of the Society of Friends, formed during the Famine, declared itself in favour of free trade in land: see p. 128 of its *Transactions* (Dublin, 1852).

[5] Pim, *Condition of Ireland*, p. 288.

this group was Neilson Hancock, then Professor of Political Economy at Dublin University and an uncompromising supporter of *laissez-faire*. Although he named legal impediments to the sale and transfer of land as the main cause of backward agriculture in Ireland, Hancock supported the legalisation of tenant-right, on the ground that tenants were always more likely than landlords to be improvers, and that no fair distinction could be maintained between agriculture and other trades as regards the ownership of 'fixtures' installed by a tenant.[1]

This was similar to the view of John Bright, whose interest in the Irish land problem dated from before the Famine. Bright was a confirmed believer in free trade in land, but a visit to Ireland in 1849 convinced him of the need to combine a measure for securing tenants' compensation for improvements with legislation for facilitating transfer of ownership.[2]

While at this time most of the advocates of free trade in Irish land would not have countenanced any legislation to establish peasant proprietorship generally in Ireland—which Hancock denounced as 'open confiscation of property'—it is clear that they would not have opposed the idea of tenants buying up their own holdings where market conditions made it possible. Pim especially favoured 'the creation of a class of small proprietors, or yeomanry', and Bright, in his later years, came more and more to view this as the ultimate basis for a solution of the problem.

Such were the opinions which were current during and immediately after the Famine, when the condition of Ireland seemed to require prompt and radical action on the land question. Varied as they were, it can fairly be said that they fell into two main classes—proposals for the improvement of agriculture through emigration, consolidation of holdings and the introduction of new capital, and proposals for the improvement of the condition of the existing population through schemes of reclamation of waste combined with occupying ownership of small-holdings. The general trend of ideas had long been in favour of the first approach, and such legislative action as there had been accorded with it. It is not to be expected that such a trend would be reversed quickly, even by such a catastrophe as the Famine. The Famine may have ruined many Irish landlords, but it did not shake the strength of the landed interest at Westminster. No measure which appeared to threaten 'the just rights of property' could have been carried through the House of Lords at that time, and there can be no question that such schemes as those of Mill and Thornton fell into this category. Apart from this, even a much more vigorous administration than that over which Lord John Russell presided

[1] W. N. Hancock, *Impediments to the Prosperity of Ireland* (London, 1850), pp. 80–4. Hancock here explained that, since the time of Queen Anne, the courts had exempted fixtures used in trade or manufactures from the rule of law that whatever is affixed to a freehold becomes a part of it.

[2] R. A. J. Walling (ed.), *The Diaries of John Bright* (London, 1930), pp. 99–100. Trevelyan, *John Bright*, p. 164.

from 1846 to 1852 could hardly have put a scheme such as Mill's into effect on the scale necessary for it to succeed in a short space of time. Mill had argued that the introduction of capitalist farming was impracticable, and so it was with the existing cottier population. But inability to pay rents during the Famine years gave a powerful stimulus to clearances, later reinforced by the 'quarter-acre clause', and once the people began to emigrate in large numbers, the possibility of consolidation was greater than ever before.

Yet if all this made it unlikely that any Government, Whig or Tory, would introduce radically new measures to deal with the land problem, it was equally impossible to propose no measures at all. Lord Devon had followed up the work of his Commission by preparing a number of Bills to extend leasing powers, to facilitate the sale of incumbered estates, as well as the Bill to provide compensation to tenants for improvements which was introduced into the Lords by Stanley in 1845, but dropped.[1] The Bill to facilitate the sale of incumbered estates was introduced into the Commons in 1846, but lapsed with the change of ministry in July of that year. In this it shared the fate of another tenant-compensation Bill, similar to Stanley's, which the Chief Secretary, Lincoln, had introduced in June.

There is evidence that the intentions of the Whigs, on taking office, were not greatly different from those of Peel's ministry. They intended to introduce a plan for selling incumbered estates, and felt that some measure of security for tenants' improvements would be desirable.[2] But although both Whigs and Tories thus appear to have accepted the idea of tenant-right at this time, it must be remembered that by this they meant simply the tenant-right of compensation for improvements, generally confined to improvements carried out with the approval of the landlord, and making no allowance for the value of those already existing. This was something very different from the legal recognition of Ulster tenant-right sought by Sharman Crawford and his supporters in Ireland.[3]

Yet when Lord John Russell brought forward his Irish measures in the Commons on 25 January 1847, tenant compensation even in the narrowest sense did not figure among them. A measure for facilitating the sale of incumbered estates was stated to be 'in contemplation', but the only Bills affecting land actually introduced were one for the improvement of landed property by advances to proprietors, and one

---

[1] See above, p. 28, and, for details of the other Bills, Devon to Peel, 29 November 1845, B.M. Add. MSS. 40580.

[2] This is suggested by Russell's correspondence at this period. Bessborough to Russell, 10 January 1846, Cottenham to Russell, 3 February 1847 (Russell Papers, P.R.O. 30/22/4 and 6). Also Russell to Clarendon, 10 November 1847, quoted by Spencer Walpole, *Life of Lord John Russell* (London, 1889), vol. I, pp. 462–4.

[3] See W. A. Dunning, 'Irish Land Legislation since 1845', *Political Science Quarterly*, vol. VII (1892), p. 64.

to enable the State to undertake the reclamation of certain waste lands in Ireland.[1]

This last would appear to have been a concession to the views of Mill and Poulett Scrope: in fact, in the words of the *Spectator*, Lord John appeared to have 'something adopted from every suggester, in order to please people all round'.[2] The waste lands Bill, however, signally failed to achieve this end. The *Morning Chronicle* characterised it as 'excellent in *principle*, but likely to be so limited in its operation that we should be sorry to stake the credit of the principle upon any practical results which can be expected to flow from it'.[3] In the House, the Bill was coldly received: Peel opposed it on the ground that private enterprise, when freed by the sale of incumbered estates, would undertake all the reclamation of waste which was desirable; while other members, stoutly refusing to distinguish between a small proprietor and a small tenant, pointed to the ruin which sub-division had brought on Ireland in the past as an argument against the creation of small-holdings on reclaimed land.[4]

In the face of this opposition, the Government first reduced the sum intended to be spent on waste-land reclamation from £1,000,000 to £500,000, and subsequently dropped the Bill in favour of a plan of Charles Wood's to advance £620,000 to certain Irish railway companies.[5]

The Incumbered Estates Bill was introduced in the House of Lords in March 1847, and was there passed, but Russell was compelled to withdraw it when it had reached the Committee stage in the Commons, as 'very great alarm had been excited by it'. In fact, a number of insurance companies who were lending on the security of Irish land had refused to complete any further arrangements of this kind while the Bill was in prospect, and threatened to call in money already lent to Irish landlords if the Bill passed. Not wishing to risk the consequences of a sudden and general foreclosure of mortgages, the Cabinet acceded to a request by representatives of the Irish proprietors to defer the Bill.[6] No Government measure for tenant compensation was brought forward during the session; Sharman Crawford therefore introduced a tenant-right Bill of his own, but this was defeated at the second reading.[7]

After the somewhat inconclusive general election of 1847, the Russell administration continued to pursue a vacillating course with regard to

---

[1] *Annual Register*, 1847, pp. 23–4.   [2] *Spectator*, January 1847.

[3] *Morning Chronicle*, 26 January 1847, p. 6.

[4] *Hansard*, 3rd ser. vol. LXXXIX, cols. 699–764 (2 February 1847). In fact, Russell had not specifically stated that the people settled on the lands reclaimed by his scheme would automatically become proprietors, although he had given the impression that this was to be the ultimate outcome, *loc. cit.*, col. 443.

[5] *Hansard*, 3rd ser. vol. XCII, cols. 215 and 284 (30 April 1847); and see below ch. VI, p. 197.

[6] Clarendon to Shannon, 12 October 1847 (Clarendon Papers, Bodleian Library, Oxon); *Hansard*, 3rd ser. vol. XCIII, col. 1192 (5 July 1847).

[7] *Annual Register*, 1847, p. 178; *Hansard*, 3rd ser. vol. XCII, cols. 55–7 (28 April 1847), vol. XCIII, cols. 630–46 (16 June 1847).

Irish land problems. In October, the Prime Minister and his colleagues were preoccupied with the crisis on the money market, but found time to decide that a measure for the sale of incumbered estates must take priority over any tenant-compensation Bill for Ireland. Accordingly Clarendon set to work with the Attorney-General to design an incumbered estates Bill which would meet the objections raised by the insurance companies and others against the scheme of the previous session.[1] The Bill which resulted was introduced, again in the Lords, in February 1848, and was successfully passed into law before the end of the session, although it encountered some opposition and was much amended in the Commons.[2] The new Act did not fulfil the expectations of the advocates of free trade in land, for although its main purpose was to shorten proceedings in Chancery, it still made use of the mechanism of that Court, and as a result proved largely inoperative.[3]

In the matter of a tenant-compensation Bill, the autumn of 1847 witnessed a prolonged series of disagreements between the Lord-Lieutenant, Clarendon, and the Cabinet, with Russell taking an indecisive position as mediator. Clarendon was anxious for a measure which would be strongly in the tenants' favour, but the majority of the Cabinet were not willing to go further than Lincoln's Bill of 1846 had done. Philip Pusey's attempt to introduce a tenant-right measure for England was still fresh in the minds of ministers, and Charles Wood in particular was fearful lest any scheme which 'infringed the rights of property' in Ireland might be held up as a precedent for England.[4] Clarendon, acutely conscious of the social disintegration setting in around him, found this approach exasperating; Russell admitted that the Cabinet's proposals were unsatisfactory, but could suggest nothing better than to 'bring in a very mild bill and refer it to a select Committee...if they agree to go further we can do so'.[5]

A few weeks later Russell had swung over to a much more radical position. He pointed out to Clarendon that no measure of compensation for improvements could be of value to evicted cottiers who had lost their only means of livelihood, since most of them had made no improvements. It was in this connection that Russell made the statement, often quoted, that 'you might as well propose that a landlord should compensate the rabbits for the burrows they have made on his land'—but the conclusion

[1] Russell to Clarendon, 21 October 1847; Clarendon to Lansdowne, 26 October 1847 (Clarendon Papers).
[2] *Hansard*, 3rd ser. vol. c, cols. 94–108 (4 July 1848); *Annual Register*, 1848, pp. 117–20. The Act was 11 and 12 Vic. c. 48.
[3] See statement of Sir John Romilly on the working of the Act, *Hansard*, 3rd ser. vol. civ, col. 893 (26 April 1849).
[4] Wood to Clarendon, 26 October 1847 (Clarendon Papers). For debates on Pusey's Bill, see *Hansard*, 3rd ser. vol. xc, cols. 383–5; xci, 541–3; xcii, 719–21 (February–May 1847).
[5] Russell to Clarendon, 28 October 1847 (Clarendon Papers).

that he drew from this was not that tenant compensation was absurd, but that 'a remedy for this evil must strike deeper and wider. It must embrace all who have occupied the land for a certain number of years, and must give them something like the tenant right of Ulster.'[1] This was the very point which Sharman Crawford and his supporters had been making, but it found favour neither with Clarendon on the one hand nor the Cabinet on the other. Clarendon pressed for the acceptance of his Bill, which would have given compensation for both prospective and retrospective improvements, and provided a mechanism of arbitration to determine their value. Russell agreed to support this Bill, rather against his own convictions, but it came before the Cabinet in his absence, and, as he told Clarendon, they 'played Old Gooseberry with it', deleting all its most essential clauses.[2] Eventually the course adopted was the cautious one which Russell had originally proposed—Somerville, the Irish Chief Secretary, came before the Commons with a mild tenant-compensation Bill, virtually identical with Lincoln's of 1846; this was referred to a Select Committee, from which it never emerged.[3] Sharman Crawford and his associates reiterated their objections to compensation which was not retrospective and applied only to improvements made with the landlord's consent; Crawford reintroduced his own Bill to legalise the Ulster custom, and met with his customary defeat.

In the next session, Peel seized the initiative in Irish matters by propounding what came to be known as 'the Plantation Scheme'.[4] This was a comprehensive scheme for the relief of Irish distress, involving the establishment of a Commission to supervise public works and land improvement schemes, and to give assistance to emigration. Peel, however, made clear that all this would be of no avail without changes in the state of landed property: 'Almost the only measure from which I derive a hope of safety is the introduction of new proprietors who shall take possession of land in Ireland, freed from its present incumbrances, and enter upon its cultivation with adequate capital, with new feelings, and inspired by new hopes...what I now recommend you to consider is, whether you ought not still further to facilitate the voluntary transfer of incumbered estates.'

The last part, at least, of this advice was followed by the Government, for within a month the Solicitor-General sought 'to bring in a Bill further to facilitate the sale of Incumbered Estates in Ireland'. In this the Court of Chancery was altogether by-passed, and a Commission set up empowered to sell estates on the application of owners or incumbrancers,

---

[1] Russell to Clarendon, 10 November 1847 (Clarendon Papers).
[2] *Idem*, 22 January 1848, *op. cit.*
[3] Spencer Walpole, *History of England* (London, 1886), vol. IV, p. 328; *Hansard*, 3rd ser. vol. XCVIII, col. 69 (7 April 1848).
[4] Peel outlined his scheme in two speeches made during the debates on the Rate in Aid Bill, 5 and 30 March 1849: *Hansard*, 3rd ser. vol. CIII, cols. 179–93 and vol. CIV cols. 87–117.

and to give a clear legal title to the purchaser. The measure was cordially received by Peel and Bright, but the *Morning Chronicle* (which had become the organ of the Peelites in 1848) commented shrewdly: 'It is a good Bill—for, what it does, it does remarkably well. But it is not a policy, and we do not yet know that it is even one item of a policy. Everything turns, in short, on whether it is to be regarded as the *beginning*, or the *end*, of Lord John Russell's Irish statesmanship.'[1]

As events proved, it was in fact the end, and consequently when the Bill passed into law its effects were not those which the advocates of free trade in land had hoped to see. Such men as Bright and Sir James Graham thought that the sale of incumbered estates might solve the Irish problem through allowing Irish tenants to purchase their holdings and obtain the security of proprietorship.[2] Perhaps the more widely held view, typified in Peel's speeches, was that the new owners would be English capitalists, either purchasers of whole estates who would carry out the improvements which the 'Rakes of Mallow' could not, or smaller men, of the yeoman sort, who would undertake the efficient cultivation of their own properties.

This latter view seems to have been the one held by Russell's ministry: there is some evidence for the belief that they envisaged the replacement of the improvident Irish landlords by an improving Whig gentry.[3] But while Peel was shrewd enough to see that no English capitalist would be easily tempted by the prospect of purchasing a broken-down Irish property, however cheaply, the Whigs apparently were not. Charles Wood, the Chancellor of the Exchequer, was probably expressing a view which his Cabinet colleagues would not have challenged when he wrote:

I do not expect to see much improvement in Ireland till parties buy land for investment, meaning to improve it, and make it pay.... This is not an encouraging prospect for existing Irish proprietors, I admit, and it implies great ruin, great change of property, and great suffering for the people in the meantime. I see no help for it. The more I see of government interference the less I am disposed to trust to it, and I have no faith in anything but private capital employed under individual charge. At some number of years purchase, capitalists will begin to buy, and then the reconstructing process begins. Meanwhile the old fabric is falling to pieces and must be cleared of what really encumbers the new building.[4]

Wood does not seem to have envisaged purchase of their holdings by tenants as forming any part of the reconstructing process, and certainly the 1849 Act contained no provision to facilitate their doing so. On the

[1] *Morning Chronicle*, 28 April 1849, p. 5.
[2] Cf. *The Diaries of John Bright*, pp. 100–5, and Trevelyan, *John Bright*, p. 163. Graham's views are quoted in the *Annual Register*, 1848, p. 120.
[3] Passages in Charles Lever's novel *Davenport Dunn*, for example, imply that this view was commonly accepted in the eighteen-fifties.
[4] Charles Wood to Monteagle, 22 November 1848 (Monteagle Papers, National Library of Ireland).

other hand, Wood's confidence in the efficacy of the unaided working of the market as a solution for the problem proved to be unjustified. In the first eight years of the working of the Act, 3197 properties were sold to 7216 purchasers, of whom only 314 were English.[1] Peel's vision of an influx of English yeomen into Munster and Connaught thus did not materialise; but this in itself would have been unimportant had the majority of Irish purchasers been conscientious improvers. In fact, they proved to be largely speculators, undoubtedly anxious to make the land pay, but unwilling to lay out anything more than the purchase money on it, and many tenants found their new landlords more exacting than the old.[2]

For the protection of the tenants, some measure to enforce tenant-right, even in the narrow sense, was undoubtedly necessary. Otherwise there was nothing to prevent the new landlords from confiscating tenants' improvements through increases of rent. No measure of protection for tenants was forthcoming, from the time when Somerville's Bill was dropped in 1848, until he brought forward another in February 1850. This Bill was substantially the same as that introduced by Stanley in 1845, but once again it was carried no further than the second reading.[3]

Thus only one half of the programme of land legislation originally mapped out by Russell was carried into effect, and Government policy seemed to tend increasingly towards a purely 'commercial' interpretation of landlord-tenant relationships.[4] Various reasons have been suggested by historians for this development; perhaps the most generous interpretation is that given by R. Barry O'Brien, who asserts that the intention of the Incumbered Estates Act was to create a class of landlords who would carry out their own improvements, and thus make any measure of tenant compensation unnecessary.[5] This seems to conflict with Russell's earlier expressions of intent to legislate for the protection of tenants, and there may be more of truth in Halévy's suggestion that the rebellion in Ireland in 1848 had turned Russell into 'a hardened conservative', believing more

[1] W. E. Montgomery, *History of Land Tenure in Ireland* (Cambridge, 1889), p. 125.

[2] See the evidence of Mountifort Longfield, Judge of the Landed Estates Court, before the Select Committee on Tenure and Improvement of Land (Ireland) Act, 15 May 1865, *Minutes of Evidence* (1865 (402), vol. XI), p. 2.

[3] R. B. O'Brien, *Parliamentary History of the Irish Land Question* (London, 1880), pp. 83–4. On 2 July 1850, Pusey moved the third reading of his Landlord and Tenant Bill, a permissive tenant-right measure, and the House agreed to include Ireland in it. Irish members characterised this as 'a mere trifling with the problem', but the Bill in any event did not pass the Lords. See *Hansard*, 3rd ser. vol. CXII, cols. 850–5.

[4] It could be argued that this was inevitable once it had been decided to facilitate the sale of incumbered estates, since any effective tenant-right measure, especially if it had retrospective effect, must greatly have diminished the vendibility of landed property. Yet Russell himself never appears to have been conscious of any incongruity between these two parts of his programme.

[5] R. B. O'Brien, *Fifty Years of Concessions to Ireland, 1831–1881* (London, 1885), vol. II, p. 149.

in coercion than concession.[1] Yet perhaps the soundest judgment of all is to be found in John Bright's Diary for 1850: 'Conversation with Lord J. Russell on Irish Tenant Question. Lord John admitted the extreme hazard of leaving the question unsettled.... He was evidently anxious on the question, but, not understanding it, he seems hardly to know how to deal with it.'[2]

Not knowing how to deal with the question, Russell was prepared to entrust its solution to *laissez-faire*, but there were others who were not. At this time the tenant cause attracted the interest and support of the younger Nationalists remaining in Ireland after the suppression of the 1848 rising. The most able of them, Charles Gavan Duffy, has told how 'I summoned a private conference of the most experienced Nationalists left in Dublin, who still made a very impressive show.... I told them that the protection of the farmers who were flying daily before the Exterminator seemed to me the most urgent business. For nationality we could do little just now, except keep alive its traditions.'[3] On the land problem, at this stage Duffy's ideas took two forms: 'We might make a new plantation in Ireland, not for strangers this time, but for the natives, under the Incumbered Estates Act. We might unite with the Ulster tenantry in obtaining a reform of the Land Code, which they desired as much as we did.'[4]

Both these ideas Duffy proceeded to carry into action without delay. As to the first, his project was to assist tenants to purchase their land when sales occurred under the 1849 Act—'help from Parliament there was none, but I bethought that we might perhaps help ourselves'. The method was to be the establishment of a Freehold Land Society, on the model of others then appearing in England, which would buy land 'wholesale' and resell it by instalments to small-holders. This scheme of Gavan Duffy's, which followed the lines of an earlier suggestion of John Marnell to Fintan Lalor, was warmly approved by John Bright, as well as by Mill and Thornton;[5] but in putting it into operation he fell foul, not for the last time, of that romantically sinister financier, John Sadleir.[6] When Sadleir sought to have the funds of the Society placed in his own Tipperary Bank, and to foist upon it some properties he had already acquired in the

[1] E. Halévy, *The Age of Peel and Cobden: A History of the English People, 1841-1852* (London, 1947), p. 256.
[2] *Diaries*, pp. 106-7.
[3] Sir C. Gavan Duffy, *My Life in Two Hemispheres* (London, 1898), vol. II, p. 7.
[4] *Ibid*. vol. II, p. 14.
[5] John Bright to C. Gavan Duffy, 13 May 1851 (Yale University Library); J. S. Mill to C. Gavan Duffy, 17 June 1851 (Gavan Duffy Papers, National Library of Ireland). These letters are reproduced in part, together with Thornton's, in Duffy, *Life*, vol. II, pp. 17-18.
[6] Sadleir is best known historically as the leader, with William Keogh, of the 'Pope's Brass Band'—the Catholic Defence party which opposed Russell's Ecclesiastical Titles Bill, but his rise and fall as a banker and company promoter were more dramatic. He is said to have inspired the character of 'Mr Merdle' in Dickens's *Little Dorrit*, and to have been the hero of Lever's novel *Davenport Dunn*.

Incumbered Estates Court, Gavan Duffy became suspicious and resigned from the managing committee.[1] From that time onwards the Freehold Land Society languished, and so a worthy attempt to achieve Bright's ideal of occupying ownership through free trade in land came to nothing.

Duffy's other project, of establishing a union of northern and southern interests to seek a reform of the land law, seemed for a time likely to achieve success. Circumstances were favourable for such a development; in Ulster the habitual security of the tenants seemed threatened, while in the rest of the country their condition was at its lowest ebb. The contrast between the virtual fixity of tenure which the Ulster custom conferred, and which Sharman Crawford and his followers wished to see legalised, and the very restricted compensation for improvements which Somerville's Bill of 1850 provided was obvious and inescapable. A deputation was sent from Ulster to protest against Somerville's Bill, led by James M'Knight, the editor of the Presbyterian *Banner of Ulster*. Returning from London 'exasperated at the apathy of Lord John Russell', he was persuaded by Gavan Duffy to support a National Conference on the Land Question in association with the representatives of the newly formed Tenant Protection Societies of Munster and Connaught.

The ensuing developments form a well-documented chapter of Irish history, fully, if not always objectively, reported by Gavan Duffy and A. M. Sullivan.[2] The Tenant League, which was formed in 1850, adopted the basic principles of fixity of tenure, rents fixed by valuation, and the right of the tenant to the market value of his tenancy; no candidate who would not endorse these principles was to be supported at the next election. The League received the commendation of Poulett Scrope and J. S. Mill, although the latter felt himself obliged to decline Gavan Duffy's offer to find him an Irish seat as a Tenant League member.[3] Carlyle, who had toured Ireland with Gavan Duffy in 1849, was also complimentary as to the work of the League, but qualified his compliments very shrewdly:

'Rent by a valuation' is not intrinsically so unfeasible—nay, so *unusual*—witness the old *usury laws* only abolished in these years; but it is utterly at variance with all the free trade, *laissez-faire* and other strongest tendencies of this poor time; and though said tendencies appear to me mostly mean and wooden, and nine-tenths untrue, yet it is precisely the true tenth that rules at present. In fact, to succeed altogether, you must have a new era, no less! Nay, I cannot but perceive that 'fixity of tenure', with such a set of tenants as you now have in Ireland, would never

---

[1] Duffy, *Life*, vol. ii, pp. 19–20; also, *idem, Conversations with Carlyle* (London, 1892), pp. 171–5.

[2] Sir C. Gavan Duffy, *The League of North and South, An Episode in Irish History, 1850–1854* (London, 1886); A. M. Sullivan, *New Ireland: Political Sketches and Personal Reminiscences of Thirty Years of Irish Public Life* (2nd ed. London, 1877).

[3] J. S. Mill, *Autobiography* (London, 1873), p. 279; H. S. R. Elliot (ed.), *Letters of John Stuart Mill*, vol. i, p. 159.

do, though you even could get it—that in fact, independently of all obstacles on the landlord's, parliament's, and official sides of the question, there is a total unpreparedness on the part of the population: 'more ado than a dish to wash', as the proverb says, before you attain this same new era of justice on the land question!¹

In the early days of their success, Gavan Duffy and his followers were unlikely to admit such unpalatable truths as this, and when the general election of 1852 put the balance of power in the hands of the Tenant League members, it must have seemed that the parliamentary obstacles to the attainment of their goal could soon be swept aside. At the opening of the new session, Shee and Greville introduced a Bill incorporating the principles of the League, Sharman Crawford having lost his seat in County Down. At the same time, Napier, the Attorney-General in Lord Derby's new ministry, introduced a land code comprising four Bills, including one recognising the principle of retrospective compensation for tenants' improvements. Both Bills were, after an attempt at delay by the Government, read a second time and referred to a Select Committee for examination. Subsequently Derby stated in the Lords that it was not the intention of the Government to accept the principles of the League Bill; at this the League members voted against the ministry and turned it out. In the new administration formed by Lord Aberdeen, Sadleir and Keogh, who had hitherto supported the Tenant League principles, accepted office, without any assurance as to Aberdeen's intentions on the tenant question. This was a clear violation of the resolution of the League's conference of 1852, 'that the members of parliament elected on tenant-right principles, should hold themselves perfectly independent of, and in opposition to, every government not supporting a measure fully embodying the principles of Mr Crawford's bill'.² In consequence, the tenant party was irretrievably split, one section, led by Gavan Duffy and Frederic Lucas, holding that independent opposition must be maintained in order to secure 'the Bill, the whole Bill and nothing but the Bill'; the other, led by Sharman Crawford and William Shee, holding that 'regard being had to the very valuable provisions of the Tenants' Improvements Compensation Bill, it would be time enough to condemn the conduct of Messrs Sadleir and Keogh should they retain office after the abandonment or injurious modification by the Government, of the essential provisions of that Bill'.³

From 1853 until 1860, the tenant party remained divided on the question of whether to press for fixity of tenure and all its corollaries, or to accept the less comprehensive measures which English Governments might be willing to support. In consequence, inevitably, nothing was achieved in the form of legislation,⁴ and public interest in the tenant case gradually

---

¹ Carlyle to Gavan Duffy, 15 September 1850; published in Duffy, *Conversations*, p. 160.
² W. Shee, *Papers, Letters and Speeches in the House of Commons, on the Irish Land Question* (London, 1863), p. 198.
³ Shee, p. 203.   ⁴ See O'Brien, *Parliamentary History*, pp. 100–3.

faded. Even had the split in the League not occurred, it is not clear that it could have achieved its aims. It may be, as Sir James O'Connor suggested,[1] that Gavan Duffy and his followers were not men of the calibre to have forced their measure through Parliament, but apart from this there is the fact which Carlyle had seen, that the people of Ireland were not ready for it. The small tenants were demoralised by the Famine, and inclined to seek their salvation in emigration;[2] the more substantial farmers, on the other hand, were turning increasingly to pasture farming, and the rising price of cattle on the English market brought them a new prosperity which made them indifferent to questions of rent and tenure.[3]

III

During the eighteen-fifties, Irish agriculture underwent a considerable transformation, as a result of emigration and price changes. The average size of farms increased considerably, and the larger farms were increasingly devoted to pasture rather than tillage. There can be no doubt that this change considerably raised the value product of Irish agriculture and improved the prosperity of the country. Visitors to Ireland testified to the remarkable recovery of the country after the Famine[4] and the annual publication of the Agricultural Statistics of Ireland by the Registrar-General was the occasion for favourable, if not complacent, comment by the Irish executive and newspapers favourable to it.[5] Year after year, Larcom, the Irish Under-Secretary, prepared speeches to be delivered by successive Lord-Lieutenants at agricultural shows and dinners, unvarying in their optimistic and hopeful tone. With equal regularity, the nationalist press assailed the executive and its policy, pointing to the continuing emigration of small tenants and the reduction of tillage as evidence of decay rather than prosperity.[6]

This undercurrent of discontent, though persistent, appeared to most contemporary observers trivial in comparison with the solid evidence of recovery and political and social stability which accumulated with the passing years. In 1861, *The Times* special correspondent could sum up his account of a tour in Ireland by saying, 'Compared with a few years

---

[1] Sir James O'Connor, *A History of Ireland, 1798–1924* (London, 1925), vol. II, p. 5.

[2] Robert Murray, Memorandum on the State of Ireland drawn up for Lord Clarendon, January 1850, January 1851 (Larcom Papers, 7600, National Library of Ireland), and see Jules de Lasteyrie, 'L'Irlande depuis la dernière famine', *Revue des deux mondes*, vol. VII (August 1853), p. 509.

[3] See J. O'Donovan, *Economic History of Live Stock in Ireland* (Cork, 1940), ch. X, especially pp. 209–10.

[4] De Lasteyrie, *passim.*

[5] For example, *Dublin Evening Packet*, 25 September 1858; *Daily Express*, 23 September 1858.

[6] Both the manuscript drafts and the printed reports of these speeches are preserved in the Larcom Papers—see especially vols. 7600–7603. For examples of the nationalist reaction, see *The Nation*, 16 October and 25 December 1858.

back, the agriculture of Ireland, as a whole, is greatly advanced. . . . Many wise men have propounded schemes for the regeneration of Ireland; but it would appear that this much-pitied country is really, though tardily, undergoing that delightful process—not necessarily by the force of any scheme at all.'[1]

The Times correspondent was shrewd enough to point out that this regeneration process might slow down or be reversed by any new growth of population 'unless ampler means of employment be provided'; but for the most part at this time English opinion was that the Irish problem had been largely solved. Good had come out of evil, for the Famine had allowed the land question to be dealt with in the manner which orthodox opinion had so long advocated—removal of the cottiers, increase in the size of farms, and more capitalistic methods of farming.

In the light of these developments, the continuance of agitation for tenant-right legislation appeared as sometimes irritating, sometimes merely ludicrous. After the subject had been debated on the motion of J. F. Maguire, M.P. for Dungarvan, on 14 April 1858, a leading article in *The Times* asserted that as England did not possess a law for tenant protection, nothing of the kind could be given to Ireland. 'England has submitted to the change necessitated by the consolidation of farms and the migration of small freeholders and copyholders into towns, and so must Ireland.' *The Times* was not often required to rebuke the tenant-righters so sharply at this time, for it could assure its readers that 'the old Irish howl has become faint and attenuated in its modern instances'.[2]

It was in this atmosphere that Edward Cardwell, the Irish Chief Secretary, introduced his Bill, to amend the law relating to the tenure and improvement of land in Ireland, at the end of March 1860, making 'one more attempt to settle a question of great difficulty and importance'.[3] This Bill, together with another introduced by the Attorney-General, Deasy, on the same night, was passed into law before the end of the session. The two Acts[4] between them constituted a comprehensive revision of Irish land law in its most important aspects and were clearly intended as a final treatment of a vexed question; as such their form has particular interest. Cardwell's Act extended the leasing powers of limited owners and gave them power to charge improvements made by them against the estate: it also gave tenants a right to compensation for improvements of certain specified kinds, when carried out with the consent of the landlord. This compensation was to take the form of a charge on the lands improved

---

[1] *The Times*, 22 October 1861.
[2] *Ibid.* 16 April 1858; 27 December 1858.
[3] *Hansard*, 3rd ser. vol. CLVII, col. 1553 (29 March 1860).
[4] 23 and 24 Vic. c. 153—Tenure and Improvement of Land (Ireland) Act, 1860 ('Cardwell's Act').
23 and 24 Vic. c. 154—Landlord and Tenant Law Amendment Act (Ireland), 1860 ('Deasy's Act').

of an annuity of £7. 2s. for every £100 expended by the tenant payable for such part of a period of twenty-five years as might be unexpired when the tenant was evicted. Existing improvements were not recognised at all.

The essential provision of Deasy's Act was Section 3, by which it was enacted that 'the relation of landlord and tenant shall be deemed to be founded on the express or implied contract of the parties and not upon tenure or service'. Here was the 'commercial principle' of landlord-tenant relationship stated in plain words and put upon the Statute Book; the theory of free contract had become established policy.

In one sense, this was the culmination of a trend long in operation; in another, it was the outcome of a direct and obvious influence. Examination will show that the terms of the two Land Acts of 1860 follow very closely the 'Suggestions for Legislation' accompanying the *Report on the Landlord and Tenant Question in Ireland from 1835 till 1859* which Neilson Hancock presented to Cardwell in October 1859. Those suggestions are such as might have been expected to come from the author of *Impediments to the Prosperity of Ireland*, the indomitable believer in *laissez-faire*; yet they are hardly such as might be expected to come from an Ulster man, the brother of a Lurgan land agent, well acquainted with the benefits of tenant-right. The explanation of this is that Hancock, by 1859, had come to believe that the interests of Ulster tenants could best be protected by encouraging the making of express contracts between landlord and tenant into which the customs of different regions could be written, rather than by attempts on the part of the government to interpret such customs in general legislation.[1] The object of the legislation of 1860 was largely to encourage such 'written engagements' between the contracting parties, as Cardwell himself emphasised in introducing his Bill.[2]

In principle, all this was eminently reasonable, as economists' plans always are. It simply left to be settled by express contract what Sharman Crawford and others had tried to establish by legislation—and if the contract were inadequate or not observed, the law recognised the tenant's right to compensation for approved improvements. In practice, the Acts had the serious defect that they established an unduly complicated mechanism of which neither landlords nor tenants would wish to avail themselves, and encouraged, but did not enforce, the granting of leases and making of contracts. Hence the tenant's position was hardly strengthened at all, and it needed only an adverse turn of economic circumstances to reveal its weakness anew.

Such unfavourable developments in the Irish economy were beginning even before the Acts of 1860 were passed. The harvest of 1859 was deficient, though not to a serious extent; another bad season followed in 1860, and in 1861 there was a serious decline in both crops and livestock,

[1] See Hancock, *Impediments* (1866 reprint), pp. 43 and 44.
[2] *Hansard*, 3rd ser. vol. CLVII, col. 1565.

the latter resulting mainly from a shortage of fodder. When 1862 brought no improvement farmers were seriously affected and began to fall behind with their rents; that summer saw the revival of agrarian crime, with several murders in Tipperary. A confidential adviser of the Irish Government, G. J. Goold, of Clonmel, reported to the Castle that these crimes arose directly from demands for rent and eviction proceedings by the landlords attacked.

You may remember [he added], that I have held persistently that the surface was no indication of what was underneath, and that whilst all was calm and orderly in the former, the latter was, if anything, more bitter and disaffected than at any previous time... if the harvest turns out as indifferent as it promises, I fear the winter will be *very* bad... the assertion of the ordinary rights of a Landlord is becoming a matter of personal danger. When you consider the number of small farmers who will be totally unable to pay their rents and their debts next November, every one of whom you may reckon as a member of the same lawless fraternity, from the date of a distress for rent or ejectment process, you must admit the prospect is not of the brightest.[1]

This gloomy trend of events, forming so sharp a contrast with the seemingly tranquil prosperity of the later eighteen-fifties, stimulated public discussion of the land problem once more. Considerable controversy arose over the question of whether the decline was a merely temporary one, due to a succession of bad seasons, or of longer duration and the result of deep-seated defects in social organisation. This latter view was taken by D. C. Heron,[2] who began the controversy by delivering a paper on 'Historical Statistics of Ireland' to the Statistical and Social Inquiry Society of Ireland in January 1862.[3] Relying primarily on statistics of emigration and cultivation, Heron contended that

Ireland during the last thirty years has not shared in the prosperity which has so abundantly befallen the rest of the United Kingdom.... Great legislative enactments are said to have passed for Ireland during the last thirty-five years. No person can now say that the result has been successful.... What is one remedy for this present decline in prosperity and population? The answer is—emancipate the land, give the tenant security for improvements on his land.[4]

Heron was answered by one Randal MacDonnell a few months later, in a paper entitled 'Statistics of Irish Prosperity'. MacDonnell admitted the existence of present distress, but denied that there was any proof of a long-period decline. The Irish executive deemed the matter sufficiently important to require investigation, and in March 1863 Hancock, who now was semi-official adviser on economic questions, produced a *Report on the Supposed Progressive Decline of Irish Prosperity*, in which he concluded

[1] Goold to Larcom, 10 August 1862 (Larcom Papers, 7605).
[2] Professor of Political Economy and Jurisprudence, Queen's College, Galway, 1849–59.
[3] *Journal* of the Society, vol. III, p. 235.
[4] *Ibid.* pp. 246–7.

'All the statistics I have examined appear to me to refute the theory of progressive decline'; but he asserted plainly that there had been considerable diminution of produce in 1860, 1861 and 1862, and that the resultant losses had fallen heavily on the farming classes.[1]

The parties to this debate were in fact arguing at cross purposes. If population and acreage of land under crops be taken as the test of national prosperity, then Heron's contention that there had been a long decline was correct; if reliance be placed on customs and excise returns, deposits in banks and such figures, used by McDonnell and Hancock, then it could be proved that recovery had merely undergone a temporary setback. But behind these statistics lie two radically different views of social organisation. The official view, as represented by Hancock, envisaged prosperity in terms of increased real net returns, considering the means by which these were obtained as relatively unimportant. The nationalist view, moderately represented by Heron, considered security on the land for the existing population more important than increasing productivity.

Even so, Hancock and Larcom, who were probably the most influential people in the framing of economic policy for Ireland at this time, saw clearly enough that changes in the land system were a necessary corollary of the new economic situation.

It was truly observed [wrote Hancock to Larcom in 1863], that before Free Trade farmers' losses were dismissed in bad years by a rise of price which transferred the burden to the consumers, and in good years the profits of abundant crops were diminished to the farmers by the great fall in price which a local abundance produced. The effect of free trade is to limit these fluctuations so that prices neither rise so high in bad years nor fall so low in good years as formerly.... This circumstance of farmers having to undergo greater fluctuations [in their net income] for good or ill, than formerly explains the necessity of farmers having more capital quite independent of the size of their farms—it explains too the absolute necessity of some arrangement more permanent than a bare yearly tenancy.[2]

Larcom shared these views, and himself stated that

the operation of this unjust state of the law as to yearly tenancies is increasing year by year in Ireland, because the leases are falling out, and new leases are not being granted to anything like the former amount. In former times the franchise being dependent on tenure, leases were the rule; but since 1850, the franchise is on a valuation and I was assured on a recent inquiry that on estates sold in the Incumbered Estates Court now there are not one-third of the number of the leases there were on the estates sold in 1850.[3]

[1] W. N. Hancock, *Report on the Supposed Progressive Decline of Irish Prosperity* (Dublin, 1863), pp. 82–3.

[2] Hancock to Larcom, 17 August 1863 (Larcom Papers, 7606).

[3] Larcom, 'Observations on the Landlord and Tenant Question, June 1863', Larcom Papers, 7706. This paper, which is without signature or heading, begins: 'I have read as you requested the Draft Bill on the Landlord and Tenant Question proposed by an Irish landlord.' This was probably J. F. Maguire, who drafted a Bill in 1863, but never brought it in. Internal evidence indicates Larcom as the author of the paper.

On this account, Larcom was prepared to advocate that 'the doctrine of emblements, that he who sows shall reap, should be extended to all improvements which the tenant bona fide makes in carrying out the purpose for which the farm was let to him'.

Apparently these principles were not acceptable to the Cabinet of the day, for when J. F. Maguire moved for a Royal Commission to inquire into the land problem in Ireland in 1863, his motion was heavily defeated, Palmerston taking the opportunity to denounce plans for fixity of tenure as 'communistic and totally at variance with the social organisation to which the country has attached so much value, and on which the interest of the country depends. I say', he added, 'let the owner and the tenant settle their own affairs—give each full liberty to do so.'[1]

At this time, the Irish members were backed by only a small amount of agitation for land reform in their own country, despite the agricultural depression. There was some petitioning for a tenant-right measure from Cork and Westmeath,[2] and later a 'monster petition' was got up by the Corporation of Dublin.[3] This was contemptuously dismissed by *The Times*: 'They simply don't know what it is they ask for, and if they don't know nobody else is likely to know....Parliament did not make Ireland, nor can Parliament make it anew to suit the golden visions of landless peasants and penniless agitators.'[4]

The tenant cause gained more authority, however, in November 1864, when Judge Mountifort Longfield declared, publicly and in the presence of the Lord-Lieutenant, that although fixity of tenure was a 'wild and impracticable' proposal, 'the claim for compensation for improvements is one that ought not lightly to be passed over'.[5]

At this period, the majority of those who claimed to speak for the tenants would have been willing to accept a fair measure legalising compensation as a settlement of the question. More extreme nationalist journals, such as the *Irishman* and the *Irish People* (the organ of the Fenians) were urging that peasant proprietorship was the only true solution,[6] but when the National Association of Ireland was formed at the end of 1864, its first object was stated to be merely 'a reform of the law of landlord and tenant, securing to the tenant full compensation for valuable improvements'.[7]

In the face of such moderate demands, Palmerston was still unyielding,

---

[1] Speech in the House of Commons, 23 June 1863; *Hansard*, 3rd ser. vol. CLXXI, col. 1375.
[2] See *Freeman's Journal*, 11 February 1863.
[3] *Ibid.* 23 and 24 April 1864.
[4] *The Times*, 26 April 1864.
[5] M. Longfield, Address at the Opening of the 18th Session of the Statistical and Social Inquiry Society of Ireland, *Journal S.S.I.S.I.*, vol. IV, p. 129.
[6] See *The Irish People*, 7 May 1864; *The Irishman*, 28 May 1864.
[7] *Freeman's Journal*, 30 December 1864.

and coined his famous epigram 'tenant-right is landlord wrong';[1] but when J. F. Maguire, in March 1865, sought to obtain the appointment of a special Committee to inquire into the existing state of the law of landlord and tenant in Ireland, the Prime Minister thought it politic to yield, partially at least. Accordingly, a Select Committee was appointed with the more limited duty of inquiring into the operation of Cardwell's Act.

This Committee had achieved little by the end of the session, save the collection of some valuable evidence from Longfield and Lord Dufferin on tenant-right.[2] Maguire and his supporters wished to report this evidence, and ask for the reappointment of the Committee in the next session, but Peel and the representatives of the landlords, who were in a majority on the Committee, were anxious to bring it to an end and keep tenant-right issues out of the coming election campaign. As a result, the Committee merely recommended some minor changes in the Act, which witnesses had clearly shown to be inoperative in its existing form. At the general election of 1865, the Liberals were returned again, but before the new ministry was well in office, events in Ireland had taken on a more menacing aspect with the discovery of the Fenian conspiracy: but as yet the government did not seem to see in this any need for a more forward Irish economic policy.

In the early spring of 1866 the Irish Liberal members drafted a Land Bill intended to replace Cardwell's Act; this Bill divided tenants into two classes, those holding on leases for thirty-one years and over, and those holding for shorter terms. In the case of tenants of the former class, the question of compensation was to be regulated exclusively by contract between landlord and tenant; tenants of the latter class were to receive compensation for improvements, measured by the increase in letting value caused by such improvements, on determination of tenancy.

Chichester Fortescue, who had succeeded Peel as Chief Secretary, obtained a report from Hancock on the provisions of this Bill, and on the working of the Acts of 1860.[3] Hancock declared the Irish members' Bill to be 'simple, clear and definite in character'; accordingly when Chichester Fortescue introduced a Government measure later in the session, it was clearly based on the Irish Liberals' Bill. But a considerable section of public opinion in Ireland, led by The O'Donoghue, M.P. for Tralee, regarded that Bill as a 'minimum measure', which could not be considered a settlement of the tenants' case. On the other hand, many landlords, English and Irish, were opposed to the recognition of the tenants' right to money compensation which it gave. Consequently, Chichester

---

[1] 'As to tenant-right, I may be allowed to say that I think it is equivalent to landlords' wrong': *Hansard*, 3rd ser. vol. CLXXVII, col. 823 (27 February 1865).

[2] See *Parliamentary Papers*, 1865 (402), vol. XI.

[3] W. N. Hancock, *Report on the Landlord and Tenant Question in Ireland from 1860 till 1866* (Dublin, 1866).

Fortescue's Bill was assailed from both sides with considerable vigour, and after the change of ministry in June 1866 it was withdrawn.

One notable feature of the debates on this Bill was the speech made in support of it by John Stuart Mill, then lately elected to Parliament for Westminster. Mill made it clear that he regarded Chichester Fortescue's Bill as a *pis aller*, asserting that 'peasant farming, as a rule, never answers without fixity of tenure'.[1] 'But you do not want to perpetuate peasant farming: you want to improve Ireland in another way.... Well, then, how are the present tenantry, or the best of them, to be raised into a superior class of farmers? There is but one way, and this Bill which is before you affords the means.'

Commenting on this speech, the *Nation* argued with some truth that its main effect was 'simply to show that the proposed law falls very far short of the legislation absolutely required to place the relations between landlord and tenant in Ireland on a basis of justice'.[2] Indeed at this period there is a noticeable tendency for the development of informed public opinion, both in England and in Ireland, to outpace the growth of policy. Whilst successive ministries fumbled before an unsympathetic House with measures for limited tenant compensation, an increasing body of opinion in Ireland was massing behind the idea that fixity of tenure was the minimum acceptable solution of the land problem. In England at the same time the feeling was growing, and finding frequent expression, that if the Irish desired to have a system of peasant farming, with all that it might imply, it was not the duty of the English legislature to foist another system on them.

IV

The first and most direct exposition of the growing claims of the tenant interest in Ireland was given by Isaac Butt, in a pamphlet published in July 1866, and entitled *Land Tenure in Ireland: a Plea for the Celtic Race.* Butt had then recently distinguished himself by undertaking the defence of the Fenian prisoners, and had been profoundly disturbed by what he had learnt of their aims and convictions. In *Land Tenure in Ireland* he held that Fenianism, like the emigration from which so much of the Fenian strength had been drawn, was the outcome of a deep dissatisfaction with the land system. Butt contended that 'the great mass of the Irish population have never acquiesced in the system of landed property which successive conquests have imposed upon them'; of recent years their discontent had increased because of the attempts to sweep away the last traces of the old customs and diminish the independence of the tenant by replacing leases with tenancies at will.[3] The land grievance must be removed before Fenianism could be extinguished, and for its removal

[1] J. S. Mill, *Chapters and Speeches on the Irish Land Question* (London, 1870), p. 100.
[2] *Nation*, 26 May 1866.   [3] I. Butt, *Land Tenure*, pp. 23, 43.

Butt advocated legislation to convert the tenure of every Irish occupier into a certain term of sixty-three years at a rent 'to be fixed at the fair letting value of the land'. The rights of the landlord were to be protected by covenants against sub-division and bad husbandry, and by continuing the right to evict summarily for non-payment of the valuation rent.[1]

For this proposal Butt was promptly and vigorously assailed by the landlord interest. Lord Lifford denounced the scheme as 'communistic' and 'subversive of the rights of property';[2] Lord Dufferin also advanced criticism of the scheme less lurid, but more shrewd. It would, he argued, prove too rigid for agricultural progress and exacerbate landlord-tenant relations—'its effect will be to render the landlords jealous of the pretensions of their tenantry, and to make the tenants distrustful of the designs of their landlords, to frighten the English mortgagee, and to discourage the investment of capital'.[3]

The critics of fixity of tenure continued to denounce it as 'irreconcilable with any respect for the landlord's property in the land',[4] but the tenant interest was now little inclined to heed them. The Irish Liberals, backed by the Catholic middle class, would have accepted a moderate measure of tenant compensation as late as 1865, but after the failure of Chichester Fortescue's Bill in 1866 it became clear that no measure so limited could be acceptable in Ireland again. Sensing the change of feeling brought about by the Fenian rising and its suppression, many Irish Liberals and moderates accepted Butt's assessment of the situation and his proposals for land reform. Amongst them was Sir John Gray, M.P. for Kilkenny and highly influential through his proprietorship of the old-established *Freeman's Journal*. Gray propounded a scheme for fixity of tenure to his constituents in January 1868; significantly, when Jonathan Pim introduced a Tenant Bill in the Commons a month later, the editorial comment of the *Freeman's Journal* was: 'It does not materially differ from Mr Fortescue's bill, which the country regarded with some favour, but since then great changes have taken place in the popular mind, and the principle on which it is now intent is direct security for a definite term. Nothing else will do.'[5]

In taking this attitude, the *Freeman's Journal* had the backing of the Roman Catholic hierarchy, most of whom were very favourably disposed to Butt's ideas. The clergy had long been associated with the tenant cause,

[1] See I. Butt, *Fixity of Tenure; Heads of a Suggested Legislative Enactment; with Introduction and Notes* (Dublin, 1866).

[2] James Hewitt, Fourth Viscount Lifford, *A Plea for Irish Landlords: A Letter to Isaac Butt, Esq.* (Dublin, 1867).

[3] Marquis of Dufferin, *Irish Emigration and the Tenure of Land in Ireland* (London, 1867), p. 393.

[4] G. Fitzgibbon, *Ireland in 1868, the Battlefield for English Party Strife; its Grievances, Real and Factitious; Remedies, Abortive or Mischievous* (London, 1868), p. 117.

[5] *Freeman's Journal*, 24 February 1868. For the provisions of Pim's Bill, see *Hansard*, 3rd ser. vol. cxc, cols. 928–30 (18 February 1868).

and, when an Irish Tenant League was founded in 1869, the principal figures in it were Butt and the Roman Catholic Dean of Limerick, Richard B. O'Brien. Even the conservative Bishop of Kerry, David Moriarty, wrote to Butt:

In your principal thesis I entirely concur....I have been frequently accused of indifference on this subject, but the fact is that in the tenant-right measures proposed hitherto I saw no remedy. It riles me to see men who assume the leadership in a question like this shouting for compensation for improvements while they leave both tenure and rent in the arbitrary power of the landlord.[1]

By 1869 the desire for fixity of tenure was so widespread in Ireland, and the liaison between the clergy and Sir John Gray's followers so strong that, when Gladstone was preparing to legislate on the question, O'Hagan, the Lord Chancellor of Ireland, had no hesitation in advising him: 'the success or failure of the Land Bill depends on the *Freeman's Journal*; if it says, We accept this as a fixity of tenure, every priest will say the same, and *vice versa*.'[2]

The reaction of the leading economists of the day to these developments in Ireland was markedly different from what had been typical a generation before. Whereas Mill in 1848 had been almost alone in his advocacy of a radically new land settlement in Ireland, twenty years later he was the leading exponent of a point of view which found many supporters. Mill's *England and Ireland*, published in 1868, was probably the most influential single contribution to the extended debate on Irish land problems which was carried on in England between 1865 and 1870. The main point which Mill stressed was that in matters of agriculture 'Ireland...bears more resemblance to almost any other country in Europe than she does to Great Britain'.[3] All attempts to assimilate the Irish land system to the English were therefore bound to aggravate the Irish sense of grievance and end in failure. Only the conversion of peasant occupiers into peasant proprietors could solve the problem:

What the case requires is simply this. We have had commissions, under the authority of Parliament, to commute for an annual payment the burthen of tithe, and the variable obligations of copyholders. What is wanted in Ireland is a commission of a similar kind to examine every farm which is let to a tenant, and commute the present variable for a fixed rent....The benefit, to the cultivator, of a permanent property in the soil, does not depend on paying nothing for it, but on the certainty that the payment cannot be increased.[4]

Thus interpreted, Mill's concept of peasant proprietorship was not fundamentally different from Butt's fixity of tenure.[5] Its most important

---

[1] Bishop Moriarty to Isaac Butt, 26 May 1867 (Butt Papers, B. 40, National Library of Ireland).
[2] Viscount Morley, *The Life of William Ewart Gladstone* (London, 1903), vol. II, p. 292.
[3] Mill, *England and Ireland*, p. 14.　　　　[4] *Ibid.* pp. 36, 37.
[5] O'Connor Morris, *The Times* Special Commissioner in Ireland in 1869, in fact identified Mill's scheme with fixity of tenure: *Letters on the Land Question of Ireland* (London, 1870), p. 322.

feature, and the one which most startled and antagonised the upholders of 'the rights of property'[1] was the suggestion that rents should be controlled by law and not determined by market forces. Perhaps one of the most remarkable proofs of the changing attitude of economists to State intervention at this time is the fact that the same suggestion was put forward, independently, by J. E. Cairnes, now traditionally regarded as the most orthodox of all classical economists. Cairnes was the author of a series of articles entitled 'Ireland in Transition' which appeared anonymously in the *Economist* during the autumn of 1865. In these he combated the view that the only possible evolution of Irish agriculture was towards large farms, on the English or Scottish model, and argued that it would be quite consistent with free trade principles for the State to enact a tenant-compensation law so as to protect and encourage the small occupiers. The basis for this contention was Cairnes's view that on economic grounds the right of property in land must be considered as qualified and subordinate to 'the right of the labourer to whatever his labour has produced'.[2] Subsequently, in an article which appeared in the *Fortnightly Review* in January 1870, Cairnes carried the implications of this doctrine much further. In this he argued that the cultivator of the soil should not have to pay more for its use than the economic rent in the strict Ricardian sense—

if the cultivator be required to pay more than this—if the rent exacted from him encroach upon the domain of wages and profits—he is so far placed at a disadvantage as compared with other producers, and is deprived of the ordinary inducements to industry. It thus becomes a question of capital importance, what provision exists in the conditions of an industrial community to prevent this result; what security we have that—the land of a country being once given up to private speculation— the limits set by 'economic rent' shall in the main, be observed in the actual rent which landlords obtain.[3]

Cairnes argued that in Ireland there was not adequate security to ensure this, and his conclusion was that 'no settlement of Irish land can be effectual which still leaves with landlords the power of indefinitely raising rent' even though 'few Englishmen can hear without something of a cold tremor a proposal to fix rent by law'.[4]

Mill and Cairnes in the eighteen-sixties were using essentially the same theoretical apparatus to discuss land problems as Ricardo and Torrens had done in the eighteen-twenties, but drew from it almost a diametrically opposite policy conclusion. This was primarily due to their recognition

[1] For an example of the unfavourable reactions to Mill's pamphlet, see *The Times* editorial of 14 March 1868.

[2] *The Economist*, 25 October 1865. And see above, p. 16.

[3] J. E. Cairnes, 'Political Economy and Land', *Fortnightly Rev.* n.s. vol. VII (January 1870); reprinted as Essay VI of *Essays in Political Economy, Theoretical and Applied* (London, 1873), p. 198.

[4] *Essays*, Essay VI, pp. 202–3.

of the fact stressed by Cairnes himself—'Political Economy stands apart from all particular systems of social or industrial existence'[1]—together with the corollary that the English system of social organisation was one form amongst many and not necessarily a norm or ideal in any sense.

Acceptance of this viewpoint had in fact become remarkably widespread between 1865 and 1870; discussions of the Irish land question in the light of Indian and Prussian precedents occur frequently in the literature at this period. Mill himself had naturally used Indian parallels quite extensively in his writings on Ireland,[2] and one of the most penetrating analyses of the Irish situation in 1868 came from a former Indian civil servant, Sir George Campbell, sometime Chief Commissioner of the Central Provinces of India. He stressed a point which Mill had also made—'that as the world now stands, it is we who are abnormal, and the Irish system is that which is more general'.[3] Campbell understood and emphasised the distinction between tenure by contract and tenure by status, and the importance of the latter in Ireland. He viewed the long attempt to replace it by a system of strict contract tenure as mistaken, but recognised that it had not been altogether unsuccessful. On this account he was critical of schemes which proposed to confer a uniform fixity of tenure throughout the country, and suggested a compromise solution recognising both existing customs and the variations from them. Definite customs should be confirmed by law, whilst true contract tenures would not be interfered with; in all other cases, disputes between landlord and tenant should be referred to a commission acting on the principle that tenants are entitled to receive the full market-value of their improvements, past and present. To this, however, Campbell added significantly: 'It seems to me that if you give the tenant a right to compensation for improvements, the only course is also to give him some remedy against an increase of rent which would absorb his improvements.'[4]

Campbell's work attracted a great deal of attention at the time of its appearance—not surprisingly, for it stands out from the mass of pamphlets produced at the time by its lucidity and penetrating common sense. Campbell's long Indian experience enabled him to view the Irish land question from a fresh and constructive aspect; amongst those who were won over by his arguments was Henry Fawcett, now remembered only as the least original of Mill's disciples, but then influential as an advanced

---

[1] Essay VII, 'Political Economy and Laissez-faire', *Essays*, p. 255.
Cairnes is not usually regarded as an exponent of 'economic relativity', but there is the testimony of one of his pupils, F. Hugh O'Donnell, in support of this view: 'The old saying that "circumstances alter cases", he said continually, was the caution which all sound economists kept in mind, and which the most influential economists were habitually defying. "Never forget your *Caeteris Paribus*," he said a hundred times.' [*A History of the Irish Parliamentary Party* (London, 1910), vol. I, p. 138.]
[2] See *Principles*, bk. II, ch. IX, p. 318; *idem, England and Ireland* (London, 1868), pp. 22, 23.
[3] Sir George Campbell, *The Irish Land* (London, 1869), p. 16.
[4] *Ibid.* p. 180.

Liberal member of Parliament, with a particular interest in Indian affairs. Stressing the fact of recognition of dual ownership in land in India, Fawcett endorsed Campbell's proposals, and in fact interpreted them as amounting to a less qualified form of fixity of tenure than Campbell himself would have admitted.[1]

Outright fixity of tenure was also advocated by Thorold Rogers, who gave his support to Sir John Gray. 'I believe', Rogers wrote, 'the only remedy is that of turning the non-occupying landowner into the recipient of a fixed rent-charge, payable in money, but calculated, to save changes in the value of money, in produce. I would also put a treble income tax on the absentee owners of such a rent-charge.' Rogers, however, did not approve of Mill's plan, since it would involve the collection of the fixed rents by the State. 'Fancy the state distraining in Tipperary or Westmeath. It would require that terrible army of bailiffs which I spoke of just now, one to every ten of the population, in order to collect its rents.'[2] The substance of this objection is hard to see, since Rogers also stated that 'I have never yet met an Irish tenant who does not emphatically assert his willingness to pay a fair rent for his holding', and offered no explanation why the tenant should be any less willing to pay it to the State rather than to the individual proprietor.

Despite his eminence as an economic historian, Thorold Rogers did not enter into any historical examination of the right of the Irish tenant to be regarded as having some proprietary interest in his holding. It was left to Frederic Seebohm to undertake this, and he argued that under the various settlements of Ireland in the seventeenth century it had been intended to establish feudal tenures similar to those on English manors; had the rights which such tenures conferred on the occupiers been observed, they should have been as secure as English copyholders. Hence 'the great wrong done to the Irish peasantry, and therefore to the Irish nation, did not so much consist in the abolition of the old Irish tenures and the introduction of English ones in their place, as in the neglect or refusal on the part of England and Anglo-Irish law to recognise the just rights of the Irish under those very feudal tenures which England herself forced upon them'.[3]

Seebohm recognised and stressed that this wrong could not be righted by seeking to re-establish feudal tenures—'the wrong must be remedied in a way consistent with those economic laws which are at work in modern society'. Such a remedy, Seebohm suggested, would involve 'the invention of two new tenures—one to meet the needs of the commercial farmer,

---

[1] H. Fawcett, Lecture on 'The Land Question' delivered before Brighton Liberal Registration Association, as reported in the *Freeman's Journal*, 23 October 1869.

[2] James E. Thorold Rogers to Sir John Gray, dated Oxford, 28 September 1869 (published in *Freeman's Journal*, 6 October 1869).

[3] Seebohm, 'The Land Question: Part I. English Tenures in Ireland', *Fortnightly Review*, n.s. vol. VI (1869), p. 627.

who hires a farm in the open market at the market price; the other, adapted to the circumstances of a peasantry born and dependent on the land for a living'. This other 'must needs be an approach to what is involved in the words, so odious to landlords, "fixity of tenure"'.[1]

Hence the comparative and historical studies of the economists and economic historians lent weight to the case for a legal recognition of fixity of tenure. But the idea of a more direct peasant proprietorship, involving land purchase by occupiers, was not without its advocates; where the supporters of fixity of tenure referred to Indian precedents, these believers in occupying ownership frequently cited Prussian experience. Since the time of von Raumer the Stein and Hardenberg decrees had formed a recurrent theme for Irish land reformers, but in the eighteen-sixties their most competent exponent was Henry Dix Hutton, a Dublin barrister whose interest in the philosophy of Auguste Comte had led him to the study of sociology.

Hutton had travelled in Prussia, and studied the operation of the Stein–Hardenberg reforms at first hand: his conclusion was that peasant proprietorship did not lead to that excessive sub-division and poor agriculture which its opponents alleged. He also shared Mill's views in holding that 'English land tenure...does not furnish a universal standard....There is no country to which English tenure, considered as an absolute test, is less applicable than Ireland.'[2] On the other hand, 'a mixed proprietary system of larger and small farms' would be well suited to Ireland, and could be introduced through a system akin to the Prussian land banks. Hutton's plan was for the gradual introduction of occupying ownership through an extension of the machinery of the Landed Estates Court to allow tenants to buy up their own holdings. Up to twenty years' purchase of the annual value of the holding would be advanced by the Board of Works, whom the tenant would repay over thirty-five years by an annuity of $5\% - 3\frac{1}{2}\%$ interest and the balance redemption of principal.

Hutton later combined these ideas with a proposal for the disestablishment of the Church of Ireland, which he published as a pamphlet in 1868.[3] Acknowledging a copy of this, John Bright wrote to Hutton—'I am ready to state my general approval of your great plan', but added 'I fear the scheme is so broad, and so good, and so complete that Parliament would stand aghast at it'.[4]

---

[1] *Ibid.* pp. 639, 640.

[2] H. D. Hutton, 'The Stein–Hardenberg Land Legislation: its Basis, Development and Results in Prussia'; 'A Plan for the Gradual Creation of a Farmer Proprietary in Ireland': *Transactions of the National Association for the Promotion of Social Science, Belfast Meeting, 1867* (London, 1868), pp. 628, 637.

[3] Hutton, *Proposals for the Gradual Creation of a Farmer Proprietary in Ireland* (London, 1868).

[4] Bright to Hutton, 27 January 1868 (Princeton University MSS., AM 9553).

Bright was himself at this time the advocate of a plan for creating small proprietors in Ireland—a plan very similar to Hutton's, but more restricted in some respects. His proposal was to have 'a Parliamentary Commission empowered to buy up the large estates in Ireland belonging to the English nobility, for the purpose of selling them on easy terms to the occupiers of the farms and to the tenantry of Ireland'.[1] The 'easy terms' would have been essentially the same as Hutton's, but the lands to be sold would have been only those of absentees, themselves willing sellers and their tenants willing buyers.

This scheme of Bright's rested on no study of Prussian or other precedents, but solely on his own belief in free trade and dislike of the laws of primogeniture and entail. It was simply 'Free Trade in Land' all over again, with the emphasis on occupying ownership now. There is here a significant divergence between the Manchester School and the classical theorists which is tellingly revealed by some of Bright's own comments in his correspondence with Gladstone in 1869: 'As to the land question, I am sorely puzzled....I have great faith in political economy, a science unknown, I suspect, in Ireland, and so far as it will carry me, I am willing and eager to go courageously—but I shrink from nearly all the propositions which are offered.'[2] Bright's political economy certainly would not carry him as far as Cairnes's, for the latter's proposal to introduce fixed rents Bright confessed 'alarmed him a good deal'.

To sum up the debate on Irish land which preceded Gladstone's first legislation in 1870, it might be said to have resulted in two proposals for policy—one, land purchase, the other fixity of tenure. The latter commanded much the greatest support, not merely from the Irish tenant interest, but from the majority of informed opinion in England. Land purchase at this time was neither sought after by the tenants nor advocated by many economists; but the authority and influence of John Bright was sufficient to redress the balance somewhat and secure considerable attention for the scheme he supported.

Until the session of 1868 at least, the debate proceeding in Ireland and England had little reflection in the debates in Parliament. By comparison with the great question of Electoral Reform, the Irish land problem was for the moment of secondary importance; in any event, it was not expected that the Conservative administration would make any vigorous attempt to deal with it. At the beginning of the session of 1867 the Irish Chief Secretary, Lord Naas, did introduce a Tenants Improvements Bill; in doing so he remarked that 'with regard to the extremer measures which had been proposed elsewhere, they had seldom found their way to that House in the shape of a substantive proposition. Such

[1] J. Bright, Speech at Dublin, 30 October 1866; reprinted in *Speeches on Questions of Public Policy by John Bright, M.P.*, ed. J. E. Thorold Rogers (London, 1868), p. 373.
[2] Bright to Gladstone, 15 October 1869 (B.M. Add. MSS. 44112).

extreme proposals had been generally confined to the platform, hustings and pamphlets, and had seldom been submitted in detail to the consideration of Parliament.'[1] Certainly there was nothing extreme in the Bill which Naas brought forward, and his critics were not slow to point out that it fell far short of the measures which had been proposed by the first Derby administration in 1852.

Naas proposed in this Bill to set up a Special Commissioner of Public Works, who would be authorised to advance money to tenants to enable them to undertake certain classes of improvements, much in the same manner as loans were made to landlords under the Land Improvement Acts. The Bill also provided that where the tenant laid out his own money or labour on his holding, he could apply to the Commissioner to have the outlay made a charge upon the land; on his giving up or being evicted from the holding the tenant would be entitled to receive back from the Commissioner a proportionate part of the sum charged on the land, in cash.

In introducing the Bill, Naas mentioned that since the Devon Commission reported, no fewer than twenty-five Irish land Bills had been introduced into the House. 'It was not his intention', he said, 'to raise again this dreamy row of ghosts.' Yet his own measure had a curious resemblance to the oldest of all these spectres, the Bill which Derby (then Lord Stanley) had introduced in 1845. The landlord interest in 1867 showed themselves little better disposed towards this Bill than their predecessors had been towards Stanley's in 1845; but now the tenant interest had a greater voice in the Commons, and used it to oppose this Bill also. The Irish members were quick to point out that the right to borrow money for improvements and charge it on the land was of little value to a tenant who might be evicted in six months, and the Bill made no provision to increase security of tenure. To this the Government response was that the Bill was not intended as a full settlement of the land question; but no partial measure was any longer acceptable to Irish interests. Thus Lord Naas's land Bill was attacked from both sides, just as Chichester Fortescue's had been in the previous session, and it eventually suffered the same fate.

Two other measures to deal with the land question were brought forward in 1867, and proved equally abortive. One was introduced by the member for County Clare, Sir Colman O'Loghlen, and attempted to encourage the granting of leases, providing that where no written contract existed the law should presume a twenty-one-years lease instead of a tenancy at will. The other was introduced in the Lords by the Marquess of Clanricarde 'and it was based upon the great principle that everything was to be done by voluntary contracts between landlord and tenant'.[2]

[1] *Hansard*, 3rd ser. vol. CLXXXV, col. 532 (18 February 1867).
[2] Speech of the Marquess of Clanricarde, *Hansard*, 3rd ser. vol. CLXXXV, col. 796 (22 February 1867).

O'Loghlen's Bill was ultimately withdrawn; Clanricarde's was referred to a Select Committee of the Lords both in 1867 and again in 1868, but never progressed further.

In the session of 1867 almost the only repercussion in Parliament of 'the extremer measures which had been proposed elsewhere' was a motion by J. L. O'Beirne, the member for Cashel, seeking to obtain authority for an advance of £1,000,000 to be applied in the carrying out of Bright's scheme of land purchase in Ireland.[1] Clanricarde had already seen fit to refer to this scheme in the Lords, characterising it as 'utterly wild and nonsensical' and asking 'Was there a single principle of political economy or of any other science to recommend the proposition?..'[2] The Commons did not seem disposed to view it in any more enthusiastic light, and O'Beirne withdrew his motion.

At the beginning of the session of 1868 there is the first evidence of a changed temper on Irish questions in the lower House. The general feeling, inside and outside the House, was that the condition of Ireland required major measures, but that little could be done by a Parliament so near the end of its life, and about to be replaced by one elected on a very different basis. In this atmosphere, Jonathan Pim obtained leave to bring in a moderate land Bill, similar to Fortescue's of 1866,[3] but proceeded no further with it. Matters stood thus on 10 March 1868, when John Francis Maguire moved his motion, 'That this House will immediately resolve itself into a Committee, with the view of taking into consideration the condition and circumstances of Ireland'.

In the four nights' debate which ensued it became clear, as H. A. Butler-Johnstone, the member for Canterbury, said, that if 1867 had been the 'Reform Session', 1868 was to be the 'Irish Session',[4] and the position of leading personalities on both sides of the House in regard to Irish questions was made clearer than it had been for years past. From the point of view of economic thought, the most remarkable feature of the debate was the controversy it produced between Robert Lowe, the most able representative of the old school of Whig economists, and J. S. Mill. Lowe declared that

there is an oasis in the desert of politics upon which we may safely rest, and that is afforded us by the principles of political economy....I entertain a prejudice, derived from Scotland and adopted by Adam Smith, that a man is at liberty to do what he likes with his own, and that having land, it is not unreasonable that he should be free to let his land to a person of full age upon the terms upon which they shall mutually agree. That I believe to be reason and good political economy.[5]

1 *Hansard*, 3rd ser. vol. CLXXXVIII, col. 1628.
2 *Ibid.* vol. CLXXXV, col. 795 (22 February 1867).
3 See above, p. 52.
4 *Hansard*, 3rd ser. vol. CXC, col. 1700 (16 March 1868).
5 *Ibid.* col. 1493.

The contrast between this appeal to absolute maxims and Mill's own relativism could not be more clearly pointed than in Mill's own words:

In my right hon. Friend's mind political economy appears to stand for a set of practical maxims....My right hon. Friend thinks that a maxim of political economy if good in England must be good in Ireland....I do not know in political economy, more than I know in any other art or science, a single practical rule that must be applicable to all cases, and I am sure that no one is at all capable of determining what is the right political economy for any country until he knows its circumstances. ...Political economy has a great many enemies; but its worst enemies are some of its friends, and I do not know that it has a more dangerous enemy than my right hon. Friend.[1]

Mill defended and elaborated his own proposals at length in the debate, but they were not too favourably received, even on his own side of the House. John Bright declared of them: 'I do not believe the time is come in Ireland, and I do not believe it will ever come when it will be necessary to have recourse to so vast and extraordinary a scheme as that which he [Mill] has proposed to the House',[2] and repeated his own plan for the establishment of 'a steady class of moderate proprietors'. However, from the point of view of actual policy neither Mill's speech nor Bright's mattered in comparison with Gladstone's, for it was clear that as the prospective leader of any Liberal ministry he alone could say whether plans such as theirs would have any prospect of being translated into action.

As to Mill's proposal, Gladstone was frank: 'I own I am one of those who are not prepared—I have not daring sufficient—to accompany my hon. Friend the Member for Westminster.' Bright's proposal startled him less—'no one, after the explanation of that plan by the hon. Gentleman, would object to it as an interference with the rights of property'[3]—and he suggested that the experiment might be tried with the lands of the Irish Church, if they should come under the control of the State. For more general land legislation, Gladstone was not prepared to advocate more than 'the frank recognition of the principle of perfect security to the tenant for the proceeds of his capital and industry expended on the soil'. It is significant that the ideas he expressed accorded closely with those of Chichester Fortescue, who again advocated legislating on the principle embodied in his 1866 Bill—'the principle which reversed the rule of English law that the improvements effected by the tenant became at once the property of his landlord'.[4]

Lord Mayo (as Naas had become) would not go even so far as this in announcing the policy of the Government. So far as land tenure was concerned, that policy was to consist of a Bill similar to that of 1867, and the appointment of a Royal Commission with a remit similar to that of the Devon Commission. Disraeli stoutly maintained that this was the

[1] *Ibid.* col. 1525.
[2] *Ibid.* col. 1650.
[3] *Ibid.* cols. 1758–9.
[4] *Ibid.* col. 1602.

normal programme of Irish legislation of his ministry which would have been brought forward in any event, and flatly denied Gladstone's assertion that 'we have reached a crisis in the affairs and in the state of Ireland'. But the change in the climate of opinion was undeniable, and in the face of it the Government policy appeared to be, as Mill characterised it, 'a beggarly account of empty boxes'.

However, once Gladstone had declared himself in favour of prompt action for the disestablishment of the Irish Church[1] the question of land reform became secondary, not merely in the debate on Maguire's motion, but in all the debates of the session of 1868. Lord Mayo's new land Bill was never in fact introduced, and it was not until the end of the session of 1869, after Gladstone had been returned to office and completed the first task which he had set before himself in his 'mission to pacify Ireland', the disestablishment of the Irish Church, that he turned to the second, the land, and the question again came to the fore in politics.

The problem of Irish land tenure was one in which Gladstone had never displayed any particular interest, even though his parliamentary experience went back to the earliest days of Sharman Crawford's agitation. 'I suspect', wrote Bright to Hutton early in 1868, 'he [Gladstone] has not studied the land question, and knows little about it.'[2] Even before the Irish Church Bill had passed into law Bright was attempting to remedy this defect in Gladstone's education, and win his support for a scheme of land purchase—'I am most anxious to meet the evil before it is too great for control, and my plan *will meet it*, without wrong to any man',[3] he assured him. The attempt met with something very like a rebuke from the Prime Minister, who replied: 'I have this advantage for learning the Irish land question, that I do not set out with the belief that I know it already: and certainly no effort that I can make to acquire the mastery of it will be wanting.' Having expressed his doubts as to the wisdom of the State entering the market for land, Gladstone then summed up the prospect for legislation most acutely:

There is no doubt of three things in my mind. First, we must take this question to heart as our No. 1, the moment that we see our way out of the question of the Irish Church. Secondly, we must approach it in the spirit in which we approached that first question. Thirdly we must anticipate both more difficulty and less support: and we shall have nothing to set against this expectation except our own hope of combining together in the formation of our measure the qualities of circumspection and resolution. If we succeed with the Church, and fail with the land, we shall have done less than half our work.[4]

[1] *Hansard*, 3rd ser. vol. CXC, col. 1767.
[2] John Bright to H. D. Hutton, 27 January 1868 (Princeton MSS. AM 9553). Bright also expressed this view to Charles Villiers in January 1868; see Trevelyan, *John Bright*, p. 410.
[3] Bright to Gladstone, 21 May 1869 (B.M. Add. MSS. 44112).
[4] Gladstone to Bright, 22 May 1869 (B.M. Add. MSS. 44112).

Gladstone did in fact 'take the question to heart' at the beginning of August 1869, and began to study the available sources with his customary thoroughness. The main source of his information was the Irish Chief Secretary, Chichester Fortescue, who in turn relied much on Neilson Hancock and Sir Edward Sullivan, then Attorney-General for Ireland. In addition to the material supplied by Dublin Castle, and Blue Books such as the Devon Commission Report, Gladstone appears to have read most of what had been published on the land question in the preceding five years. Campbell's work especially impressed him, and he also paid a good deal of attention to Fitzgibbon's *The Land Difficulty of Ireland, with an Effort to Solve It*.[1] Gladstone rightly regarded this latter pamphlet as 'a very important sign of the times', for Fitzgibbon, who was a bitter critic of Gladstone, had declared in 1868 that there was no need for exceptional legislation on Irish land tenures; in 1869 he retracted this view, and proposed a scheme to give tenants parliamentary leases proportioned in length to the magnitude of their improvements.

In the early stages of Gladstone's study of the problem, Bright again attempted to influence him in favour of peasant proprietorship. He urged Gladstone to read Hutton's papers, and even to send Hancock or 'someone in good repute with the public' to Berlin to study the Prussian land reforms at first hand.[2] Gladstone did not follow this suggestion, but he did obtain, through Fortescue, some information about the Prussian land system from Sir Robert Morier, then secretary of the British legation at Darmstadt, and the author of the Cobden Club essay on land tenure in Prussia. But Gladstone confessed himself 'unwilling to force a peasant proprietary into existence', and Fortescue agreed with him.

From the outset, Gladstone was unwilling to contemplate any fundamental revision of the landlord and tenant relationship, and the first thoughts which he committed to paper on the subject did not carry him much beyond the Liberals' compensation Bill of 1866.[3] Fortescue, the author of this Bill, was already convinced that it should be 'enlarged in very important respects' and was working on the idea of legalising the Ulster custom, and providing tenants outside Ulster similar protection, by giving them a right not only to compensation for improvements, but also to compensation for disturbance. 'This is very important and novel', he wrote to Gladstone on 13 September 1869, 'and I am working it out carefully.' He added that 'the Bill, as it cannot go to the extent of the popular demand in the way of fixity of tenure and rents fixed by public

---

[1] (London, 1869). References to this pamphlet and Campbell's *The Irish Land* occur several times in Gladstone's correspondence with Fortescue between August and October 1869; see B.M. Add. MSS. 44121 and 44122.

[2] Bright to Gladstone, 30 July 1869 (B.M. Add. MSS. 44112).

[3] See Gladstone's Memorandum on Irish Land Tenures, dated from Balmoral, 15 and 17 September 1869 (B.M. Add. MSS. 44758).

valuation, should be as comprehensive as possible and make up in *breadth* for what it may want in length'.[1]

The ideas set out in this memorandum were quickly accepted by Gladstone, and became the foundation of the Bill. Morley says of Fortescue 'it is believed that he was instigated to adopt the new and bolder line by Sir Edward Sullivan'[2] but there is evidence that Fortescue actually took the main ideas from Neilson Hancock, and, directly or indirectly, from his brother, John Hancock, who was still Lord Lurgan's agent, as he had been at the time of the Devon Commission.[3] Neilson Hancock, more influential perhaps in the counsels of the Irish Government in 1869 than he had been in 1859, had evidently been convinced by the failure of Cardwell's Act that free contract was not the solution of the land problem, and was now developing and advocating the idea of giving the Ulster custom the force of law.

While Gladstone was willing enough to accept new ideas, there were others in the Cabinet who were not so ready—mainly Lowe, now Chancellor of the Exchequer, Argyll, Clarendon and Cardwell. So the Prime Minister had to warn Fortescue:

This question has been moving onwards for some time, and of late at an accelerated pace. You have watched this movement, and, as far as I can apprehend your views, I enter thoroughly into the spirit of them. But many members of the Cabinet, laden sufficiently with their own labours, have probably not so closely followed up the matter, and, as I think it likely, are at a point not far removed from our Bill of 1866. The proposition, that *more* than compensation to tenants for their improvements will be necessary in order to settle the Irish Land Laws, will be unpalatable, or new, to several, and naturally enough.[4]

Fortescue, indeed, would have been willing to send a draft of a Bill involving the principle of compensation for disturbance as well as improvements to the first Cabinet meeting on the subject, but Gladstone warned him that they must secure authority before proceeding so far.

The Cabinet did not meet to discuss the land Bill until the end of October, and in the meantime Gladstone prepared the ground with some care. He arranged for Fortescue to come over before the meeting from Dublin, and meet Granville and Bright—who was having qualms about interference with freedom of contract[5] and still felt anxious to

---

[1] Fortescue to Gladstone (Memorandum), 13 September 1869 (B.M. Add. MSS. 44121).
[2] Morley, *Gladstone*, vol. II, p. 283.
[3] This is borne out by a passage in a letter from Fortescue to Gladstone, 28 September 1869: '...I am working this out as thoroughly as I can, with Hancock, and will bring Sullivan's mind to bear on it, as soon as I see him. He went to Galway for the Special Commission the day I arrived [25 September].' (B.M. Add. MSS. 44121.) Another letter, 23 October 1869, refers to 'a long and useful discussion today upon the Ulster custom, and the means of legalising it, with Mr Hancock, Lord Lurgan's agent'.
[4] Gladstone to Fortescue, 27 September 1869 (B.M. Add. MSS. 44121).
[5] See his letter to Gladstone, 15 October 1869, quoted above, p. 58.

press his land purchase plan. *The Times* was already producing a considerable effect on public opinion by the publication of O'Connor Morris's letters from Ireland. Gladstone saw the editor, Delane, on 26 October, and on the 27th a judiciously worded leader appeared, advocating 'a careful study of those deeply-rooted usages exemplified by Ulster Tenant Right'.[1]

Gladstone was able to write in his diary on 30 October 'Cabinet, 2–5½....We broke ground very satisfactorily on the question of Irish land' but on 3 November he had to record 'Cabinet. Chiefly on Irish land, and stiff.'[2] In these meetings Gladstone's colleagues had agreed readily enough to his proposals to reverse the presumption of law as to improvements, and to extend the tenants' claim in this respect to improvements already made, for which they had a precedent in Napier's Bill of 1852. They had even accepted the idea of legalising the Ulster custom, in Ulster, but Lowe and his group could not be persuaded to concede the principle of compensation for disturbance. A position intermediate between those of Lowe on the one hand and Fortescue on the other was adopted at this time by Dufferin, who had joined Gladstone's administration as Chancellor of the Duchy of Lancaster. Though much concerned to prevent any infringement of the landlord's rights by schemes for fixity of tenure, he was prepared to concede the tenant's right to compensation for loss of 'anticipated profits' in case of sudden eviction. He stated these in a memorandom of 29 October 1869, which, significantly enough, was more favourably received by Gladstone than by Fortescue.[3] By this time, however, Gladstone had come to agree with Fortescue that a mere 'tenant compensation Bill' would be a failure in Ireland, and they returned to the task of working out the broader principle in a form which the Cabinet would accept. The fact that Gladstone was now at Hawarden, and Fortescue back at Dublin Castle did not make matters any easier. Gladstone contemplated going to Ireland, but decided that it would be 'highly imprudent'. Fortescue offered to send Hancock to England, but Gladstone, who found the Irish economist distressingly long-winded even on paper, declined; instead he took a senior civil servant, Lambert, from the Poor Law Board, and used him as a liaison officer between Dublin, Hawarden and London.

Apart from this the discussions continued through the difficult medium of correspondence and memoranda; nor did Gladstone seek advice from

[1] *History of 'The Times'* (London, 1939), vol. II, p. 411.
[2] Morley, *Gladstone*, vol. II, p. 289.
[3] Dufferin to Gladstone, 29 October 1869; Gladstone to Dufferin, 3 and 13 November 1869 (Dufferin Papers, P.R.O., N.I.); Fortescue to Gladstone, 3 November 1869 (B.M. Add. MSS. 44122). When the Land Bill was in the Commons, Gladstone wrote to Dufferin praising 'the valuable aid derived from friendly critics...most of all... Bessborough and yourself'; but when the Bill came into the Lords the reluctant support which Dufferin gave it was more an embarrassment than a help to the Government. See Sir A. Lyall, *Life of Lord Dufferin* (London, 1906), pp. 168–74.

Butt, Gray, or any other representatives of the Irish tenants.[1] It would seem that he had now made up his mind that the demand for fixity of tenure could not, and should not, be met, but that the measure must go beyond mere compensation for improvements; the problem was to find a middle course which would be acceptable to Cabinet and Parliament alike. Towards this end, the Irish executive set on foot, through the local Poor Law guardians, an inquiry as to customs regarding tenant-right throughout Ireland.[2] This revealed the existence of compensation customs in many places outside Ulster, a point which Gladstone was anxious to establish, for as he worked on the problem he began to see the desired middle course more and more in the recognition of existing customs. Fortescue, on the other hand, wished the tenant to have the alternative of claiming compensation for disturbance either under custom or under a definite scale established by the Act. By way of compromise, Gladstone suggested that where evidence of custom was inadequate, the Bill could provide that the Court charged with assessing compensation could take evidence as to what a 'solvent person' would be willing to pay for the tenant's interest in the holding. The fatal objection to this was pointed out to Fortescue by McCarthy Downing, one of the Irish Members—if a small tenant were forced to abandon his holding by rack-renting, no solvent person would pay anything for his interest. Lord Monck also saw this, and told Fortescue that the only solution was a compulsory settlement of rents. Fortescue could not bring himself to agree with this, but, seeing the force of the point, attempted to design means whereby the Courts could reduce rack-rents. Even this was too much for Gladstone, who confessed himself 'a good deal staggered at the idea of any interference with present rents'.[3]

The eventual solution adopted was proposed by the Lord Chancellor, Hatherley; this was the idea of allowing the tenant to claim damages for eviction according to a scale based on the rent.[4] Normally, a tenant evicted for non-payment of rent would be debarred from claiming damages, but in the original scheme the case of rack-rented tenants was provided for by enacting that the Court might award damages even to tenants evicted for non-payment of rent, where there were 'special grounds'. To appease the believers in freedom of contract, Gladstone

[1] Lord Eversley, *Gladstone and Ireland: The Irish Policy of Parliament from 1850–1894* (London, 1912), p. 44.
[2] Published, in 1870, as *Relations between Landlords and Tenants in Respect of Improvements in Farms. Poor Law Inspectors' Reports* (1870 [C. 31], vol. XIV).
[3] Gladstone to Fortescue, 5 December 1869; quoted in Morley, *Gladstone*, vol. II, p. 291. The correspondence summarised above is mainly in B.M. Add. MSS. vols. 44121 and 44122. Fortescue's proposals on rack-rents are outlined in J. L. Hammond, *Gladstone and the Irish Nation* (London, 1938), pp. 97–8.
[4] Tenants of holdings with an annual rateable value of less than £10 could claim damages equal to seven years' rent; tenants of holdings with an annual rateable valuation above £100, damages equal to, at most, one year's rent.

softened this proposal by inserting a clause which provided that a land-lord could bar all claims to compensation by giving the tenant a lease for thirty-one years. Gladstone feared that this proposal might alienate the Irish farmers, but he told Fortescue that it was a proposal 'which the Cabinet appeared to relish a good deal', and evidently this decided him in its favour.

In fact, even to get these compromise proposals accepted by the Cabinet, Gladstone had to conduct a battle on three separate fronts. He had first to meet the determined opposition of Lowe, Argyll and those who, like them, thought on the old landlord lines. Morley speaks of Gladstone trying to lead Argyll 'over one or two of the barest rudiments of the history of Irish land, and occasionally showing in the process somewhat of the quality of the superior pupil teacher acquiring today material for the lesson of tomorrow'.[1] Lowe proved even more difficult to convince, but eventually conceded the force of Gladstone's arguments, although not abandoning his own convictions.

Gladstone's second difficulty was the attitude of Bright, who continued to press the case for his land purchase scheme, urging that it was 'not against political economy', whereas Fortescue's proposals undoubtedly were. Gladstone had to rebuke Bright for thus undermining the case he was trying to build up at a critical stage,[2] but added: 'No part of what I have said is an argument against your propositions.' Ultimately, Bright's convictions were met by the incorporation in the Bill of clauses to facilitate the purchase of their holdings by occupiers.

Thirdly, Gladstone had to contend with some opposition from Fortescue himself. Fortescue had grave misgivings about the wisdom of Gladstone's scheme to make custom the essential basis of the legislation, for he had little faith in the value of such custom outside Ulster. Eventually, he suppressed his scruples in the face of a stiffly worded reminder from his chief that 'what we have to do is to obtain the consent of the Cabinet to a bill, on the substance of which you and I are agreed: and this, it is my duty to say, will in my judgment be greatly endangered by any further prolongation of the subaltern controversy between us'.[3]

Finally, on 25 January 1870, Gladstone was able to enter in his diary: 'Cabinet. The great difficulties of the Irish Land Bill *there* are now over. Thank God!'[4] He introduced the Bill in the Commons on 15 February; it was on the whole well received, both inside and outside the House. The comment of the *Spectator*—'Mr Gladstone has, we believe, solved the problem'[5]—was echoed by most of the London press. But in view of

---

[1] *Gladstone*, vol. ii, p. 290.
[2] See Gladstone to Bright, 4 December 1869 (B.M. Add. MSS. 44112): partly quoted in Morley, *Gladstone*, vol. ii, p. 291.
[3] Gladstone to Fortescue, 12 January 1870 (B.M. Add. MSS. 44122).
[4] Morley, *Gladstone*, vol. ii, p. 293.   [5] *Spectator*, 19 February 1870.

O'Hagan's warning to the Liberals that in Ireland all would depend on the reaction of the *Freeman's Journal*[1] it was significant that its editorial comment on the Bill was: 'it will pass into law, but it will leave the old sore unhealed, the Land Question unsettled.'[2]

In its passage through Parliament, the Bill was attacked from two sides: on the one hand by those whom Gladstone termed 'the popular Irish party', the advocates of fixity of tenure, led by Sir John Gray; on the other by the supporters of 'freedom of contract' and 'the rights of property', Liberals and Conservatives alike.

Gray and his supporters sought, at the Committee stage, to bring the Bill more nearly into line with their own doctrine by introducing a new clause designed to establish a 'permissive parliamentary tenant-right'. Under this scheme the tenant would have been recognised to have a saleable chattel interest in his holding, and the right to continuous occupation provided that he duly paid a rent to be fixed by arbitration every fourteen years, and did not sub-divide or dilapidate the holding. Walter Morrison, an English member, at the same time sought to introduce a similar proposal which was generally known as the 'Longfield Scheme', being based on an idea which Mountifort Longfield had put forward in his Cobden Club essay on Irish tenures.[3] By this scheme, the tenant would have been permitted to buy the tenant-right of his farm by giving the landlord ten years' purchase of the rent; thereafter he would be entitled to continuing occupation and if the landlord sought to increase the rent, the tenant could surrender his holding and obtain ten years' purchase of the increased rent demanded as compensation.

Both these plans, but particularly Longfield's, had influential support: Gladstone, however, declared that either would involve a radical change in the Bill and virtually grant fixity of tenure, and, he added, 'I am irreconcilably opposed to granting fixity of tenure'.[4] Both Gray and Morrison were defeated in their attempts to modify the Bill, but *The Times* commented next day: 'the Bill remains a good Bill...but an opportunity of greatly improving it has been lost.'

Those who saw in the Bill a dangerous interference with freedom of contract naturally directed their attacks mainly against the provisions giving compensation for disturbance. Disraeli himself assailed the relevant section (clause 3) as conceding that 'occupation involves a right of property';[5] but on the whole the Government was less discomfited by the attacks of the Opposition than by the criticisms and qualifications of

[1] See above, p. 53.
[2] *Freeman's Journal*, 19 February 1870.
[3] See M. Longfield, 'The Tenure of Land in Ireland', *Systems of Land Tenure in Various Countries: a Series of Essays published under the sanction of the Cobden Club* (London, 1870), pp. 47–9; also *The Longfield Scheme of Parliamentary Tenant-Right* (n.p., 1870), *passim*.
[4] *Hansard*, 3rd ser. vol. CCI, col. 1025 (19 May 1870).
[5] *Ibid*. vol. CC, col. 1182 (4 April 1870).

one of their supporters, Sir Roundell Palmer, who set himself to guard against any undue infringement of the rights of the landlord as he conceived them. Campbell, watching the passage of the Bill through the Commons, saw the main danger to it in Palmer's attitude: 'There is the real obstacle to the peace of Ireland, the candid friend, the essence of English-lawyer respectability, who squares and measures, and would give an exact quantum of justice measured by English ideas, but "*not one inch beyond*"; who whittles away in every direction till nothing worth having is left.'[1]

Although Palmer's tactics increased Gladstone's difficulties, they did not prevent him from getting the Bill, in its essential form, through the Commons. As might have been expected, it was the Lords who most effectively weakened the measure. They at first passed numerous amendments which would have made the Bill worthless to the tenants, but were later persuaded by the Government to withdraw most of these. But the Government were forced to concede a vital point in regard to compensation for disturbance: the Lords would not have the provision that a tenant evicted for non-payment of rent should receive damages if the Court were of opinion that 'on special grounds' such damages should be paid. Eventually they accepted a clause allowing the Court to award damages 'if, in case of any such tenancy of a holding held at an annual rent not exceeding fifteen pounds, the Court shall certify that the non-payment of rent causing the eviction has arisen from the rent being an exorbitant rent'.[2]

Thus altered, the Bill passed into law, but it was fatally weakened. Gladstone had written to Cardinal Manning that the Bill was designed 'to prevent the Landlord from using the terrible weapon of undue and unjust eviction by so framing the handle that it shall cut his hands with the sharp edge of pecuniary damages'.[3] The Irish priests and the tenant party were not convinced that the Bill in its original form made the handle sharp enough: they would have preferred that direct control of rents which 'staggered' Gladstone and 'alarmed' Bright; as the clause was finally accepted by the Lords it left the handle of the weapon of eviction so smooth that no landlord need fear to wield it.

The Land Act of 1870 was at once a major success and a major failure. It was a success because it was the first measure placed on the Statute Book to recognise that the occupier as well as the owner had a right in the land; the first measure, in other words, which reversed the trend towards insistence on 'free contract' as the basis of landlord-tenant relations, and was based, partially at least, on concepts of status and custom. It was a failure because it recognised the status of the tenant, and the rights

---

[1] Sir G. Campbell, *The Progress of the Land Bill* (London, 1870), p. 7.
[2] *Hansard*, 3rd ser. vol. CCIII, cols. 820–1 (25 July 1870).
[3] Gladstone to Manning, 16 February 1870. Quoted in Hammond, p. 100.

which that status conferred, in too limited a form and with too many qualifications.

No fairer comment on the Act, perhaps, could be made than that of Isaac Butt, who wrote:

I am bound to say that, imperfect and inadequate as they are, I can trace in its provisions an earnest and sincere desire to protect the Irish tenant—a struggle to escape from principles by which the framers of the Bill believed themselves bound, but which, in favour of the Irish tenant, they made every effort to evade. I fear the result has been only an elaborate failure to do the justice which it was so elaborately attempted to work out.[1]

Inevitably, after that failure, the tendency grew in Ireland to feel that the legislation which Ireland required could never pass through English parliaments. 'Mr Gladstone has closed the line of Statesmen in whom I had any hope' wrote the moderate Dean O'Brien. 'English wisdom has failed to see the nature of the crisis—and Irish warning has spoken in vain. We stand on the brink of the future which the "Limerick Declaration" two years ago shadowed forth.... Landlords and statesmen have only one remaining chance of saving us from coming confusion, and that is to permit us to make our own laws.'[2]

The Limerick Declaration of 1868 was a manifesto by an assembly of Roman Catholic priests in favour of the repeal of the Union, and one of the reasons which they advanced in favour of Repeal was that 'Ireland had had enough of political economy'. To them, and to most Irishmen, it is clear, political economy meant *laissez-faire* and freedom of contract, not the doctrines of Mill and Cairnes.

It would be easy to say that this was a crudely mistaken view, that the subject of protest was not political economy but the bowdlerization and misapplication of it. But when the history of thought on the Irish land problem in this period is surveyed as a whole, it can be clearly seen to be composed of two main strands—on the one hand, a line of thought which, looking to the maximum real product as a goal, conceived the best agricultural economy to be that of medium and large farms, held by capitalist tenants under lease from improving landlords, and worked by wage-paid labour. On the other hand, there was the line of thought which, looking to the security of the existing rural population as a goal, sought to see established a system of peasant proprietorship or copyhold tenancy.

In the first half of the nineteenth century, the first school of thought represented undoubted orthodoxy: the second was then not a school of thought at all, but little more than an incoherent feeling of the small tenants, sometimes finding vent in the speeches and pamphlets of those

[1] Butt to Wm. Bolster (Chairman of Limerick Farmers' Club): published in the *Freeman's Journal*, 22 February 1870.

[2] R. B. O'Brien, Dean of Limerick, to Isaac Butt, 17 February 1870. (Butt Papers, B. 34, National Library of Ireland.)

whom established thinkers regarded as demagogues and quacks. Only after 1848 did this second view come to be held by a respectable minority, who recognised the unsuitability of contract tenures for the Irish social system, and, looking to Continental examples, were prepared to assert that small properties could be made as efficient economically as large tenant farms.

It can hardly be denied then that, for a vital half-century, the virtue of the English land system for Ireland was asserted and upheld not merely by powerful vested interests, but by powerful independent minds. Hence it is hardly to be wondered at if, in 1868 or 1870, the majority of Irishmen had come to fear the application of classical political economy in Irish land policy. For, in the words of Keynes, 'the power of vested interests is vastly exaggerated compared with the gradual encroachment of ideas. Not, indeed, immediately, but after a certain interval; for in the field of economic and political philosophy there are not many who are influenced by new theories after they are twenty-five or thirty years of age, so that the ideas which civil servants and politicians and even agitators apply to current events are not likely to be the newest.'[1] The Irish Land Act of 1870 might serve as a classic example of the truth of this. That it contained too much of the old political economy and too little of the new was the fault of civil servants and politicians rather than of economists; yet it is difficult to exempt the economists from the charge of having offered the wrong advice at the right time, and the right advice at the wrong time.

[1] J. M. Keynes, *General Theory of Employment, Interest and Money* (London, 1936), pp. 383–4.

CHAPTER III

THE ABSENTEE LANDLORD

I

THROUGHOUT the period covered by this study a considerable proportion of the Irish proprietors resided, temporarily or permanently, in England or abroad, and this fact of absentee ownership was usually prominent amongst the causes of Irish misery listed by contemporary writers.

Absenteeism was no new phenomenon in Ireland. Petty, in his *Political Anatomy of Ireland* (1672) made reference to absentee landlords, but opposed the view that they should be deprived of their estates 'as both unjust, inconvenient and frivolous'.[1] In general, however, the absentee was a subject for condemnation, and Swift, Madden and Prior, amongst eighteenth-century authors, all inveighed against him.[2] In the beginning of the nineteenth century there was renewed censure of absenteeism, strengthened by the prevalent opinion that the Act of Union had reinforced the tendency for the Irish gentry to live in England; the popular opinion was well summed up in the phrase which Lady Morgan, in 1825, put on the title-page of her romantic volume on the subject: 'Les absens ont toujours tort.'[3]

Without doubt the Irish were inclined to use their absentees as convenient scapegoats, and name them as the cause of many evils which the most conscientious resident landlords could not have eradicated. Yet in a country so completely agricultural as nineteenth-century Ireland, the absence of perhaps as much as a third of the landed aristocracy,[4] including

[1] Sir Wm. Petty, 'Political Anatomy of Ireland', in *Economic Writings of Sir William Petty*, ed. C. H. Hull (Cambridge, 1899), vol. I, p. 193.

[2] Jonathan Swift, *The Truth of Some Maxims in State and Government, Examined with Reference to Ireland* (written in 1724, published in Deane Swift's 1765 edition of J. Swift's works).

[T. Prior] *A List of the Absentees of Ireland, and the Yearly Value of their Estates and Incomes Spent Abroad. With Observations on the Present State and Condition of that Kingdom* (Dublin, 1729).

[S. Madden], *Reflections and Resolutions Proper for the Gentlemen of Ireland, As to their Conduct for the Service of their Country* (Dublin, 1738).

[3] Sydney, Lady Morgan, *Absenteeism* (London, 1825).

[4] This is the proportion commonly cited in works of the period: see M. Staunton, *Reasons for a Repeal of the Legislative Union between Great Britain and Ireland* (Dublin, 1845), p. 63. In the *Return of Owners of Land (Ireland)*, which Isaac Butt obtained in 1876, only 13·1 % of all proprietors owning more than 100 acres were recorded as absentees from Ireland, but another 10 % were recorded as residence 'not ascertained'. Of the total area of land in Ireland, 15·7 % was recorded as owned by proprietors 'rarely or never resident in Ireland', 6·8 % as owned by those 'resident usually out of Ireland, but occasionally on the property', 2·9 % as owned by public institutions and companies, and 3·0 % as 'not ascertained'. *Owners of Land (Ireland)* (1876 (412), vol. LXXX, pp. 184–6.

many of its important members, could not be without significance, whilst the debates to which it gave rise throw considerable light on the doctrines and attitudes of the time. It was customary in the discussion of the subject to separate the economic from the social and moral aspects of it and it is therefore convenient in attempting to review the thought of the period on absenteeism to maintain this same distinction.

II

In so far as eighteenth-century criticism of absentees rested on economic grounds, it was usually mercantilist in form. The drain of specie which the payments of rents to absentees caused, and the resultant damage to the balance of trade, were the normal grounds for complaint.[1] These arguments were revived during the Bank Restriction period, when the depreciation of the Irish exchange was frequently attributed to absentee remittances.[2] Contradictions of such exploded theories were not slow in forthcoming; Lord King, John Leslie Foster and Sir Henry Parnell all wrote to prove that the unfavourable exchange resulted from over-issue rather than from increased transfers of rents, and the 1804 *Report of the Committee on the Circulating Paper of Ireland* demonstrated that the remittances must ultimately be made in goods and not in specie, along the lines of the classical trade analysis.[3]

In fact these works contain all the essentials of the classical doctrine on absentee remittances as a type of unilateral international transfer. Their central contention was that the payment of the remittances must result in increased Irish exports to Britain, which would compensate for the diminished demand in the home market. That this would involve some transfer of resources within Ireland was conceded, but it was held that there would be no net reduction in income or employment; generally it was taken for granted that the shift of demand would be adequate to effect the transfer without any change of price levels or movement of specie.[4]

---

[1] See Anon., *A List of the Absentees of Ireland* (Dublin, 1767), p. 39. This is one of several anonymous lists, based on Prior's, which appeared in the later eighteenth century.

[2] Anon. ['Merchant of Dublin'], *Observations on the Exchange between London and Dublin* (Dublin, 1804), especially pp. 9 and 16.

[3] Lord King, *Thoughts on the Effects of the Bank Restrictions*, 2nd ed. (London, 1804); J. L. Foster, *An Essay on the Principle of Commercial Exchanges, and More Particularly of the Exchange between Great Britain and Ireland* (London, 1804); Sir H. Parnell, *The Principles of Currency and Exchange Illustrated by Observations upon the State of the Currency of Ireland, the High Rates of Exchange between Dublin and London, and the Remittances of Rent to Irish Absentees* (London, 1805); *Report from the Committee on the Circulating Paper, the Specie, and the Current Coin of Ireland* (1803–4 (86), vol. IV, and 1826 (407), vol. V), reprinted, with an Introduction and selections from the Evidence, in F. W. Fetter, *The Irish Pound, 1797–1826* (London, 1955).

[4] See Foster, pp. 23–5; Parnell, *Principles of Currency*, pp. 83–4. For a full discussion of the theory of demand shifts and its history, see W. E. Mason, *The Classical Theory of Adjustment to Unilateral Capital Transfers* (Ph.D. thesis, Princeton University, 1952: University Microfilms, Ann Arbor, Michigan, no. 5155), and also his article: 'Some Neglected Contributions to the Theory of International Transfers', *J. Political Economy*, vol. LXIII (1955), pp. 529–35.

In 1804 and 1805 the discussion of absenteeism and its effects was incidental to the wider issue of currency depreciation, and so attracted little notice. By contrast, in 1825 when J. R. McCulloch used the classical analysis to demonstrate the unimportance of landlords' residence or non-residence, a storm of protest and dispute resulted. McCulloch first stated his views in evidence before a Select Committee of the House of Commons on the State of Ireland, in June 1825, and amplified them in an article in the *Edinburgh Review* for November 1825.[1] The core of his argument was that whether an Irish landlord were resident or absent from his estate 'it is certain he must still purchase an *equivalent amount of Irish commodities of some sort or other*. How idle then is it to accuse absenteeism of lessening the demand for labour!'[2] There was nothing in this proposition, or the development of it, which went beyond what had been said by Foster and Parnell twenty years before; but McCulloch asserted his conclusion with all his customary dogmatic arrogance, once before a parliamentary committee and once in the best-known literary review of the day, so that it had no lack of publicity. The resulting criticism came mainly, though by no means entirely, from Irish sources. Much of this was ill-informed, and based on sentiment rather than reasoning;[3] much of the reasoned criticism even was fallacious or beside the point, but when all this is sifted away there still remains a valuable residue of analysis, and a survey of the controversy reveals much that is fundamental about the presuppositions of classical economics and the use and limitations of its technique.

McCulloch's contention that absenteeism could not lessen the demand for labour was a long-term proposition intended in an overall sense. 'It is certainly true that absenteeism may have the effect to occasion a *partial change in the species of labour demanded*; but that is all it can do; and for anything that we can *a priori* know to the contrary, this change may be advantageous.'[4] McCulloch was prepared to admit that the process of effecting this partial change would occasion some disturbance and even distress, but he regarded this as a purely temporary phenomenon. It was the permanent effects which concerned him, and to him it seemed clear that these could not be adverse to the demand for labour.

[1] *Fourth Report from Select Committee on the State of Ireland, 1826*, Evidence, p. 813 [8 June 1825] (1825 (129), vol. VIII); *Edinburgh Rev.* no. LXXXV, pp. 54–76. This article was ostensibly a review of Lady Morgan's *Absenteeism*.

[2] *Edinburgh Rev.* no. LXXXV, p. 60.

[3] At least one of McCulloch's critics expressed himself in heroic couplets:
> 'Oh come, return, resume your former reign
> Ye absentees, be Irishmen again!...
> ...Let vain McCulloch bawl with all his might
> That absentees are wholly in the right
> ...Fly to your parent, fly, each duteous son
> And strive to do what Grattan would have done!'

From 'Three months in Ireland' by 'an English Protestant', *Eclectic Rev.* vol. XXVIII, p. 185.

[4] *Edinburgh Rev.* no. LXXXV, p. 60.

The basis for this view was the accepted classical doctrine that 'industry is limited by capital'. It was the capital of society which formed the fund for employment of productive labour and to McCulloch it seemed evident that 'the absentee takes no part either of his own capital, or of the capital of the tradesmen and manufacturers of the country he has left, along with him. These remain where they were, and are employed equally to support and employ labourers when the landlords are abroad as when they are at home.'[1]

Given the 'stock' or 'fund' approach of classical economics as a pre-supposition of analysis, McCulloch's proposition follows with perfect logic, but to those less thoroughly schooled in the Ricardian method, it naturally appeared paradoxical. This difference in approach was actually quite clearly seen and stated by McCulloch himself. 'Those who raise an outcry against absenteeism', he wrote, 'take for granted that all retail dealers, tradesmen and manufacturers, live at the expense of those who employ them, or who buy their products. It is certain, however, that they do no such thing—that they live by means of their own capital and industry and that these would support them, though their customers were annihilated.'[2]

Aside from any question of the validity of this theory, there is the further point of the relevance of its postulates to the circumstances of Ireland in 1825, and it seems fair to suggest that that relevance was not very great. McCulloch's argument implicitly assumes mobility of factors and flexibility of factor prices; in Ireland no range of employments outside agriculture existed and the land system gave no encouragement to agricultural investment, and hence employment. To such a condition of chronic under-employment the analysis of the *Edinburgh Review* article, however consistent, was merely inappropriate.

This is the reason for much of the apparent barrenness of the absentee-ism controversy; McCulloch, looking to his theory, and his critics, looking to Irish conditions, were simply arguing different questions. But this was not always the case; for example, a leading article in the *Morning Chronicle* attacked McCulloch's suggestion that the small tradesmen employed by landlords could find other employment in agriculture, on the ground that in Ireland there was already a greater population than agriculture could employ.[3]

Similar considerations seem to have prompted Senior, when discussing

---

[1] *Edinburgh Rev.* no. LXXXV, p. 64. And see his evidence before the Select Committee on the State of the Poor in Ireland, 1830: 'I never argued or spoke about absenteeism in any way but under the express or implied condition that it was with reference to the spending of revenue.... I never dreamed of saying that if instead of vesting [his] capital at home, [a landlord] goes abroad and vests it there, that would not be injurious to this country' (1830 (665), vol. VII), p. 592.

[2] *Edinburgh Rev.* no. LXXXV, p. 61.

[3] *Morning Chronicle*, 19 September 1825.

absenteeism, to make the distinction between countries which export raw produce, and those which do not, contending that absenteeism can injure the former, but not the latter.[1] Senior's discussion is based on the wage-fund analysis (in a 'real' sense) and his contention is that Irish absenteeism diminishes the fund of goods available for the support of Irish labour and increases that available for the support of English labour. If it could be assumed that both Ireland and England possessed developed money economies, Senior's argument would appear to fall to the ground with the general wage-fund fallacy. But if it be remembered that comparatively few of the Irish peasantry in Senior's time worked for money wages, and that their normal diet did not include any of the cash crops or products which were sold and exported to pay rent, his argument seems to become of more importance. In fact, what Senior seems to have been seeking to emphasise was the secondary employment which a landlord's expenditure on local manufactures might produce, a point which McCulloch had glossed over.

Senior was by no means the first writer to make this distinction between raw produce and manufactures in regard to absentee expenditures; the point was perhaps most clearly made by Poulett Scrope in 1833:

The case of Ireland differs from that of Britain in this remarkable point, that, while the latter exports solely manufactures, the exports of Ireland consist almost solely of *food*—corn, butter, pork, beef, etc. In her case, therefore, that portion of the raw produce of the soil which accrues to the landlord as rent, will, if he is an absentee, be directly exported, as the only means of remitting his rent, instead of being consumed by manufacturers at home while working up goods for exportation, as in England. The English absentee landlord may be considered as feeding and employing, with the surplus produce of his estate, that portion of our manufacturing population which is engaged in fabricating the goods that are sent abroad to pay his rent. The Irish absentee, on the contrary, can only have *his* rent remitted in the shape of food; there is no secondary intervening process whatever; and the more food is in this way sent out of the country, the less, of course, remains behind to support and give employment to its inhabitants. If these were all fully fed and employed, no harm would result from the exportation of food; as is the case, for example, with some parts of North America. But so long as the people of any country are, as in Ireland, but half employed and half fed, so long, to export food from thence will be to take away the means existing in the country for setting them to work and improving their condition.[2]

In thus recognising the significance of under-employment in Ireland, Scrope showed himself more realistic than Senior, who confined his conclusion to wage-changes, thus again implying the inappropriate

[1] N. W. Senior, *Outline of the Science of Political Economy* (London, 1836). (Library of Economics reprint, London, 1938, pp. 155–62.)

[2] G. P. Scrope, *Principles of Political Economy, Deduced from the Natural Laws of Social Welfare and Applied to the Present State of Britain* (London, 1833), pp. 394–5.
For an interesting contemporary comment on this passage, see A. Atkinson, *Principles of Political Economy* (London, 1840), pp. 30 and 31. Atkinson holds that this passage, while correct in itself, is inconsistent with Scrope's general (classical) reasoning.

assumption of flexible wage-rates. In reality, the Irish peasants could not accept a lower wage, in any employment, for none was offered to them. The response which they could, and frequently did, make to their situation was to follow the landlord's example by emigration, temporary or permanent. This undeniable fact was recognised by Senior and some of his contemporaries, notably Torrens,[1] and incorporated into the analysis, with dubious consistency, as a factor mitigating the fall in wages which otherwise would result from the reduction of the wage-fund without an alteration in the quantity of labour it must support.[2]

Although Scrope and Senior attached more importance to the secondary employment given by the landlord and the difficulties of supplying an alternative than did McCulloch, the difference is still only of degree; the discussion remains within the long-term static framework of the wage-fund analysis.

At the same period, however, a number of lesser-known writers approached the subject with the aid of embryonic income-analysis. The contrast between their mode of thinking and the orthodox classical method is well exemplified by this passage from Pettman's *Resources of the United Kingdom*:

Were Irish landlords to reside on their estates, and expend the money they derive from rents among their countrymen, the Irish people would, in such case acquire an ability to purchase and consume the corn and cattle they now annually export to England; and such money would circulate among all classes, and might be acquired by their tenants, in exchange for their produce, many times within the year, provided they re-expend it, as they receive it, with tradesmen, and in wages to labourers, and also provided they advance their prices in proportion to the quickness of its return in exchange for more of their produce. An advance in prices, *so produced*, would enable farmers and tradesmen to employ a greater number of labourers in raising and creating products; a larger supply would therefore be produced, which the alternate changes of the money from the producer to the labourer, and from the labourer to the producer, would enable each class to purchase a larger proportion of. Hence, by such a process more products would be raised and created, and more purchased and consumed by every class.[3]

A similar type of argument had been used in 1827 by Lord Stourton[4] and is to be found again in Longfield's *Three Lectures on Commerce and One on Absenteeism*.[5]

---

[1] Speech of Colonel Torrens, in the debate on the Repeal of the Union, 28 April 1833: *Hansard*, 3rd ser. vol. XXIII, cols. 183–6.　　　　[2] Senior, *Outline*, p. 156.

[3] W. R. A. Pettman, *Resources of the United Kingdom: or, the Present Distresses Considered; their Causes and Remedies Pointed Out; and an Outline of a Plan for the Establishment of a National Currency, that would have a Fixed Money Value, Proposed* (London, 1830), pp. 201–2.

[4] Lord Stourton, *A Letter to the Rt. Hon. George Canning on the Nature of Absenteeism and its Influence on the State of Ireland, in Reply to an Article of the Edinburgh Review* (London, 1827), pp. 27 and 41.

[5] M. Longfield, *Three Lectures on Commerce and One on Absenteeism, Delivered in Michaelmas Term, 1834 before the University of Dublin* (Dublin, 1835), pp. 83–4.

At first sight, the main difference between these discussions and McCulloch's appears to be that they lay special emphasis on the short-term disturbance to employment created by the landlords' removal, whereas McCulloch had concentrated on long-term permanent effects. But this is symptomatic of a more fundamental difference of approach; whereas McCulloch started from the classical premiss that capital was the source of employment, Pettman and others like him assumed that revenue, used even in 'unproductive consumption', was the basis of effective demand and employment. Only Longfield, however, perceived and explained the relationship between the two analyses. In a passage which displays greater insight into the true nature of the wages-fund doctrine than most of his contemporaries, and many of his successors, possessed, Longfield pointed out that the defenders of absenteeism

say that industry is set to work and maintained, not by income, but by capital; and that if the capitalist is in the country, it is no matter where the rich consumer resides.... But let us look at the different forms of expenditure and labour; and we shall see how far it is from being true, that the wages of labour depend solely upon the amount of capital in the country, compared with the number of labourers in it. It is certainly at least not true in the sense in which it must be taken to sustain the argument, for that requires that the wages of labour should depend upon the amount of capital in the country, and upon nothing else; and that capital in this proposition should mean, wealth employed for the purpose of making a profit thereby, and that it should not extend to any part of a man's income, however analogous in other respects the latter might be to capital. All these assumptions are necessary to convert the argument into any proof of the harmlessness of absenteeism, since it evidently supposes that if the absentee remained at home, no part of his income would be employed as capital.

Now, is it true that the same quantity of capital however laid out, will afford the same employment and wages to labourers? Is not the contrary proposition evident? A capital of £1,000, if employed in a manufacture which returns it in two years, will give an income of £50 a year to ten labourers, but if it is employed in a business where the return is made in a period of six months, it will give the same employment and wages to forty labourers. Is not this such a difference as should make us cautious how we draw any deductions from the proposition that the employment of labourers depends upon the capital, not the income of the country? The returns to capital are all derived ultimately from income, and the capitalist may be considered as the mere agent of the incomist.[1]

The view that 'unproductive consumption' is necessary to the maintenance of effective demand and employment is in fact of special relevance to the question of absenteeism for, as has been shown by Dr R. L. Meek,[2] under-consumption theories at this period were closely linked to agrarian ideas. The view of the wealthy landlord as providing support for a mass of dependants is to be found very frequently repeated, and not merely in

---

[1] Longfield, *Three Lectures on Commerce*, pp. 85–6.
[2] 'Physiocracy and the Early Theories of Under-Consumption', *Economica*, n.s. vol. XVI, no. 71 (August 1951), pp. 229–69.

reference to Irish conditions.[1] In its more *simpliste* forms such a proposition could be adequately refuted by classical analysis. In the particular case of Ireland, however, it could be argued, as was done by the Dublin economist James A. Lawson,[2] that when the landlord became an absentee and ceased to demand the services of local tradesmen, the effect was to force labour from more into less productive types of employment. It could be argued too that although the landlord's removal implied no direct abstraction of capital from the country, it did diminish the sources from which saving and accumulation of capital and hence further permanent increases of employment and income could come. Comparatively little attention was paid to this side of the question; W. E. Mason has suggested that the first reference to it is to be found in J. Broadhurst's *Political Economy*, published in 1842,[3] but in fact the point was made by Lord Stourton in 1827.[4]

It may be suggested then, that McCulloch's conclusion that the absence of the landlords could not influence the demand for labour adversely was true only as a long-term proposition for an assumed money economy with flexible prices and hence full employment, and that those who, free from the static limitations of the wage-fund doctrine, approached the subject through a consideration of expenditure flows, not merely drew attention to the short-period decline of employment resulting from the landlord's removal but were able to point to possible causes of continuing injury, having regard to actual conditions in Ireland.

Although it was the problem of the effects of absenteeism on the demand for labour which secured most attention after McCulloch wrote, more attention has since been given to the related problem of the adjustment of the balance of payments to accommodate the unilateral transfer of the rents.

It has long been accepted that the classical economists, from Hume onwards, explained the adjustment of the balance of payments, in consequence of any disturbance in the trade relations of two countries, in terms of specie flows and price changes. Professor Viner has shown that many of them took account of the part played by relative changes in demand in restoring equilibrium,[5] but this was never regarded as more than a secondary element in the generally accepted notion of classical transfer theory. Yet in the explanation of absenteeism shifts in demand as between

---

[1] See, for example [Sir W. H. Sleeman], *On Taxes, or Public Revenue, the Ultimate Incidence of Their Payment, Their Disbursement, and the Seats of Their Consumption* by An Officer in the Military and Civil Service of the honourable East India Company (London, 1829), *passim*.

[2] Lawson, *Five Lectures on Political Economy, Delivered before the University of Dublin in Michaelmas Term, 1843* (London, 1844), p. 125.

[3] W. E. Mason, *The Classical Theory of Adjustment to Unilateral Capital Transfers* (Ph.D. thesis, Princeton University, 1952), pp. 233-4.

[4] Stourton, *Letter to Canning*, p. 48.

[5] J. Viner, *Studies in the Theory of International Trade* (New York and London, 1937), p. 293.

THE ABSENTEE LANDLORD

the two countries were generally assumed to be the sole cause of the readjustment.[1] This is the clear implication of McCulloch's argument, and it was endorsed by J. S. Mill in the letters which he wrote to the *Morning Chronicle* during the correspondence on absenteeism in 1825.[2] In view of the long-run character of McCulloch's theory and his innocence of effective demand ideas this unquestioning acceptance of the concept of a unilateral transfer being effected entirely by shifts of demand appears somewhat strange. On the whole, there seems no reason to doubt the explanation offered by Dr Mason—that the absentee case was the only one where a prolonged continuing transfer was envisaged, and where the transfer of purchasing power was direct and evident, requiring no income analysis.[3]

McCulloch's many critics did not generally trouble themselves with the subtleties of the transfer problem. An exception must be made for Henry Gardiner[4] who pointed out that the bills which might be purchased to make remittances to absentees were the outcome of previous exports and not the cause of subsequent exports. This might seem to suggest a possible alteration in the terms of trade, but Gardiner did not in fact work out this analysis correctly, and in other passages admitted that absenteeism would cause increased demand for Irish exports abroad, making the transfer possible without price changes.[5]

Longfield appears to have been the first to question the adequacy of changes in demand to effect the transfer of remittances, although he was also one of those who most clearly appreciated the short-run consequences to income and employment of the landlord's removal—at least for the paying country, Ireland. His argument was that 'if the home market is destroyed or diminished, more goods are forced into the foreign market by a reduction of price'[6]—which implies that there will not be a fully compensating expansion of demand in the 'foreign market' of the receiving country to prevent any deterioration of the terms of trade. 'It is this,' he adds, 'rather than the exportation of the necessaries of life, that creates, or at least increases the pernicious influence of absenteeism upon Ireland', and this seems to suggest, as Mason points out,[7] that Longfield believed the contraction of home demand resulting from absenteeism would outweigh any possible increase of demand for Irish exports that might result.

---

[1] See above, p. 73, and see McCulloch, *Edinburgh Rev.* no. LXXXV, pp. 56–7, 63. Dr Mason (*Classical Theory*, p. 167) has pointed out that the implicit reference to the demand-shift as effecting the transfer in the 1825 article was made explicit in the 1853 reprint of it in McCulloch's *Treatises and Essays on Money, Exchange and Interest*.
[2] *Morning Chronicle*, 16 and 20 September 1825, letters signed 'J. S.'.
[3] Mason, *Classical Theory*, p. 458.
[4] H. Gardiner, 'Absenteeism Considered, with some Remarks on a Part of Mr McCulloch's Evidence', *Pamphleteer*, vol. XXVII, no. LIII (1826). See also his *Essays on Currency and Absenteeism* (London, 1827).
[5] Gardiner, *Essays on Currency*, pp. 185–6.
[6] Longfield, *Three Lectures on Commerce*, p. 82.   [7] Mason, *Classical Theory*, p. 225.

Some time before Longfield wrote, J. S. Mill appears to have altered the opinions which he expressed in the *Morning Chronicle* in 1825. In his essay 'Of the Laws of Interchange between Nations', which was written in 1829 or 1830, but not published until 1844, Mill presented a general explanation of the process of unilateral transfers entirely cast in terms of price movements and specie flows and neglecting the factor of alterations in aggregate demand.[1] Absentee remittances are specifically included in this explanation, and Mill suggests that in view of the deterioration of the terms of trade 'Ireland pays dearer for her imports in consequence of her absentees; a circumstance which the assailants of Mr McCulloch, whether political economists or not, have not, we believe, hitherto thought of producing against him'.[2]

There appears to be no obvious reason for this change of opinion on Mill's part, save that in his later essay he was considering the problem in a broader light, and may have thought fit to bring the particular case of absenteeism into line with his generalised theory. Yet certainly in so doing he was making his view of the consequences of absenteeism an exceptional one, for the great majority of those who touched on the subject were content with the demand-shift explanation, explicit or implicit, for the mechanism of transfer. Only Longfield, his disciple Butt,[3] and J. S. Mill seem to have put forward what Professor Samuelson can now call 'the orthodox doctrine of a presumption that unilateral transfer payments will tend to deteriorate the terms of trade of the paying country'.[4]

III

Undoubtedly Longfield expressed a widespread opinion when he described the indirect social effects of absenteeism as 'infinitely more important' than the direct economic ones,[5] and a great many who wrote on the subject concurred with him in the opinion that absenteeism was injurious in its social and moral results. McCulloch had stated this point of view fairly enough when he wrote: 'Absentee landlords are said to be injurious...because the country is deprived of the moral benefits that would have resulted from their residence, and the peasantry left to be

---

[1] J. S. Mill, *Essays on Some Unsettled Questions of Political Economy* (London, 1844). See Preface, p. v, for the statement that the essays were written in 1829 and 1830.
[2] *Ibid.* p. 43. The last statement may have been correct when the essay was written, but not when it was published, in view of the appearance of Longfield's *Three Lectures on Commerce* in 1835. See Viner, *Studies*, p. 321.
[3] I. Butt reproduced Longfield's views, with acknowledgment of the work of Mill also, in an appendix to his *Protection to Home Industry: Some Cases of its Advantages Considered. The Substance of Two Lectures Delivered before the University of Dublin in Michaelmas Term, 1840* (Dublin, 1846), p. 122.
[4] P. A. Samuelson, 'The Transfer Problem and Transport Costs, II: Analysis of Effects of Trade Impediments', *Econ. J.* vol. LXIV, no. 254 (June 1954), p. 264.
[5] Longfield, *Three Lectures on Commerce*, p. 89.

fleeced and plundered by those who have no permanent interest in their welfare, and whose only object is to enrich themselves.'[1]

The 'moral benefits' of a resident proprietary were often assumed rather than explained; many advocates of residence held that it would induce the landowners to take a more serious view of their responsibilities, without making clear how this would come about. Those who were more specific, for example Longfield, held that residence would bring the problems of his tenantry before the landlord more effectively than could the most conscientious agent, and that he might be prompted to an interest in agricultural techniques and their improvement. Others believed that the return of the landlords must inevitably be beneficial—as gentry they required no stimulus to do good, but must inevitably set a meritorious example to their tenants.[2]

Senior gave qualified approval to this view. 'We have no doubt', he wrote, 'that a well-regulated gentleman's family, removing the prejudices, soothing the quarrels, directing and stimulating the exertions, and awarding praise or blame to the conduct of the villagers round them, is among the most efficient means by which the character of a neighbourhood can be improved.'[3] But this was true only of gentlemen of 'moderate fortune'—persons with incomes over £2000 a year were more likely to do harm than good by the example of their lavish expenditure.

Senior was here considering absentees in general, but not a few of those who referred particularly to the Irish proprietors held that their return would serve only to increase the demoralisation of the peasantry—because of what the *Westminster Review* bluntly termed their 'corruption and ineptitude'.[4] In addition it was often pointed out that the proprietors were in no position to make improvements whether they were resident or absent, because of the extent to which their estates were financially incumbered.

A more important point than any of these, perhaps, was the fundamental lack of sympathy between many Irish landlords and their tenantry, the result of differences in religion and outlook, which was as likely to be sharpened as modified by the landlords' residence. McCulloch showed that he was not always out of touch with reality when he said that 'before the residence of the landlords can be advantageous to Ireland, they must learn in some degree to sympathise with the feelings of the people'.[5]

Yet on the whole the balance of public opinion was certainly against the absentee landlord, and legislative action against him was frequently advocated. In general, these proposals took the form of various schemes

---

[1] McCulloch, *Edinburgh Rev.* no. LXXXV, p. 56.
[2] Cf. J. G. V. Porter, *Some Irish Questions Calmly Discussed* (London, 1843), p. 87.
[3] Senior, *Political Economy*, p. 159.
[4] *Westminster Rev.* vol. VIII (1827), p. 70.
[5] McCulloch, *Edinburgh Rev.* p. 68.

of discriminatory taxation, most frequently a poor-rate of some type.[1] The absentees' indifference towards the poor was a frequent ground of complaint, but aside from emotional considerations it was clear that a thorough system of poor relief would require an assessment on property, which absentees should not be able to evade. Torrens, indeed, was of opinion that the introduction of the workhouse system into Ireland would compel the use of an absentee tax.[2]

Those who advocated discriminatory taxation of absentees usually justified their intention to interfere with the liberty of the subject on the ground that no man should have liberty to injure others, and indeed this contention was even put forward in the *Quarterly Review*.[3] But proposals to tax absentees were naturally met with the cry of 'interference with the rights of property'; in Parliament in 1833 Spring Rice, himself an Irish proprietor, declared that absenteeism could not be remedied 'without degrading the people of Ireland, by leaving them without the power of free agency and making them mere *adscripti glebae*'.[4] It was further pointed out that proprietors forced into unwilling residence could not be expected to be zealous improvers.[5] Besides this, there were obvious difficulties in defining absenteeism for tax purposes, and many proprietors could claim that their absence was the necessary result of parliamentary or official duties. It is therefore not surprising that proposals to penalise the Irish absentees, though sometimes heard of in the House of Commons, never reached the Statute Book during this period.

The Irish Parliament had in fact established a limited form of absentee tax during the eighteenth century; it was first imposed in 1715, upon 'all persons...having...any office, salary, imployment, fee or pension, upon His Majesty's establishment...as shall live or reside out of this kingdom for the space of six months in one whole year'.[6] So many exemptions were granted under this Act that it was largely ineffective, and was allowed to lapse in 1753. The tax was reintroduced in 1767, at the rate of four shillings in the pound,[7] and continued until the time of the Union. No general tax upon the lands of absentees as such was ever imposed; an attempt, of dubious sincerity, by Lord North's administration to

---

[1] See, for example, W. Parker, *A Plea for the Poor and Industrious* (Cork, 1819), p. 82; J. F. Murray, *Ireland Contrasted with Scotland* (Belfast, 1832), p. 19; Stanley, MSS. headed 'Extracts from Remedial Measures for Ireland', submitted to Sir Robert Peel, January 1835 (B.M. Add. MSS. 40611, fos. 168–70).

[2] Torrens, *The Budget*, part v (London, 1842), p. 117. Torrens's argument here again was based on wage-fund theory—'The increased subsistence given to the poor within the workhouses must be taken from the labouring poor without the workhouses' unless an absentee tax be introduced 'such as may retain within the country, a portion of the agricultural produce now exported in payment of rent, sufficient to supply the inmates of workhouses....'

[3] *Quarterly Rev.* vol. XXXIII, p. 460.

[4] *Hansard*, 3rd ser. vol. XIX, col. 587.

[5] R. Slaney, *Essay on the Employment of the Poor*, 2nd ed. (London, 1822), pp. 93–4.

[6] 2 Geo. I, c. 3 (Ir.), sect. v.

[7] By 7 Geo. III, c. 2 (Ir.).

6-2

introduce such a tax in Ireland in 1773, was defeated through the activities of Lord Rockingham and some other prominent absentee proprietors.[1] If the chances of acceptance of such a measure were small in the time of the Irish Parliament, they were even less under the Union; but official disapproval of absenteeism did at times prove real enough to prevent the extension of patronage or advancement to non-resident Irish proprietors. Thus in 1815, Whitworth expressed to Sidmouth his 'conviction of the absolute necessity of reserving this distinction [a representative peerage] for those who are residents, as a means of encouragement to those who are so, and an inducement to those who are not, to become so'.[2]

IV

Although Irish absenteeism continued to be the subject of periodic comment throughout the period up to 1870, there were really no new developments in thought on the subject after the controversy stimulated by McCulloch in 1825 had died down. In general, economists accepted McCulloch's theory as established, and more than thirty years later he was able to say that 'it has yet to be answered'.[3] Certainly, if its premisses could be granted, the conclusion to which McCulloch's argument led was sound, at least as a long-term proposition, and it emerged largely unscathed from criticism. But, as has been suggested above, the premisses did not accord very closely with the facts of the position in Ireland.

It was this divergence between assumptions and actual conditions which led practical observers, both Irish and non-Irish, to regard the theory as a mere collection of paradoxes, 'a spell muttered from the mystic legends of modern political economy'.[4]

The true standing and influence of the theory is well summarised by Leonce de Lavergne's comment:

Many English economists, Mr McCulloch in particular, whose authority in these matters is great, have disputed the evil influence generally attributed to the non-residence of proprietors. The reasons advanced in favour of this opinion are purely theoretical. They would merit a careful examination if this were a didactic exposition of the principles of the science: but as far as regards Ireland at least, the question appears to me to be settled by the facts.[5]

For the critics of absenteeism, the facts were indeed sufficient evidence, but there were a number of more balanced observers who saw that so far

[1] See J. A. Froude, *The English in Ireland in the Eighteenth Century* (London, 1874), vol. II, pp. 149–60.
[2] Whitworth to Sidmouth, 13 November 1815 (H.O. 100/187).
[3] McCulloch, *Treatises and Essays*, p. 224.
[4] *Blackwood's Magazine*, vol. XXIV, p. 758.
[5] L. de Lavergne, *Rural Economy of England, Scotland and Ireland* (Edinburgh, 1845), p. 353.

as the condition of the people was concerned, the presence or absence of the proprietors was largely irrelevant so long as the conditions of land tenure remained unchanged.[1] McCulloch was probably guilty of an understatement when he allowed that absenteeism was 'not entirely innocuous', but in itself it was only a symptom of more deep-seated evils in the Irish economic and social system.

[1] See H. D. Inglis, *Ireland in 1834* (London, 1835), vol. II, p. 296.

CHAPTER IV

THE POOR LAW

I

AT least up to the time of John Stuart Mill, the classical economists were agreed that no change in the system of landed property was necessary to the improvement of Ireland; economic development could best be achieved through the retention of that system, and the adjustment of Irish agriculture to the capitalist type of mixed farming.

This conviction followed logically from the economists' method of viewing economic development in terms of the comparative rates of increase of population and capital.[1] In 1817, it seemed clear to such writers as Malthus and Ricardo that the extremely low standards of the majority of the Irish people were the result of a continuing tendency for population growth to outstrip capital increase. Employment opportunities were thus few, and money wages in them extremely low, but the people were able to support themselves, because of the comparative ease with which land could be obtained, through sub-division, and a sufficient quantity of potatoes raised from it.[2] The system gave no incentive to produce more than this, and thus the great majority of the people were idle and indolent.

If they were to be raised out of this condition and given higher material standards, then the growth of population must be checked, and the increase of capital promoted.[3] That it was desirable thus to raise material standards most political economists of the time did not doubt, although Ricardo pointed out that it was not the only course that might be chosen. 'Happiness is the object to be desired', he reminded Malthus, 'and we

---

[1] By capital was normally meant circulating capital—'funds destined for the support of labour'—but the term was often used in a looser sense. See the present author's article 'The Classical Economists and the Irish Problem', *Oxford Economic Papers*, vol. v, no. 1 (March 1953), especially p. 28.

[2] See Malthus to Ricardo, 17 August 1817: '...the predominant evil of Ireland, namely a population greatly in excess above the demand for labour, though in general not much in excess above the means of subsistence on account of the rapidity with which potatoes have increased under a system of cultivating them on very small properties rather with a view to support than sale' (*Works and Correspondence of David Ricardo*, ed. Sraffa, vol. III, p. 175).

[3] Most economists tended to regard increase of capital as a long-term remedy, and reduction of population as the main source of short-term improvement. Ricardo, however, classed Ireland amongst those 'poor countries where there are abundant means of production in store' in which accumulation of capital would be the 'only safe and efficacious means' of reducing the pressure of population against subsistence. So long as the people remained ignorant and indolent, reduction of their numbers would cause an equal fall in food production, and thus be of no benefit—*Principles, Works and Correspondence*, ed. Sraffa, vol. I, pp. 99–100; and cf. below, p. 134.

cannot be quite sure that provided he is equally well fed, a man may not be happier in the enjoyment of the luxury of idleness than in the enjoyment of the luxuries of a neat cottage, and good clothes. And after all we do not know if these would fall to his share. His labour might only increase the enjoyments of his employer.'[1]

However, once granted the premiss that improvement of material standards was to be sought, it clearly followed that capital growth must be made to outstrip population growth, and the classical economists reasoned that the most effective single step that could be taken to achieve this was the abolition of the cottier system, and the introduction of the English type of agriculture in its place. Such a change would in fact operate to check population and stimulate investment simultaneously.

Malthus, and all who shared his beliefs, constantly stressed that population would be stimulated where it appeared easy for the labourer to obtain food and shelter for a family.[2] Nowhere did it appear easier than in Ireland, so long as sub-division of land was permitted. By the consolidation of holdings and the conversion of the cottier into a wage-labourer, buying his food and renting his cottage, a deterrent might be imposed on improvident marriages, and population be checked. At the same time, the loss of potato ground would make the labourer dependent on the employer for his subsistence, and give him a new incentive to work. This was Ricardo's argument: to Malthus's contention 'That the necessity of employing only a small portion of time in producing food does not always occasion the employment of a greater portion of time in procuring conveniences and luxuries' he replied: 'Certainly not, if the choice be in the power of the labourers, in which case their wages must be high, or rather they must be well paid for their work. As certainly yes, if labour be low, and the choice be in the power of the capitalists.'[3] Left to themselves, the Irish labourers might prefer potatoes and idleness: employed by capitalists, either in agriculture or industry, they could be made to produce 'conveniences and luxuries' and might develop a taste for their products, which would come to be a part of their accepted standard of life, as with the English labourer. In other words, if industry replaced idleness a very considerable increase in the wages-fund would be possible,

---

[1] Ricardo to Malthus, 4 September 1817, *Works and Correspondence*, ed. Sraffa, vol. vii, p. 185. See Ricardo's note (no. 225) to p. 382 of Malthus's *Principles* in his *Works*, ed. Sraffa, vol. ii, pp. 336–8: 'It has been well said by M. Say that it is not the province of the political economist to advise: he is to tell you how you may become rich, but he is not to advise you to prefer riches to indolence, or indolence to riches.'

[2] 'Such is the tendency to form early connections, that with the encouragement of a sufficient number of tenements, I have very little doubt that the population might be so pushed and such a quantity of labour in time thrown into the market, as to render the condition of the independent labourer absolutely hopeless....'—Malthus, *A Letter to Samuel Whitbread, Esq., M.P., on his Proposed Bill for the Amendment of the Poor Laws* (London, 1807) reprinted in Glass, p. 193.

[3] Ricardo, *Works and Correspondence*, vol. ii, pp. 349–50.

but the abolition of the cottier potato-truck system would be the condition precedent for this.

With the land minutely sub-divided neither an increase of productive efficiency, nor an influx of fresh capital to aid it, could be hoped for.[1] Hence the population and capital aspects of the problem were inter-related: to improve agriculture and give scope for investment in it, it was necessary to clear the land of the improvident cottiers who encumbered it and consolidate it into more efficient farm units: to employ the displaced population and raise their real income, it was necessary to encourage investment.

So, as the classical economists saw the problem, the replacement of the cottier system by a capitalistic agriculture was the key to the economic regeneration of Ireland; but though this was necessary to the solution of the problem, it was not sufficient. The adjustment must be accompanied by a series of other measures designed to promote capital growth and control population. The remainder of this book will be devoted to the examination of the proposals which stemmed from this conception of the problem, and the manner of their transition into policy.

Analysed in classical terms, the situation in Ireland appeared as one mainly of chronic under-employment, which must compel steps to increase the demand for labour, and reduce the supply of it. Yet however vigorously and judiciously such a programme might be pursued, it could only succeed after a period of some years. In the meantime 'the boundless multiplication of human beings satisfied with the lowest condition of existence'[2] created a serious problem. Not all could succeed in the competition for land, so that to the crowds of under-employed cottiers in rural areas were beginning to be added crowds of unemployed labourers in the towns and villages, and a poor potato crop, which was a frequent occurrence, brought the majority of the working population to the brink of destitution.[3] These conditions might be eradicated by measures for economic development, but until they were the question of immediate relief for those without means of support was too large to be ignored. Moreover, it was recognised by economists and administrators alike that cottiers could not always be transmuted into wage-labourers without delay; there was bound to be a difficult 'period of transition' during which the population displaced by clearances would require assistance.[4]

[1] This is clearly indicated by statements such as those of Torrens, quoted above, ch. II, p. 19.
[2] From *Report of the Select Committee on the State of Disease, and the Condition of the Labouring Poor in Ireland* (1819 (409), vol. VIII), p. 97.
[3] See above, ch. I, pp. 9 and 10. Though the condition of the majority of the Irish labourers was certainly one of under-employment, there seems to be ample evidence that many 'landless men' were unemployed in the modern sense. See evidence of A. Nimmo before the Select Committee on the Condition of the Labouring Poor in Ireland: (1819 (409), vol. VIII), p. 101.
[4] See above, ch. II, p. 21, and references quoted there; also Lewis, *Local Disturbances in Ireland* (London, 1836), pp. 313-21; *Report of Geo. Nicholls, Esq., on Poor Laws, Ireland* (1837 [69], vol. LI).

The problem of poor relief in Ireland in the early years of the nineteenth century was thus a considerable one, and likely to grow in proportion to the success of the policy which the economists advocated, in its first stages. The existing mechanism of assistance was wholly inadequate to meet the situation. The poor in Ireland were almost entirely relieved by private charity alone. An Act had indeed been passed in 1772[1] containing provisions for the establishment of corporations charged with the relief of the poor in every county,[2] but this had proved largely inoperative, and in the early nineteenth century Irish property was subject to no compulsory assessment for poor-rates. This was the period when Poor Law reform was being hotly debated in England; the importance of the part played by the classical economists in this debate is well recognised, and has been much discussed.[3] Whether a Poor Law should be introduced into Ireland, and if so in what form, was an equally live issue in which the economists were no less interested; but their views on this question have received little attention, although they provide interesting light on classical attitudes to social policy. Before entering on consideration of the classical economists' prescriptions for Ireland in their wider aspects, it therefore seems appropriate to examine their contributions to the debate on Poor Laws for Ireland, and the resultant effects on policy.

II

Long before 1817, the condition of the poorer classes in Ireland had been such as to compel discussion of means of relieving their distress. The legislation of 1772 was in part the result of the exertions of Richard Woodward, bishop of Cloyne, who in 1768 published *An Argument in Support of the Right of the Poor in the Kingdom of Ireland to a National Provision* in which he asserted 'That it is the indispensible duty of the Rich to provide a competent maintenance for the Poor' and that 'the interest of the state demands some compulsory law, that the Rich may provide a competent subsistence for the Poor'.[4]

There was no legislative action in regard to poor relief between 1772 and the Act of Union, and the subject did not come to the fore again until the fall of agricultural prices after the end of the Napoleonic wars and the partial famine of 1817 brought widespread distress in Ireland. Select Committees were appointed in 1819 and again in 1823 to investigate 'the

---

[1] 11 and 12 Geo. III, c. 30 (Ir.).

[2] For a fuller account of the provisions of the Act, see Sir G. Nicholls, *A History of the Irish Poor Law, in Connexion with the Condition of the People* (London, 1856), pp. 51–4.

[3] See, for example, S. and B. Webb, *English Poor Law History*, Part II, *The Last Hundred Years* (London, 1927), vol. I; M. Bowley, *Nassau Senior and Classical Economics*, (London, 1937), pt. II, ch. 2; K. Polanyi, *Origins of our Time, the Great Transformation* (London, 1945), *passim;* Robbins, *Theory of Economic Policy*, pp. 93–100.

[4] Woodward, pp. 25 and 43.

condition of the Labouring Poor in Ireland'[1] and some pamphlets appeared[2] but the real public debate on the desirability of Poor Laws for Ireland did not begin until about 1828–30.

The subject attracted attention in both England and Ireland at this time. The effect of land clearances in increasing the numbers of homeless poor was beginning to be noticeable in Ireland, and the introduction of steam navigation made it increasingly easy for Irish labourers to migrate to England. There they sometimes became a charge on the poor-rates, sometimes competed so severely with English labourers that these in turn became subjects for parish relief. With the increasing cost of the allowance system Poor Law reform had become an urgent question in England: the influx of cheap Irish labour underlined its urgency, and suggested the desirability of a measure for Ireland also. English property owners felt that they had burdens enough without undertaking to support, or bear the cost of removing, a mass of Irish paupers whose former landlords escaped poor-rates altogether.

On the face of things, the issue in debate appears straightforward enough—should a compulsory Poor Law be introduced into Ireland? In fact, the question was greatly complicated and obscured by the fact that the participants in the discussion often meant quite different things by 'a Poor Law' and did not always trouble to define the term. It is evident that a clear distinction must be maintained between measures for elimination or reduction of poverty through overall economic development, and measures for the immediate relief of distress, but many writers used the term 'Poor Law' to cover the former as well as the latter. Others still argued that a Poor Law in the narrower sense was the necessary foundation for measures of economic development. Since such measures are separately considered in later chapters, only the arguments advanced for and against a Poor Law in the narrower sense need be considered here.

At the outset, the classical economists were virtually unanimous in their opposition to the idea of introducing a general system of poor relief into Ireland. The demoralising effects and the immense cost of the operation of the unreformed English Poor Law were only too plain, and had led Malthus to declare himself in favour of the total abolition of poor relief.[3] Ireland had so far escaped this scourge; why should it now be

---

[1] See *First and Second Reports from the Select Committee on State of Disease, and Condition of the Labouring Poor in Ireland* (1819 (314, 409), vol. VIII); *Report from Select Committee on Employment of the Poor in Ireland* (1823 (561), vol. VI).

[2] The most notable pamphlet published in Ireland was Parker's *Plea for the Poor*, only the first part of which appears to have been published. Parker advocated relief to the infant, sick, and aged poor only, but urged legislative action to increase employment for the able-bodied. See *Plea for the Poor*, p. ix, and Parker's earlier work, *A Plan for the General Improvement of the State of the Poor of Ireland* (Cork, 1816).

One of the earlier English pamphlets is Sir C. T. Waller, *A Plan for the Relief of the Poor in Ireland, in a Letter Addressed to His Grace the Duke of Devonshire* (Bath, n.d. [1826 or 7]).

[3] T. R. Malthus, *Essay on the Principle of Population*, 6th ed. (London, 1826), vol. II, p. 109.

imposed upon her? Certainly it was true that the absence of Poor Laws had not rendered Ireland more prosperous or less pauper-infested than England, but it did not follow from this that the introduction of such laws would not make the condition of Ireland worse rather than better.

The standard arguments of the classical school against Poor Laws which conferred a general right to relief were that they tended to weaken thrift and industry, promoting improvidence and idleness in their place; that by affording a guarantee of subsistence they encouraged the growth of population, while at the same time they merely diverted funds which would have been used to employ productive labour to the support of idleness. All these arguments could be applied to Ireland with added force—administrative experience in local affairs being less general there than in England, the operation of a Poor Law system would doubtless prove more difficult and costly. So many cottiers were on the verge of destitution that at some seasons the majority of the population might become a charge on the rates: small farmers would never be able to meet the assessments, and the whole rental of the country might be absorbed. Inevitably, the introduction of a compulsory poor-rate would dry up the sources of private charity, which would further augment the cost of public relief.

When the question of Poor Laws for Ireland first began to be widely discussed, most economists assumed it to imply the introduction of the allowance system, and this they unreservedly condemned, on the grounds just outlined. On the other hand, many were prepared to approve proposals for the relief of the aged and infirm, orphans and foundlings, so long as no right of assistance were given to the able-bodied poor.

Generally it may be said that the classical economists who turned their attention to the Irish situation between 1820 and 1835 were convinced that the condition of the population necessitated remedial measures, but that the introduction of relief to the able-bodied ought not to be one of those measures. Ricardo, for example, did not anywhere express himself directly on the question of Poor Laws for Ireland, but he was a member of the Select Committee of the House of Commons on the Condition of the Labouring Poor in Ireland in 1823[1] and subscribed to its Report, which included the statement that 'relief purely gratuitous can seldom in any case be given without considerable risk and inconvenience; but in Ireland, where it is more peculiarly important to discourage habits of pauperism and of indolence, and where it is the obvious policy to excite an independent spirit of industry, and to induce the Peasantry to rely upon themselves and their own exertions for their support, it is obvious that gratuitous relief can never be given without leading to most mischievous consequences'.[2] This same report, however, stressed the fact that the

---

[1] *Works and Correspondence*, vol. v, p. xxvi.
[2] *Report from Select Committee on Employment of the Poor in Ireland* (1823 (561), vol. VI), p. 5.

employment of the people of Ireland was 'essentially necessary' in the general interests of the United Kingdom, and recommended Government assistance to promote it where necessary.[1]

There is more direct evidence of Malthus's views on Poor Laws for Ireland, for he stated them unequivocally in evidence before the Emigration Committee of 1827: asked whether such legislation 'would have a tendency to alleviate or to increase the misery that now prevails there?' he replied 'I think on the whole, and finally, it would aggravate it'.[2] Nor had his views changed six years later when the question—'What would be the effect of establishing Poor Laws in Ireland?' was discussed at the Political Economy Club: Malthus then expressed the gravest misgivings about their effects, and argued that poor relief would impede Irish economic development, since it would tend to 'fix the surplus and unemployed population in Ireland instead of putting them upon means of providing for it by emigration'.[3]

Senior can be considered representative of the school of thought which would have denied relief to the able-bodied, but not to other classes of the poor. In his *Letter to Lord Howick on a Legal Provision for the Irish Poor*, published in 1831, he showed himself opposed to any system which would give the able-bodied a right to public assistance. On the other hand, he declared: 'Without wishing to give to the poor, when in sickness, a right to assistance, I am anxious that public provision should be made for such assistance, as far at least as medical treatment is concerned', while in the cases of blindness, 'chronic infirmity' and lunacy—'No public fund for the relief of these calamities has any tendency to diminish industry or providence. They are evils too great to allow individuals to make any sufficient provision against them, and too rare to be, in fact, provided against by them at all....I wish therefore to see these evils met by an ample compulsory provision.'[4]

Senior would not have extended this provision to the aged: inability to earn in old age, he contended, was entirely foreseeable, and could be provided for by personal thrift. The weakening of the motives to private charity was another reason against a public provision for the aged poor. In condemning relief to the able-bodied Senior assumed that it must take the form of outdoor relief, on the English model: but even when the workhouse system had been evolved, he still did not consider general relief practicable in Ireland, for the low living standards of the people

[1] *Report from Select Committee on Employment of the Poor in Ireland* (1823 (561), vol. VI), p. 11; and see below, ch. v.

[2] Answer to Q. 3228: evidence of Rev. T. R. Malthus before the Select Committee on Emigration from the United Kingdom (1827 (550), vol. v), p. 313.

[3] From J. L. Mallet's Diary, 6 December 1833, *Political Economy Club, Centenary Volume* (London, 1921), p. 253.

[4] N. W. Senior, *A Letter to Lord Howick, on a Legal Provision for the Irish Poor; Commutation of Tithes, and a Provision for the Irish Roman Catholic Clergy*, 2nd ed. (London, 1831), pp. 13–14.

made the principle of 'less eligibility' inapplicable.[1] This rigid opposition to a Poor Law in the narrow sense caused Senior to be strongly criticised by Poulett Scrope and other supporters of 'legal provision for the Irish Poor', but actually Senior qualified his views to a great extent by advocating a comprehensive development programme for Ireland, including both public works and subsidised emigration.[2]

The weapons of classical theory were wielded frequently and bluntly against the idea of an Irish Poor Law by Colonel Torrens. In his speeches in the House of Commons, Torrens displayed impatient contempt of all those who reasoned on the problem without regard to the principles of political economy.[3] His own thinking on it was wholly conditioned by classical concepts; he used strict Malthusian principles to show that by the introduction of Poor Laws 'the progress of population in Ireland would be accelerated' so that 'at no distant period the whole rental of the country would be inadequate to the maintenance of those for whose labour there would be no demand'—for while a Poor Law would increase population, it would not augment resources. Nor would England benefit from the introduction of Poor Laws into Ireland, Torrens contended; for 'the confiscation of the whole property of the country, and applying the entire rental to the increase of wages, would be insufficient, without any increase of the existing population of Ireland, to prevent the influx of Irish labourers.'[4]

Economic arguments against the idea of Poor Laws for Ireland were thus plentiful, and used by powerful authorities, but other arguments were also employed. Senior's belief that assistance to the aged would weaken the motives of benevolence and private charity has already been mentioned: this was an idea often urged by Dr Thomas Chalmers, the Scots divine and tireless advocate of private charity as the answer to all Poor Law problems. 'I look upon a compulsory provision', said Chalmers, 'to be that which acts as a disturbing force upon certain principles and feelings, which, if left to their own undisturbed exercise, would do more for the prevention and alleviation of poverty than can be done by any legal or artificial system whatever.'[5] A compulsory provision for poor relief, Chalmers asserted, would 'deteriorate the condition of any country'. Ireland formed no exception to this rule, in his view: he concurred with Malthus in thinking that a Poor Law would slow down the transition to

[1] *Idem, Letter to His Majesty's Principal Secretary of State for the Home Department on the Third Report from the Commissioners for Inquiring Into the Condition of the Poor in Ireland* (1837 [90], vol. LI).

[2] For a fuller account of Senior's views on these subjects, see Bowley, pt. II, ch. I; also below, chs. V and VII.

[3] See, for example, his speech against Sadler's motion for an Irish Poor Law, 29 August 1831, *Hansard*, 3rd ser. vol. VI, col. 818.

[4] *Ibid.* col. 821.

[5] Answer to Q. 3394: evidence of Rev. Thomas Chalmers, D.D., *Second Report of Evidence from the Select Committee on the State of the Poor in Ireland* (1830 [654], vol. VII), p. 287.

capitalist farming, 'and prevent that natural distribution of the people which is best adapted to the new state of things'. It would promote improvidence and increase population, and instead of reducing the gap between English and Irish standards of life, would widen it still further. Chalmers, like Senior, was prepared to concede that the blind, the insane, and the chronically ill, though not the aged, might safely be relieved at the public expense; but for 'general indigence' he could offer no other cure than education to inculcate 'Christian principle' in the people, encouraging self-reliance and leaving the relief of genuine destitution to private charity.[1]

These moral arguments of Chalmers carried great weight at the time, and they were widely approved and supported. Thus J. E. Bicheno, a Fellow of the Royal Society with an interest in political economy, who was later a member of the 1833 Royal Commission on the State of the Poor in Ireland, declared in 1830 that 'one great objection to the introduction of Poor Laws into Ireland, would be the inevitable consequence of breaking in upon the humane and charitable disposition which actuates the people at present'. Bicheno was quite prepared to contend that the moral cost of 'blunting the natural affections of the poor' might outweigh the economic benefit of relieving their sufferings through a public agency. 'Above all, I would wish to avoid that narrow treatment of the question which regards it as one of political economy. How the labouring poor are to improve the wealth of the country is, no doubt, of great moment; but how they, with the rich, are to be made happy, is a subject of more vital importance.'[2]

There can be no doubt that this attitude of mind played a significant part in forming the social philosophy, and so the social policy, of the whole period from 1817 to 1870, and beyond. It is a thread which will be found to appear again and again in the pattern of social and economic thought in this era. Those who advocated this stern morality undoubtedly did so in the belief that it was in the best interests of the poor themselves, but not all humanitarians were prepared to accept this belief. It was never contested by anyone at this time that the condition of the poorer classes in Ireland was miserable in the extreme; but to many observers it seemed that the sufferings of the poor were so great as to make all talk of prudence, forethought and thrift a sad mockery. Perhaps the best known of these writers was James Warren Doyle, the Roman Catholic Bishop of Kildare and Leighlin, whose *Letters on the State of Ireland*, published under the pseudonym of 'J. K. L', attracted wide attention when they appeared in 1825, and established him as a leading advocate of Poor Laws for Ireland.

[1] Chalmers, answers to Questions 3553–5, 3570–84, *State of the Poor, loc. cit.* pp. 316–20.
[2] J. E. Bicheno, *Ireland and its Economy: being the Result of Observations made in a Tour through the Country in the Autumn of 1829* (London, 1830), pp. 251 and 258.

'A legal provision for the poor invites to idleness, and renders the poor themselves improvident' [wrote Doyle]. Good God! How bewildered in useless theories must not the minds of those men be, who rest their opposition to a Poor Rate on this objection!...It would, if it were true, lead us to conclude that to excite men to labour, you have only to strip them naked, and give them no food....A man habitually devoured by hunger, or perishing with cold, may, if a Christian, be a saint; but abstracting from religion he is deranged, he is supersitious, improvident, reckless of life and character, and liable to be agitated by every species of passion. It is impossible to introduce him, or restore him a to state of civilisation, of labour, or industry, until you provide for him the necessaries of life.[1]

The objection that Poor Laws might weaken charity and 'blunt the natural affections of the poor' served equally to rouse Doyle's righteous indignation, and he classed those who employed it as 'Pharisees and hypocrites'.[2] Yet righteous indignation was not Doyle's only weapon against the critics of Poor Laws, and he was prepared to meet the economists on their own ground. Doyle can be regarded in this respect as one of a group of humanitarians and unorthodox economists, both Irish and English, who supported the introduction of Poor Laws into Ireland at this time, and most of the arguments which he employed to refute the classical indictment were common to all the group.

Rejection of the Malthusian doctrine of population was the starting-point for all these writers. On this, Doyle confined himself to the simple assertion that the population of Ireland would not be 'redundant' if the resources of the country were properly employed, but added a much more significant comment as regards the tendency of Poor Laws to stimulate population: 'I who am daily and hourly conversant with the poor and with the middling classes of society, find that early and improvident marriages occur amongst the former much more frequently than with the latter...so that in order to check this supposed evil [of increasing population] no remedy could be devised more effectual than to raise somewhat the condition of the poor.'[3] The view that destitution encouraged reckless marriage, while Poor Laws, by raising the condition of the poor, tended to check population, was also expressed by J. B. Bryan, an Irishman to whom 'the Malthusian *philosophes*' were a constant *bête noir*.[4]

Undoubtedly the best-known, as well as the most verbose, anti-Malthusian of the day was Michael Thomas Sadler, who earned the

---

[1] J. W. Doyle, *Letter to Thomas Spring Rice, Esq., M.P., on the Establishment of a Legal Provision for the Irish Poor, and on the Nature and Destination of Church Property* (Dublin, 1831), pp. 22–3. Essentially the same argument had been used by James Mill in his Essay on Education; see *James and J. S. Mill on Education*, ed. F. Cavenagh (Cambridge, 1931), p. 45.

[2] Doyle, *Letter to Thomas Spring Rice*, p. 34. Doyle here makes clear that he is thinking of the affections of the poor towards each other, but he also attacked the idea that a poor law might 'dry up the sources of benevolence amongst the well-to-do'—*ibid.* pp. 30–3.

[3] [J. W. Doyle], *Letters on the State of Ireland; Addressed by J. K. L. to a Friend in England* (Dublin, 1825), p. 363.

[4] J. B. Bryan, *A Practical View of Ireland* (Dublin, 1831), pp. 137–43.

contempt of the whole classical school by producing 'a Treatise in Six Books' designed to prove that the true law of population 'is simply this: The fecundity of human beings is, caeteris paribus, in the inverse ratio of the condensation of their numbers.'[1] Whilst preparing this work, Sadler turned his attention to Ireland, and became a strong exponent of the case for Irish improvement. Both in his writings and from his place in the House of Commons he constantly advocated a Poor Law for Ireland, using the argument, against Malthus, that population had increased more rapidly in Ireland without a Poor Law than in England with one.[2] Neither Malthus nor any of his followers had ever denied this, in point of fact, but Sadler's answer to the contention that the introduction of Poor Laws would now make matters worse rather than better was always that what he wished to see introduced into Ireland was 'the Poor Laws of England restored to their original purity and efficiency', whereas the consequences which Malthus feared flowed only from the misinterpretation and abuse of those laws, chiefly in affording relief to the able-bodied without requiring labour from them in return.

This view was shared by G. Poulett Scrope, a much clearer thinker and more able economist than Sadler. Scrope frequently asserted that the opponents of Poor Laws tended to 'confound the abuses introduced into the administration of the English poor-law *within the present century*, with the law of Elizabeth, as previously acted upon with the most beneficial results for more than two centuries'.[3] As to the effect of Poor Laws on population, Scrope took much the same position as Doyle, declaring that 'no economical fallacy was ever more completely opposed to fact, as well as reasoning, than that which induced so humane a man as the late Mr Malthus to preach the revolting doctrine that the poor should be left to starve, lest they should propagate their numbers too rapidly. Ireland incontestably demonstrates that it is when they are on the verge of starvation that they multiply the fastest'.[4]

Scrope, however, grounded his defence of Poor Laws for Ireland not so much on anti-Malthusian arguments as on the contention that Poor Laws would increase rather than reduce productive employment. Lack of security, he held, was the reason for reluctance to invest in Ireland:

[1] M. T. Sadler, *The Law of Population: a Treatise in Six Books, in Disproof of the Super-fecundity of Human Beings, and Developing the Real Principle of their Increase* (London, 1830).

[2] M. T. Sadler, *Ireland: its Evils, and their Remedies: being a Refutation of the Errors of the Emigration Committee and Others, touching that Country* (London, 1828), p. 261.

[3] G. P. Scrope, *Plan of a Poor-Law for Ireland, with a Review of the Arguments For and Against It* (London, 1833), p. 1.

[4] [G. P. Scrope], 'Foreign Poor Laws—Irish Poverty', *Quarterly Rev.* vol. LV (December 1835), p. 65.

For the attribution of this article to Scrope, see R. Opie, 'George Poulett Scrope: a Neglected English Economist', *Quarterly J. Economics*, vol. XLIV (November 1929), pp. 101–37.

establish Poor Laws and crime and outrage would be reduced, security, and thus investment, promoted.[1] This was a common argument with the supporters of Poor Laws for Ireland, usually supplemented by the proposition that a poor-rate might induce landlords to give more productive employment, rather than support the poor in idleness on the rates.[2]

Doyle, who employed these arguments also, went further in undertaking a direct refutation of the classical view 'that what is given to [the poor for] their support, is deducted from capital to be otherwise employed in productive labour'[3] but here he moved somewhat out of his depth, for he did not understand the significance of the distinction between capital employing productive labour, and revenue employing unproductive labour. The view just quoted he held to be advanced

without remorse by those who justify luxurious living—the keeping of dogs, and horses, and servants, without limit or employment. These persons say, that what is thus expended or consumed, returns to the tradesman, the merchant and agriculturalist. Be it so. But if the rich encourage arts and agriculture by useless and luxurious consumption; if the capital thus expended by them be not withdrawn from productive labour, how can it be said that the food and raiment furnished to the pauper is a drawback from the resources of the country?

No one who had read, for example, McCulloch's article on Absenteeism, with any care, could have imagined that this was a fair summary of current economic thinking on employment processes. Yet Doyle's criticism on this point cannot be wholly dismissed: for Malthus, the great opponent of Poor Laws, was also certainly the great advocate of unproductive consumption. Even within the limits of Ricardian orthodoxy, it could still be argued that the majority of Irish landlords did *not* employ all, or even most, of their capital in the support of productive labour.

While many of the arguments of the supporters of Poor Laws were, like those just discussed, developed as simple negations of opposing views, they also contained some positive points. Many of these were straightforward appeals to humanity, but these were frequently supported by an ethical argument with economic implications—the argument that the poor have a right to support from society. Sadler held that 'It was a principle in morals, immutable as any principle in nature, that the poor inherited this claim to support as part of their birth-right.'[4] Like many others before him, he justified this on the ground that the State permitted the appropriation of property, and enforced the rights of ownership; therefore it must enforce the right to subsistence of those who had no

---

[1] See, for example, Scrope's *Poor Law for Ireland*, p. 41.
[2] Bryan, *A Practical View of Ireland*, pp. 91–3; Murray, *Ireland contrasted with Scotland*, p. 19.   [3] Doyle, *Letter to Thomas Spring Rice*, p. 14.
[4] *Hansard*, 3rd ser. vol. XIII, col. 831 (19 June 1832). See Scrope's *Plan of a Poor-Law for Ireland*, which carried on the title-page the words: 'God gave the earth to mankind in common; and the right to Property is subordinate to the rights of every man, to the means of Existence which his Maker has placed within his reach.'

property if they could not, through no fault of their own, earn their bread. Doyle supported this in a qualified fashion, saying that, while the poor man has a right to support, 'it is one which, as a general rule, it may be said it is never lawful for him to enforce'.[1]

This doctrine of the rights of the poor had been used by Woodward in 1768,[2] and, as Sadler himself pointed out to an uninterested House of Commons, it can be traced back through the writings of Paley to its origins in Locke.

As Halévy has shown[3] the right to subsistence can be directly deduced from the principle of utility, but was regarded by Bentham as dangerous to both property and industry. The idea that the State should guarantee the right to subsistence, or at least the right to work for subsistence, had fallen before the idea of a spontaneous economic system and a natural harmony of interests. In reasserting the right, Sadler and others like him were going against the trend of social philosophy, since it was coming more and more to be accepted that the free economy provided the right to subsistence automatically, through the opportunity to work, for all who would take it.

That the economic system which existed in Ireland did not, as it stood, provide the right to work or subsistence was manifest. Where the difference in philosophy between men such as Sadler and Scrope on the one hand, and Torrens and Malthus on the other, became evident was in their views as to the course of policy made necessary by this situation. Torrens, for example, wished to create through emigration and consolidation of farms a situation where the right to work would be provided through market processes. Sadler and Scrope felt that the State must assume the duty of providing subsistence, in return for labour in the case of the able-bodied, as they believed had formerly been done by the Elizabethan Poor Law. Thus, particularly in the case of Scrope, the distinction between a Poor Law and a system of public works frequently became indistinct.

The essential issue in the debate on Irish Poor Laws can thus be narrowed to this point—what is the duty of the State towards the able-bodied poor? Most opponents of Poor Laws held that to offer support to the able-bodied, even in return for labour, was to encourage over-population and idleness. Such men as Senior and Spring Rice held that the State or local authority could not usefully employ paupers without threatening unfair competition to private enterprise, and that pauper labour employed on parish work would always be inefficient from lack of incentive.[4] The supporters of Poor Laws answered such charges with a

[1] Doyle, *Letters on the State of Ireland*, p. 319.
[2] *Argument in Support of the Right of the Poor* (Dublin, 1768).
[3] E. Halévy, *Growth of Philosophic Radicalism*, trans. Morris (London, 1928), p. 205.
[4] See Senior, *A Letter to Lord Howick*, pp. 25, 52, and *Journals relating to Ireland*, vol. I, pp. 171–83; [Spring Rice], 'Proposed Introduction of Poor Laws into Ireland', *Edinburgh*

denial, pointed to the absence of private employment in Ireland and urged the duty of the State to do what private individuals did not.

Here was the area of disagreement, but as to the desirability of relieving those who could not help themselves—infants, the blind, and the infirm, both sides were agreed. Relief could be given to such classes without any tendency to improvidence, the most rigid economists agreed, while the strongest advocates of general Poor Laws admitted that a grant of relief to these classes would meet many of the worst evils of which they complained.

III

An examination of the literature of this question, such as has just been given, might suggest that the controversy involved only a comparatively small group of economists and humanitarians, but by the beginning of the eighteen-thirties the Irish Poor Law was rapidly becoming a national issue throughout the United Kingdom. Numerous and varied interests were involved, and many public men who were normally opponents in politics found themselves drawn together by their convictions in favour of or against a Poor Law.

In Ireland, the main opposition to Poor Laws came, naturally, from the landowners, who saw themselves and their property as threatened by the worst evils of the Speenhamland system. This point of view was well represented by the Earl of Limerick, a prominent absentee, who, when the question of the introduction of Poor Laws into Ireland was being debated in the House of Lords, declared that 'neither by march of intellect, nor by political economists, nor by any other influence would he be persuaded to support any such wild schemes of innovation'.[1]

The opposition of Irish landowners was not always merely obscurantist. Spring Rice (afterwards Monteagle), a talented Whig who had done much to secure reforms in Irish affairs, often urged the case against an Irish Poor Law in the Commons, and was widely regarded as the spokesman of uncompromising opposition to such a measure. His own view of his position was that sympathy with the poor need not imply sympathy for the Poor Laws.

I fear you are somewhat of a heretic on the Poor-Law question, [he told Bishop Doyle], but you must not misconceive me on that most important point—I never will argue against the poor laws if it can be shown that their establishment would be for the benefit of the poor themselves. It is that I doubt. The prosperity of the bulk of the people must depend on the profitable demand for their labour, and I cannot see that Poor Laws tend to augment the demand for labour in any respect.[2]

Rev. vol. LIX, p. 246 (April 1834). The idea of pauper labour giving unfair competition to labour in normal employment can be found in such eighteenth-century works as Defoe's Giving Alms No Charity (1704).

[1] Hansard, 2nd ser. vol. XXIII, col. 368 (16 March 1830).   [2] Spring Rice to Bishop Doyle, 26 April 1829 (Monteagle Papers, National Library of Ireland).

Spring Rice was frequently a strong opponent of Daniel O'Connell, but in the matter of Poor Laws they found themselves in the same camp. Since O'Connell was certainly 'King of the Beggars'[1] there was no easier way in which he could have courted popularity than by championing the cause of poor relief, but his attitude was one of general, though not consistent, opposition to any Poor Law for Ireland.[2] O'Connell adopted most of the moral and economic arguments against Poor Laws common at this time, and took the view that such laws were one scourge from which Ireland could escape through repeal of the Union.[3] Certainly while O'Connell showed himself willing to abate his agitation for Repeal in the hopes of Irish reforms by the Whigs, a Poor Law does not seem to have been amongst the measures he desired.

In this respect, O'Connell was at odds with some influential Irish liberals of the time. Lord Cloncurry, always sympathetic to the cause of Repeal, though not always to O'Connell, was an advocate of Poor Laws, and hoped that the Whig ministry of 1830-4 might legislate upon the subject. Cloncurry was a believer in relief to the able-bodied, somewhat along the lines suggested by Scrope, and would have wished to make it compulsory for landowners to employ at least one labourer for every ten acres of their property.[4] This scheme of a labour-rate was also supported, and urged upon the Government of the day, by the Marquess of Anglesey, who was Lord-Lieutenant of Ireland from 1830 to 1833, and in frequent personal contact with Cloncurry. Anglesey desired to see introduced a Poor Law for the helpless and aged, and a labour-rate for the able-bodied; but although he argued that 'O'Connell's dislike of it should be with you all conclusive in its favour' he gained little sympathy for his views amongst his Whig colleagues.[5]

In fact there would have been no practical possibility of introducing legislation on the lines desired by Cloncurry and Anglesey at this time. Where a labour-rate had been tried in England it had not succeeded, and

---

[1] This is the title of Mr Sean O'Faolain's biography of O'Connell (London, 1938).

[2] In March 1830, O'Connell declared that he could not wish Poor Laws to be introduced into Ireland; in May 1830, he stated that 'he had always advocated the principle of the Poor Laws: his only difficulty was, in what way they should be applied' (Hansard, 2nd. ser. vol. xxiv, col. 767). In August 1831, he declared himself opposed to Poor Laws but admitted that 'in the present condition of Ireland, they had no other resource than to adopt some measure of the sort' (Hansard, 3rd ser. vol. vi, col. 158). While in 1837 he said that he would not vote against the Government measure for Irish Poor Laws, in 1838 O'Connell announced his intention of opposing the measure 'because Ireland was too poor for a Poor Law'.

[3] See O'Connell to R. Barrett, 11 July 1831, Correspondence of Daniel O'Connell, ed. Fitzpatrick (London, 1888), vol. i, pp. 268-9.

[4] Lord Cloncurry, Design of a Law, for Promoting the Pacification of Ireland, and the Improvement of the Irish Territory and Population submitted to His Majesty's Government, the Legislature, and the Public (Dublin, 1834), pp. 9-12.

[5] Anglesey to Holland, 20 December 1831; also 20 April 1831, 12 August 1831, 4 July 1831; and see Cloncurry to Anglesey, 3 April 1833 (Anglesey Papers, P.R.O., N.I., T. 1068/7).

the whole weight of opinion against the allowance system extended to the labour-rate also.[1] All this testimony the Irish landlords could employ against any scheme of compulsory employment, and Anglesey admitted that 'it would be difficult to get any money for the purpose, and the scheme would be fiercely opposed'.[2] On the other hand, less ambitious schemes were quite widely supported in Ireland; the urban traders and many landholders were advocates of a system of relief to the infant and helpless poor: proposals for legislation on these lines were several times advanced by William Smith O'Brien and Sir Richard Musgrave,[3] and Sharman Crawford was also among the supporters of an Irish Poor Law.

By opposing these views, which were shared also by a number of English Radicals, O'Connell did not merely set himself apart from many of his usual allies in the House of Commons; he also took the risk of antagonising a majority of the Irish Catholic priesthood, who followed Bishop Doyle in wanting a measure of public relief for their suffering parishioners. Indeed, the occasional wavering in O'Connell's opposition to Poor Laws seems mainly to have been due to a desire to conciliate Doyle and his supporters.[4]

In England, public opinion on the Irish Poor Law question was much more nearly unanimous. Scrope's opinion, that only 'a sect of Political Economists' was opposed to Poor Laws for Ireland[5] was reasonably near the truth, although one of the most able tracts against the proposals was written by Sir John Walsh (later Lord Ormathwaite), a Berkshire land-owner.[6] Popular support for the idea of an Irish Poor Law, against the advice of the economists, was widespread and growing. The basis of this feeling was a compound of increasing knowledge of Irish conditions, producing greater sympathy with the Irish poor, with fear of the possibilities of competition from cheap Irish labour. The natural result of this was to generate resentment against the Irish landlords, who were frequently accused of neglecting their duty towards the poorer tenants on their estates.[7] While in 1817 and 1822 large subscriptions were raised in England

[1] Labour-rates, in the sense of agreements amongst the rate-payers to employ labourers with settlements in the parish in proportion to the acreage occupied by the rate-payer, were quite common in Surrey and Sussex before the Poor Law Amendment Act of 1834, but worked inequitably. See *Report of the Poor Law Commissioners* (1834 (44), vol. xxxviii), pp. 195–226.
[2] Anglesey to Holland, 9 March 1833 (Anglesey Papers).
[3] E.g. in the Commons, 8 February 1831, 19 March 1835, 9 February 1836; *Hansard*, 3rd ser. vol. ii, col. 246; vol. xxvi, col. 1206; vol. xxxi, col. 429.
[4] Thus in the Commons on 10 August 1831, Crampton, the Solicitor-General for Ireland, taunted O'Connell: '... when did the honourable and learned Gentleman become a convert to the opinion that Poor Laws were necessary in Ireland? Only a few weeks ago: on the appearance of a pamphlet, written by a very clever Catholic Bishop' (*Hansard*, 3rd ser. vol. v, col. 1113).   [5] *Poor Law for Ireland*, p. 1.
[6] Sir J. Walsh, *Poor Laws in Ireland, Considered in their Probable Effects upon the Capital, the Prosperity and the Progressive Improvement of that Country* (London, 1830).
[7] See J. Wade, *History of the Working Classes* (London, 1835), p. 386.

for the relief of Irish distress, in later years the argument that 'Irish property must support Irish poverty' was more and more frequently advanced, supported by the contention that the callousness of Irish landlords made clear that this could only be done through a compulsory provision.[1]

Many petitions from English constituencies in favour of such a provision for the Irish poor were laid before Parliament in the eighteen-twenties and eighteen-thirties; while many of these expressed a sympathy with the sufferings of the poor which may have been genuine enough, there can be little doubt that the main motive behind them was fear—fear of cheap corn and cheap labour, imported from Ireland by the new steam packets under no restrictions of any kind. It was generally contended in England that if communication between Ireland and England was to be made as easy as communication between Lancashire and Yorkshire, the result must be either to bring England, and the English labourer, down to the Irish level, or else to raise Ireland and its people to the English level. Fears that natural forces would produce the former result led to advocacy of State intervention to secure the latter, and the introduction of Poor Laws into Ireland seemed the obvious step.[2] The Poor Laws were relied on to reduce migration by giving the Irish a right to subsistence at home, and, by giving the landlords an incentive to increase employment, to raise wages in Ireland.

The extent of Irish migration to England and Irish exports of corn was probably exaggerated by those who thus argued the necessity of measures to reduce them[3] and not all English authorities regarded them as constituting a danger: Senior, for example, was disposed to consider Irish immigration as necessary and beneficial to the English economy.[4] In any event, it was by no means certain that Poor Laws would stop immigration, as opponents were quick to point out. O'Connell argued that if Poor Laws were in force in Ireland, the landlords would be all the more eager to eject their tenants and drive them abroad, while the labourers would be all the more willing to go to England when they could leave their families to be supported from the rates.[5] Senior and other economists used the wage-fund analysis to prove that Poor Laws would not raise wages:[6]

[1] See, for example, *Morning Chronicle*, 13 May 1836.

[2] See, for example, Wilmot Horton, *Causes and Remedies of Pauperism: Third Series* (London, 1830), pp. 28–9; *Hansard*, 2nd ser. vol. XXIII, cols. 183–222 (11 March 1830); H. Burgess, *A Letter to...Canning...with a Postscript on the Tendency of the Wages of Labour in England and Ireland to Become Equal* (London, 1826), p. 135.

[3] In a pamphlet entitled *The Present Poverty of Ireland Convertible into the Means of Her Improvement under a Well-administered Poor Law* (London, 1838), Lord Clements used the available statistics to show that the effect of Irish imports on English grain prices was comparatively slight (pp. 4–11).

[4] Senior, *A Letter to Lord Howick*, p. 47. Senior's argument was that the immigration was largely temporary, taking place at harvest time, and that without its aid cultivation would have to be reduced.

[5] *Hansard*, 3rd ser. vol. XVII, col. 874 (2 May 1833).

[6] *A Letter to Lord Howick*, pp. 47 et seq.

considerations of this sort had already led some thinkers, including James Mill,[1] to advocate a more direct control of movement between the two islands. Since this would have been a contravention of the Act of Union, it was not very widely supported or canvassed. But the fear of Irish immigration remained strong, and the belief that Poor Laws could reduce or prevent it was probably the most important single factor in creating popular English support for their introduction into Ireland.

This popular feeling was aided by the writings and speeches of Radicals like Cobbett, who advocated a Poor Law for the Irish labourer on the ground of the right to subsistence, and held that 'if there is not something done in this way, a dreadful convulsion must take place'.[2] Cobbett's warm-hearted and sometimes hot-headed championship of the poor was as attractive to the general public as the cold Malthusian reasoning which he attacked was repulsive. No one earned sharper condemnation from him than the 'Scotch feelosofers' who accepted Malthus's arguments against poor relief and stressed the virtues of thrift and charity.

By 1830, however, the popular view and the economists' doctrines were no longer altogether opposites. McCulloch, who has some claim to be regarded as the archetype of the 'feelosofers', had recanted his views, and appeared as a supporter of Poor Laws—in general, and for Ireland in particular. Examined before Spring Rice's Committee on the State of the Poor in Ireland, McCulloch declared: 'In the opinion that I stated before the Irish Committee in 1825, I expressed myself as hostile to the introduction of poor laws into Ireland, supposing that it would be impossible so to manage them but that they would be pernicious: but further reflection upon their operation in England, as far as I have been able to ascertain it from studying their history, has convinced me that this opinion was not well founded, and that poor laws may be administered so as to be made productive of good rather than evil.'[3] The reasons which McCulloch gave for this alteration in his ideas were, however, scarcely such as would have appealed to Cobbett or his sympathisers. McCulloch had become convinced that, before the introduction of the allowance system in 1795, the English Poor Laws 'operated to diminish and not to increase the population' because 'the laws made every gentleman, who allowed any poor person to establish himself upon his estate, aware that if he resided there

[1] See his article 'State of the Nation' in *Westminster Rev.* vol. vii (October 1826), p. 264; H. Booth, *Thoughts on the Condition of the Poor in Large Towns* (Liverpool, 1824), pp. 44–7; G. Strickland, *Discourse on the Poor Laws* (London, 1827), expresses the view that legislative control of migration inside the United Kingdom would be impolitic—see pp. 68–9.
[2] *Three Lectures on the Political State of Ireland, Delivered in Fishamble Street Theatre, Dublin, by Wm. Cobbett, Esq., M.P.* (Dublin, 1834), p. 14. See also *Cobbett's Manchester Lectures, in Support of his Fourteen Reform Propositions...to which is subjoined a Letter to Mr O'Connell, on his Speech made in Dublin, on 4th of January, 1832, against the proposition for the Establishing of Poor-Laws in Ireland* (London, 1832).
[3] *Third Report of Evidence from the Select Committee on the State of the Poor in Ireland* (1830 (665), vol. vii), p. 575.

for three years...he would be obliged in the event of such poor person afterwards falling into poverty...to support him in all time to come: that circumstance naturally made him very much disinclined to allow cottages to be built upon his estate, or people to establish themselves on it'.[1] His new advocacy of Poor Laws for Ireland thus rested not on any fresh access of sympathy for the sufferings of the poor there, but on the belief that such laws would compel landlords to stop sub-division and new settlements on waste land, and so check the growth of population.

McCulloch was not the only economist to change his views on Poor Laws at this period; in 1835 J. L. Mallet recorded with some dismay that at a meeting of the Political Economy Club where McCulloch, Tooke, Torrens and Chadwick were present the members 'with a few exceptions were nearly all favourable to the fearful experiment' of introducing Poor Laws into Ireland.[2] J. S. Mill afterwards attributed this development largely to the leading articles written by John Black for the *Morning Chronicle*: '...Black, as I well remember, changed the opinion of some of the leading economists, particularly my father's, respecting Poor Laws, by the articles he wrote in the *Chronicle* in favour of a Poor Law for Ireland. He met their objections by maintaining that a Poor Law did not necessarily encourage over-population, and he convinced them that he was in the right.'[3]

Important as the *Chronicle* leaders were in moulding informed opinion, the passing of the English Poor Law Amendment Act of 1834 was undoubtedly of more significance. In 1830 Sir John Walsh had written: 'Could a system be devised for the relief of the poor, which should so work, as, by its own operation, steadily to diminish the number of claimants upon its funds, there is no doubt that it would confer a solid benefit upon society: but such a system seems impossible.'[4]

With the introduction and initial success of the New Poor Law, it seemed that such a system, or at least one with no tendency to increase the number of claimants, was a practical possibility. In the light of this fact, many of the objections to a Poor Law for Ireland seemed to diminish in force, and compensating possibilities of advantage became evident. Instead of tending to increase the population and attach it more firmly to the soil, a properly designed Poor Law could be made to facilitate the transition from a cottier economy to capitalist farming, by giving the cottier another alternative besides land or starvation. Moreover, the right of the poor to relief could be justified on the ground that the transition to a new state of agriculture was not a foreseeable event, for which the labourer might reasonably be expected to provide himself.

[1] *Third Report of Evidence from the Select Committee on the State of the Poor in Ireland* (1830 (665), vol. VII), p. 579.   [2] *Political Economy Club Centenary Volume*, p. 267.
[3] J. S. Mill to Robert Harrison, 12 December 1864, quoted in Elliott, *Letters of John Stuart Mill* (London, 1910), vol. II, p. 14.   [4] Walsh, *Poor Laws in Ireland*, p. 65.

These arguments were employed in 1836 by George Cornewall Lewis, who was closely connected with official enquiries into the state of the Irish poor.[1] He was supported later by Herman Merivale, who in a series of lectures from the Drummond Chair at Oxford, held that in the existing state of Irish agriculture a Poor Law could be of no value, but that when combined with, and designed to aid, measures for introducing an improved agriculture, it might be an important instrument of economic progress.[2]

IV

These movements of opinion can be seen reflected with remarkable clarity in the course of policy. A Select Committee of the Commons in 1823 produced, as has already been noticed,[3] a report hostile to Poor Laws, though not to public works. The matter did not again receive the attention of Parliament until 1829, when Villiers Stuart moved a resolution which was intended to commit the Commons to 'early consideration' of the condition of the Irish poor, with a view to the introduction of Poor Laws.[4] Peel refused to pledge the Government to any measure, but undertook to give the problem 'his full and deliberate consideration'; on the strength of his pledge Villiers Stuart withdrew his motion.

In the following session, Spring Rice moved for, and obtained, the appointment of a Select Committee to inquire into the state of the poorer classes in Ireland.[5] The speech in which Rice introduced his motion was more unfavourable to the introduction of Poor Laws into Ireland than otherwise, and many people, inside and outside the House, believed that the object of the Committee was really 'to get rid of the poor law question' by producing an unfavourable report.[6] When the Committee did report, it recommended the introduction of no less than nineteen Bills designed to improve the condition of the poor, but a measure for compulsory relief was not amongst them. On this subject the Committee 'contented themselves with recommending that the consideration of this subject may be resumed at a future time, and that in the meanwhile the most severe and scrutinizing attention may be applied to the important evidence already before the House'.[7]

[1] Lewis, *On Local Disturbances in Ireland*, ch. vi. For some further account of Lewis's part in the preparation and administration of the Irish Poor Law, see below, pp. 108, 112.
[2] Merivale, *Legislative Provision for the Poor in Ireland*, especially p. 38. An earlier instance of a similar argument can be found in F. Page, *Observations on the State of the Indigent Poor in Ireland* (London, 1830), pp. 56–7.
[3] Above, p. 91.
[4] *Hansard*, 2nd ser. vol. XXI, col. 1130 (7 May 1829).
[5] *Ibid.* vol. XXIII, col. 183 *et seq.* (11 March 1830).
[6] Bryan, *A Practical View of Ireland*, p. 76. *Hansard*, 2nd ser. vol. XXIV, cols. 1329–30 (3 June 1830).
[7] *Fourth Report from Select Committee on the State of the Poor in Ireland* (1830 (667), vol. VII), p. 55. The measures recommended included Bills for the promotion of public works and emigration: *Report*, pp. 56–7.

This was as much as, perhaps more than, might have been expected from any committee of which Spring Rice was chairman, but it certainly gave no spur to governmental action. In ensuing sessions quite a good deal of parliamentary time was occupied by discussions on petitions in favour of Irish Poor Laws,[1] and in 1831 Smith O'Brien obtained leave to introduce a Bill for the relief of the 'aged, helpless and infirm poor' of Ireland: 'it was met by repeated delays on the part of the government, and at last postponed until the dissolution took place'.[2] Sadler several times tried the patience of the House by introducing resolutions on the subject in general terms, but produced no reaction from the Government, whose representatives continued to stress the need for 'careful consideration' before taking any action.

By 1833 there was growing pressure, inside and outside Parliament, for some official move in the matter of Poor Laws for Ireland. There had been some expectation in Ireland that Catholic emancipation would be followed by remedial measures for the economic condition of the country, and a Poor Law seemed the most immediately useful.[3] From the time of his return to Ireland, in December 1830, to become Lord-Lieutenant for the second time, Anglesey had been constantly reiterating the need for such measures to his Cabinet colleagues in London, and pressing the merits of his scheme for poor relief combined with a labour-rate.[4] In England, the anxiety over Irish immigration was growing, particularly in the northern manufacturing towns, while the appointment of the Poor Law Commission, with the prospect of reform in the English law, brought the issue of extending its provisions to Ireland to the fore. The consistent advocacy of such a step by the *Morning Chronicle* was not without influence on Whig circles: Black himself was friendly with Melbourne.[5]

After the passage of the Reform Act, these various pressures could not be resisted indefinitely. In May 1833, Lord Althorp, then Chancellor of the Exchequer, met an attempt by a Yorkshire member, Richards, to commit the Commons to the principle of Poor Laws for Ireland, by moving, as an amendment to Richards's resolution, that a Royal Commission should be appointed to investigate the problem. The amendment was carried, some members protesting that this was merely another way of shelving the problem.[6]

---

[1] See *Hansard*, 2nd ser. vol. XXIII, col. 389 (March 1830, petition from King's Co.); *Hansard*, 3rd ser. vol. VI, col. 58 (August 1831, petition from Dublin); *Hansard*, 3rd ser. vol. IX, col. 709 (January 1832, petition from Leeds).

[2] Smith O'Brien, speaking in the Commons, 19 March 1835 (*Hansard*, 3rd ser. vol. XXVI, col. 1207).

[3] See the speech of Chas. Brownlow, M.P. for Armagh, on presenting a petition for Poor Laws signed by 24 Irish Catholic bishops: *Hansard*, 3rd ser. vol. V, col. 1106 (10 August 1831).

[4] See Anglesey correspondence 1830–3, as quoted above, p. 100.

[5] C. Mackay, *Forty Years' Recollections* (London, 1877), vol. I, p. 95.

[6] *Hansard*, 3rd ser. vol. XVII, cols. 846–64 (2 May 1833).

The Commission, with Archbishop Whately as its chairman, undertook the most thorough survey of the condition of the Irish poor yet attempted; so thorough, in fact, that the whole of its Report did not become available until 1836.[1] In the meantime those private members, English and Irish, who were specially interested in the problem grew impatient and came forward with measures of their own. In the sessions of 1835 and 1836, Poulett Scrope, William Smith O'Brien and Sir Richard Musgrave all introduced Bills for the relief of the Irish poor, but these were never pressed beyond a second reading; in 1835, because the Government spokesman (Morpeth) asked that the matter be allowed to stand over until the following session, when the Royal Commission's Report could be fully considered; in 1836, because he promised the early introduction of a ministerial measure.[2]

The first report of the Royal Commission became available in July 1835; the final report and recommendations did not appear until 1836. In it, Whately and his colleagues decisively rejected the idea of applying the principles of the New Poor Law of 1834 to Ireland. The workhouse, they argued, might be valuable where the able-bodied could always obtain work—but in Ireland 'we see that the labouring class are eager for work, that work there is not for them, and that they are therefore, and not from any fault of their own, in permanent want'.[3] Because of the numbers of able-bodied persons, and their dependants, thus constantly requiring assistance, the Commissioners reported against the introduction of either indoor or outdoor relief, as being impracticable except for the aged and infirm. To assist the able-bodied they recommended a scheme of assisted emigration 'to relieve the labour market', and the establishment of a Board of Improvement to supervise drainage schemes and other public works designed to promote employment and national economic development.

Considered as a scheme for economic development, the Commissioners' proposals were comprehensive and far-sighted, but they far exceeded the limits of poor relief, as that term was being interpreted in England in 1836. The Government displayed little enthusiasm for the proposals of the Report, Lord John Russell remarking that 'they certainly had found in it a great variety of important matters; at the same time he must add, that the suggestions in it were not of that simple and single nature as to allow them to be adopted without the caution which was recommended by the Commissioners themselves'.[4]

[1] For a fuller account of the Commission and its work see Nicholls, *A History of the Irish Poor Law*, pp. 118–52; R. B. McDowell, *Public Opinion and Government Policy in Ireland, 1801–46* (London, 1952), pp. 190–1.
[2] *Hansard*, 3rd ser. vol. xxix, col. 308 (8 July 1835); vol. xxxiv, col. 211 (8 June 1836).
[3] *Third Report of Commissioners for Inquiring into the Condition of the Poorer Classes in Ireland* (1836 [43], vol. xxx), p. 5.
[4] *Hansard*, 3rd ser. vol. xxxii, col. 1167 (18 April 1836).

Accordingly, Russell proceeded to obtain the advice of Nassau Senior and G. C. Lewis on the contents of the Report. Senior, who had strongly recommended Whately for the Commission,[1] could hardly have been unduly critical, for the proposals in the Report closely resembled his own suggestions in *A Letter to Lord Howick*. 'On the whole', he commented, 'the Report seems to me to have exposed many mischievous errors, and to contain, among much that I have ventured to disapprove, many valuable suggestions.'[2]

The points which Senior 'ventured to disapprove' were considerable, but not essential, ones: Lewis, on the other hand, attacked the whole principle of the Report. The son of J. Frankland Lewis, the original chairman of the English Poor Law Commission under the Act of 1834, George Cornewall Lewis had acted as an assistant commissioner on the Irish inquiry, and prepared an Appendix on the State of the Irish Poor in Great Britain.[3] An enthusiast for the workhouse system, he unhesitatingly recommended its extension to Ireland, contrasting its comprehensive simplicity with the complex proposals of the Commission for relieving different classes of the poor by different means. He dismissed the recommendations of the Commission for national improvement by saying:

A Government can only, as it seems to me, attempt to accelerate the improvement of the soil by *indirect* means. In this, as in most other cases connected with the material part of civilisation, its functions are simply negative; it can do no more than remove obstacles to amelioration, and suffer a society to proceed unchecked in its natural career of advancement....Government, in my opinion, cannot interfere more directly for the improvement of land in Ireland than by a well-guarded Poor Law.[4]

Even before the Final Report of the Royal Commission reached them, the Government of the day had received other testimony in favour of extending the workhouse system to Ireland. This came from George Nicholls, a colleague of Frankland Lewis on the English Poor Law Commission, who, although 'he did not pretend to any personal knowledge of the state of Ireland' presented Russell with a set of suggestions for an Irish Poor Law in January 1836. 'These "Suggestions" were framed in considerable detail, and recommended the application of the amended system of English Poor Law to Ireland.'[5]

[1] See Senior to Spring Rice, 5 May 1833 (Monteagle Papers, National Library of Ireland).
[2] *Letter from N. W. Senior, Esq. to His Majesty's Principal Secretary of State for the Home Department, on the Third Report from the Commissioners for Inquiring into the Condition of the Poor in Ireland, dated 14 April 1836* (1837 [90], vol. LI), p. 11.
[3] Appendix G (1836 [39], vol. XXXIV).
[4] *Remarks of G. C. Lewis, Esq., on Poor Laws, Ireland* (1837 [91], vol. LI), p. 30.
[5] Nicholls, *History of the Irish Poor Law*, p. 130. Even before this Russell had been inclined to favour the extension of the workhouse system to Ireland; Whately afterwards recalled 'receiving a pretty broad hint, once or twice while the inquiry was going on, what Government expected us to report...there was a very great desire among many persons in England, to assimilate the two countries, as far as regarded poor laws'. E. J. Whately, *Life and Correspondence of Richard Whately, D.D.* (London, 1866)), vol. I, p. 199.

In August 1836, at the instigation of Cornewall Lewis, Russell wrote to Nicholls and instructed him to proceed to Ireland and investigate the practicability of the recommendations of the Royal Commission in comparison with a possible workhouse system of relief. 'Your attention', Russell added, 'need not be very specially given to the plans for the general improvement of Ireland, contained in the Report of the Commissioners of Inquiry: but you will generally remark upon those, or any other plans, which may lead to an increased demand for labour.'[1]

After a nine weeks' visit to Ireland, Nicholls submitted his report in November 1836. His tour had done nothing to shake his belief in the applicability of the new English Poor Law to Irish conditions. He echoed Lewis's opinion that a Poor Law would assist the agricultural transition, and demolished the argument that the workhouse could never be made less attractive than the normal condition of the Irish peasant, by pointing out that it was not the diet or lodging which made the workhouse unattractive to the poor, but the confinement and discipline involved. Hence he concluded 'that the workhouse system which has been successfully applied to dispauperise England, may be safely and efficiently applied, as a medium of relief, to diminish the amount of misery in Ireland'.[2]

When the report was considered by the Cabinet, some members were in favour of making an experimental introduction of workhouses before applying the system to the whole of Ireland, and the Marquis of Lansdowne also told Spring Rice that 'a great point will be to launch the emigration system so as to let it work ahead of the workhouse system, and it should if possible be made sweet in proportion as the other must be made bitter to the national taste'.[3] Nevertheless, within a month of submitting his Report, Nicholls was instructed by Russell to prepare a Bill embodying its main recommendations and this Bill Russell introduced into the Commons on 13 February 1837.

According to Nicholls's own account, 'doubts were of course expressed, and objections stated; but on the whole the measure was not received unfavourably'.[4] This may have been true of the proceedings in the House; it was hardly true of the reception of the measure in the country as a whole. In Ireland particularly, the confidence with which Nicholls asserted the applicability of the English system to manifestly different conditions gave rise to considerable resentment. Whately was naturally

---

[1] *Report of Geo. Nicholls, Esq., on Poor Laws, Ireland* (1837 [69], vol. LI), p. 2.
[2] *Ibid.* p. 15.
[3] Lansdowne to Spring Rice, 15 December 1836 (Monteagle Papers, National Library of Ireland). In his report, Nicholls had advocated that the introduction of the workhouse system into Ireland should be accompanied by a measure to assist emigration, and Lansdowne apparently believed that this recommendation would be accepted: see ch. VII, p. 223.
[4] *History of the Irish Poor Law*, p. 194.

incensed at the manner in which the detailed reports and recommendations of his Commission, the outcome of three years' careful work, had been passed over in favour of Nicholls's brief and dogmatic survey.[1] Many commentators confessed themselves surprised and perplexed by the course which the Government had taken, and also by the remarkable discrepancy between the two reports—for while the Royal Commission estimated the numbers likely to require assistance at 2,385,000, Nicholls declared the correct figure to be 80,000.[2]

In fact, the explanation of both these points was comparatively simple and very closely related. Whately and his commissioners had sought to estimate the amount of poverty in Ireland, and to propose measures for reducing or eliminating it: Nicholls had estimated the extent of actual destitution and proposed a plan for relieving it. However desirable the measures asked for by the Royal Commission might be, from an administrator's point of view they were certain to prove difficult to frame, more difficult to enact, and costly to operate. Yet the state of public opinion, in England particularly, made it impossible not to propose some measure for the relief of the Irish poor. Nicholls's proposals were simple and limited and, it might be hoped, would meet the immediate need. So, as Isaac Butt said, 'the truth is, that it has been brought in to meet the desire on the part of the public, that some remedial measure should be applied to the destitution which is known to exist in Ireland. The necessity of meeting this desire determined the Cabinet to prepare *some* Poor-law.'[3]

Those who, like Butt, believed that public measures of economic development were essential to solve the Irish problem, were bound to protest against Nicholls's ideas and favour the plans of the Royal Commission. Those who, like Cornewall Lewis, believed that all must be left to the power of natural economic forces, were bound to favour the clear-cut, economical proposals of Nicholls. And these latter were the men who had the sympathetic ear of Melbourne's ministry.

The prorogation of Parliament on the death of William IV prevented the Bill passing in 1837. Nicholls made use of the delay to visit Ireland again and prepare a second Report, meeting some of the objections which had been raised to the Bill. The only one of these which involved a point

[1] Whately, *Life and Correspondence*, vol. I, pp. 394–405. Whately expressed his feelings about Nicholls's proposals in a letter to Senior dated 13 November 1837, partly printed, *op. cit.* p. 394. He sent a copy of this to Spring Rice, who showed it to the Cabinet: 'This comes of appointing university tutors to great offices' was Melbourne's only comment on reading the Archbishop's chagrined protest (Monteagle Papers, National Library of Ireland).

[2] Third Report from Commissioners (1836 [43], vol. xxx), p. 5. *Report of Geo. Nicholls, Esq.* (1837 [69], vol. LI), p. 37. For contemporary criticism of Nicholls's proposals, see I. Butt, *The Poor-Law Bill for Ireland Examined* (London, 1837); J. P. Kennedy, *Analysis of Projects Proposed for the Relief of the Poor of Ireland* (London, 1837); Sir F. Workman-Macnaghten, *Poor-Laws—Ireland: Observations upon the Report of George Nicholls, Esq.* (London, 1838).

[3] Butt, *The Poor-Law Bill for Ireland Examined*, pp. 4–5.

of principle was that concerned with outdoor relief; some Radical members had suggested that the Bill should be extended to allow of this being granted in certain circumstances. Nicholls's reply was to reassert that a Poor Law must be limited to cases of actual destitution, and not extended to help all the needy.[1]

Slightly modified, the Bill was reintroduced in December 1837, and passed the Commons with little alteration, in spite of the opposition of O'Connell. In the Lords the Irish proprietors set out to oppose the measure strongly, but the Duke of Wellington gave it his support, Nicholls having been at pains 'to settle the differences between his grace and the government'.[2] Thus the essential requirement[3] for the passage of the Bill was secured, and on 31 July 1838, 1 and 2 Vic. c. 56, 'An Act for the more effectual Relief of the Poor in Ireland', became law.

For all their change of heart on the subject of Poor Laws, the classical economists received the Act with little more enthusiasm than did the Irish people. Torrens again applied the whole mechanism of classical theory to predict the consequences of the measure, and concluded:

The case stands simply thus—there is in Ireland a redundant population, which must continue to occasion the most frightful misery, unless maintained in workhouses, or assisted either to migrate to Great Britain, or to emigrate to the colonies; but the workhouses to be erected under the Irish Poor Law, will contain only about one-thirtieth part of the redundant population, and the remainder cannot be permitted to migrate to Great Britain; because, if permitted to do so, they would bring down English wages to the level of Irish starvation: therefore, the poor law for introducing the workhouse system into Ireland, cannot have any perceptible effect in removing, or even in mitigating the destitution of Ireland, unless accompanied by an extensive scheme of emigration.[4]

This is not a surprising conclusion, coming from Torrens. It is more interesting to find that McCulloch, who by no means approved the proposals of the Whately Commission, declared after the Act had been in operation for some years that 'the idea of making workhouses tests of destitution in Ireland is as absurd as can well be imagined'.[5]

The framers of the Act, however, were entirely convinced of its value, and set to work with vigour and enthusiasm to put its provisions into effect. It had been decided to empower the English Poor Law Commissioners to carry the Act into effect, and for this purpose their number was to be increased to four. Despite Chadwick's eager efforts to secure

---

[1] Nicholls, *History of the Irish Poor Law*, p. 203.

[2] *Ibid.* p. 221.

[3] For an explanation of the extent to which the passage of Irish measures through the Lords at this time depended on Wellington's support, see D. Large, 'The House of Lords and Ireland in the age of Peel, 1832–50', *Irish Historical Studies*, vol. IX (September 1955), pp. 367–99.

[4] R. Torrens, *A Letter to Lord John Russell, on the Ministerial Measure for Establishing Poor Laws in Ireland* (London, 1837), pp. 56–7.

[5] J. R. McCulloch, *The Literature of Political Economy* (London, 1845), p. 301.

the position, the place of fourth Commissioner was given to G. C. Lewis.[1] Before this, Drummond, perhaps the most able and certainly the most popular Under-Secretary in Ireland throughout the century, had advised his superiors: 'Before the Bill has passed I take it Nicholls will be anything but popular here, and *pray be cautious* as to sending *him over* to carry it into effect.'[2] In spite of this, Russell instructed Nicholls to go to Ireland and carry the law into effect, aided by four assistant commissioners. Nicholls, who shared some of the personal characteristics of Chadwick, set about the task with great zeal and a complete lack of tact.[3] By 1841, all the Unions, 130 in total, had been formed and guardians elected; by 1845, 118 workhouses in these unions were open for the relief of the poor, and on 1 January of that year about 40,000 persons were receiving relief.[4] Thus the mechanism of the Irish Poor Law had scarcely been completed and put into operation, when the advent of the potato blight subjected it to an unprecedented strain.

V

The strict limitation of relief to the workhouse may possibly be objected to, on the ground that extreme want is found occasionally to assail large portions of the population in Ireland, who are then reduced to a state bordering upon starvation: and ought, therefore, it may be asserted, to be relieved at the public charge, without being subjected to the discipline of the workhouse. This, however, is an extreme case, and it would not, I think, be wise to adapt the regulations of Poor Law administration in Ireland to the possible occurrence of such a contingency....The occurrence of a famine, if general, seems to be a contingency altogether above the powers of a Poor Law to provide for.[5]

So Nicholls had written in his First Report of 1836, and he had not designed the Act of 1838 to meet the possibility even of a partial famine, much less a general calamity of the magnitude produced by the potato disease. Previous experience of such partial famines had, however, established a commonly accepted pattern of relief measures: it was normal practice for the Government to vote special sums for public works, and to encourage private charity by supplementing the sums raised by relief committees. Employment to provide the distressed with the means of supporting themselves was always preferred to direct relief, but when employment could not be given, food might be supplied.[6]

[1] See Chadwick to Lord John Russell, 2 July 1838, and other correspondence on Irish Poor Laws, 1836-8, in Chadwick MSS., University College, London; S. E. Finer, *Life and Times of Sir Edwin Chadwick* (London, 1952), bk. III, ch. II.

[2] Drummond to Morpeth, 6 January 1838 (Russell Papers, P.R.O. 30/22/3).

[3] See a letter from Spring Rice to Nicholls, 9 December 1838, criticising the latter's proposals and complaining of the carelessness and ignorance of local conditions displayed by his assistants (Monteagle Papers, National Library of Ireland).

[4] Nicholls, *History of the Irish Poor Law*, ch. IV *passim*.

[5] *Report of Geo. Nicholls, Esq., on Poor Laws, Ireland* (1837 [69], vol. LI), p. 38.

[6] For a statement of the policy proposed to meet the partial famine of 1822 in Ireland, see Goulburn to Wellesley, 29 March 1822 (B.M. Add. MSS. 37298).

When, in the late autumn of 1845, it became clear that Ireland was faced with the prospect of a more general failure of food supplies than had ever been known before, the consensus of informed opinion was that special measures, along the lines indicated by previous experience, would have to be promptly taken. Sir James Graham wrote to Peel: 'The peasantry without potatoes cannot go to market, and must starve at home: but an effort must be made, both by public and by private charity, to assist them.'[1] Monteagle took the same view, and recalled his own work on the London Tavern Committee during the distress of 1822:

We adopted the principle as far as we could of giving our aid in furtherance of local effort, and through local bodies regularly constituted, responsible, and rendering an account of their expenditure....At present, unfortunately, I anticipate no such effort of a private nature in England. Various causes, some rational, others unreasonable, have diminished, if they have not totally extinguished, the sympathy on which in 1822 we relied. I therefore fear that if an extreme case should render the interposition of others necessary, it must be public assistance alone that can be looked to.[2]

The memorandum which Peel read to his Cabinet on 1 November 1845 reflects these views closely.[3] It included proposals for giving employment through aid to works of local improvement, conceding, however, that 'there may be many cases in which there will be no opportunities for giving employment, and in which subsistence must be provided without any equivalent given in return'. There is no suggestion that relief should be given through the mechanism of the Poor Law. Indeed at this stage neither economists nor legislators seem to have questioned the appropriateness of an *ad hoc* policy of public works. Senior wrote to Monteagle:

No course seems practicable except considering ourselves in a state of war against scarcity, and drawing upon the national resources to wage it. A portion of the Irish population must be considered as an army to be fed and employed—and fortunately the means of employing them are ready. We need not dig holes and fill them again, or look out for public works. The railways are ready. Could not Government contract for finishing certain lines, and be entitled to participate in the profits?[4]

While, for reasons discussed below,[5] the Government did not undertake railway construction, Peel did introduce the system of aid to local public works, which was, on the whole, successful in its primary object, which was to provide the people with the means of buying food. The natural corollary of the policy was to ensure that food was available to be purchased, and the necessity of ensuring the largest and cheapest supply to this end was the main foundation of Peel's arguments for the repeal of the Corn Laws;[6] his own preference was for the necessary imports to be

---

[1] Graham to Peel, 22 October 1845; C. S. Parker, *Sir Robert Peel* (London, 1899), vol. III, p. 226. [2] Monteagle to Peel, 24 October 1845 (B.M. Add. MSS. 40576).
[3] Sir R. Peel, *Memoirs* (London, 1857), vol. II, pp. 141–5.
[4] Senior to Monteagle, 14 November 1845 (Monteagle Papers, National Library of Ireland). [5] See ch. VI, pp. 195–7.
[6] Fuller discussion of this point is beyond the scope of this chapter. But cf. Peel, *Memoirs*, vol. II.

made 'through the ordinary medium of private adventure, stimulated as it would have been by the suspension of the import duty'.[1] As an immediate suspension did not prove possible, Peel, in November 1845, authorised the purchase of £100,000 worth of Indian corn by the Treasury from the United States, since he considered it 'of so much importance to provide, by any means, for an increased supply of food'. The transaction was carried out secretly to avoid any effect on markets, and later in the season this and other supplies of corn were sold at low prices from official depots in Ireland. Hence during the season 1845–6 the Government continued to meet the potato failure through the provision of both food and employment. Although the numbers receiving relief in the workhouse rose to over 51,000 in June 1846[2] the mechanism of the Poor Law was not unduly strained, and in the summer of 1846 official opinion was that the crisis had been effectively met—a view which the majority of people in Ireland appear to have shared.[3]

The harvest of 1846 showed the effect of the potato blight to be more extensive than in the previous year: the failure of the crop was almost complete. Lord John Russell's newly formed ministry was thus confronted with the task of organising measures of relief on an even larger scale. The main reliance was again placed on public works, but the method of organising these was altered in important respects. The expense of the works authorised under Peel's administration[4] was met from advances of public money, half of which was a grant, the other half a loan to be repaid by the barony; these terms were favourable enough to have caused applications for public works beyond what was necessitated by the actual distress. To prevent a recurrence of this, the Whig Government decided to make the whole cost of public works a local charge, to be met by a rate assessed in the same fashion as the poor-rate. This was therefore a labour-rate in the proper sense of that term, and the Act under which it was levied[5] was commonly referred to as 'the Labour Rate Act'. By its provisions, able-bodied but destitute persons were to be employed on 'works of a public character, which were not likely to be undertaken except for the purpose of giving relief';[6] they were to be paid in proportion to the work they did, at a rate somewhat below the current average rate of wages.

This method of conducting relief works was much resented by Irish

[1] Peel, Memoirs, vol. II, p. 173.
[2] J. O'Rourke, History of the Great Irish Famine (Dublin, 1875), p. 121.
[3] See Correspondence Explanatory of the Measures Adopted by Her Majesty's Government for the Relief of the Distress Arising from the Failure of the Potato Crop in Ireland (1846 [735], vol. XXXVII); Statements of Daniel O'Connell in the House of Commons, 25 May 1846, Hansard, 3rd. ser. vol. LXXXVI, col. 1203; [Butt], 'The Famine in the Land', Dublin University Magazine, vol. XXIX, p. 507.
[4] By 9 and 10 Vic. c. 1.   [5] 9 and 10 Vic. c. 107.
[6] [C. E. Trevelyan], 'The Irish Crisis', Edinburgh Rev. vol. LXXXVII, p. 259 (January 1848).

landed proprietors, who argued that if they were to be taxed to employ the people, the people should at least be employed productively. The official view was that the landlords should themselves extend employment and keep the people off the relief works: 'the landlords must feel that their only way of escape from the relief works is by employing the people themselves in more profitable ways', wrote the Chancellor of the Exchequer to the Lord-Lieutenant of Ireland, 'Why cannot Irish gentlemen do as English gentlemen do, and borrow their money from private lenders? It seems to me to be the misfortune of Ireland that every man looks to the government for everything.'[1]

The landlords' case found a more sympathetic hearing at Dublin Castle, not unnaturally, for Bessborough, the Lord-Lieutenant, was himself a major Irish proprietor. In mid-September 1846, he sent forward to London a proposal to employ the labour which was being paid out of public funds on profitable schemes on private estates, instead of 'very useless and unprofitable work' such as the making of unnecessary roads. Since the landowners were eventually to repay the sums so advanced, Bessborough regarded the plan as 'in fact a labour rate on property', but Russell's view was that 'it proposes to confound two things essentially distinct—the one, public works on roads and all analogous works to be paid for by a public vote—the other, loans to proprietors for improvements'.[2]

Nevertheless, in a memorandum for the Cabinet Russell admitted that there might be some case for the scheme in the special circumstances of Ireland; normally landlords might be expected to try to lower the poor-rates by getting people off relief and employing them themselves, but Irish landlords were discontented and apathetic about improvements, and it might be well to give a stimulus to improve agriculture through relief works.[3] After the Cabinet meeting on 25 September, the Irish executive was asked to supply more details of the proposals and Redington, the Irish Under-Secretary, travelled to London to explain the plan. 'Trevelyan gave him a great deal of sound political economy, which Redington declares to be wholly inapplicable to Ireland', wrote Sir George Grey after a meeting at the Home Office.[4] Trevelyan's rigid attitude as Assistant Secretary to the Treasury dismayed not only Redington, but also the Lord-Lieutenant and some leading Whig supporters in Ireland, notably Lord Monteagle, himself a former Chancellor of the Exchequer and a member of the Political Economy Club. It was well known that Trevelyan's views carried great weight with Charles Wood, and that he had the main responsibility for decisions on Irish relief measures. Hence Bessborough felt obliged to remind Russell that 'it is quite useless, as Mr Trevelyan

---

[1] Charles Wood to Bessborough, 9 September 1846 (Russell Papers, P.R.O. 30/22/5).
[2] Bessborough to Russell, 20 September; and Russell to Wood, 21 September 1846 (loc. cit.).   [3] Memorandum by Russell, 24 September 1846 (loc. cit.).
[4] George Grey to Russell, 28 September 1846 (loc. cit.).

appears to do, to compare Ireland with Scotland—there is no capital here among the lower classes, and I fear not a great deal among the higher'.[1]

Monteagle told Bessborough: 'I am both an Economist and Treasury man, but after what I have seen and know, the government must be prepared to face much responsibility if they wish to keep society together.'[2] He wrote in the strongest terms to Russell, Wood and Trevelyan: '"Why not help yourselves as in England and Scotland" it is asked, you might as well ask a child why he does not perform the functions of a man... remember as Wilberforce said, that England owes us a debt for the wrongs of centuries. Endeavour to repay it, not by pauperizing us, but by raising us above our present condition.'[3]

Monteagle's indignation against the Treasury attitude was quite understandable, but at the time when he was giving vent to it, the Cabinet had already decided to override Wood's objections to the plan submitted by Redington and give it a trial in a modified form. Wood foresaw the worst possible consequences from this step; he told Labouchere that 'poor Trevelyan is terribly discomfited by the departure from sound principle' and replied to Monteagle: 'Russian despotism never undertook such duties as you are imposing on the government of this country. Where the agency is to be found for executing it all I can hardly conceive.'[4] On the other hand Lansdowne, who was amongst the majority in the Cabinet who favoured the experiment, told Russell afterwards that the Chancellor was 'disposed to be too severe, even upon Irish landlords... on the whole, they seem to me to be behaving well—to wish that such large sums as those proposed to be levied on them should not be thrown away on useless works is not unreasonable'.[5]

The practical outcome of this clash of opinions was that the Lord-Lieutenant obtained the sanction of the Cabinet to authorise the making of presentments for certain improvements to private estates, provided the owners allowed their estates to be charged with repayment of the advances made.[6] The effect was slight, only about £180,000 being expended in this way. The officials in Whitehall continued to be exasperated by the supine attitude of the proprietors: the proprietors' reply was that if they borrowed money and charged it on the land, they simply increased their incumbrances, without reducing their liability to the labour-rate.[7] Trevelyan alleged that 'Landlords competed with each other in getting

[1] Bessborough to Russell, 30 September 1846 (Russell Papers, P.R.O. 30/22/5).
[2] Monteagle to Bessborough, 1 October 1846 (Monteagle Papers).
[3] Monteagle to Trevelyan, 1 October 1846 (Monteagle Papers).
[4] Wood to Labouchere, 2 October 1846 (Russell Papers, loc. cit.); Wood to Monteagle, 10 October 1846 (Monteagle Papers).
[5] Lansdowne to Russell, 18 October 1846 (Russell Papers, loc. cit.).
[6] This was the measure usually referred to as 'the Labouchere Letter' since the authorisation was published in a letter from Labouchere, the Chief Secretary, to the Board of Works on 5 October 1846.
[7] Wood to Russell, 1 September 1847 (Russell Papers, P.R.O. 30/22/6); for the landlords' view, see J. Ball, *What is to be Done for Ireland?* (London, 1849), *passim.*

the names of their tenants placed on the lists; farmers dismissed their labourers and sent them to the works', while the landlords countered with the accusation that, through jobbery, wages on the public works were often fixed above, rather than below, the average for the district, so that no private employer could compete with them.[1] Whatever the cause, the indisputable fact was that the numbers dependent on the public works for their livelihood increased steadily through the winter of 1846–7, reaching a peak in March 1847, when 734,000 people were directly employed by the Board of Works.

As in 1845–6, the necessary counterpart of the public works was the provision of an adequate food supply, but here Russell's Government made important departures from Peel's policy. Believing that Treasury purchases in the previous season had 'paralysed the provision trade' so that 'the general expectation of the Government again interfering would inevitably have created a necessity for that interference, on a scale which it would have been quite beyond the power of the Government to support' the Cabinet let it be known that no Government orders for food would be placed abroad, that food depots would only be established in those parts of Ireland where no provision trade existed, and even these would not be opened while supplies could be obtained from private dealers at 'reasonable prices'.[2]

The official view was strictly deduced from free trade doctrine—'there is a general scarcity throughout all Western Europe, and we are almost wholly dependent upon Commerce for the means of relieving it. We must abstain from any attempt to tamper with prices. We must pay the true value for each article of food and encourage its importation upon that principle. Any other line of conduct would expose us to the most fatal results.'[3] Under the influence of this policy food prices rose as the winter wore on,[4] until it became impossible for the poor to purchase an adequate

---

[1] [Trevelyan], 'The Irish Crisis', *Edinburgh Rev.* vol. LXXXVII, p. 256. Senior, 'Journal of a Visit to Ireland in 1852', *Journals*, vol. I, p. 290.   [2] Trevelyan, *loc. cit.* pp. 252–3.

[3] Sir Randolph Routh to Monteagle, 22 October 1846 (Monteagle Papers).

[4] The absence of an organised trade in the western districts makes it difficult to establish the prices charged to the people in those areas, but quotations from the markets in east coast ports show the trend. The following are the quotations from Belfast:

	Indian corn (per ton)	Indian meal (per ton)	Wheat (per cwt.)	Potatoes (per cwt.)
26 June 1846	£9	£9 to £9. 10s.	9s. 6d. to 10s. 3d.	3s. to 4s.
28 September 1846	£12. 10s.	£14	11s. 3d. to 12s. 3d.	No fixed price
28 December 1846	£17. 15s.	£18. 10s.	15s. to 15s. 9d.	8s. to 9s. 6d.
28 January 1847	£18. 15s.	£19. 10s.	17s. to 18s.	9s. to 9s. 6d.
26 February 1847	£18	£19	17s. 3d. to 18s. 3d.	9s. to 9s. 6d.
29 March 1847	£12. 5s.	£13. 10s.	17s. to 18s.	9s. to 9s. 6d.
29 April 1847	£14	£14. 10s.	17s. 3d. to 18s.	—
27 May 1847	£15	£16	18s. 6d. to 19s. 6d.	8s. 6d. to 9s.
28 June 1847	£11. 15s.	£12. 15s.	16s. 6d. to 17s.	8s. to 10s. 4d.
30 September 1847	£9	£10	12s. to 13s.	3s. 6d. to 4s.

In March 1847, it was reported that 'large arrivals of Indian Corn caused quite a panic in the trade here' (*Belfast News-Letter*, 30 March 1847).

diet even from the wages paid on public works. Not unnaturally an out-cry against the policy arose in Ireland, but the Government and their supporters remained convinced of the value of the principle they had espoused: 'Ignorant people cannot see the absurdity of their notions, or the mischief naturally, and of course done by an attempt of government to feed the people', Clanricarde, who held the office of Postmaster-General in Russell's Government, assured his Prime Minister.[1]

However, not all those who questioned the soundness of the policy could be dismissed as ignorant. In an article in the *North British Review* for May 1847, it was pointed out that 'the argument in favour of Free Trade, and against the interference of government, requires, not only that there shall be an unshackled competition, *but that there shall be enough of it*'[2]—a condition certainly not fulfilled in many parts of Ireland. But by far the most telling attack on the policy of leaving emergency food supply to private enterprise was made by Isaac Butt, who pointed out that the necessary diversion of resources would only be made when it was clear to merchants that a large and persistent increase of demand had occurred, and that even then the process must take considerable time. To expect private dealers to send large cargoes rapidly to Ireland 'was to expect men suddenly to embark in the trade of supplying Ireland with food, not by any of the ordinary processes by which merchants are led into the affording of additional supplies, by orders coming in the usual way of trade, but upon some vague and uncertain speculation that a country of which they knew nothing would have a demand for corn, and the still more uncertain speculation that the pauper inhabitants of that country would have the means of paying for that demand'. In the event, the supplies had proved inadequate, and 'the application of the best established principles of political economy would have enabled any man of ordinary sagacity to have foreseen this result. All the ordinary demands of civilised life are doubtless best met by those spontaneous processes in which the self-interest of man directs his activity and energy in the channels best adapted to supply these demands; but sudden and extraordinary emergencies must be met by other means.'[3]

That the policy had been a mistaken one, and that some traders had taken advantage of it to profiteer by holding up supplies was recognised within the Irish executive at least. 'I fear from what Sir Randolph [Routh] tells me that there has been a mistake in providing food by too strict an adherence to the principle of not allowing the government to interfere', the Lord-Lieutenant reported to Russell, 'there is no doubt that the merchants in the great towns have taken advantage

---

[1] Clanricarde to Russell, 17 December 1846 (Russell Papers, P.R.O. 30/22/5).
[2] 'Political Economy of a Famine', *North British Rev.* vol. VII, p. 253. Evidence in the Monteagle Papers identifies this article as the work of one Dr Auster.
[3] [Butt], 'The Famine in the Land'.

of it, and in some places are keeping up the prices by the most unfair means.'[1]

The policy of relief works to enable the people to buy imported food thus proved inadequate to meet the crisis of 1846–7 and starvation and disease produced widespread mortality. Even though food prices began to fall in the spring of 1847, it was clear that the policy could not be continued, and a critical dilemma arose—'If the people were retained on the works, their lands must remain uncultivated. If they were put off the works, they must starve.'[2] To meet this problem, it was decided to revert, temporarily at least, to a system of providing relief directly, in the form of rations of cooked food, the cost of providing the food being met out of the poor-rates. Although the system represented a movement towards Poor Law principles, neither a labour test nor a workhouse test was imposed on applicants for relief; since the cooked food would not keep, it could not be sold or hoarded and it was thought that the requirement of personal attendance to collect the ration was a sufficient safeguard against fraud.

This mode of relief proved comparatively successful, but it was intended to be purely temporary, ending with the harvest of 1847. From 1 October 1847, it was intended that all distress in Ireland should be relieved through the mechanism of the Poor Law, newly extended for the purpose.

The decision to abandon special measures of relief, and revert to the use of the Poor Law at this stage, can only be understood in the light of the public controversy on methods of meeting the crisis in Ireland which went on throughout 1846 and the early part of 1847—a controversy in which many of the arguments used before the passing of the 1838 Act were again brought out.

During 1846 the English public began to grow restive about the cost of the relief works in Ireland. Stories of extensive abuse of the system appeared in the newspapers, and gave rise to suspicions that much public money was being wasted, and that the sums advanced by the Exchequer would never be recovered. There was a widespread impression that everyone in Ireland, from the lowest to the highest, expected to be assisted indefinitely from the British Treasury. From all this arose a very real sense of exasperation, and a determination not to be imposed upon further. The prospect of additional taxation for the relief of Ireland was evident, but highly unpopular, and the old argument that 'Irish property must support Irish poverty' was heard again in many quarters, both in and out of Parliament.[3]

[1] Bessborough to Russell, 19 January 1847 (Russell Papers, P.R.O. 30/22/6). This is in sharp contrast with the optimistic account given by Trevelyan in 'The Irish Crisis', *loc. cit.* pp. 261–5.
[2] Trevelyan, 'The Irish Crisis', *loc. cit.* p. 257.
[3] See *Greville Memoirs* (2nd pt.), vol. II, pp. 426, 434; *Hansard*, 3rd ser. vol. LXXXVII, cols. 781, 791 (17 August 1846); vol. LXXXIX, cols. 810–15 (4 February 1847).

In its crudest form, not infrequently heard, this argument would have suggested that the whole problem was vastly exaggerated—rich and poor alike were guilty of imposture, and must be taught a lesson by being thrown back on their own resources—the poor to seek employment or go to the workhouse, the rich to give employment or pay the rates. But the whole weight of evidence was against the view that the Irish crisis could be reduced to these terms: the whole principle of the New Poor Law rested on the assumption of a normally functioning economy in which both employment and food might be obtained, and no one could seriously maintain that the Irish economy was working normally in 1846.

On the other hand, it was quite possible and reasonable to maintain that the existing organisation of relief works was such as to prevent any return to normal, and that while Ireland could not be simply left unaided, it would be better to design measures which would tend towards the establishment of a sound economy there, and help the people to become self-dependent. A wide variety of proposals for achieving these ends appeared during 1846 and 1847, but a definite common pattern can be discerned in them. On the one hand they proposed the introduction of a permanent mechanism capable of meeting recurrent distress to the fullest extent; on the other they proposed schemes to limit and reduce that distress by positive economic development. A permanent mechanism for meeting distress already existed in the Poor Law, but this had not been primarily used to meet the distress of the famine years because of its deliberately limited scope; the common suggestion therefore was that the Poor Law should be extended so as to become the only channel of relief. 'Extension of the Irish Poor Law' was a slogan widely employed in 1846–7, but not always with the same connotation.

The widest interpretation of it was given by Poulett Scrope, who had long regarded a 'properly administered Poor-Law' as a fundamental agency for Irish improvement.[1] The 1838 Act did not come within Scrope's definition of a properly administered Poor Law; he considered it 'a law, the main purpose of which was to *pretend* to be a Poor Law'.[2] In a series of pamphlets, published between 1846 and 1850, Scrope urged that the Poor Law should be extended to give a right to relief to all destitute persons; such relief should not necessarily be provided in the workhouse— outdoor relief might be given to the aged and infirm unconditionally, and to the able-bodied in return for labour of a productive nature. While he believed that the effect of such a law would be to stimulate private employment by landowners, Scrope always insisted that it should be accompanied by other measures to improve the economic condition of Ireland. First among these was his project for the reclamation and reallocation of waste lands, but he advocated legislation to provide

[1] See above, p. 96.
[2] G. P. Scrope, *How is Ireland to be Governed?* (London, 1846), p. 46.

security for small tenants and facilitate the sale of incumbered estates.[1] To Scrope these proposals appeared as strictly complementary; while the extended Poor Law could not succeed without legislation for the permanent improvement of the country, all such legislation must equally fail without an extension of the Poor Law.

Scrope, as he readily admitted, was here merely reiterating the views which he had put forward in the eighteen-thirties. It still seemed to him that a Poor Law could and should be not only an agency for the relief of immediate distress but also an instrument of economic regeneration. Hence, as in 1833, while his proposals were for a combination of Poor Laws with schemes of public works, it would not always be easy to say where the one plan ended and the other began.

In view of the accumulating experience of relief works in 1846 and 1847, it is not surprising that Scrope's proposals met with more criticism than support. The most powerful attack on them came from Senior, who argued that if such schemes were put into effect they would almost immediately necessitate the levying of rates, which would amount to a virtual confiscation of property and put an end to all attempts at employment on private schemes of improvement. Senior supported these contentions, not only with much evidence drawn from the working of the unreformed Poor Law in England, but also with examples of the ill-effects of relief works in Ireland during 1846.[2] To such points, Scrope's answer was that the relief works of 1846 were unproductive and only partially financed from current rates, whereas his plan was to have productive work wholly financed from local sources.[3] It was not perhaps a very convincing answer, since the works which Scrope envisaged could only have been productive in the long period, while their immediate finance from local rates would have imposed a very great burden on the already embarrassed landowners.

A much more original case for 'setting the poor on work', and one of some interest from the standpoint of the history of ideas, was made by Jasper Rogers, always an acute observer of the peculiarities of the Irish economy.[4] Rogers argued that the potato blight had destroyed not merely the food supply, but also the circulating capital of Ireland, because of the potato-truck system. Hence the farmers could not produce food, because they had no means to employ labour, and neither they nor their landlords had sufficient credit to enable them to borrow. While this situation per-

---

[1] See Scrope, *How is Ireland to be Governed?* and *Letters to...Lord John Russell, on the Expediency of enlarging the Irish Poor Law to the full Extent of the Poor Law of England* (London, 1846); *Letters to...Russell...on the Further Measures required for the Social Amelioration of Ireland* (London, 1847); as well as the other works quoted in the Bibliography.

[2] Senior, *Journals Relating to Ireland*, vol. I, pp. 143–207.

[3] G. P. Scrope, *The Irish Relief Measures, Past and Future* (London, 1848), pp. 19–23.

[4] See the references to his work on the potato-truck system above, p. 7.

sisted, England must go on importing food, suffering a loss of gold and financial stringency as a result. Rogers therefore suggested that the able-bodied poor should be sent by the Poor Law Commissioners to work for the farmers, without charge at the moment; at a later date the farmers would be required to repay the cost plus interest at whatever rate the State had paid for the money borrowed to support the labourers.[1]

Rogers appears to have been the only author who at this period contemplated the finance of relief works from borrowed funds rather than current rates.[2] His proposals seem to have attracted little attention, and indeed they were scarcely likely to commend themselves to current opinion, which was already disturbed by the pressure of borrowing for railway finance on the London capital market.

All schemes which envisaged the combination of relief to the able-bodied with some form of labour test invariably aroused opposition on the ground that they were simply a return to the evils of the unreformed English Poor Law. Scrope was able to produce direct evidence that the labour test was used and approved by the Commissioners under the Act of 1834,[3] but Senior judiciously ignored this point and devoted a good many pages to quoting examples of the idleness and demoralisation which had followed from the old system of parish labour. The argument that there could be no means of enforcing industry amongst those employed at the public expense, and no security that independent labourers would not transform themselves into paupers, was employed by many writers besides Senior at this time, amongst them J. R. Godley and W. Neilson Hancock.

Senior, however, stood apart from all others in that he was not prepared to countenance any extension of the existing Poor Law beyond some measure of public assistance to voluntary charitable associations. Hancock and Godley agreed in wishing to see outdoor relief given to the aged and infirm, and workhouse relief to the able-bodied, Godley advocating that a right to relief should be given to all, as under the English law.[4]

Considering the extent of distress in Ireland at this time, the grant of a general right to relief necessarily involved contemplating either a major

---

[1] Rogers, *Employment of the Irish Peasantry the best means to prevent the Drain of Gold from England* (London, 1847).

[2] Relief schemes similar to Scrope's were proposed by William Pulteney Alison, a Scots physician with a long-standing interest in Poor Law questions (*Observations on the Famine of 1846–7...as Illustrating the Connection of the Principle of Population with the Management of the Poor* (Edinburgh, 1847)) and by A. Shafto Adair, an Ulster landlord (*The Winter of 1846–7 in Antrim, with Remarks on Out-Door Relief and Colonisation* (London, 1847)).

[3] Scrope, *Letters to Russell on Enlarging the Irish Poor Law*, p. 45.

[4] J. R. Godley, *Observations on an Irish Poor Law* (Dublin, 1847). W. N. Hancock, *Three Lectures on the Questions, Should the Principles of Political Economy be Disregarded at the Present Crisis? and if Not, How Can They be Applied Towards the Discovery of Measures o, Relief?* (Dublin, 1847).

expansion of workhouse accommodation, or a large amount of outdoor relief, with corresponding increases in the poor-rates. Anyone who advocated such a policy had therefore either to believe firmly that the landlords could, and would, give considerable employment when confronted with the duty of relieving all the poor, or else to propose other means of creating employment opportunities.

Only Hancock possessed a sufficient faith in *laissez-faire* to be able to accept the former point of view, and even he in after-years admitted that 'during the recent famine...the absurdity of attempting in such times to diminish pauperism by putting the pressure on the poor became manifest' because 'the assumption that in ordinary times all who are able and willing can find means of support by their labour' was no longer applicable.[1] Godley relied on his schemes for assisted emigration to relieve the position and keep the poor rates within bounds.[2] Since Senior opposed any extension of the Poor Law, he apparently considered himself exempt from the necessity of proposing any accompanying measures of positive economic improvement. Indeed, Senior's 1846 article has an extraordinarily negative and detached air about it; his opposition to all schemes of public employment contrasts strangely with the attitude he had taken in his *Letter to Lord Howick* and in his private correspondence with Monteagle as late as November 1845.[3] It is impossible to say whether this was due to a change of opinion on Senior's own part, a suggestion from official quarters as to the standpoint the *Edinburgh Review* should take, or simply to Senior making a sharper distinction between poor relief and public works than did Scrope and others.

Whatever the reason, in stating that any extension of the Irish Poor Law to allow outdoor relief, with or without a labour test, must prove ruinous, Senior was voicing an opinion shared not merely by the majority of Irish proprietors, but by experienced Poor Law administrators also. The relief of the destitute poor in Ireland was the subject of an investigation by a Select Committee of the House of Lords, which sat between February and June 1846,[4] and heard evidence from a number of well-known authorities on the Poor Laws, such as G. C. Lewis, Nicholls and Twisleton;[5] all were questioned about outdoor relief, and all agreed that its introduction into Ireland would have disastrous effects; in their Report, the Committee also expressed 'their decided opinion, that the introduction

[1] W. N. Hancock, 'The Workhouse as a Mode of Relief for Widows and Orphans', *Journal of the Dublin Statistical Society*, vol. I, p. 84 (April 1855).
[2] See J. R. Godley, *An Answer to the Question, What is to be Done With the Unemployed Labourers of the United Kingdom?* (London, 1847), *passim*. And below, ch. VII, pp. 229–31.
[3] See quotation above, p. 113.
[4] *Report of the Select Committee of the House of Lords on the Laws relating to Relief of the Destitute Poor in Ireland* (1846 (694, 694—II), vol. XI).
[5] E. T. B. Twisleton became an Assistant Poor Law Commissioner in England in 1839, was appointed a Commissioner to inquire into the Scotch Poor Laws in 1843, and was Chief Poor Law Commissioner in Ireland from 1845 to 1849.

of any system of outdoor relief would be dangerous to the general interests of the community, and more particularly to the interests of the very class for whose wellbeing such relief was intended'.[1]

In June 1846, some fifteen major Irish landlords petitioned the Government against any introduction of outdoor relief;[2] it seems doubtful if Peel then had any such measure in contemplation, but Lord John Russell and his ministers certainly had the extension of the Irish Poor Law under active consideration before the end of the year.[3] In view of the growing resentment in England against the Irish landlords, and the political inexpediency of continuing heavy Treasury advances for assistance to Ireland, Russell and his Cabinet appear to have resolved that the system of emergency relief works would not be continued beyond the season 1846–7, even before that system was evidently breaking down. While they may have hoped that an improved harvest in 1847 would ease the problem, the Whig ministers did not imagine that they could simply transfer the burden of relief on to Irish shoulders without any accompanying assistance to reduce it; they accepted the view that they must seek to lay the foundations of an improved economy in Ireland.[4] As to the means for doing this, Russell and his colleagues debated the alternatives of aiding emigration or seeking to provide employment in Ireland at some length. For a time, Russell vacillated between the two.

'I am inclined to think the Scotch Poor Law, with the aid of the work-house, and plenty of public works, and great facilities for borrowing by landlords the best system', wrote Russell to Bessborough at the beginning of December 1846. Presumably by the 'Scotch Poor Law' Russell meant a limited system of outdoor relief, financed from voluntary contributions where possible, but he did not make himself clear to Bessborough, who replied—'I hardly know what you mean by the Scotch Poor Law, but I do not think that workhouses will give much facility at present in providing for future years of destitution.'[5]

This warning made no difference to the trend of policy; Russell had made up his mind that an extension of the Poor Law in Ireland was the only way of avoiding unpopular additions to Imperial taxation, but some two weeks later he was able to tell Bessborough that the Cabinet had agreed that such an extension should be combined with Bills to aid

[1] P. xxiv.

[2] Peel Papers (B.M. Add. MSS. 40593, fos. 28–32).

[3] Parker, *Sir Robert Peel*, vol. III, p. 502. Russell to Bessborough, 1 December 1846 (Russell Papers, P.R.O. 30/22/5).

[4] 'I am sure that we must look forward in Irish matters, and pay regard not only to the temporary, but the ultimate tendency of our measures'—Wood to Russell, 28 September 1846 (Russell Papers, *loc. cit.*). For opposing Whig and Tory views of Wood's competence to evolve these measures, see *Greville Memoirs* (2nd part), vol. II, p. 434; and Parker, *Sir Robert Peel*, vol. III, p. 469.

[5] Russell to Bessborough, 1 December 1846; Bessborough to Russell, 4 December 1846 (Russell Papers).

drainage, purchase and reclaim waste lands, and give some help to emigration.[1]

From Russell's correspondence with the Lord-Lieutenant during December 1846, it would seem that a substantial degree of help to emigration was in contemplation, but the difficulties of evolving a practicable scheme proved great,[2] and when Russell came before the Commons with his proposals for Irish legislation on 25 January 1847, he announced that the Government did not 'mean to propose any scheme of a great or extended nature' to aid emigration. On the other hand, he declared that 'if a good agricultural system was introduced into Ireland; if there was good security for the investment of money in land; if the proprietors themselves would undertake the task of improving the country, and if other classes would co-operate with them—I say I do not think the present population of Ireland is excessive'.[3] Hence the main emphasis was placed on the measures to improve agriculture by assisting drainage, waste-land reclamation and the sale of incumbered estates.

The Bill for extending the Poor Laws conceded a right to relief only to the aged and infirm, and those permanently disabled; these might be relieved either in or out of the workhouse, but generally the workhouse was to be maintained as a test of destitution for the able-bodied. Where, however, the workhouses 'could not afford accommodation to all who crowded to their doors' even the able-bodied might be granted out-relief, though in the form of food only.

When the Bill containing these proposals was brought forward in March 1847, it found support amongst English members, but Irish members were divided on the issue involved. The landlord representatives opposed the Bill, resting their case on the demoralising effects of indiscriminate outdoor relief and the inevitable confiscation of property which must follow in the attempt to levy poor-rates sufficient to meet the cost. Most of the 'popular' Irish members, Repealers and others, did not follow this lead, being reluctant to oppose any measure for the relief of distress, especially when proposed by their traditional political allies, the Whigs.[4]

Hence there was no concerted opposition to the Bill, which passed into law on 8 June 1847,[5] with only one substantial amendment. This was the subsequently infamous 'quarter-acre clause', proposed by William Gregory, the Tory member for Dublin, and accepted by the Government

---

[1] Russell to Lansdowne, 2 December 1846; Russell to Bessborough, 16 December 1846: G. P. Gooch, *Later Correspondence of Lord John Russell* (London, 1925), vol. I, pp. 162–4.

[2] For a fuller account of the framing of emigration policy at this time see O. MacDonagh, 'Irish Emigration to the United States of America and the British Colonies during the Famine'; *The Great Famine*, ed. R. D. Edwards and T. D. Williams (Dublin, 1956), especially pp. 340–6; and see below, ch. VII.

[3] *Hansard*, 3rd ser. vol. LXXXIX, col. 449.

[4] See K. B. Nowlan, 'The Political Background', *The Great Famine*, pp. 160–3.

[5] It became 10 and 11 Vic. c. 31, usually known as 'The Poor Law Extension Act'.

as a concession to the Irish landlords. Its effect was to prevent any person holding more than a quarter-acre of land from receiving relief until he had parted with possession of the land.

Although the extension of the Poor Law was thus carried into effect easily enough, few of the complementary projects for agricultural improvement reached the Statute Book. The waste-lands measure and that for facilitating the sale of incumbered estates were both given up;[1] the Land Improvement Act passed, but this in itself could be of little immediate value—even had the financial difficulties of many landowners not prevented them from taking advantage of its provisions, the benefits were bound to be of a long-term character.

Thus the situation which Senior had viewed with such foreboding became a fact; from the autumn of 1847 the whole burden of Irish distress was placed on the ratepayers through the mechanism of the extended Poor Law. The harvest of 1847 was good, and the potato blight did not return, but the acreage planted in Ireland had been so much reduced that the food supply was still far below normal. Nevertheless, Wood and Trevelyan were optimistic about the prospects for success of the new system, although Clarendon, Bessborough's successor as Lord-Lieutenant, sent some harsh warnings of the difficulties which were to be expected in the poorer areas of the south-west.[2]

Most of the workhouses were already filled almost to capacity in the summer of 1847, but places for applicants under the new law were made by removing the aged and disabled to their homes for out-relief, and by renting temporary accommodation. At first reluctance to enter the workhouse was general, but as the winter wore on more and more families were left destitute, and by February 1848, the workhouses were crowded to capacity, with over 135,000 inmates.[3] Conditions in the workhouses were appalling; many of the entrants were already in poor health, and in the overcrowded wards disease spread rapidly, while in some unions the funds did not permit even of the prescribed minimum diet being provided.[4]

[1] See above, ch. II, pp. 36–7.
[2] Wood to Russell, 1 September 1847: 'Clanricarde...speaks much more cheerfully and thinks the workhouse test will much reduce the number of applicants for relief.'
Trevelyan to Russell, 30 October 1847: 'Our prospects in Ireland are in my opinion brightening....'
Clarendon to Russell, 30 October 1847: 'I quite understand the disinclination of the Treasury, the Cabinet, and the House of Commons to give further relief to Ireland—heaven knows I see all the difficulty of it in the present state of public opinion and of the Exchequer, but what is the alternative? Can you announce to the House of Commons that in certain districts where the people habitually live upon potatoes and have never known anything else, and where they were unable to sow any last year for want of seed, and where there are no rates because those who should pay them are *bona fide* applicants for relief, deaths by starvation are daily taking place, but that the Government has no measure of relief to propose?' (Russell Papers, P.R.O. 30/22/6).
[3] Nicholls, *History of the Irish Poor Law*, p. 345.
[4] T. P. O'Neill, *The Great Famine*, pp. 248–9.

Resort to outdoor relief on a considerable scale was thus inevitable, even for the able-bodied, and in February 1848, 703,762 persons were receiving such relief. A labour test was introduced for the able-bodied, but the labourers were not employed on any more productive work than stone-breaking, in return for which they received rations of food.[1]

The situation grew worse after the harvest of 1848, when the potato blight again appeared. In the south and west the position was as bad as in 1846, and the people were less able to bear it after the long-continued distress. Numbers in the workhouses and on out-relief rose steadily until in June 1849 there were 215,000 in the former class, 769,000 in the latter.[2] The system of relief was not changed, but it certainly failed to meet the crisis. On the one hand, adequate relief was not provided, mortality from starvation as well as disease being heavy;[3] on the other, the burden of the rates proved crushing in some of the poorer unions. Responsibility for poor-rates was divided equally between landlord and tenant in the case of holdings valued at above £4 per annum; on small-holdings the tenant was exempt, but the long series of bad years brought distress even to the middle class of farmers. In 1848 and 1849 it was reported that in many areas there was 'a race between the land agent and the rate collector' to seize their due, and in many cases the ratepayers themselves became subjects for relief.

Early in 1849, Russell admitted that 'the poor law, although it might have succeeded according to expectations in some parts of Ireland, had in other parts been found unequal to contend with the distress'.[4] The Government proposed the appointment of committees of both Lords and Commons to inquire into the operation of the Irish Poor Law, for they had pledged themselves to allow such an inquiry if the law did not seem to be working satisfactorily, and it was now painfully clear that it was not. Clarendon's gloomy prophecies[5] had been proved correct; many unions could not support their poor out of their own resources, and from 1847 to 1849 Parliament had of necessity to sanction special advances by the Treasury to the Irish Poor Law Commissioners. Since such votes were

---

[1] At this time Clarendon favoured the employment of the able-bodied poor on 'reproductive' schemes by Poor Law guardians, but the Cabinet opposed this, on the grounds that it might discourage private employment and revive many of the difficulties of earlier public works projects. See G. Grey to Clarendon, 17 January 1848, Clarendon to Somerville, 13 February 1848 (Clarendon Papers).

[2] Nicholls, *History of the Irish Poor Law*, p. 351.

[3] O'Neill, *The Great Famine*, p. 252. The actual number of deaths from starvation in Ireland at this time cannot be established, but between 23 April 1848 and 20 April 1850 a verdict of 'death from want' was returned at 814 inquests: *Second Annual Report of the Poor Law Commissioners for Ireland*, pp. 222–5; *Third Annual Report*, pp. 125–7.

[4] *Hansard*, 3rd ser. vol. CII, col. 436 (7 February 1849).

[5] Clarendon to Russell, 27 December 1847: 'I kept repeating that only a certain number of Irish could be allowed to die of starvation, and that sooner or later, repayable or not, relief must be advanced by England—This country can no more get on unaided till next harvest time than it can fly into the air' (Russell Papers).

becoming increasingly unpopular, Russell put forward in February 1849, a scheme for levying a rate-in-aid of the distressed unions on the whole of Ireland, but on Ireland alone. This proposal was strongly resisted by Lansdowne, who threatened to resign on account of it, and was only with difficulty persuaded by Russell to remain in the Cabinet and support the scheme in a modified form.[1] This was for a rate-in-aid of sixpence in the pound to be levied in every union in Ireland for the next two years towards a general fund for the relief of the poor.

This proposal drew strong objections from Irish members, the representatives of the richer areas, particularly Ulster, being averse to paying for what they considered the consequences of mismanagement in the poorer ones. Suggestions were made that to impose separate national taxation on Ireland was unconstitutional, since the Exchequers of Britain and Ireland had been amalgamated, and that the distress should be met from the Imperial Treasury. To this the Government reply was that Ireland was in fact exempt from a number of taxes which were paid in Britain; if the Treasury was to bear the whole cost of relief to Ireland, these taxes would necessarily have to be extended to that country, and they would constitute a much heavier, and perhaps more lasting, burden than the rate-in-aid.[2]

The scheme for a rate-in-aid was carried into law in May 1849, and succeeded in tiding the insolvent unions in the west of Ireland over their difficulties; but the measure gave fresh cause for resentment, for it was widely felt that instead of enacting the promised schemes of improvement, the Whig Government was simply forcing the less afflicted parts of Ireland to share the poverty of the more afflicted, and Poor Law guardians in the solvent unions complained that this was a curious lesson in that self-reliance which had so often been preached to Irishmen.[3]

Meanwhile, the two Select Committees continued their deliberations, but, like many committees on Irish matters, they accumulated much evidence without producing many significant conclusions. They were still sitting when the Government came forward with further proposals for amendment of the Irish Poor Law. That amendment was essential was by now everywhere admitted, but the changes put forward by Russell were mainly of a technical character. Scrope declared, with some justification, that 'the improvements proposed by the noble Lord...involved merely the shifting of the burden of taxation as regarded the ratepayers; but what he wished to see was some improvement in the law as regarded the poor themselves, for whose benefit the law professed to have been passed;

[1] See Gooch, vol. II, pp. 233–5; Spencer Walpole, vol. II, p. 82.
[2] *Hansard*, 3rd ser. vol. CIII, cols. 109–12 (2 March 1849). For the Irish case against the measure, see Butt, *The Rate in Aid: A Letter to the Rt. Hon. the Earl of Roden, K.P.* (Dublin, 1849).
[3] See Lifford, *Who is Blacker?* (Dublin, 1865), p. 9; Butt, *The Rate in Aid, passim.*

and he could perceive nothing in the noble Lord's plan at all relating to them'.[1]

In the form in which it was finally enacted, the amending Bill contained a clause empowering guardians to apply money towards the expenses of emigration of poor persons,[2] but this was little availed of, since in most unions the guardians were hard enough pressed to find funds even for immediate relief. Otherwise, the Act was concerned mainly with administrative matters, and made no essential change in the principles of relief laid down by the Act of 1838 and the Extension Act of 1847.

Trevelyan wrote that through the Poor Law Extension Act 'a principle of great power' had been introduced into the social system of Ireland, 'which must be productive of many important consequences besides those which directly flow from it'.[3] This proved to be true, but the consequences were not those which Trevelyan envisaged. The hope of the Whigs was that the Poor Law would force Irish landlords to carry out their responsibilities and give profitable employment, but the fact was that, however willing they might have been, most landlords were simply unable to do this in the circumstances of 1847–9. For the most part, the proprietors had little land in their own hands on which they could give immediate employment, but apart from this many of them merely owned life-interests in estates already so much incumbered that they could not well be charged with the cost of further borrowing. As the weight of the poor-rates increased, even the best landowners hesitated at the thought of investing money in their estates, for however much employment they gave on their land they might still not escape the burden of supporting the poor in other parts of the rating area.[4] For the more improvident proprietors, the poor-rates eventually amounted in many cases to what Senior had warned they would be—a confiscation.

Over many parts of the country, the Poor Law Extension Act can fairly be said to have disintegrated the fabric of rural society. Since the landlords had to pay the full rates on all holdings of a valuation below £4 per annum, they were naturally anxious to get rid of the smallest tenants, and the 'quarter-acre clause' gave a powerful stimulus to the process of clearance. When the cottiers could no longer support themselves from their potato ground, some of the better landlords assisted them to emigrate, but the 'Gregory clause' gave a much cheaper way of clearing an estate, for once the tenant was compelled to surrender his holding in order to obtain relief, the responsibility was taken off the landlord's shoulders. In one respect, this merely served to hasten the proprietors' ruin by increasing the rates, but this was true only in a collective sense; the individual land-

[1] *Hansard*, 3rd ser. vol. CIV, col. 874 (26 April 1849).
[2] 12 and 13 Vic. c. 104 (Irish Poor Law Further Amendment Act, 1849), Clause 26.
[3] Trevelyan, 'The Irish Crisis', *loc. cit.* p. 301.
[4] Senior, *Journals Relating to Ireland*, vol. I, pp. 265–9.

 BE

owner could partly shift the burden to his fellows and the more substantial tenant-farmers. Ultimately, however, the rise in poor-rates and the decline in rent receipts served to send many proprietors into the Incumbered Estates Court once its operations began in 1849.

Hence those who had forecast dire results from the introduction of a system of outdoor relief in Ireland were able to declare their forebodings justified. Senior did not lose the opportunity to do so; in an article in the *Edinburgh Review* for October 1849[1] he was able to produce a wealth of recent evidence to support his former views. While declaring that he did not feel himself bound to answer the question 'What do you propose to substitute?' Senior made clear that he thought the only remaining remedy for the economic situation was extensive and rapid emigration.

Scrope, on the other hand, did not consider the results of the Poor Law Extension Act constituted a refutation of his ideas. He had advocated a Poor Law in which the able-bodied would be employed on useful work, accompanied by auxiliary measures for economic development. The Government had enacted a Poor Law which confined the labourers in workhouses or employed them uselessly, and had failed to accompany it with the necessary auxiliary measures. Scrope therefore held to his opinion that the situation could have been met by his proposals, and that agricultural improvement was still preferable to any scheme of emigration.[2]

In attempting to assess both the proposals and the policies of these years, it is necessary to keep in mind the distinction between immediate relief and ultimate improvement. For the immediate relief of a starving population, public works were the obvious remedy, and their character made little difference so long as employment was provided—but the essential counterpart of this was that food should be obtainable with the wages given. None of the works proposed by Scrope or others would have effected an immediate increase in the food supply. In trusting to private enterprise almost entirely to make food available in 1846-7 the Government made a grave mistake, but a mistake resulting from a too rigid application of the economic doctrines of the time. Amongst contemporary writers, only Scrope supported Butt in his contention that the Government should have gone into the market itself.[3]

The decision to rely on the extended Poor Law from 1847 onwards was in fact a decision to shift the emphasis of policy from immediate relief to permanent improvement. In the event only one half of the intended policy came into effect, with the consequences already described. These were, in a sense, the contrary of what the ministry had planned, for Lord John

[1] 'Relief of Irish Distress in 1847 and 1848', *Edinburgh Rev.* vol. LXXXIX, pp. 221–268; reprinted in *Journals Relating to Ireland*, vol. I, pp. 208–82.
[2] See G. P. Scrope, *The Irish Difficulty: and How it Must be Met. From the Westminster and Foreign Quarterly Review, January, 1849. With a Postscript* (London, 1849); idem, *Draft Report on the Kilrush Union* (London, 1850).
[3] Scrope, *The Irish Relief Measures*, pp. 52–4.

Russell had declared himself in favour of supporting the Irish population at home through improved agriculture, and against emigration; yet the forces set in motion by the Poor Law Extension Act all tended to increase emigration. Even so, the Poor Law measure did help to produce a long-term solution of the economic difficulties; it may be questioned whether, in 1849, any scheme of development in agriculture could have succeeded without some emigration, and it was certainly necessary that Ireland should be rid of uneconomic holdings and insolvent proprietors. Much of this was achieved as a consequence of the new Poor Law, but in a harsh and erratic fashion. Here was no solution through the ordered application of a well thought-out plan; it was, in the most starkly literal sense, a solution by trial and error.

VI

As a result of increases in workhouse accommodation, the growth of emigration, and an improved harvest, the Irish Poor Law Commissioners found it possible in October 1849 to withdraw all orders for outdoor relief granted because relief could not be afforded within the workhouse;[1] by 1852 'the transition from out-door to in-door relief was said to be complete throughout Ireland'.[2] In the following year Nicholls visited Ireland, after an absence of eleven years, and reported to Lord John Russell that there were no able-bodied persons in the workhouses. 'The total number of inmates of all classes is now 84,000, which is about the number I estimated at the outset as requiring to be provided for. The cost of relief is moreover about the same as I then estimated that it would probably amount to; and it is not a little gratifying to find that our calculations in these respects are so far verified.' Nicholls did not seem to find any incongruity between these remarks and the statement at the beginning of his letter that 'since I quitted Ireland...the country has suffered from famine and pestilence, and the Poor Law has been subjected to a most severe trial'[3] nor did he point out that to meet that trial the Poor Law of 1838 had been first by-passed, then vastly extended.

During the eighteen-fifties, the cost of poor relief per head of population became considerably lower in Ireland than in England or Scotland, a fact to which Nicholls and others pointed with gratification.[4] The reason for this situation was that in Ireland no one would be granted outdoor relief when the workhouse was not full, whereas in England and Scotland such relief was quite frequently afforded. The severity of the Irish administration was criticised by Hancock and, later, John Kells Ingram. Hancock, in 1855, argued strongly against the refusal of out-relief to widows and

[1] *Third Annual Report of the Poor-Law Commissioners for Ireland*, 25 May 1850, p. 4.
[2] Nicholls, *History of the Irish Poor Law*, p. 378.
[3] Nicholls to Russell, 16 September 1853, quoted in *ibid.* p. 399.
[4] *Ibid.* p. 403.

orphans, but went on to state that neither theory nor fact any longer supported the necessity for rigorous enforcement of the workhouse test: '...the Malthusian doctrine that all the sufferings of the poor are of their own creating, and the remedy within their own control, is exploded. Thus the principal danger which the new Poor Law was intended to meet no longer exists, and the theory on which it was framed is no longer believed.' In Ireland, emigration had reduced the danger of excessive demands for relief, while the operation of the Incumbered Estates Court had changed the proprietary into one well able to bear the cost of poor-rates. 'In short, the principles on which the Irish Poor Law is to be administered for the future must be learned not from the traditions of the changes introduced in England in 1834 but, from a careful consideration of the present state of the poor and of the country in which they are to pass their lives.'[1]

The consequences of the rigorous enforcement of workhouse relief fell most severely on children brought up 'in the house', as Hancock stressed; inadequate diet caused a very high rate of mortality amongst them, and left many more deformed and diseased.[2] But when the deficient harvests of 1859–62 brought to an end the deceptive prosperity of the eighteen-fifties, hardship became widespread amongst all classes of the poor. In parts of the south and west, the destitution of the people was comparable with that experienced in 1846. Cardwell, the Chief Secretary, admitted as much in reply to a parliamentary question in April 1860, but declared that the ordinary resources of relief were considered sufficient to meet the distress, and it was not proposed to introduce any special measures.[3]

Nevertheless, in view of the many protests voiced in Ireland about the severity of the Poor Law administration, it was decided to renew the powers of the Irish Poor Law Commission, then due to expire, for two years only, and to appoint a Select Committee to inquire into the administration of poor relief. This Committee was appointed in March 1861; a number of officials of the Irish Poor Law Commission, and members of Boards of Guardians, gave evidence before it. While they generally testified that the existing system was satisfactory, several independent witnesses roundly asserted the contrary, and called for a wider use of outdoor relief and a system of boarding out pauper children.[4]

The Committee took the view that no alteration of the powers of guardians in regard to the granting of indoor or outdoor relief was 'necessary or desirable',[5] but reported in favour of the repeal of the

---

[1] Hancock, 'The Workhouse as a mode of Relief for Widows and Orphans', *Journal of the Dublin Statistical Society*, vol. I, p. 91.

[2] See Sir John Arnott, *The Investigation into the Condition of the Children in the Cork Workhouse* (Cork, 1859).

[3] *Hansard*, 3rd ser. vol. CLVII, col. 1885 (17 April 1860).

[4] See evidence of Denis Phelan, M.D., and George Place, Select Committee on Poor Relief (Ireland): *Minutes of Evidence* (1861 (408), vol. X), pp. 154, 156, 209.

[5] *Report from the Select Committee on Poor Relief (Ireland)* (1861 [408], vol. X), p. iii.

quarter-acre clause, and permitting guardians to board out orphan and deserted children up to the age of twelve years.

A Bill embodying the substance of these recommendations was introduced by Sir Robert Peel (who had in the meantime succeeded Cardwell as Chief Secretary) in 1862[1] and passed into law in the same session.[2] Despite the modifications thus introduced, when Ingram turned his attention to a comparison of the Irish and English Poor Laws in 1863, he was able to show that the former was still much the more severe. In illustration, he pointed out that in January 1863 only 12 % of all those who received relief in England were made to enter the workhouse, whereas in Ireland the proportion was 91 %. Ingram argued that so long as this stringency in the administration of the Irish Poor Law continued, it would hinder attempts to convert small-holders into wage-paid labourers; since the Irish labourer had no prospect of obtaining outdoor relief if he became unemployed, he would always tend to cling to the occupation of land as the only safeguard against the workhouse for himself and his family. Apart from this, the knowledge of a difference between the treatment of English and Irish labourers tended to increase discontent and foster disaffection. Ingram, like Hancock, held that the grounds for resisting an extension of outdoor relief were no longer valid—'The emigration has greatly reduced the population, the poor rates have fallen to a very low amount, wages are rising, and the time seems to have arrived when the law in this country should be made identical with that of England.'[3] These suggestions, however, led to no further modification of the Poor Law in Ireland within the period of this study.[4]

[1] The Bill provided for the boarding out of pauper children up to the age of five years only.
[2] 25 and 26 Vic. c. 83 (Irish Poor Law Further Amendment Act, 1862). Although this Act repealed the quarter-acre clause, it provided that holders of more than one rood of ground could be relieved only within the workhouse.
[3] Ingram, 'Address at the Opening of the Seventeenth Session', *Journal of the Statistical and Social Inquiry Society of Ireland*, vol. IV, p. 25 (Read 18 November 1863).
[4] The Poor Law Commission in Ireland had a number of administrative functions, not directly connected with poor relief, assigned to it in the years after 1848. Consequently, by an Act of 1872 (35 and 36 Vic. c. 69) it was replaced by the Local Government Board, but this made no immediate difference to the conditions of relief.

CHAPTER V

PRIVATE ENTERPRISE AND FREE TRADE

I

REFERENCES to 'the lack of Capital in Ireland' recur constantly throughout the whole period of this study, in the columns of *Hansard*, in *Parliamentary Papers*, and in general writings on Irish economic problems.[1] The consequent proposition that the prosperity of Ireland could best be advanced by the introduction of capital, in some sense not exactly defined, was a safe generalisation, sure to command popular assent, in Ireland or England.

The task of the economist should be to give precise content to such generalisations and assess their value. As has been pointed out in the previous chapter, most of the classical economists had clearly defined views on this subject, which they conceived in terms of the relative rates of growth of population and the funds for its employment, that is circulating capital. In theory, a relationship between these two variables more favourable to economic development might be achieved either by increasing capital or reducing population, *simpliciter*; the latter might be regarded as a short-term expedient, attainable through emigration, the former as a long-term process.

Most economists were careful to qualify this view by reference to Malthusian population theory. Care must be taken to ensure that any improvement of standards brought about by adjusting the population-capital ratio was not merely dissipated through a fresh growth of population. It was on this ground that both Ricardo and McCulloch opposed tackling the Irish problem, at least in the first instance, by a mere reduction of population—Ricardo because he felt that a parallel reduction of food supplies would be the consequence,[2] McCulloch for the more obvious reason that he feared any gap in the population created by emigration would quickly be filled up again by early marriages and large families.[3] But if these objections could always be offered against plans for the mere

[1] See, for example, E. Wakefield, *An Account of Ireland, Statistical and Political* (London, 1812), vol. I, p. 586; *Report from the Select Committee on the Employment of the Poor in Ireland* (1823 (561), vol. VI), pp. 7 and 8; J. O'Connell, *An Argument for Ireland* (Dublin, 1844), p. 216; Sir J. Forbes, *Memorandums made in Ireland* (London, 1853), vol. I, p. 84.

[2] See Ricardo, *Principles, Works and Correspondence*, ed. Sraffa, vol. I, p. 100, and above, ch. IV, p. 86.

[3] [McCulloch], 'Ireland', *Edinburgh Rev.* vol. XXXVII (June 1822), p. 108. In a later article, McCulloch expressed the conviction that a plan of emigration could be combined with effective measures 'for preventing the vacuum that would be made in the population from being filled up'. The measures suggested were consolidation of farms and a tax on cottages, levied from the proprietor. *Idem*, 'Emigration', *Edinburgh Rev.* vol. XLV (December 1826) p. 72. And see below, ch. VII.

reduction of population, similar ones could be brought against proposals to increase the wages-fund, unaccompanied by any measures to check the ensuing increase in the labour force.

For Ireland then, the investment problem could be conceived in classical terms as one of finding an increased supply of capital and channelling it into the most effective uses so as to produce a rise in living standards which would not be quickly cancelled out by population growth. Although in the early nineteenth century observers most frequently talked in terms of 'lack of capital', it could be argued that the situation in Ireland was the outcome of absence of investible funds, absence of incentives to invest, or both.

The class structure in Ireland at that time was certainly not favourable to the accumulation of capital. The majority of the landlords were 'unproductive consumers' on a large scale, and since those who were not absentees tended largely to purchase imported commodities, their expenditure did not generate much local employment. At the other end of the scale, the cottiers were at the very margin of subsistence and frequently burdened with debt. In between there were only the more substantial farmers and the tradespeople of the towns. There were certainly farmers, mostly in the eastern counties, who were capitalists in a genuine sense, but they were generally graziers, whose circulating capital was almost wholly invested in livestock. Most other farmers who employed labour outside their own families, paid for it by giving the labourers patches of ground and in effect used potatoes as a wages-fund. There is a considerable volume of evidence that such small farmers accumulated cash from the sale of their crops, but hoarded it or placed it in savings banks, because the insecurity of their tenure gave them no incentive to use it on improvements, and any display of affluence might be made the ground for a demand for increased rent or other exactions.[1]

The virtual absence of a middle class in Ireland was so frequently stressed that the comment was almost platitudinous; but if the middle classes were not numerous some of them were prosperous enough, particularly those engaged in import and export business. Even so, they did not always share the habits of thrift so typical of the English middle classes—partly because the Penal Laws, which were designed to prohibit Roman Catholics from acquiring wealth and property, had prevented those habits from growing up, partly because the well-to-do Irish merchant was inclined to 'ape the gentry' and spend his profits in lavish hospitality or keeping horses and dogs, rather than add them to his capital.[2]

[1] See *Digest of Evidence taken before Her Majesty's Commissioners of Inquiry into the State of the Law and Practice in Respect to the Occupation of Land in Ireland* (Dublin, 1847), pt. I, pp. 197–9.
[2] See Inglis, *Ireland in 1834*, vol. II, p. 217. Inglis, like many others before and since, here points out the difference between the businessmen of Ulster and their counterparts in Dublin or Cork; but on this see below, p. 157.

Those who had capital to invest frequently preferred to place it in the British funds or in business ventures outside Ireland[1]—for the same reasons which deterred British and foreign capitalists from investing in Ireland—the simple absence of safe and profitable opportunities there.

Before 1849 there was not usually a great deal of land in the market, but if the 'moneyed man' did buy land it usually paid him best to go on rack-renting the tenants as his predecessor had done. Certainly he would have been foolish to rent land and try to invest his capital in cultivating it efficiently; no prudent investor would destroy his change of profit by outbidding the reckless offers of rent which the small tenants made. Even had he done so, he would probably have seen his property destroyed in turn by the outrages committed by the former occupiers of the land.

Investment in industrial projects offered prospects little less bleak as a rule. The extreme poverty of the mass of the people made the Irish market a small one for most manufactured products, while the absence of raw materials and the force of English competition, unfettered by any tariffs after 1826, were further deterrents in many lines.

Most of the classical economists, from Ricardo to John Stuart Mill, were familiar with this drab picture, and their writings give a clear indication of how they felt the situation should be handled. To all of them, the fundamental point was security: here was the necessary condition for encouraging investment and economic development, and a condition which was not fulfilled in Ireland as matters stood. Ricardo appears to have regarded this as a question quite distinct from the problems of land tenure,[2] but others, notably Senior and J. S. Mill, recognised that insecurity was a product of the attitude of the people to the land.[3] Only to J. S. Mill did this seem to argue a case for altering the institutions of land tenure. Trower's judgment was much more typical of the classical view: 'The two great deficiencies in Ireland are *want of capital*, and *want of Industry*. By destroying small tenancies you would obtain both.'[4] A sentence from Malthus completes the diagnosis: 'The *Land* in Ireland is infinitely more peopled than in England; and to give full effect to the natural resources of the country, a great part of this population should be swept from the soil into large manufacturing and commercial towns.'[5] Once an efficient system of agriculture had been thus established, the same volume of produce might be obtained by a greatly reduced labour force (or, possibly, a somewhat increased produce by a somewhat less reduced

---

[1] For a striking instance of this, see W. O. Henderson, 'W. T. Mulvany: an Irish Pioneer in the Ruhr', in his *Britain and Industrial Europe, 1750–1870* (Liverpool, 1954), pp. 179–93.
[2] See his letter to Trower, 25 January 1822, quoted above, ch. I, p. 19. And see T. R. Malthus, *Principles of Political Economy Considered with a View to their Practical Application*, 2nd ed., L.S.E. reprint (London, 1936), p. 349. [3] See above, pp. 23 and 31.
[4] Trower to Ricardo, 10 January 1822, quoted above, p. 18.
[5] Malthus to Ricardo, 17 August 1817 (*Works and Correspondence of David Ricardo*, vol. VII, p. 175).

quantity of labour). The population 'swept from the soil' could then be employed in the manufacture of 'comforts and enjoyments', even 'luxuries',[1] which the cottiers under the existing system held in less esteem than idleness, but for which they and others would soon develop a taste under the stimulus of regular wage-paid employment.

That 'a taste for other objects besides mere food' was a primary necessity for economic development in Ireland was a point much emphasised by classical authors. Ricardo and Malthus were essentially in agreement upon it, despite the divergence in their views on effective demand, and it was also stressed by McCulloch.[2] That much surplus labour could be released from agriculture to produce the goods and services to gratify such tastes is unquestionable; what is more difficult to determine is how the economists expected it to be drawn into industrial employment. Malthus was the most nearly explicit on this point, indicating that the change in tastes and the resultant growth of demand must precede the introduction of capital for manufactures, which capital he seems to have thought must come from England.[3] Other formulations, such as Ricardo's, seem to imply that the reorganisation of production would afford the means of employing all the labour in manufactures without any import of capital; in this case, it would seem that the landowners must be presumed to invest in industry, or even become entrepreneurs themselves.[4]

Granted the achievement of this reorganisation of production, a brilliant future could be forecast for Ireland. 'If', wrote Malthus, 'under a state of things where all kinds of property were secure an improved system of agriculture were to raise the food and raw materials required for the population with the smallest quantity of labour necessary to do it in the best manner, and the remainder of the people, instead of loitering about upon the land, were engaged in manufactures and commerce carried on in great and flourishing towns, Ireland would be beyond comparison richer than England.'[5]

[1] See Ricardo, *Principles, Works and Correspondence*, vol. I, p. 100, and his letter to Trower of 15 July 1816 (*ibid.* vol. VII, p. 48).
[2] See references to Ricardo given in the last footnote; Malthus, *Principles*, pp. 346–51; [McCulloch], 'Ireland', *Edinburgh Rev.* vol. XXXVII, pp. 97–100.
[3] Malthus, *Principles*, p. 350.
[4] In some of Ricardo's remarks on the question the terms 'landlord' and 'capitalist' are used interchangeably. See *Notes on Malthus, Works and Correspondence*, vol. II, pp. 344–5.
The possibility that 'the use of disguised unemployment for the accumulation of capital could be financed from within the system itself' is discussed in R. Nurkse, *Problems of Capital Formation in Underdeveloped Countries* (Oxford, 1953), p. 38. Nurkse describes this as 'a relationship between consumption and investment which stands midway between the classical and the Keynesian approach'. If the interpretation given here is correct, the relationship was one which leading classical authors recognised and used. See E. W. McKinley, 'The Problem of "Underdevelopment" in the English Classical School', *Quarterly J. Economics*, vol. LXIX, no. 2 (May 1955), pp. 235–52.
[5] Malthus, *Principles*, p. 350.

Malthus did not discuss the question of possible difficulties in getting the displaced cottiers into employment in manufactures and commerce,[1] but in the circumstances of Ireland after the Union it was probable that any increased demand for manufactures would be met largely by imports from England, rather than home production. This point was explicitly recognised by McCulloch in his 1822 article, but his main concern was with increased consumption, rather than increased employment, in Ireland. To McCulloch the important point was to raise the standard of living of the Irish labourer, and make him a more contented citizen; to this end, cheap products were requisite, and it was immaterial whether they came from Ireland or England. In this regard McCulloch argued that the retention of the 10% duty on English goods imported into Ireland since the Union had damaged English manufacturing interests without benefiting Irish. The duty was too low to be a real protection to the Irish producer, but high enough to make imported goods too dear for the poorer classes of Irish consumers. Even from the standpoint of employment in Ireland, the tariff had probably been injurious, McCulloch suggested, for since a countervailing duty of 10% was imposed on Irish manufactures exported to England, this had served to deter English manufacturers from taking advantage of the cheap labour available in Ireland to produce there, for example, the coarser grades of cotton textiles.[2]

In general, McCulloch did not envisage a growing Irish market supplied by Irish industry, as Malthus at times seems to have.[3] The fullest and most explicit treatment of this problem came from Torrens, who admitted that improvement in Irish agriculture 'would create a demand for an additional *town* population equal to, and perhaps greater than, the portion of *country* population which had been displaced', but agreed that 'in the sequence of cause and effect, the extinction of a portion of the agricultural population of Ireland must precede the creation of an equivalent town population. Whatever might be the *ultimate* operation of agricultural improvement in increasing the general demand for labour, its *immediate* consequence, unless averted by an extensive plan of Emigration, would necessarily be a frightful aggravation of the existing misery.'[4]

---

[1] In evidence before Wilmot Horton's Emigration Committee in 1827, Malthus classed cultivation of waste lands, public works, and bounties to private industry together as 'partial and temporary stimulants, and on that account...prejudicial'. The natural growth of non-agricultural employment is not discussed, but the whole tenor of Malthus's evidence suggests that this growth would be inadequate to employ the ejected cottiers without some emigration, *Minutes of Evidence before the Select Committee on Emigration* Qs. 3340–8: 1826–7 [550], vol. v.   [2] [McCulloch], 'Ireland', pp. 98–100.
[3] In 1826, McCulloch wrote: 'What is to become of the wretches who are ejected? They can obtain no employment in the towns, which are already gorged with unemployed inhabitants', *Edinburgh Rev.* vol. XLV (December 1826), p. 53.
[4] *Substance of a Speech delivered by Colonel Torrens...15th February 1827* (2nd ed. London, n.d.), p. 41.

In this 1827 speech, Torrens recognised that the increased demand resulting from growth of agricultural production would divide itself between imported goods and home-produced articles, yet nevertheless felt that it could ultimately provide urban employment for the whole population. Even before the removal of the 'Union duties' in 1826 this would have been an optimistic assumption; thereafter it was even less likely to be fulfilled. In later years Torrens came to recognise this, and in 1833 he gave expression to the consequent conclusion that there could be little profitable opening for investment in Irish industry:

He broadly asserted and he was prepared to prove the assertion, that the introduction of capital into Ireland, instead of making things better, would make them worse. No person was so absurd as to suppose that any capital, however large in amount, would be able to create manufactures in Kent and Sussex that could compete with those of Lancashire and Yorkshire. There could be no manufactures, except in places where fuel was cheap, and where they had been established by the habits of the people. Apply, then, this argument to Ireland, and the conclusion was, that while coal was cheap in Lancashire, and while Ireland was subject to the competition of England, manufactures could not be established there. If capital were introduced into that country, it must be employed in the cultivation of the soil, and the consequence would be an improved mode of cultivation, rendering less labour necessary on any given surface of ground, and increasing, in a like proportion, the unemployed surplus population.[1]

This astringent speech startled Sir Robert Peel, who declared that 'if it was one of the new discoveries of political economy that the voluntary transfer of capital into Ireland would entail a curse on that country and not a blessing, he must say that his faith in the science would be greatly shaken'.[2] Unfortunately, Torrens's analysis was substantially correct, and emphasises a vital point which Malthus seems to have overlooked— 'while Ireland was subject to the competition of England, manufactures could not be established there'. Having shown the difficulty of the Irish situation, Torrens proceeded to consider various remedies for it, and amongst these was 'to raise a wall of Custom house duties round the country. That, he admitted, would for a time cause a portion of the surplus population to be employed in manufactures, but he would tell the Irish landlords that it would reduce the value of their estates fifty per cent.'[3]

Hansard's compiler did not record Torrens as having enlarged at all on this rather cryptic threat,[4] but the implication of the speech is that protection to manufactures would afford no solution to Ireland's problems. On this point the classical economists were in agreement, but the opposite view was never without a substantial volume of support during most of the

---

[1] Speech in the House of Commons, 8 February 1833, *Hansard*, 3rd ser. vol. xv, col. 416.
[2] *Ibid*. col. 602.   [3] *Ibid*. col. 417.
[4] It seems reasonable to infer that Torrens had in mind the possibility of Irish tariffs provoking retaliation against her exports of agricultural produce.

nineteenth century. There has been a traditional association of protectionist thinking with nationalist movements[1] and much, though not all, of the advocacy of protection for Irish industry came from nationalist sources. The arguments of Irish nationalists on the subject of industrial development during the period here covered must be pieced together from speeches, articles and pamphlets; there is no reasoned statement of any generally accepted view. They must therefore be cautiously interpreted; it may not always be fair to either group to compare the carefully thought out, and often abstract, ideas of academic economists with the *ad hoc* utterances of politicians, and the polemical writings of journalists.

As might be expected, the argument most commonly employed by nationalists was some variant of the infant industry case, but this was more often used in a negative than a positive sense. Thus Daniel O'Connell and his supporters in the Repeal Association never hesitated to list 'the premature withdrawal of the protecting duties' amongst the evil consequences of the Union,[2] but they were usually careful not to commit themselves on the question of whether a restored Irish parliament would introduce protection again. Generally, Repealers laid most stress on the drain of capital which they alleged Ireland suffered as a result of the Union, through increased taxation and absenteeism. They contended that Repeal would bring an end to these drains, and so provide an abundant supply of capital, sufficient in itself, perhaps, to give new life to Irish industry.[3]

These views were accepted and adopted by the Young Ireland group; 'aristocratic extortion' and 'foreign taxation' were frequent targets for criticism in the early days of the *Nation* newspaper.[4] The Young Irelanders, however, were sometimes more explicit than the earlier Repeal writers in their use of the infant industry argument. Thomas Davis argued that Repeal 'would secure the mechanic from premature competition'[5] and a later article confidently assumed the ability of an Irish parliament 'to create vast manufactures here by protecting duties in the first instance and to maintain them by our general prosperity'.[6]

From such statements, it could be inferred that a period of protection was alone necessary to bring about that rapid rise of Ireland to a level with England's prosperity, which Malthus had envisaged. In general,

[1] See Nurkse, *Capital Formation in Underdeveloped Countries*, p. 104.
[2] See Report of the Committee of the Loyal National Repeal Association of Ireland on the Disastrous Effects of the Union on the Woollen, Silk and Cotton Manufactures of Ireland: *Second Series of Reports of the Loyal National Repeal Association* (Dublin, 1840), no. 4, p. 108; John O'Connell, *An Argument for Ireland* (Dublin, 1844), p. 217
[3] See O'Connell, *An Argument for Ireland*, p. 216.
[4] See *The Nation*, 31 December 1842, 30 September 1843.
[5] [T. Davis], 'Slaves' Vices and Freemen's Duties', *The Nation*, 30 September 1843. For the identification of authorship of this and other *Nation* articles, see McGrath, 'Writers in *The Nation*, 1842–45', *Irish Historical Studies*, vol. VI (1948–9), pp. 189–223.
[6] *The Nation*, 2 December 1843.

those who were not prepared to consider the possibility of Ireland
becoming a separate political entity were also unable to concede the
possibility of tariffs between Britain and Ireland; but in 1849 Sir John
Byles, swimming against the full tide of free-trade thinking, argued that
Irish industry should receive such protection 'as would place Ireland, not
on a seeming and pretended level, as now, but on a *true and actual level
with England*. It should be no more than is absolutely necessary for this
first purpose, and last no longer than the necessity continues; which time
would be very short.'[1] This was no more than had been admitted to be
desirable at the time of the Union, and had been intended to be achieved
by the continuance of tariffs for a period thereafter. Byles, indeed, drew
specific attention to the decline of Irish industries since the cessation of
the 'Union duties' and implied that they might have remained prosperous
if the duties had continued. He never attempted to reconcile this with his
statement that the period of protection necessary to raise Irish industry
to English levels would be 'very short'. In fact, once industry had come
to be based on coal and iron, it must inevitably have been difficult for
more than a few trades ever to flourish unprotected in Ireland. This hard
fact, which Torrens recognised, was ignored or played down by those who
used the infant industry argument in the Irish case.[2]

A case for protection, which did not employ the infant industry argument, was made by Isaac Butt in his lectures from the Whately Chair in
1840.[3] 'It appears to me', wrote Butt, 'that in all the arguments which
attempt to prove, as a general proposition, the injury of protective duties,
it is assumed, that the industry of a country must always be fully
employed.'[4] He contended that where this assumption was not fulfilled
protection could be used to generate employment; this, indeed, might
involve consumers in accepting products inferior in quality or quantity—
but in a country situated as Ireland was, employment must be considered
a more valuable end than consumer satisfaction.

Butt was clearly much influenced by Senior's argument that absenteeism
could injure a country which exported mainly raw produce,[5] which he
extended to include the case of expenditure on imported commodities by
landlords and others resident in Ireland. His case for protection rested
on the idea that it could divert such expenditure to home-produced

---

[1] Sir J. B. Byles, *Sophisms of Free Trade and Popular Political Economy Examined*,
1st ed. (London, 1849), p. 149.
[2] The publication of Sir Robert Kane's *Industrial Resources of Ireland* in 1844 lent
support to optimistic views of Irish manufacturing potential, but Kane's discussion dealt
with technical rather than economic possibilities.
[3] Published under the title *Protection to Home Industry: Some Cases of its Advantage
Considered* (Dublin, 1846).
[4] Butt, *Protection to Home Industry*, p. 133.
[5] See above, ch. III, p. 76. Butt refers to Senior's argument (*Protection to Home
Industry*, pp. 92–3) but does not seem to have been aware of Scrope's treatment of the same
case.

articles, so creating employment and giving to labourers the means of purchasing the food-stuffs which would otherwise be directly exported to pay for foreign goods. With a frankness and vigour unusual in the writings of his day, Butt made the welfare judgment that the employment of the poor was more important than the gratification of the desires of the rich. Thus to him, protection appeared as a form of redistributive taxation, and he argued that tariffs 'may act the part of the most wise and wholesome poor law'.[1] These views were unorthodox, but not uniquely so: Butt had in fact been anticipated in them by an obscure pamphleteer, Beare, who wrote on the question of free trade in relation to Ireland in 1827. Beare also contended that 'to speak on such a question, without treating it with reference to *employment*, is to look at it incorrectly' and pointed out that if the effect of imports was to produce unemployment, the cost of supporting the idle labourers from poor-rates or charity, ought to be added to the price of the imports and the total compared with the cost of producing the goods at home.[2]

While protection as a means of developing Irish industry was thus advocated at various times and on various grounds, it was never more than an uninfluential minority which advocated it. Other forms of intervention to stimulate investment and employment in industry were occasionally suggested,[3] but the generally accepted view was that Irish industry must stand or fall by its own unaided efforts.

Protection to agriculture was a cause with more powerful support, at least up to 1846. Hence it is not surprising to find that arguments favouring the development of Irish agriculture, by protection and other means, occur more frequently than proposals for the development of Irish industry. Some of these arguments took a positive form, suggesting plans for improving the market for Irish produce in Britain and abroad. Since under the Union Ireland enjoyed free access to the British market and protection from the competition of foreign produce, further discrimination was not usually proposed, but reduction of transport costs and improvements in communication were urged to help the Irish farmer and the British consumer at the same time. Thus Rooke, one of the company of neglected British economists rediscovered by Seligman,[4] asserted that 'the surest method to enforce large farms, and cause a

---

[1] Butt, *Protection to Home Industry*, p. 15. See also pp. 62–67.

[2] J. Beare, *Improvement of Ireland: A Second Letter to the King, on the Practical Improvement of Ireland* (London, 1827), p. 42.

[3] Thus in 1828 J. R. Elmore proposed to abolish the Irish executive and 'let one or two years' savings from that source be invested in commissioners for the purpose of forming manufacturing establishments throughout Ireland', *Letters to the Earl of Darnley on the State of Ireland, in Advocacy of Free Trade* (London, 1828), p. 70. In the same year, an anonymous writer proposed to solve the problem of employing the Irish population by enforcing a suppression of machinery and a return to domestic hand spinning and weaving of textiles: *Practice Opposed to Theory*, by 'A Practical Man' (London, 1828), pp. 139–40.

[4] Seligman, 'On Some Neglected British Economists', *Econ. J.* vol. XIII (1903), pp. 511–14.

division and co-operation of labour, is to promote cheap means of inter-course between one part of the country and another, by the extension of public roads, railways, and inland navigation'.[1] To Rooke, like most of his contemporaries, large farms were synonymous with efficient agriculture, and the profits which they might yield could form the basis for increased accumulation of capital and employment, directly and indirectly. That capitalist farming does not always give increased employment was more clearly recognised by Keating Trenor, a member of the staff of the Commissariat Department of the British Services, who proposed to create employment directly in Irish agriculture by prohibiting the export of meat from Ireland and producing wheat there 'to supply the army, the navy and the mercantile marine, and those colonies in which wheat is not grown'.

'These propositions', Trenor admitted, 'are not only not in agreement, but are directly at variance, with that theory of political economy which is pithily expressed in the French phrase *laissez nous faire*: but, however applicable this theory may be to philanthropic or peacable society, it cannot be ceded in this time to the Irish peasantry.'[2]

Trenor, however, was alone in his desire to plan the output of Irish agri-culture. Most writers on this subject were willing to leave the Irish farmer to produce according to market trends, but many who made no positive proposals to assist him were prepared to urge negatively that the privileges which Irish agriculture enjoyed in the British market should not be reduced or removed. Whenever modification or repeal of the Corn Laws came under discussion, it was pointed out that this would be a fundamental blow to Ireland, whose population so largely depended on agriculture. To this was sometimes added the argument that since England had dis-couraged Irish industry by her mercantilist policy in the eighteenth century, she was morally bound to protect Irish agriculture in the nineteenth.[3]

When the repeal of the Corn Laws became an issue of practical politics in the eighteen-forties, the nationalist interest in Ireland came out strongly against it, essentially on these grounds. The Young Ireland group stressed that this was a case—to them, only one of many cases—where Britain and Ireland had conflicting interests, Britain being largely a consumer of corn, Ireland largely a producer.[4]

Against all arguments for the protection of Irish agriculture in this

---

[1] J. Rooke, *An Inquiry into the Principles of National Wealth, Illustrated by the Political Economy of the British Empire* (Edinburgh, 1824), p. 137. For an earlier instance of the same argument, see J. Dawson, *Canal Extensions in Ireland, Recommended to the Imperial Legislature* (Dublin, 1819), p. 36.

[2] Keating Trenor, *An Inquiry into the Political Economy of the Irish Peasantry, as Connected with the Commissariat Resources of Ireland* (London, 1822), pp. 4 and 5.

[3] See, for example, W. Graydon, *Reflections on the State of Ireland in the Nineteenth Century*, 2nd ed. (London, 1825), p. 278; M. Gore, *A Free Trade in Corn Considered in its Influence on Ireland* (London, 1834), pp. 7 and 8.

[4] See 'The New Tariff—Ireland' and 'Commercial Policy of England', *The Nation*, 31 January 1836.

period the accusation could be made that they were ultimately arguments in the landlord interest. The cottier might indeed be made worse off by the removal of protection, but the continuance or increase of protection could not make him better off so long as nothing was done to curb rack-renting. Exemption from the charge of neglecting this fundamental point can be given to the Young Ireland writers, for measures to end the evils of rack-renting were always part of their programme.

In fact the Young Irelanders did not believe in the appropriateness of English land tenures and agricultural forms for their country, but shared and helped to express the Irish desire for fixity of tenure or peasant proprietorship. While, as has been pointed out above, these nationalist writers did not doubt the ability of a native Government to foster industry, their belief was that if a system of occupying ownership were established it could 'put the people above the need of hazarding purity or content in great manufactures'.[1] Thomas Davis and his colleagues frequently contended that the Irish people could achieve greater happiness under a system where peasant agriculture would be combined with domestic handicrafts than by seeking to follow the pattern of British economic development. This was a reflection of the romantic philosophy which underlay all their thinking and which they consciously opposed to the Utilitarianism in which the classical economists were schooled.[2]

The Young Ireland group were somewhat naïvely optimistic in thinking, as they did,[3] that the simple peasant economy of which they dreamed could provide the entire population of Ireland, at its pre-Famine level, with a standard of living at least as high as that achieved in England. It could scarcely have provided the whole of the 1841 population with even a bare subsistence; but it might well have provided a rural population much denser than could be maintained under a capitalist agricultural system with food and work in their native districts. This was as much as the majority of Irish people wished for at that time, and if it were accepted as a sufficient objective for economic development, then such schemes as the Young Irelanders put forward might well be regarded as more practicable than the policy which Malthus and Ricardo contemplated.

II

Viewed objectively, the classical economists' plan for effecting a favourable adjustment of capital to population in Ireland would seem bold and difficult of attainment, for it involved nothing less than a fundamental reorganisation of the social structure and institutions of the country. A scheme of peasant proprietorship, confirming the existing population

---

[1] *The Nation*, 2 December 1843; and see the issue of 15 June 1844.
[2] See Gavan Duffy, *Thomas Davis* (London, 1890), pp. 100–1; McDowell, *Public Opinion*, p. 232.
[3] This point emerges from many *Nation* articles, including those cited above, note 1.

in their tenure of the soil and giving them the incentive to cultivate it more effectively, would seem to involve far less dislocation, while the improvement it produced, if less spectacular, would be more certain.

Yet in practice policy followed what would logically appear to be the more difficult course, because of the distribution of land ownership and political power. A doctrine which started from the premisses of landlord-tenant relations on the English model, and advocated medium- and large-scale farming, was acceptable to the landed interests and their representatives in Parliament, where a simpler scheme which involved 'tampering with the rights of property' could not be. It is, however, doubtful if many of the governing classes had ever thought out the implications of the classical model as applied to Ireland, or considered the problems involved in putting it into practice as a whole. They were willing enough to believe in the necessity of clearing the land and consolidating farms, but there was no agreed view as to what should be done with the 'surplus population' so created. Could, and should, the people displaced from the land be re-employed in Ireland, or should they be aided to emigrate? Here was the crucial question, which successive ministries either ignored or met with conflicting answers.

If sufficient capital were forthcoming, then the people might be found employment in Ireland either in industry or agriculture. What steps, then, were taken officially to assist private investment and so develop employment?

Even at the opening of our period, the trend of parliamentary opinion was sufficiently firmly set in the direction of *laissez-faire* to make it improbable that any Government would propose measures for the deliberate fostering of industry by any form of subsidisation or protection. The history of the regulation of the linen industry in Ireland during the early nineteenth century forms a good example of this trend. During the eighteenth century the Irish Parliament had passed various Acts for the encouragement and control of the linen trade, and their enforcement was the responsibility of a Board of Trustees, founded in 1711. In addition to regulating the marketing of the cloth and enforcing prescribed standards for various types of it, the Board attempted to develop the industry by distributing premiums and bounties. Numerous endeavours were made to encourage the domestic production of coarse linens in the south and west, the Board distributing spinning wheels and other equipment free or at low cost, and giving technical instruction. These efforts were continuing in the years of depression after Waterloo, and in 1823 a number of witnesses before the Commons Committee on the Employment of the Poor in Ireland concurred in the view that they were of great value to the cottiers and small farmers.[1] The Committee 'looked with the

---

[1] See evidence of Thomas Oldham, p. 59; Henry Grattan, p. 128; Countess of Glengall, p. 183, *Minutes of Evidence Before Select Committee on Employment of the Poor in Ireland* (1823 (561), vol. VI).

greatest solicitude' to the development of the linen trade in the south, but gave only tepid support to official encouragement for it by grants of equipment and premiums. 'Aid might be given in all these respects to the people, not substituting public for private effort, but assisting and encouraging the latter, and making all public assistance strictly dependent upon local contributions.'[1]

Such care and economy had never been characteristic of the Linen Board, whose Trustees were constantly under fire from the Commissioners of Accounts for their slackness and extravagance. Their activities came in for serious criticism from Joseph Hume and other Radicals, who considered the Board a survival of a discredited system. In 1825, Hume moved a reduction of £10,000 in the annual grant to the Board;[2] this did not succeed, but shortly afterwards a committee was appointed to investigate the whole state of the Irish linen trade.

While the Committee made no secret of the fact that they considered the organisation of the Irish industry to be backward by comparison with similar trades in England and Scotland, they confessed to 'an unwillingness to force any hasty changes upon the settled habits of a people long engaged in an established manufacture' and therefore recommended the continuance, with some slight modifications, of the system of regulation by the Linen Board.[3]

However, many of the larger manufacturers in Ulster seem to have felt that the Linen Board had become more an encumbrance than a help to them. In deference to their views and the opinions expressed in the House, the Government decided to wind up the Board in 1828.[4] Regulations governing the marketing of yarn and cloth were continued until 1842, but while they met with the approval of those in the trade, there was always strong parliamentary criticism when the regulations came up for renewal. Thus in 1835 Hume attacked the Linen Trade (Ireland) Bill as being 'founded upon principles opposed to all those on which the manufactures of this country were founded'. Several Ulster members declared that the Bill was wanted by all concerned in the linen trade, and Hume's attempt to have it thrown out was defeated, Peel saying that 'it was

[1] Report, p. 10, loc. cit. The principle of 'aiding local effort' on which the Committee, like many of their contemporaries, laid such stress, was strongly criticised by J. P. Kennedy, an able engineer officer who was later Secretary to the Devon Commission and to the first Famine Relief Commission. 'Nine out of ten of the very few who are to be found where the "local effort" is required to be made, have no inclination whatever to make the "local effort"', wrote Kennedy. 'Had the Committee urged the necessity of *forcing forth the local efforts of the rich*, instead of "only aiding" them, the recommendation would have been admirable.' *Instruct; Employ; Don't Hang Them* (London, 1835), p. 60.
[2] *Hansard*, 2nd ser. vol. XII, cols. 1078–81 (18 March 1825).
[3] *Report from the Select Committee on the Linen Trade of Ireland* (1825 (463), vol. v), p. 4.
[4] For a fuller account of these developments, see C. Gill, *The Rise of the Irish Linen Industry* (Oxford, 1925), ch. XV.

inexpedient to force even right principles on those who were engaged in the manufacture in question....But he confessed he had some doubts respecting it, and could not clearly see that that must be good for Ireland which was not considered good for other countries.'[1]

With the whole trend of legislative thought thus set against the continuance of existing forms of regulation and protection, it was scarcely likely that any extension of such intervention would be possible. So in 1825 when a deputation led by the Duke of Devonshire proposed to the Prime Minister that the Government might encourage manufacturers to invest their circulating capital in Ireland by granting a loan to be used in providing buildings and machinery, Lord Liverpool replied that 'loans were expedients and contrary to political economy—and that as such it was the determination of His Majesty's Ministers not to use them'.[2]

While direct intervention to aid industry might be neither good political economy nor sound practical politics, it was everywhere admitted to be a first essential for the growth of private enterprise that Government should provide a stable framework within which such enterprise could flourish. It has already been pointed out that the classical economists constantly stressed the importance of 'security' as a condition precedent for investment and recognised that the condition was not fulfilled in Ireland. Here was a field in which Government action was not merely desirable, but imperative; when Senior wrote that 'to explain what are the causes of the relative increase of subsistence and population is rather the business of a writer on politics than of a Political Economist',[3] he had in mind the need for political security as the foundation for economic development.

'Security' in itself is a vague term, but it is not difficult to draw up an agreed list of the essential elements comprised in it from the writings of the classical school. Such a list would include, primarily, security of property—a fundamental economic incentive according to the Utilitarian code—sound enforcement and administration of the law, civil and religious liberty, and the availability of general education. To this basic list might be added measures to promote freedom of exchange and facility of communication.[4] A list specifically applicable to Ireland was drawn up by McCulloch, and this included Catholic emancipation, reform of the tithe system and reduction of the Church of Ireland establishment, abolition of the separate Irish executive and reform of the magistracy, and the extension of education.[5]

---

[1] *Hansard*, 3rd ser. vol. xxix, cols. 273–6 (6 July 1835). The final abolition of the regulations governing the Irish linen trade came soon after their condemnation in the Report of the Commission on the Condition of the Hand Loom Weavers, drafted by Senior. See *Report* (1841 [296], vol. x), pp. 94–8.
[2] Quoted in Elmore, p. 127.   [3] Senior, *Political Economy*, p. 49.
[4] Cf. Ricardo, *Principles, Works and Correspondence* ed. Sraffa, vol. I, p. 99; Malthus, *Principles*, pp. 226, 309, 350; Mill, *Elements*, p. 44; Senior, *Political Economy*, p. 49.
[5] [McCulloch], 'Ireland', p. 64.

In this field at least, the achievements of the policy-makers did not fall far short of the desires of the political economists. The first half of the nineteenth century did witness a considerable overhaul of the machinery of government in Ireland, many abuses and sinecures being abolished. The magistracy was overhauled, and the appointment of sheriffs reformed; after 1835 an effective police force was introduced.[1]

Catholic emancipation was achieved, albeit somewhat belatedly, in 1829, and under the Whig administration of Morpeth and Drummond from 1835 to 1841 some attempt was made to bring into force that 'equal admissibility to rank and power' which Senior regarded as important to economic progress. The reform of the tithe system was begun in 1823 and completed, after much controversy, in 1838, while some redistribution of the funds of the established Church was achieved by the Irish Church Temporalities Act of 1833.[2]

Under pressure of public opinion, which strongly favoured education as a panacea for Irish problems, Stanley, the Chief Secretary for Ireland in Grey's administration, decided to set up a National Board of Education. The Board achieved considerable success in establishing a national system of free primary education, and also provided agricultural instruction in district model schools.[3]

Stanley was also responsible at this period for the establishment of the Board of Works and for certain reforms in the grand-jury system, which greatly facilitated and encouraged the undertaking of those public works which the economists had always regarded as the essential foundation for private enterprise.[4]

Thus the 'Age of Reform' was not without its impact on Ireland, and it could be said that successive Governments did virtually all that the economists required of them in creating an appropriate environment for the growth of private enterprise.[5] Anything more than this would not be

[1] See McDowell, especially chs. 3 and 7; idem, 'Ireland on the Eve of the Famine', in The Great Famine.

[2] 3 and 4 Will. IV, c. 37; see Emerson, 'The Last Phase of the Establishment', History of the Church of Ireland, ed. W. Alison Phillips (London, 1933), vol. III, pp. 302–5.

[3] See McDowell, 'Ireland on the Eve of the Famine', pp. 55–62; Auchmuty, Irish Education: A Historical Survey (Dublin and London, 1937), ch. IV.

[4] See below, ch. VI. The establishment of the Irish Poor Law might be added to the list of reforms: its effects for economic advance were debatable, but many contemporary observers considered it an important means of ensuring 'tranquillity'. See memorandum of Larcom to Lord St Germans, January 1854; Aberdeen Papers, B.M. Add. MSS. 43208.

[5] There was one further respect in which the Government might have aided enterprise in Ireland, but did not—by lightening the burden of taxation. Complaints against over-taxation were common in Ireland, from the beginnings of the Repeal movement, but became numerous and specific after the extension of the income tax to Ireland in 1853. The ensuing debate culminated in the appointment, in 1894, of a Royal Commission whose members reported 'That the Act of Union imposed upon Ireland a burden which, as events showed, she was unable to bear' and 'that whilst the actual tax revenue of Ireland is about one-eleventh of that of Great Britain the relative taxable capacity of Ireland is very much smaller, and is not estimated by any of us as exceeding one-twentieth' (Royal Commission on the

undertaken, as previous instances have shown. Even when, in 1828, Anglesey put forward a scheme to guarantee those establishing manufactures in Ireland against arson and malicious damage—a proposal which might have been thought to come within the definition of 'creating security' —Peel rejected it flatly, saying that 'there are real and solid objections to the direct interference of the Executive Government in the establishment of manufactures—either by pecuniary advances or guarantees'.[1]

In addition to creating the appropriate background for the growth of private enterprise, it was always agreed that the State must assume the duty of providing the economy with a stable currency—a task which would necessarily involve exercising some control over the activities of bankers.[2] Great Britain and Ireland possessed separate currencies until 1826; in the early part of the nineteenth century the Irish currency was in a somewhat disordered state, with many counterfeit coins and tokens in circulation, whilst in consequence of the suspension of specie payments in 1797, there was considerable expansion of the note issue, both of the Bank of Ireland and private banks, causing depreciation and an adverse Dublin—London exchange rate both in 1803–4 and again in 1815–16.[3]

The laws governing banking in Ireland at the opening of the period here under consideration were broadly similar to those of England. The Bank of Ireland had been founded in 1783 by an Act which prohibited any other corporation or body of persons more than six in number from issuing notes.[4] While this prevented other joint-stock concerns from competing with the Bank of Ireland, it did not prevent the establishment of private banks, and during the Restriction period a great many small and dubious firms began to issue notes, especially in the country districts. Many of these proved unable to stand up to the consequences of the period of depression and falling prices which came after the end of the Napoleonic war. A serious banking crisis developed in the south in the early summer of 1820, which only ten private banks outside Dublin ultimately survived.[5] The result was to leave most areas without any banking facilities—since the Bank of Ireland had then no branches—and with a much contracted

---

Financial Relations between Great Britain and Ireland, Final Report (1896 [C. 8262], vol. XXXII), p. 2).
The 'over-taxation issue' did not come into much prominence until after the period covered by this study, and hence no full account of the public discussion is given here. A fairly detailed, though by no means impartial, survey of it is given in T. Kennedy, *History of the Irish Protest against Over-Taxation, from 1853 to 1897* (Dublin, 1897).
[1] Anglesey to Peel, 14 May 1828; Peel to Anglesey, 20 May, 26 July 1828 (Anglesey Papers, T 1068/1 and D.O.D. 619; V).
[2] See Adam Smith, *Wealth of Nations*, bk. II, ch. II (Cannan's ed. vol. I, pp. 305–12); Ricardo, *Principles, Works and Correspondence*, ed. Sraffa, vol. I, p. 356.
[3] For a full account of these conditions, see Fetter, *The Irish Pound, 1797–1826.*
[4] 21 and 22 Geo. III. c. 16 (Ir.).
[5] See F. G. Hall, *The Bank of Ireland, 1783–1946* (Dublin and Oxford, 1949), p. 130. On p. 120 Mr Hall lists forty-four private banks in operation outside Dublin in 1804.

circulating medium. Not only was great hardship inflicted on those who held the issues of the many banks which failed, but a continuing check was given to economic activity generally.

At first the crisis was so serious in its effects that the Government was compelled to the unusual step of making advances, usually on the security of goods in stock, to traders who were solvent but not liquid. These advances were made by a specially constituted Commission for the Relief of Trade and Manufactures, out of the balance of funds voted in 1817 for public works and measures of relief to meet the partial famine of that year. By 1823, Goulburn was able to tell the Lord-Lieutenant that 'latterly (the advances) have not been much called into operation',[1] but the disastrous exposure of the weakness of the private banks led to widespread pressure for legislative changes which would allow the establishment of other joint-stock banks besides the Bank of Ireland. Business interests in the north-east, where industry was developing rapidly, were particularly anxious for such reforms, and in 1824 the Government yielded to an influential petition from Belfast, and put through an Act allowing banking concerns with more than six members to be set up outside a radius of fifty Irish miles from Dublin.[2] As a result of this, and an amending Act of 1825,[3] a number of joint-stock banks were established in the next decade, and the Bank of Ireland was forced to adopt a system of branches in order to meet their competition. While most of the new joint-stock banks were substantial and well-managed undertakings, such as the Provincial Bank established by Thomas Joplin, the state of the law allowed some less reputable banks to be set up and a few spectacular failures occurred, most notably that of the 'Agricultural and Commercial Bank' in 1836.[4]

These developments are a close reflection of those which were occurring in the English banking system at the same period, but the problem of banking did not stimulate any discussion in Ireland which could be compared, either in quality or extent, to the 'Banking and Currency' controversy in England—nor did the participants in that controversy give any attention to the particular problems of Irish banking.

In Ireland, discussion mainly concerned the position of the Bank of Ireland and the extension or limitation of its powers. There were many critics of the partial monopoly which that Bank enjoyed, who charged it with providing inadequate facilities and pursuing a generally restrictive

---

[1] Goulburn to Wellesley, 24 May 1823 (B.M. Add. MSS. 37301).
[2] 5 Geo. IV, c. 173.
[3] 6 Geo. IV, c. 42.
[4] This concern was founded by two men of no substance or banking experience, whose names chanced to be identical with those of two reputable Dublin merchants; consequently many were induced to take up shares in the Bank through a misapprehension about the integrity of its directors. See [M. Longfield], 'Banking and Currency', *Dublin University Magazine*, vol. XVI (October 1840), pp. 373–80; M. Dillon, *History and Development of Banking in Ireland* (London and Dublin, 1889), ch. VIII.

policy; to them the solution appeared to lie in encouraging competitive joint-stock banking over the whole country.[1]

The extent of actual and potential frauds in joint-stock banking led others to advocate that the Bank of Ireland monopoly should be made complete, at least in the matter of note issue. This was the view taken by Longfield, who argued that note issue must be regarded as a public function, 'which is not any part of the business of a banker'.[2]

Once Peel had become convinced of the truth of the Currency School doctrine, and incorporated it in the 1844 Act, he seems to have determined to apply the principles of that Act to Ireland, with some prior consultation with Irish bankers, but none with Irish economists.[3]

The 1844 Act prohibited the establishment of new banks of issue throughout the United Kingdom, but differences in the banking structures of Scotland and Ireland made it necessary to have separate legislation for these countries in order to implement the principles of the English Act in them. Accordingly the Bankers (Ireland) Act, 1845, was passed; this removed the partial monopoly of the Bank of Ireland, but confined the right of note issue to those banks which had issued notes during the year ended 1 May 1845. All these banks were allowed a fiduciary issue, and no provision was made for their note issues to lapse in the event of amalgamation or for any corresponding expansion of the Bank of Ireland issue to take place in that event.

Under this Act the existing joint-stock concerns and the Bank of Ireland continued their existence side by side; the composition of the Irish banking system was altered by the establishment of some new banks and the failure of a few old ones, but its structure remained essentially unaltered after 1845.[4]

Thus by the course of legislation Ireland was provided with a banking system closely similar to the English one, and intimately linked with it. How did this system meet the needs of the Irish economy for the provision of credit facilities? Not a few contemporary observers were of the opinion that it did not meet them well; common charges against the Irish banks were that they provided inadequate banking service outside urban areas, pursued an ultra-cautious lending policy, and invested most of their funds in London instead of aiding local enterprise.[5]

---

[1] G. L. Smyth, *Banking in Ireland, Remarks upon the Renewal of the Charter of the Bank of Ireland* (London, 1840). 'Report of the Committee on Joint-Stock Banking in Ireland', in *Reports of the Parliamentary Committee of the Loyal National Repeal Association of Ireland* (Dublin, 1844).

[2] [M. Longfield], 'Banking and Currency—Part II', *Dublin University Magazine*, vol. xv (February 1840), p. 121. This was one of a series of four articles under this title by Longfield, which appeared in vols. xv and xvi of the *Dublin University Magazine*.

[3] See Hall, *The Bank of Ireland, 1783–1946*, pp. 201–5.

[4] For details of the changes in the composition of the Irish banking system, see Hall, *The Bank of Ireland*.

[5] See *Reports of the Parliamentary Committee...Repeal Association*, vol. 1 (1844); C. Dennehy, *Letters on the Banking Systems and Industrial Resources of Ireland* (Dublin,

The first of these charges appears to have had more substance in the years before the Famine than after it. The Bank of Ireland monopoly retarded the spread of banks, and it was very slow to embark on the opening of branches itself. Apart from this, there was little incentive to extend banking facilities in many parts of the country; the potato-truck system minimised the use of money, and the frequent disturbances which occurred in rural areas made the transfer of funds between branches appear a risky matter. After about 1850, however, there was quite a rapid expansion of banking facilities, due mainly to the improvements in transport and the increase of cash transactions.

That the banks lent cautiously was true, and it followed inevitably from this that much of their business was done outside Ireland. Yet while this might be accepted as a fact, to claim, as critics did, that the banks were to blame for the existence of such a state of affairs, is a wholly different matter. The banks' duty to their depositors automatically involved caution in lending, and if they lent little in Ireland, it was because few sound projects were offered to them. The main outlet for lending was agriculture, and many farmers could have used loans to advantage, but so long as they possessed no security of tenure, bankers could not treat them as a good credit risk. Nor could they create investment opportunities in industry where none existed; where industry did gain a footing, as in Ulster, there were no complaints of growth being handicapped for lack of credit facilities.

The joint-stock banking system always endeavoured to follow the English tradition of short-term lending—in fact, aiding the provision of working capital. There remained two other aspects of the investment process in which attempts could be, and to some extent were, made to aid economic progress by improved organisation. One was the collection of small savings and the making of small loans; the other, the provision of long-term capital.

The ordinary processes of banking generally lay outside the economic horizon of the Irish cottier and small farmer in the early nineteenth century, but many of them contrived to accumulate some savings, which were commonly hoarded. The charitable savings bank movement, with its aims of encouraging self-reliance and providence, took early root in Ireland, and considerable sums were deposited by the poorer classes.[1] The security afforded the depositors in these banks was unfortunately defective,

1873); W. N. Hancock, 'Complaints against Bankers in Ireland', *Journal of the Statistical and Social Inquiry Society of Ireland*, vol. VI (1875), p. 523.
[1] The first savings bank in Ireland was established at Stillorgan, near Dublin, in 1815; see H. O. Horne, *A History of Savings Banks* (London, 1947), p. 69. According to a report furnished to the Lord-Lieutenant in 1830, £46,615 was paid into Irish savings banks in 1821, and £213,020 in 1830, at which date 'about one Million remains in the savings in Ireland' (Anglesey Papers, D.O.D. 619). The total deposits amounted to £2,143,082 in 1860 (Hancock, *Decline of Irish Prosperity*, p. 52).

and some considerable frauds occurred. Serious defalcations at Dublin, Tralee and Killarney came to light in 1848, and Lord John Russell's Government procured the passing of an Act which increased the liability of savings bank trustees in Ireland. This was little more than a stop-gap measure, and depositors did not in fact obtain real security until the establishment of the Post Office Savings Bank in 1861 and the passing of the Trustee Savings Bank Act of 1863.[1] This lack of security was frequently exposed and condemned by Hancock, who was one of the first to propose that the Post Office should undertake savings bank functions.[2]

From 1817 onwards the law required that the funds of the savings banks should be invested in public securities through the National Debt Commissioners, so that these balances were not invested in Ireland.[3] It was clearly undesirable that small savings should be used in any way which did not afford the highest possible security; small traders often stood in need of small advances, which involved too little profit and too much risk for joint-stock banks to make them. Such borrowers were therefore often driven into the clutches of village usurers, the ill-famed 'gombeen men'. To meet this situation charitable loan funds were established in many areas. Some such funds existed in the eighteenth century, but their number greatly increased in the nineteenth. From 1823 onwards, there were two distinct loan fund systems in operation in Ireland, for the London Tavern Committee, which had been formed to administer the subscriptions made for the relief of distress in the partial famine of 1822, wound up its operations with a surplus of some £55,000, which it was decided to form into an 'Irish Reproductive Loan Fund'. Since the money had been subscribed for relief in ten counties of the south and west, it was decided to form loan funds in each of these counties.[4] Other private loan funds continued to exist, and an Act was passed in 1823 to protect their funds and encourage their extension.[5]

This Act was not very carefully drawn, and a number of abuses in the

---

[1] See Horne, *Savings Banks*, especially chs. IX and XII.
[2] See his papers: 'What are the Duties of the Public with Respect to Charitable Savings Banks?' (April 1852), and 'Present State of the Savings Bank Question', *Journal of the Dublin Statistical Society*, vol. I (1855), p. 58.
[3] But the possibility of their being so invested was discussed in official circles once at least. On 20 September 1847, Clarendon wrote to G. R. Porter at the Board of Trade, saying that he 'liked the notion of making the deposits in Savings Banks applicable for loans on good security'. The proposal did not meet with the approval of Charles Wood, who wrote: 'I do not think it would do to employ Savings Bank money in such a way— they are a very ticklish concern—the obvious object for a run, and I should be sorry to expose them to a chance of that kind'—Wood to Clarendon, 23 October 1847 (Clarendon Papers).
[4] Some of the funds were employed for advances in kind—of flax, flax-seed and hand looms—to encourage domestic production of linen in the counties concerned. See evidence of Wm. Hyett, *Minutes of Evidence before the Select Committee on Employment of the Poor in Ireland* (1823 [561], vol. VI), pp. 17–19.
[5] 4 Geo. IV, c. 32.

management of loan funds grew up under it. Some of these arose from benevolence rather than dishonesty, but in a number of cases the trustees and officers of the funds converted moneys to their own use, for while the Act forbade the payment of salaries to them, it allowed 'all necessary expenses', a conveniently elastic phrase. The local officers of the Irish Reproductive Loan Fund, to whom the funds had been entrusted by the London Committee, were also lax in their management, and much of the capital remained either unused or misused.[1]

In an attempt to meet these abuses, a new Act was passed in 1836, which placed the loan societies under the supervision of a Loan Fund Board.[2] This Act fixed the maximum rate of interest chargeable at 6d. in the £ for loans from £1 to £10 repayable over a period of 20 weeks.[3] The societies were also authorised to receive money on deposit, paying interest up to 6% on it. For the next ten years, the numbers and capital of loan funds continued to grow steadily, but the Famine was, inevitably, a serious set-back to them. Many societies were wound up at this time and the operations of the Irish Reproductive Loan Fund were completely terminated. For some years the directors of that institution had begun to realise that they could not effectively control their local officers in the use of the funds, and they decided to wind up the Fund and hand the balance over to the Treasury to be used for charitable purposes.[4]

In 1852 and 1853 the Central Loan Fund Board urged the necessity of inquiry into the management of loan societies, and accordingly a Select Committee was set up to investigate the whole system in 1854.[5] Some witnesses expressed the feeling that loan funds tended to encourage improvidence and habits of contracting debts amongst the poor, but the Committee approved the principle of the funds as conferring substantial benefits on small farmers and traders, whilst suggesting various improvements in their management. Although in later years the system of charitable loan funds continued in operation, it never regained the importance which it had had before 1846.[6]

At the opposite end of the scale, those risk factors which tended to deter

---

[1] See Inglis, *Ireland in 1834*, vol. I, pp. 310–11.

[2] 6 and 7 Will. IV, c. 55. The Irish Reproductive Loan Fund Institution was exempt from the provisions of this Act.

[3] In 1844, the maximum rate of interest was reduced to 4d in the £ for twenty weeks. Even at this rate borrowing was expensive, but the trustees argued that the risk element necessitated a high interest rate. See *Report and Minutes of Evidence...Select Committee on Loan Fund Societies (Ireland)* (1854–5 (259), vol. VII).

[4] See Evidence of F. R. Bertolacci in the *Minutes* cited in note 3. An Act of 1848 (11 and 12 Vic. c. 115) transferred the funds of the Irish Reproductive Loan Fund Institution to the Treasury, to be distributed on the recommendation of the Lord-Lieutenant.

[5] See *Fifteenth Annual Report of the Loan Fund Board, Ireland* (1852–3 [1638], vol. XLI), p. 6.

[6] Between 1848 and 1868 the number of Loan Funds fell from 177 to 90, and their circulation from £717,000 to £581,000: Dillon, *History and Development of Banking in Ireland*, p. 109.

investment in Ireland naturally operated with particular force in regard to the provision of long-term capital. It was often suggested that these deterrents might be offset if the investor were given the protection of some simply obtainable form of limited liability. Thus in 1836 Senior recommended 'that the introduction of capital into Ireland be encouraged by permitting the establishment of partnerships *in commandite*, as allowed by the laws of France'.[1] In point of fact, a law which permitted the formation of such partnerships had been passed by the Irish Parliament in 1782: it provided that firms could take in 'anonymous partners' who would not be subject to the bankruptcy laws nor liable for debts of the partnership beyond the amount they originally subscribed. Such partnerships were limited to fourteen years' duration, and were required to have a total capital of not less than £1000 or more than £50,000.[2] Very few capitalists had ever taken advantage of this law, the reason given being 'the risk attending any accidental non-compliance with the strict and minute provisions of the Act'.[3] In three successive parliamentary sessions, 1818, 1819, and 1820, Bills were introduced by the member for the city of London, Alderman Matthew Wood, to promote employment in Ireland by consolidating and extending the provisions of the Act of 1782, but none of these passed. In later years, limited partnership in Ireland continued to have its advocates, not a few of whom seem to have been unaware of the existence of the law of 1782,[4] but no official steps were taken to give investors in Ireland the protection of limited liability before the legislation of 1855–6 conceded the privilege for the United Kingdom as a whole.[5]

III

It remains to consider the actual development of investment which occurred within the framework created by policy. It has already been pointed out that conditions at the beginning of the nineteenth century were not such as to encourage investment either in agriculture or industry, and nothing that was done during the period covered here was sufficient

---

[1] *Letter from N. W. Senior, Esq. on the Third Report from the Commissioners for Inquiring into the Condition of the Poor in Ireland* (1837 [90], vol. LI), p. 12.

[2] 21 and 22 Geo. III, c. 46 (Ir.).

[3] *Report from the Select Committee on Joint-Stock Companies*, Appendix no. 1 (1844 (119), vol. VII), p. 260.

[4] Senior cannot have been unaware of it when he wrote the passage quoted above, for his attention had been specifically drawn to it in the course of an examination before a parliamentary committee on 15 March 1836. He then admitted to the Chairman that he had not previously known of the Act. See extract no. 14 printed in Appendix no. 1 cited above.

For contemporary discussion of limited partnership for Ireland, see H. Colles, 'Inquiry as to the Policy of Limited Liability in Partnerships', *Social Inquiry Society Papers* (1852); J. Pim, 'Partnership of Limited Liability', *Transactions of the Dublin Statistical Society*, vol. III (1852); P. McKenna, 'Partnerships with Limited Liability', *Trans. D.S.S.* vol. III (1853) and *J.D.S.S.* vol. I (1856), p. 136.

[5] See L. C. B. Gower, *Principles of Modern Company Law* (London, 1954), pp. 40–7.

to stimulate it to the extent necessary to bring about that relation of capital to population which the economists regarded as desirable.

In the years before the Famine, the wholly inadequate capitalisation of agriculture might be blamed on the state of the law, which hindered the sale and purchase of land, as well as investment in the land by tenants and landlords alike. After the Famine the prospects for investment in and on the land would seem, on the face of things, to have been much enhanced by the Land Improvement Act of 1847 and the Incumbered Estates Act of 1849—but the expectations generated by these were not realised, for reasons which have already been discussed.[1] There was no marked influx of improving landlords or enterprising capitalist tenants. Nassau Senior's brother, Edward, who was one of the Irish Poor Law Commissioners, discussed the question of investment in Irish land with him in 1858. '...the profit must be very great', he told the economist, 'for profit is the only motive for buying land here. In England, one may wish to live among one's own tenants, to be useful to them, to enjoy the rank and position of a proprietor. These motives do not exist in Ireland, except in the case of a purchase on a very large scale....If I were a purchaser, therefore, I should be an absentee.'[2] This was the attitude which most purchasers did in fact take, and so long as they did they were scarcely likely to attract improving tenants.

So far as investment in industry is concerned, none of the legislative measures which were introduced during the period altered the basic conditions which inhibited it at the outset—although it might be argued that those conditions were altered for the worse by the growing strength of English industry and the removal in 1826 of such protection as Irish manufactures had possessed. Yet while industrial development never occurred to an extent sufficient to employ the whole population surplus to the needs of agriculture, it was certainly not wholly absent. In the north-east it was considerable and varied, sufficient to give Belfast at least a close similarity to the rapidly growing industrial cities of the north of England. This pattern was not repeated anywhere else, but the south was not without examples of successful enterprise. Flour milling, brewing and distilling, natural concomitants of agriculture, were always standard cases of home industry, but not all Irish capitalists were to be found in these trades. In the eighteen-thirties, William Malcolmson employed 900 people in his cotton factory at Portlaw, Co. Waterford, and Charles Bianconi, an Italian immigrant, provided cheap transport throughout the south of Ireland, before the coming of railways, with his famous 'long cars', while in the next decade William Dargan gained a fortune and a high reputation as the contractor responsible for almost every railway built in Ireland. But these were isolated examples of success, all the more

[1] Above, ch. II, pp. 40–1.
[2] Senior, *Journals Relating to Ireland*, vol. II, pp. 109–10.

admired and extolled by contemporaries because of their rarity. Viewed overall, industrial development in the south of Ireland was trifling, in comparison either with the development in England or the numbers of the local population.

The vital point which requires explanation in all this is the disproportion between the growth of industry in the north-east and in the rest of Ireland. Ulster was no better provided with power sources or raw materials than the rest of Ireland, and the trades unions which were said to have driven industry from Dublin were no less violent in Belfast.[1] It is true that Ulster industries did not depend on the impoverished and limited Irish market, and that being based on imported materials and exported products they thrived under a free-trade regime. Yet this only puts off the real question— if such industries could be successfully located in Belfast, why could they not also grow in Dublin, Cork or Limerick?

Many contemporary observers thought that the cause could be found in the Presbyterianism of the north and the Roman Catholicism of the south. An alternative explanation was suggested by H. D. Inglis, who argued that both Protestants and Catholics were more prosperous in the north than in the south and traced the difference to the fact that 'the people of the north are of Scotch descent; and there cannot be found, throughout the north, any of that improvidence which is so detrimental to the condition of society in the south and west'.[2] Actually this theory was not so clearly distinct from the explanation on religious grounds as Inglis appeared to believe, for most of those in the north who could claim Scots descent were also Presbyterian.

To assess the proper weight to be given to religion and character in creating economic distinctions must always be a difficult matter, but there can be no doubt that the latter part of Inglis's statement was true enough; the people of the north did devote more time and energy to their work and less to fairs and race-meetings, 'patterns' and wakes than did the people of the south. In part this may well have been due to the fact that their religion and upbringing taught them to respect the virtues of thrift and industry more highly, but it is difficult to believe that the difference would have been so marked if the northerner had had as little chance of being allowed to retain the fruits of his industry as the southerner had. In short, while other influences may have played their part, the real key to the differing industrial development of the north and south lay in that factor which the classical economists had stressed so much—security. In the north landlord and tenant shared the same outlook, and the tenant enjoyed security by custom. Agrarian outrage was therefore absent, and money could safely be invested in farms. There was some incentive to

[1] See Edward Harland's account of his labour troubles in the early days of the Belfast shipyard in Smiles, *Men of Invention and Industry* (London, 1884), p. 303.
[2] Inglis, *Ireland in 1834*, vol. II, p. 216.

domestic industry, because the cottager, and not his landlord, obtained the proceeds of it: hence the textile industry was well established in Ulster when the Industrial Revolution came and quite capable of adapting itself to the change. Into this setting other industries could fit readily enough once the necessary foundations for profitable investment and enterprise had been shown to exist.[1]

Yet if security in the north and insecurity in the south are pointed out as the root causes of divergent economic development, it must also be pointed out that security in the north resulted primarily from the existence there of a land system which the classical economists, with the exception of such men as John Stuart Mill, neither understood nor advocated. In this regard there was a fundamental, but unperceived, contradiction in the classical prescription for Ireland. It urged the creation of a prosperous agriculture on the English model within a framework of political stability —but ignored the fact that since the Irish people believed the English land law to be essentially unjust, there could never be political stability, and hence economic security, while that law was suffered to remain unamended in Ireland. In turn, the amendments in the land laws necessary to produce stability and security would have been incompatible with the establishment of that type of economy which the economists envisaged; but that they would not have been incompatible with the achievement of some measure of prosperity was shown by the example of east Ulster.

---

[1] For some account of the processes whereby domestic industry in east Ulster was transmuted into factory industry, located mainly in Belfast, and other trades added to the basic textile industry, see E. R. R. Green, 'The Beginnings of Industrial Revolution' and R. D. C. Black, 'The Progress of Industrialization, 1850–1920', *Ulster since 1800* (London, 1954).

CHAPTER VI

PUBLIC WORKS

I

THE subject of public works receives comparatively little direct discussion in the writings of the major classical economists. The fullest treatment is that of Adam Smith, who listed amongst the duties of the sovereign 'that of erecting and maintaining those public institutions and those public works, which, though they may be in the highest degree advantageous to a great society, are, however, of such a nature that the profit could never repay the expense to any individual or small number of individuals, and which it therefore cannot be expected that any individual or small number of individuals should erect or maintain'.[1]

Amongst such public works Smith listed those 'which facilitate the commerce of any country, such as good roads, bridges, navigable canals, harbours, etc.', but argued that for the most part they might be 'so managed as to afford a particular revenue sufficient for defraying their own expense, without bringing any burden upon the general revenue of the society'.[2] Where public works could not be so managed, Smith maintained that they should wherever possible be managed by local authorities and financed out of local taxes, in preference to their being made a responsibility of the central government.

Most of Smith's followers appear to have acquiesced in these views: there is no direct discussion of public works in Ricardo's *Principles* or Mill's *Elements*, but passages in McCulloch's *Principles* appear to reflect Smith's ideas fairly closely.[3] McCulloch took a somewhat wider view than Smith, for he considered it 'the duty of government...to assist, by making grants, in enabling roads to be carried through districts, and bridges to be constructed, where the necessary funds could not otherwise be raised'. 'As a general rule, however', he added, 'government ought to be exceedingly shy about advancing funds for the prosecution of undertakings that have failed in the hands of private individuals, or that will not be engaged in by them', and gave the example of Irish canals as a case in point.

From such statements as these it has customarily been inferred that the English classical school was uniformly opposed to anything more than the barest minimum of public enterprise, and insistent on that being managed

---

[1] Smith, *Wealth of Nations*, bk. v, ch. v, pt. III.
[2] *Idem.*
[3] McCulloch, *Principles of Political Economy*, pp. 279–84.

according to the strictest criteria of economy. This is a view of their attitude which was shared by contemporaries. Even J.-B. Say, usually closely identified with the doctrine of *laissez faire*, felt that the English attitude to public works was sometimes unduly rigid:

Il me semble qu'en Angleterre on est trop porté à croire qu'un édifice public, un pont, un canal, un bassin de navigation qui ne rapportent pas l'intérêt des avances et les frais d'entretien qu'ils coutent ne méritent pas d'être construits; d'où résulte une sorte de préjugé contre les établissements que les associations particulières ne veulent pas entreprendre, et qui ont besoin d'avoir recours à l'appui et aux fonds du gouvernement, c'est à dire, de la nation.[1]

That a general presumption against the State undertaking any enterprise which could be tackled by private initiative exists in the writings of the English classical economists is beyond all question—but their whole philosophy on the subject of public works cannot be deduced from this. The presumption against public enterprise in classical economics was always associated with a recognition that a certain minimum of State activity was inevitable and essential. It is usually taken for granted that these activities were confined to defence, police and administration of justice—what modern writers refer to as 'keeping the ring'. Yet it is clear that most of the classical authors believed that the State would not merely have to keep the ring, but also build it; the passages already cited from Smith and McCulloch are typical enough in this respect. If they also show something of that narrow insistence on the criterion of profitability in public works, of which Say complained, that would seem to be because, though general in form, they were primarily made with the British economy in mind. In such a society, where the volume of trade and commerce was already large, the basic facilities of communication and exchange were largely inherited from the past, and it would be legitimate to apply fairly strict tests of profitability to any improvements or extensions of them. With a considerable volume of capital seeking investment outlets, it would also be right for the Government to be 'exceedingly shy' of undertaking works where private agencies were available.

It was the tendency to take this background for granted which led the classical economists, explicitly or implicitly, to minimise the role of government, and especially the central government, in undertaking construction and other enterprises. On the other hand, when their attention was specifically directed to societies in which the essential public works were lacking, they were quite prepared to place it amongst the essential duties of the State to undertake them. Thus when that staunch interpreter of classical orthodoxy, Miss Harriet Martineau, visited the United States and turned her attention to the question of the right of Congress to use public funds for internal improvements, she afterwards wrote that 'to an

[1] J.-B. Say, *Cours complet d'économie politique pratique*, 7th ed. (Brussels, 1844), p. 453.

impartial observer it appears...that some degree of such power in the hands of the general government is desirable and necessary'.[1] Professor Carter Goodrich has shown how, in the American discussions of the period, advocacy of Federal action on internal improvements was frequently combined with acceptance of *laissez faire*, the improvements being thought of as necessary to create the basic structure within which private enterprise could function unhindered.[2]

Similarly, when Senior came to deal specifically with the case of Ireland in his *Letter to Lord Howick* of 1831, he advocated a vigorous programme of economic development which included advances by the Government for the building of roads, canals, railways and harbours, as well as drainage and reclamation of waste lands—a programme very much akin to that which Whately later endorsed as Chairman of the Irish Poor Inquiry Commissioners in 1836, and one which seems to echo the suggestions made by Rooke for improving the market outlets for Irish agriculture in 1824.[3]

The necessity of qualifying the definition of the proper sphere of public action according to circumstances was specifically recognised and stated by John Stuart Mill:

In the particular circumstances of a given age or nation, there is scarcely anything, really important to the general interest, which it may not be desirable or even necessary, that the government should take upon itself, not because private individuals cannot effectually perform it, but because they will not. At some times and places there will be no roads, docks, harbours, canals, works of irrigation...unless the government establishes them....In many parts of the world, the people can do nothing for themselves which requires large means and combined action; all such things are left undone, unless done by the state.[4]

The expression of such views by Mill is not surprising, but it may be suggested in the light of the evidence given here that most of his predecessors in the classical tradition would not have dissented from them. That there must be a certain basis of public works to facilitate economic activity they all accepted; where possible the cost of these works ought to be borne by those who would most directly benefit from them, and where they could be undertaken by private agencies (as, for example, in the case of railways) then the Government should certainly exercise no more than a regulatory function in connection with them. But these conditions might not everywhere be fulfilled, and where they were not, then the State must assume the duty of constructing and maintaining the requisite works.

[1] H. Martineau, *Society in America*, 2nd ed. (London, 1837), vol. II, p. 215.
[2] C. Goodrich, 'National Planning of Internal Improvements', *Political Science Quarterly*, vol. LXIII, no. 1 (March 1948), see especially pp. 42–3.
[3] Senior, *A Letter to Lord Howick*, pp. 45–6; and see above, ch. IV, pp. 92 and 108; Rooke, *Principles of National Wealth*, p. 137, quoted above, ch. V, p. 143.
[4] Mill, *Principles*, bk. V, ch. XI, § 16.

Normally the orthodox economists thought of public works as contributing to the institutional framework within which private economic activity could be successfully carried on. A considerable programme of such works might be necessary to bring a country up to the point where private enterprise could function to the fullest advantage in it, but in their view it should certainly not be necessary to introduce public works into a developed private enterprise system in order to maintain the volume of employment in it. In such a case all Government expenditure would be liable to the same criticism—that of diverting funds from private to public use, since if the funds were left in private hands they might be used to employ productive labour, whereas the Government would normally employ them unproductively. In fact, transfer of funds from private to public use meant conversion of capital into revenue, and was to that extent undesirable.

The assumption underlying all this—that the fund destined for the maintenance of labour might be indefinitely increased without creating an impossibility of finding employment for it[1]—was not, however, accepted by all the economists of the period. To those who feared the possibility of general overproduction, public works naturally appeared in a more favourable light. Malthus, for example, felt that the tendency of public expenditure to convert capital into revenue might be 'to a certain extent, exactly what is wanted' and contended that 'in our endeavours to assist the working classes (in a period of depression) it is desirable to employ them in those kinds of labour, the results of which do not come for sale into the market, such as roads and public works'.[2]

Views of this kind were not uncommon in the period of distress which followed the Napoleonic wars, when under-consumption theories were enjoying a considerable vogue. The majority of these theories, including Malthus's, relate primarily to the conditions of industrial society and reflect a fear that the continued investment of capital in industry must produce a flood of manufactured products for which no market can be found. Some of their authors were nevertheless prepared to apply the theories to less-developed agricultural economies where 'redundant population' presented a problem.

A remarkable example of this is to be found in the now forgotten economic writings of Major-General Sir William Sleeman, an officer in the service of the East India Company from 1809 to 1854.[3] Sleeman mingled under-consumptionist ideas clearly derived from Malthus and

[1] See Mill, *Principles*, bk. I, ch. v, § 3.
[2] Malthus, *Principles*, p. 51.
[3] Sleeman's two economic works were: *On Taxes, or Public Revenue, the Ultimate Incidence of their Payment, their Disbursement, and the Seats of their Consumption*, by An Officer in the Military and Civil Service of the honourable East India Company (London, 1829); *Analysis and Review of the Peculiar Doctrines of the Ricardo or New School of Political Economy* (Serampore, 1837).

Sismondi with observations based upon his Indian experience. The behaviour of Indian princes who devoted their wealth to the construction of irrigation canals and aqueducts, seeking only 'the gratitude of society and the approbation of the Deity' appeared to Sleeman much more worthy of approval than the activities of Western merchants and manufacturers based on calculations of profit and the desire for accumulation of capital.[1] Like Malthus, Sleeman was impressed with the necessity of maintaining a body of unproductive consumers in society, and argued that in countries like India the great landed proprietors and the Government might confer a double benefit on the mass of the people by giving them employment in the construction of public works which would ultimately improve the productive capacity of the economy. The other country which Sleeman thought especially suited to benefit from a scheme of extended public works was Ireland. 'Perhaps the legislature could hardly confer a greater blessing upon Ireland, than the formation of a few such great works, out of means levied from Absentees, in a tax upon their incomes; and the revenues arising from these might be given to small communities, or deserving Irish families, on condition of their keeping them in a state of efficiency.'[2]

Thus Irish landlords were to be compelled by taxation to do what Indian princes did for 'the approbation of the Deity', and afford employment to their people.

Although at one stage, Sleeman does say 'I should be glad to see a public debt contracted in every district of India, provided I could feel assured that the amount of the loan would be spent in the formation of works useful to the people, and that the interest of the debt should be permanently enjoyed by people residing in these districts'[3] he is generally suspicious of the growth of public debt, and tends to adhere to Adam Smith's principles for the financing of public works from tolls and local taxes.

The proposition that where unemployment exists the Government should attempt to eliminate it by undertaking public works, financed not by taxes but by loans, is to be found quite clearly and generally stated in the work of another very little-known contemporary of Malthus, W. R. A. Pettman, a captain in the Royal Navy. In an *Essay on Political Economy*, published in 1828,[4] Pettman declared that

the burden of debt is much less to be feared than the burden of idleness; but a debt that produces incomes, and an expenditure that finds employment for millions of the population who, but for such expenditure, would not be able to sell their labour, is not a burden, but a capital.... The community at large are benefited by the public money being expended in building palaces, improving harbours, cutting canals...

---

[1] [Sleeman], *On Taxes*, pp. 182, 200–3.
[2] *Ibid.* p. 212.   [3] *Ibid.* p. 223.
[4] W. R. A. Pettman, *An Essay on Political Economy, Parts I and II* (London, 1828).

in short, on any public works that find employment for the labouring classes, and thereby create in them an ability to purchase and consume the commodities produced by each other.[1]

Amongst the 'Propositions and Suggestions' which Pettman based on this line of argument was one for the Government to borrow money and employ it in the reclamation of waste lands in Ireland.[2]

Hence a review of writings on public works in the first half of the nineteenth century reveals the co-existence of two attitudes towards public works policy, which were sharply distinct though not, in this respect, contradictory. On the one hand, orthodox writers envisaged public works as part of the necessary infrastructure of a free-exchange economy, to be built up, if need be, in order to give full scope to the natural forces of economic development. On the other hand, those who were sufficiently unorthodox to see employment as an end which must be deliberately sought, conceived of public works as a valuable means of achieving it, with the possibility of their aiding economic development thrown in as an additional advantage.

Ireland at the time was a backward agricultural region with a serious population problem, and to such a region, clearly, both these arguments for public works could be readily applied. They are to be found constantly recurring in various guises in the numerous works, English and Irish, which put forward solutions for the Irish problem year after year through the whole period covered here. 'Public works' was indeed one of the clichés of this endless debate, and, like all clichés, many writers were none too clear as to the reasons why they were using it. The most obvious reason was that so many Irish were palpably half-idle and half-starved and public employment could give them work and food. Those who advocated the expenditure of public money on these grounds usually argued that it would be counterbalanced by a consequential reduction in the outlay needed for military and political establishments in Ireland.[3] In fact, the reasons offered for giving employment were often as much political as economic; officially as well as unofficially, the hope was frequently entertained that by giving work the people might be prevented not only from joining Whiteboy raiding parties at night, but also from attending Repeal gatherings by day. 'I have got O'Connell in the net. He cannot get out', wrote Anglesey to Holland in 1831, with rather hasty optimism. 'Now, then, send me money to employ the People, without a moment's loss of time. Then, pass quickly a few popular bills...and finally, pay the Priests, and I promise you shall never hear more of O'Connell, or of any such fellow.'[4] The prophecy was not fulfilled, whether

[1] Pettman, *Essay*, pt. II, pp. 74 and 105.   [2] *Ibid.* p. 119.
[3] See, for example, *Reflections on the State of Ireland in the Nineteenth Century* (London, 1822), p. 109.
[4] Anglesey to Holland, 29 January 1831 (Anglesey Papers, T. 1068/7).

or not because the advice was not heeded, and twelve years later, when the Tories had succeeded the Whigs, Lord Devon passed on to Peel a letter from one of his land agents, who wrote: 'I wish the Government would *promptly* put in circulation a large sum of money to neutralize the labourers. All the discontented small shopkeepers, etc., would derive advantage from the extensive employment....'[1]

Those who looked beyond the immediate tranquillising effects of wages and employment usually envisaged public works as a means of creating new facilities for private enterprise, by which permanent employment could be provided after the public works were completed. This argument was very concisely summarised in 1831 by C. W. Williams, whose interest in Irish public works stemmed from his being a director of the Dublin Steam Packet Company, and much interested in the growth of inland navigation: '1. The population want employment. 2. That can only be supplied by the pursuits of agriculture, trade or commerce. 3. These cannot be promoted without intercourse and interchange.' These, in turn, depended on such public works as roads and canals in which, Williams contended, Ireland was sadly deficient.[2]

A few years later the same argument was frequently put forward in reference to railways. The building of railways would not only afford much direct employment, but when completed the lines would improve access to markets so greatly as to open many new opportunities for employment in agriculture and industry.[3]

Arguments of this type, contemplating increasing the public works equipment of the Irish economy to a point which would allow the rapid development of private enterprise, were quite in accord with classical orthodoxy. They also evaded one of the most common criticisms of public employment at the time—that the expenditure could not be continued indefinitely, and that when it came to an end the labourers would be no better off than before, possibly even worse.[4]

Some other schemes of public works proposed for Ireland rather overstepped the limits which most classical economists would have prescribed for State activity, since they aimed not merely at creating the appropriate

---

[1] Alfred Furlong to Devon, 18 June 1843 (Peel Papers, B.M. Add. MSS. 40530).

[2] C. W. Williams, *Observations on an Important Feature in the State of Ireland, and the Want of Employment of its Population* (Westminster, 1831), p. 7.

[3] See *Second Report from the Railway Commissioners, Ireland* (1837–8 [145], vol. xxxv), p. 91.

[4] 'So long as money is expended in carrying on public works, a scanty means of subsistence may be afforded the poor labourer engaged, but at the expiration of the outlay you will not find the wretched man or his miserable family improved in the least degree in their prospects; but, on the contrary, he would be found inhabiting his former hovel, with his physical strength much impaired by hard toil merely for a scanty support'—A. C. Buchanan, *Outline of a Practical Plan for the Relief of the Poor of Ireland* (Brighton, 1837), pp. 9 and 10. See also Bryan, *Practical View of Ireland*, p. 220; W. T. Thornton, *Over-population and its Remedy* (London, 1846), p. 418.

foundation for economic development, but at undertaking that development deliberately—in part at least. The proposals for arterial drainage and the reclamation of waste lands put forward by Poulett Scrope, Thornton and John Stuart Mill[1] might be regarded as coming into this category, since they aimed at a fundamental change in the conditions of occupation and cultivation of land.

Proposals of this kind were always met by the objection that they could be undertaken by private enterprise—and that the fact that they were not was proof that they would be an unprofitable speculation.[2] If Government, then, were to undertake the works it would be diverting funds from more to less profitable uses, and so retarding rather than advancing economic growth. Advocates of large-scale works met these criticisms by saying that the projects they wished to see undertaken were of a long-term character, affording a genuine return, but too slowly to interest private speculators; moreover, they were projects too large for the private investor in a country like Ireland, where capital was scarce.[3]

It was also possible to use the argument, stated generally by Mill, that where private agencies did not exist or were inadequate, the tasks which in better circumstances would fall to them must be undertaken by the public authorities. More rigid economists could counter this with a point which had considerable force in reference to Ireland, before the Famine at least—it could be said that if the Government took on these tasks it would sap the initiative of potential private employers, and encourage them perennially to look to the Government to do what properly they ought to do themselves. In Ireland the main potential employers were the landowners, and there can be little doubt that many of them were all too ready to seek the expenditure of public money which would benefit their estates or put their tenants in funds to pay increased rents; this was a tendency which Ricardo found as prevalent and as exasperating in 1823 as did Charles Wood in 1846.[4]

There was in fact something of a tradition in Ireland in the early nineteenth century that public works and jobbery went hand in hand, and that every man of any influence did his best to get whatever pickings he could from public expenditure.[5] In the light of this it is not surprising that ambitious schemes of Government enterprise were usually received with

---

[1] See above ch. II, p. 30.   [2] See Bryan, p. 220; E. Wakefield, vol. I, p. 85.
[3] See 'Hints for the Cultivation of the Peat-bogs in Ireland', *The Pamphleteer*, vol. IX (1817), p. 84.
[4] Ricardo to Trower, 24 July 1823: 'It is a favourite plan with many, for Government to lend capital to Ireland, in order that the people may be employed. Against such a scheme I have the most decided objections, which I never fail to urge. If the greater part of the Irish members could have their way, we should not only grant a vast number of charitable loans, but we should encourage all sorts of manufactures by bounties and premiums'—*Works and Correspondence*, vol. IX, p. 313; Wood to Bessborough, 9 September 1846, quoted above, ch. IV, p. 115.
[5] E. Wakefield, vol. II, p. 803; Inglis, *Ireland in 1834*, vol. I, p. 237.

more enthusiasm in Dublin Castle than in Whitehall or Westminster. Thus when Anglesey was Lord-Lieutenant in 1828 his frequent and impassioned pleas for 'money to employ the people' met with but a cool reception from Peel, then Home Secretary.

While I admit the melancholy fact that there is a great want of employment for the poor in Ireland, and admit also, that an increase in the demand for labour would be of the utmost advantage to society in that Country, I must at the same time express a doubt whether ultimate advantage would arise from the creation of such a demand by the continued application of large sums of public money [wrote Peel]. In voting the public money in aid of local improvements, it must be borne in mind that, with the best intentions on the part of Government, it is not easy to prevent occasional abuse in the expenditure....It must also be borne in mind that too great a facility on the part of Government in applying the public money in furtherance of such objects has a tendency to discourage local exertions, and to afford an excuse for the indifference and neglect of those, who ought to apply some part of their influence and their wealth in promoting the improvement of their Country.[1]

Very similar views can be found expressed in the speeches and writings of Whig statesmen, such as Russell,[2] whilst, almost forty years later, Gladstone was if anything more rigid in his attitude: speaking in 1865, he showed no inclination to relax his classic principles of public finance in the case of Ireland:

There is, I think a tendency to claim that public expenditure in Ireland shall not be limited to the amount required for the purposes in view, or fixed to the spot which is deemed most for the general convenience and efficiency of the public service, but that it shall be applied for the benefit of a particular locality and in a fixed degree. Against that principle and every modification of it I entirely protest...what is the public expenditure? What is a tax? It is money taken by the Government out of the pockets of the people. What right have the Government to take that money? Simply the necessity which exists to satisfy the public wants. And if they proceed to satisfy the public wants, are they not bound to do so in the best, most efficient, and at the same time most economic manner in their power?[3]

Much as the various ministers of the period may have wanted to limit public expenditure in Ireland, the endemic distress of the country frequently forced them to depart from the principles which they enunciated. At the beginning of the nineteenth century, many parts of Ireland lacked such fundamental works as roads and bridges, and the administrative mechanism which existed for their construction and maintenance was rudimentary and

[1] Peel to Anglesey, 26 July 1828 (Anglesey Papers, T. 1068/1).
[2] See Russell's memorandum 'State of Ireland—July 1847' (P.R.O. 30/22/6): 'In my opinion no aid similar in character to that of the public works, or the rations, should be administered by the Public Treasury. If England were to countenance, which she would not, such continued expenditure, we should run the risk of making large portions of the people permanent paupers....'
Also Wood to Bessborough, 25 September 1846: 'We are well disposed to help those who will help themselves, but we shall get into a scrape if we do nothing but make advances of money with a distant prospect of repayment' (P.R.O. 30/22/5).
[3] *Hansard*, 3rd ser. vol. CLXXVII, col. 679 (24 February 1865).

inefficient. Reform in these respects was clearly necessary and inevitable, for political as well as economic reasons. Apart from this, periodic famines compelled the undertaking of relief works and at various times more ambitious schemes seemed to provide a means of conciliating Ireland. Hence while in principle every Government was always opposed to the extension of public expenditure, in practice the State became involved in a series of public works programmes in Ireland, some undertaken *ad hoc*, others of a continuing nature.

II

In Ireland at the opening of the nineteenth century, the construction and repair of such public works as roads and bridges was the responsibility of the Grand Jury of each county, for the Grand Jury then possessed civil as well as criminal functions. By an Act of 1795,[1] anyone wishing to make or repair a road would have it surveyed by two persons, who would swear to the measurement before a magistrate. At the assizes, the Grand Jury would 'present' to the court the sum they approved for the project, and the judge would fiat the presentment. The work could then be carried out, initially at the expense of the person promoting it who subsequently, on a sworn affidavit that the work had been completed, could obtain the money granted by the Grand Jury. The funds would come from the proceeds of the county cess, a tax levied by the Grand Jury on the occupiers of land in the various baronies composing the county.

This system of Grand Jury presentments was notoriously corrupt and unjust. The members of the Grand Jury were nominated by the sheriff of the county, who owed his appointment to the influence of the local Member of Parliament. Hence the jurors were usually selected on grounds of political expediency, and not on any representative basis. The proceedings of the Grand Jury were always secret, and the time available for business was very restricted. It was calculated that some juries dealt with 132 presentments for public money in a day, and that the average time for the consideration of each was two minutes.[2]

In these conditions, abuses were inevitable, even had the public spirit of the jurors been beyond reproach, which it was not. The Grand Jury consisted of resident landholders, who naturally endeavoured to ensure that the public money was spent in places where it would most benefit their estates. Hence, contemporaries alleged, the district where a gentleman resided would be found well supplied with roads and bridges in the best of repair, while in the neighbourhood of an absentee's property there would be scarcely any public works at all.[3]

[1] 36 Geo. III, c. 25 (Ir.).
[2] *Report from Select Committee on Grand Jury Presentments, Ireland* (1826–27 (555), vol. III), p. 4.
[3] See de Beaumont, vol. I, p. 296.

It was also notorious that the landlords obtained public works for their tenantry in order that the latter should be able to pay the rent.[1] Because of the system of paying for the works only after completion, it suited the promoters to leave them until just before an assizes and then finish the work hurriedly; since the assizes took place in spring and summer, this meant that the demand for labour on public works reached its peak at the time when the tenants could least spare their labour from the land. Even this was not the worst of the defects of the system. Spring Rice, who attacked the Grand Jury system at the outset of his public career in 1815 and always remained a strong critic of it, alleged that the proprietors often did not hesitate to swear false affidavits and that by wording the presentments vaguely it was possible to obtain money for the same work on as many as twelve different occasions.[2]

The funds which were thus so lavishly misapplied and misappropriated by the landowners, came from a tax which was levied on the occupiers of the land. The valuation on which the tax was assessed was often very out-of-date—in some areas its basis was Petty's Down Survey of 1655[3]— and hence the assessment pressed very unequally on different tenants. Although in most areas the county cess, not surprisingly, had a constant tendency to increase, its amount from year to year was always uncertain, so that it was impossible for a tenant to allow for it in computing the rent he would give for a holding, even where the competition for land would allow for his making calculations of that kind.

Abuses of this extent and notoriety could not long escape attention, even in the years after Waterloo with their mixture of popular turmoil and governmental reaction. For some twenty years, from 1815 to 1836, the reform of the Irish Grand Jury system was a topic frequently considered by Parliament. A Select Committee appointed in 1815 collected ample evidence of all the abuses detailed by Spring Rice and other critics of the system, but confined itself to recommending that another committee should draw up a Bill to amend and consolidate the laws in the ensuing session.[4] This was in fact done, and the 1816 Committee produced two reports, the first recommending legislation to separate the civil and criminal business of Grand Juries, giving more time for the consideration of the former, and to appoint qualified surveyors for public works in each county. The second report recommended separate legislation to provide

---

[1] See *Report from Select Committee on the Employment of the Poor in Ireland* (1823 (561), vol. VI), p. 8. Elmore, p. 98.
[2] T. S. Rice, *Inquiry into the Effects of the Irish Grand Jury Laws, As Affecting the Industry, the Improvement and the Moral Character, of the People of England* (London, 1815), pp. 25-9.
[3] Evidence of Matthew Forde, M.P., before the Select Committee on Grand Jury Presentments, Ireland: *Minutes of Evidence* (1822 (353), vol. VII), p. 10.
[4] *Report from Select Committee on Grand Jury Presentments, Ireland* (1815 (283), vol. II), p. 254.

for a new survey and valuation of land in Ireland.[1] A Bill to amend the law was brought in late in the session, but not proceeded with: only in 1817 did any changes reach the Statute Book. Then Vesey Fitzgerald, the last Chancellor of the Irish Exchequer, brought in a Bill which incorporated the main recommendations of the Committee of 1816. Though this was passed into law with little opposition, it was not altogether popular with the Irish gentry.[2] Their fears for the sanctity of the Grand Jury system as they knew it proved almost groundless, however, for the changes made by the Act of 1817 were small: the office of County Surveyor was established and improved arrangements were made for examining presentments, but no steps were taken to alter the valuation basis of the county cess or to change its incidence.

The problem of valuation of lands was again examined by a Select Committee of the Commons in 1822, whose Report stressed 'the urgent necessity of applying to it a complete and adequate remedy without further delay'.[3] Nevertheless, the Ordnance Survey of Ireland was not ordered until two years later and the first Act providing for a new valuation of Ireland to be based thereon was passed in 1826.[4] Meanwhile the continuing defects of the Grand Jury system and the need for further reform had formed the subject of emphatic comment in the reports of the 1823 Committee on the Employment of the Irish poor, and the 1825 Committee on the State of Ireland.[5] In 1827 yet another Select Committee was appointed 'to consider what Provisions it may be expedient to establish for regulating Grand Jury Presentments in Ireland' and reported that 'when it is considered how much the peace and prosperity of the country depend on the wise administration of those Laws by which all the means of internal communication and trade are maintained, and how much the comfort of all classes in the community, the employment of the poor, and the morality of those engaged in executing the public works, are involved in the present system, your Committee cannot too strongly express their opinion, that the attention of Parliament should be called at an early period of the ensuing session to the state of the Irish Grand Jury Laws'.[6]

In the ensuing session, Catholic emancipation claimed more attention

[1] *First and Second Reports from the Select Committee on Grand Jury Presentments, Ireland* (1816 (374, 435), vol. IX).

[2] See John Foster to Vesey Fitzgerald, 25 January 1818 (Massereene Papers, P.R.O., N.I., D.O.D., 207/27). Foster condemns Fitzgerald's Act and defends the old system. The new Act (57 Geo. III, c. 107) was in fact suspended for a year at the beginning of 1818, owing to difficulties in operating it—particularly in appointing suitably qualified County Surveyors—but a Select Committee appointed to report on it in 1819 declared it to be 'wise and judicious'—(1819 (378), vol. VIII).

[3] *First Report from Select Committee on Grand Jury Presentments, Ireland* (1822 (353), vol. VII), p. 4.

[4] 7 Geo. IV, c. 62.

[5] *Parliamentary Papers:* (1823 (561), vol. VI); (1825 (129), vol. VIII).

[6] *Report from Select Committee on Grand Jury Presentments, Ireland* (1826–7 (555), vol. III), pp. 3 and 4.

from Parliament, and no measure of Grand Jury reform was brought forward: but there is evidence that the Government were considering some amendments in the system, and the possibility of codifying the whole law regarding public works in Ireland, which was then in a somewhat confused state.[1] The primary responsibility of Grand Juries was for local works, and when works of regional or national importance were called for they were usually the subject of special legislation, and their conduct was delegated to separate bodies. By this means there had been created a number of *ad hoc* commissions, whose functions sometimes overlapped and whose operations gave frequent opportunities for jobbery and the creation of sinecures. One of the most important of these bodies was the Board of Directors of Inland Navigation, established in 1800 and charged with the promotion of public works, for which a grant of £500,000 was appropriated. The original purpose of the board was the laying-out of various lines of canal, but in this respect it achieved little and in the eighteen-twenties its work had come to consist chiefly of the maintenance and control of the Shannon navigation, and the Newry and Tyrone canals; it also acted as a board of control over the affairs of the Royal Canal Company, which had become bankrupt in 1811. Apart from these duties the Directors of Inland Navigation also served, with some additional members, as a Commission for the regulation and encouragement of Irish fisheries under an Act of 1819,[2] while in 1825 they were given the responsibility of maintaining various roads in western counties which had been constructed as relief works during the distress of 1822.

In an earlier season of distress, 1817, Parliament had authorised the issue of sums up to £250,000 from the Consolidated Fund 'for the carrying on of Public Works' in Ireland, and a special body of Commissioners was set up to control the advances under this Act.[3] In the banking crisis of 1820, it was decided to apply the balance of the funds authorised by the legislation of 1817 towards 'the support of commercial credit'[4] and for this purpose also a board was established—the Commissioners for the Relief of Trade and Manufactures. In addition to all these bodies there existed another and older 'Board of Works' whose duty was the maintenance and repair of public buildings in Dublin.

This heterogeneous collection of agencies was an obvious target for 'economical reform'; many of them had outlived their usefulness in relation to the particular purpose for which they were established. The Select Committee on Irish Miscellaneous Estimates in 1829 examined James Saurin, the Chairman of the Board of Directors of Inland Navigation, and elicited from him the information that if, as was then proposed and subsequently enacted, the Newry canal were handed over to a private

---

[1] See Lamb to Lansdowne, 19 September 1827 (B.M. Add. MSS. 37305).
[2] 59 Geo. III, c. 109.   [3] 57 Geo. III, c. 34.
[4] Authorised by 1 Geo. IV, c. 39. See above, ch. v, p. 150.

company, his board would then be responsible for an annual expenditure totalling about £2000, while its establishment was costing the country £4800 a year.[1]

Reform was also beginning to be sought on wider grounds than mere economy; the eighteen-twenties witnessed a significant change in the attitude of the Government towards the question of public works policy in Ireland. In 1823 Goulburn, then Irish Chief Secretary, complained that Alexander Nimmo, one of the engineers appointed by the Lord-Lieutenant to take charge of relief works, had exceeded his duty by trying to promote 'what appeared to him great national improvements, and the misfortune is that he has thereby created an expectation that the Government considers itself bound in all time to come, without reference to seasons of distress or of plenty, to expend a large annual sum in works which ought in fact to be defrayed by the several Counties'.[2] But although Cabinet members might feel that public works were best left to local effort, except in seasons of peculiar distress, there was already widespread feeling, which was beginning to find expression in Parliament, that the condition of Ireland demanded a more systematic effort. The example of Scotland was frequently quoted, for a special Commission had been established in 1803 to aid local efforts there in the construction of public works, and had operated with considerable success.[3] In 1819, 1822 and 1823, Select Committees advocated the extension of this or a similar system to Ireland,[4] and in 1829 more specific criticisms and recommendations came from the Committee on Irish Miscellaneous Estimates, which expressed the view that

the present laws under which such public works are carried on, require revision and amendment, having been frequently passed at times of severe pressure, and not founded on any settled principle.... The Committee further consider that all works supported or erected, in the whole or in part, by Parliamentary aid, whether by loan or by grant, should, with a view to their expediency, in the first instance, and to their preservation and maintenance, be brought under the control of a fixed authority.[5]

By 1829, Wellington and his ministers were disposed to look into suggestions of this kind, even though Ellenborough might record in his diary: 'Cabinet at half-past three. The only talk we had was about Irish

---

[1] *Minutes of Evidence before the Select Committee on Irish Miscellaneous Estimates* (1829 (342), vol. IV), p. 119.

[2] Goulburn to Wellesley, 23 May 1823 (B.M. Add. MSS. 37301).

[3] A full account of the establishment and operation of the Commission is given in *Ninth Report of the Commissioners for Roads and Bridges in the Highlands of Scotland* (1821 (432), vol. X).

[4] *Second Report from the Select Committee on the State of Disease and the Condition of the Poor in Ireland* (1819 (409), vol. VIII); *Sixth Report from the Select Committee on the roads from London to Holyhead* (1822 (513), vol. VI); *Report from the Select Committee on the Employment of the Poor in Ireland* (1823 (561), vol. VI), p. 10.

[5] *Report of the Select Committee on Irish Miscellaneous Estimates* (1829 (342), vol. IV), pp. 25–6.

Poor, and Public Works in Ireland. The feeling seemed against anything like Poor Laws, and against Public Works too. This is mine. The first productive of mischief, the second useless.'[1]

That same afternoon, the Cabinet went on to appoint Peel, Goulburn and Maurice Fitzgerald, the Knight of Kerry, a committee to consider Irish measures for the ensuing session. Amongst those ultimately brought forward was a Bill for the drainage of bog lands in Ireland, which did not pass the Commons. Fitzgerald disliked the powers of taxation and borrowing which it contained, but in July 1830 he sent Wellington a memorandum proposing the establishment of a special department of public works for Ireland, following it up in October with more detailed proposals.[2] Wellington showed these to Peel, who thought the scheme would be difficult to administer, but desirable in principle.[3]

One of the arguments which Fitzgerald advanced in support of his proposal was that 'it would anticipate and substitute any hasty proposition of Poor Laws' and this was certainly a point which weighed with Peel and Wellington. Since the concession of Catholic emancipation, attention could no longer be diverted from the economic condition of Ireland and if, as seemed increasingly obvious, some measure of improvement must be brought forward, the Tory Cabinet felt convinced that public works would be a lesser evil than Poor Laws.

Much the same views were held by some Whigs, notably Spring Rice, who had obtained the appointment of his Select Committee on the Irish Poor early in 1830. Amongst the recommendations of its Report were 'A Bill for the extension and promotion of Public Works,...placing the direction of such works under a fixed superintendence and control' as well as 'A Bill to amend the Laws respecting Grand Juries, and to provide that the burden of the County Rates shall no longer be borne exclusively by the occupying tenant'.[4] In the light of Peel's correspondence with Wellington, it seems very probable that the Tories would have acted on these recommendations in the ensuing session, but with the change of Government in November 1830, the task fell to the Whigs. In the following June, Stanley introduced a Bill for the establishment of a new Board of Works for Ireland, to consist of three Commissioners. This body was to take over the duties of the various boards already existing for the conduct of public works and to have charge of a newly created fund of £500,000 to be used for making loans to individual proprietors and to Grand Juries in aid of public works. A further sum of £50,000 was provided to be used

[1] 4 July 1829; Earl of Ellenborough, *A Political Diary 1828-30*, ed. Ld. Colchester (London, 1881), vol. II, pp. 63–4.
[2] *Despatches, Correspondence and Memoranda* [of Duke of Wellington] *1819-32*, ed. 2nd Duke (London, 1878), vol. VII, pp. 63, 118, 305.
[3] *Ibid.* pp. 317–18.
[4] *Fourth Report from Select Committee on the State of the Poor in Ireland* (1830 (667), vol. VII), p. 57.

for making outright grants towards the building of roads and bridges in 'such Districts [as] are too poor themselves to bear the whole Expense of constructing such Roads and Bridges'.[1]

Although some of the Irish members were displeased by the strict security and high interest rates required for the advances,[2] the Bill passed with comparatively little opposition, and the first three Commissioners were appointed on 31 October 1831.[3] In the first years of the Board's existence most of its work was carried on in association with Grand Juries, the security and interest required being generally too onerous for individual proprietors, especially those whose estates were already incumbered. Even so, a Select Committee appointed in 1835 to inquire into the advances made found that loans to the amount of £497,000 had been sanctioned and grants of almost £33,000. 'The experiment has so far succeeded, and the funds are nearly exhausted. Your Committee strongly recommend an extension of the measure.... '[4]

The Chairman of this Committee, A. H. Lynch, the member for Galway, was a particularly strong advocate of a public works policy for Ireland,[5] which indeed continued to receive powerful support, first in 1836 from the Whately Commission on Poor Laws and later in 1839 from Drummond's Railway Commission. Although not all these recommendations were carried into effect, in the next decade Parliament continued to find additional funds for the Irish Board of Works and to place additional duties on its members. In pursuance of the recommendation of the 1835 Committee, a further £100,000 was made available to the Commissioners for loans in 1836[6] and in later years about half of the original fund of £500,000 was reissued after its initial repayment. These funds were issued in the form of Exchequer Bills, but an Act of 1843 put an end to this system, and introduced a new one whereby £15,000 was issued directly from the Consolidated Fund each quarter for public works in Ireland.[7] Under these and other Acts the Commissioners had, by the beginning of 1845, been entrusted with the distribution of a fund of some £980,000 for loans and £125,000 for grants.

In addition to their original duties, the Commissioners had been charged with the full control and encouragement of Irish fisheries in 1842, when they also began to act as Drainage Commissioners, together with

---

[1] 1 and 2 Will. IV, c. 33.

[2] See speech of Alexander Dawson, M.P. for Louth, *Hansard*, 3rd ser. vol. VI, col. 46 (15 August 1831).

[3] Treasury Outletters, T. 28/82.

[4] *First Report from Select Committee on Public Works (Ireland)* (1835 (573), vol. XX), p. 8.

[5] Unlike Spring Rice, Lynch conceived public works as supplementary, rather than alternative, to a Poor Law; his chief concern was to recommend public works in preference to emigration. See his publications, *An Address to the Electors of Galway, on the Poor Law Bill for Ireland* (London, 1838) and *Measures to be Adopted for the Employment of the Labouring Classes in Ireland* (London, 1839). And below, ch. VII, p. 221.

[6] 6 and 7 Will. IV, c. 108.   [7] 6 and 7 Vic. c. 44.

one other appointed for that purpose. Their Chairman, Colonel Burgoyne, had also been appointed to take charge of the newly established Commission for improving the Shannon navigation in 1835, and served with two other engineers in that capacity until 1846, when the Shannon Commission was absorbed into the Board of Works, whose members were then increased from three to five.

Hence before the Famine, a centralised public works agency, whose programme included various long-term projects of economic development, had become a well-established feature of the Irish Government. While this was taking place, the system of administering local works through Grand Juries continued with little alteration. In 1831 Stanley had promised to introduce a reform of the Grand Jury system soon after the Board of Works measure, but although a Bill was drafted it was not brought forward, and it was not until 1836 that any new legislation on this subject reached the Statute Book.[1] So far as public works were concerned, the main effect of the Act of 1836 was to give representation to the cess-payers at the special Presentment Sessions to be held in each barony, which examined proposals for works before their submission to the Grand Jury at the next assizes. The representation of the cess-payers proved inadequate and ineffectual in practice, while the tax continued to fall entirely on the occupiers, contrary to the recommendations of Spring Rice's Committee of 1830; but the 1836 Act remained the basic Act governing the local administration of public works until the comprehensive reform of the whole system of local government in 1898.

The inequities and anomalies of Grand Jury law continued to be a subject of discussion and protest in Ireland, and it was frequently suggested that in fiscal matters the Grand Jury should be replaced by some type of baronial or county board more truly representative of the ratepayers.[2] The system was fully investigated by a Royal Commission in 1840–2[3] which recommended that the powers of Grand Juries to present for public works should continue, but that the county cess should be based on the new general valuation of Ireland, then in progress, while the Poor Law guardians should be associated with the magistrates in presentment sessions, in order to make these latter more representative. No legislative action followed the report, and almost twenty years later a Bill brought in by Isaac Butt, incorporating this and some other changes in the

---

[1] 6 and 7 Will. IV, c. 116. See J. Muldoon and G. M'Sweeny, *A Guide to Irish Local Government* (Dublin, 1898), p. 4; J. Flach, *Le gouvernement local de l'Irlande* (Paris, 1889), pp. 69–70.

[2] See, for example, J. L. Conn's paper 'On the Reform of the Grand Jury Laws', read to the Statistical Society of Ireland on 20 April 1864 and reported in *Freeman's Journal* and *Dublin Evening Mail*, 21 and 22 April 1864. The paper is not printed in the Society's *Journal*.

[3] *Report of the Royal Commission appointed to revise the Grand Jury Laws of Ireland* (1842 [386], vol. xxiv).

constitution of presentment sessions, was lost on the second reading.[1] Various other private Bills for Grand Jury reform suffered a similar fate during the eighteen-sixties[2] and while a Select Committee of the Commons in 1868 recommended that the county cess should in future be equally divided between tenant and proprietor, it also held that the authority of Grand Juries in county fiscal matters should not be done away with, and went so far as to assert that 'however open to objection certain portions of the Grand Jury system may be in theory, its administration has generally been pure and economical'—a view which contrasted sharply with that of the experienced land agent, John Hancock, who declared the whole system to be 'bad, unsound and rotten'.[3]

The coming of the Famine was at once a proof of the failure of the system of public works so far established to resolve the Irish economic crisis, and the opening of a new period in the conduct of that system. The decision to attempt to alleviate distress through the medium of relief works placed an unprecedented burden on the Board of Works, and its hastily extended mechanism proved scarcely equal to the strain.[4] But even after the winding-up of these temporary measures, the work of the Board was considerably increased as a result of the decision of Russell's Government to rely on public works again as a means for the regeneration of the country.[5] Apart from measures to facilitate drainage, which are more fully discussed below[6] the most important piece of legislation in this respect was the Land Improvement Act of 1847, which provided a sum of £1,500,000 to be advanced to landowners on favourable terms for reclamation of waste, subsoiling, fencing and similar projects.

Subsequent amending Acts brought the total sum available for land improvement loans to three millions, and extended the purposes for which they could be claimed to include construction of farm buildings, labourers' dwellings and flax-scutching mills, as well as planting for shelter. The scheme was an immediate and a continuing success; by June 1850, no less than 1953 works of improvement were in progress under the supervision

[1] See *Dublin Evening Mail*, 11 March 1861, where the debate is fully reported. In 1848 Russell had contemplated replacing Irish Grand Juries by elective county boards, but never introduced a measure for the purpose. See Russell to Clarendon, 17 April 1848: 'I should like to have a good Grand Jury Bill founded on a representative principle—but I suppose there will be no time to carry it this year' (Clarendon Papers).

[2] For example, Grand Juries (Ireland) Bill, 1864 (Bill 35)—defeated on second reading, 20 April 1864: *Hansard*, 3rd ser. vol. CLXXIV, cols. 1379–97; Grand Jury Cess (Ireland) Bill, 1869 (Bill 60)—withdrawn 4 August 1869: *Hansard*, 3rd ser. vol. CXCVIII, col. 1247.

[3] *Report from Select Committee on Grand Jury Presentments, Ireland* (1867–8 (392), vol. x). John Hancock, speaking to J. L. Conn's paper (see above, note 2, p. 175) as reported in *Dublin Evening Mail*, 21 April 1864.

[4] Since the works undertaken during the Famine were designed to afford immediate relief only, no attempt is made to detail or discuss them here. See above, ch. IV, pp. 114–17; T. P. O'Neill, 'The Organisation and Administration of Relief', in *The Great Famine*.

[5] See above, ch. IV, p. 125.

[6] See pp. 178–89.

of the Board of Works[1] and in 1878 it was said that 'no legislative measures for Ireland have ever been more freely taken advantage of, and from no measures has the country probably derived greater benefit'.[2] While this process of land improvement was being carried forward, some of the policy-makers were beginning to feel that a stage had been reached where Ireland might well be made more self-reliant in such matters as road construction. In March 1850, Trevelyan wrote to Larcom, then one of the Commissioners of Public Works, asking him to look over a Bill concerning the fiscal affairs of Irish counties, then about to be introduced, with a view to cutting out several clauses which called for the assistance or intervention of the Treasury. Trevelyan suggested that the operation of the Poor Law and the Incumbered Estates Act had given a new stimulus to individual exertions, which might now be more readily relied upon in local matters, whilst the development of railways had made extensive future outlay on roads less necessary.[3] Larcom and his colleague, Richard Griffith, concurred in Trevelyan's views and suggested a number of modifications in the Bill, but Somerville did not afterwards bring it before the House.

In his letter of 1850 Trevelyan implied that public works financed with Treasury aid should be regarded as a temporary prop to a weakened or under-developed economy, to be removed as soon as conditions would permit. He expressed this view still more clearly at the beginning of 1853, when Larcom drew his attention to a letter written by Sir James Caird in *The Times*, pointing to what had been achieved by the Board of Works in regard to Irish agriculture as an example which England might well follow. 'I must admit', Trevelyan replied in somewhat dampening fashion, 'that Caird's proposal to provide John Bull with an Irish Board of Works outfit is a great compliment to your Board, but I doubt the wisdom of it. I think it would do more harm in discouraging the application of private capital than it would do good by applying public capital.'[4]

In close conformity with this approach, an Act was passed, with little opposition or comment, towards the end of the session of 1853, which gave to Irish Grand Juries the power to borrow money from private sources on the security of presentments, and authorised the Commissioners of Public Works to transfer piers, harbours and other works under their control to Grand Juries for maintenance. Before this measure had received the royal assent, a Treasury minute prohibited the Commissioners from lending to Grand Juries for county works.[5]

---

[1] Larcom to Somerville, June 1850 (Larcom Papers, National Library of Ireland MSS. 7746).
[2] *Report of the Board of Works Committee* (1878 [C. 2060], vol. XXIII), p. xxiv.
[3] Trevelyan to Larcom, 18 March 1850 (Larcom Papers 7746).
[4] Trevelyan to Larcom, 10 January 1853 (Larcom Papers 7746).
[5] 16 and 17 Vic. c. 136 (royal assent, 20 August 1853); Treasury minute dated 22 June 1853.

Comparatively few new works were undertaken by the Board in the ensuing ten or fifteen years, indeed the impression became widespread that the Board pursued an ultra-conservative policy—an impression fostered by its close association with the Treasury, and certainly not without some foundation.[1]

Yet the hope which Trevelyan entertained that the Irish economy had developed to a point where public works could be dispensed with was shown to be illusory by the experience of a few bad harvests in the early eighteen-sixties. In 1863, even after thirty years of public works policy and fifteen years of heavy emigration, it could still be said that 'the present distress is rather the symptom of a deep-rooted evil than a special visitation. . . . It is employment, not alms—wages, not charity—work and its requital, not bounty—that is needed.' And those who argued in this way were forced to admit that while security of tenure might provide work and wages in the long run, the immediate need of the country could only be met by yet another dose of public works.[2]

III

The public works activities so far described could for the most part be considered as falling into the category of works designed to create a foundation for economic development through private enterprise. It remains to consider what action was taken in regard to those wider schemes which aimed at undertaking development deliberately, or at least at forcing its pace by comprehensive measures. Two such schemes gained the major share of public attention over most of the period here covered; these were the reclamation of waste lands and the provision of a railway network.

Probably no single proposal for Irish improvement was so frequently and so widely canvassed, or supported by so many distinguished advocates, as the idea of reclamation of waste lands. The names of Peel, Russell, John Leslie Foster, Spring Rice, Stuart Mill, Scrope and Thornton are all to be found associated with it at various times, and it was being debated as eagerly in 1878 as it was in 1809. Its perennial popularity is not difficult to understand; once the Irish economic problem has been stated in the classical form of the population—resources ratio, it is evident that the ideal solution to it would be an increase in the available quantity of land, the fundamental resource of an agricultural country.

---

[1] Complaints against the Board ultimately became so widespread, in and out of Parliament, that a special Departmental Committee was set up to investigate them in 1877. The Committee reported it to be 'unquestionable that much of the Board's work has been attended with success' but characterised the Board as having sometimes ignored local interests, evaded its responsibilities, and displayed an 'absence of boldness' vis-à-vis the Treasury: *Report of the Board of Works Committee* (1878 [C. 2060], vol. xxiii), pp. lx and lxi.
[2] *Freeman's Journal*, 23 January 1863.

For Ireland, it could always be argued that this was a practical possibility, for it was estimated in 1845 that there were in Ireland some three-and-a-half million acres of land capable of reclamation and use lying waste.[1] The advocates of reclamation had always to meet the argument that the process must be an unprofitable one, or else it would long since have been undertaken. Generally they found no difficulty in doing this, for it could be contended that effective large-scale reclamation was beyond the means of individual proprietors. Apart from this it could also be urged that to incur the cost of land reclamation was preferable to incurring the dangers of dependence on foreign corn—a point of some political value before 1846—or to incurring the direct and indirect costs of mass emigration. This latter argument, used by opponents of emigration throughout the period, came to have more popular appeal in the late eighteen-fifties and eighteen-sixties when continuing emigration was coming to be looked on as a dangerous drain.

Thus the desirability of reclaiming waste lands was constantly being urged on successive Governments by well-meaning reformers of varying degrees of information and talent; to judge from the amount of land reclamation actually undertaken by public agencies it would seem that the advice largely fell on deaf ears. This is not a fair basis for judgment, however, for, since much of the reclaimable land was bog, the whole question of waste lands is bound up with that of drainage. State activity on land reclamation must therefore be discussed in the wider context of measures to aid drainage and inland navigation—the latter since a system of canals could be designed to assist arterial drainage as well as transport.

Advocates of land reclamation such as its indefatigable champion, Scrope, usually thought in terms of a Government project covering a large area and connected with a plan of 'home colonisation'. Ministers were generally wary of comprehensive schemes of this type, but often not unwilling to consider giving some aid to landlords in undertaking improvements of waste lands themselves. A typical instance of this was Wellington's reaction when Lord Clancarty approached him about a reclamation project in 1829. 'These are subjects more properly for the consideration of individuals or of private societies than for government, and I here leave them. Government have plenty to consider and to do in relation to Ireland without attending to schemes of this description, which can have

[1] The precise figures of the estimate, drawn up by Richard Griffith for the Devon Commission, were:

Land improvable for cultivation	1,425,000 acres
Land improvable for pastures	2,330,000 acres
Total improvable	3,755,000 acres
Unimprovable	2,535,000 acres
Total waste land:	6,290,000 acres

Appendix No. 96 to *Minutes of Evidence taken before Commissioners Appointed to Inquire into the Occupation in Ireland*, pt. IV (1845 [672], vol. XXII), p. 290.

only a partial operation'[1]—yet Wellington was quite willing to stand over a drainage Bill for Ireland at this time.[2]

A similar, but rather more positive, attitude was adopted by Grey's administration of 1830. Spring Rice's Committee on the State of the Poor in Ireland 'though they depart(ed) reluctantly from what they consider(ed) a general principle, venture(d) to recommend the trial of one or two experiments' in the draining and reclamation of waste lands. Rice, who became Secretary of the Treasury in Grey's ministry, succeeded in persuading his department to act on the recommendation. Early in 1831 the Treasury approached the Commissioners of Woods and Forests, who declared themselves 'inclined to think favourably' of the possibilities of reclamation of some Crown lands, mostly mountain bog, situated on the borders of West Cork and Kerry. The experiment was begun in 1833 under the enthusiastic supervision of Richard Griffith. Not only was the bog drained and clayed, but new roads were laid out, a complete village constructed and a model farm set up. The results were at first encouraging, but the outlay was considerable[3] and Griffith himself admitted that the land had, even before drainage, possessed advantages which many tracts of waste land lacked.[4] In 1850 Sir James Caird wrote of it: 'The land was worked by con-acre labour...as long as the potato remained sound, the experiment prospered; but now that money wages must be paid, it does not succeed.'[5]

The heavy cost of this reclamation experiment did not deter Lord John Russell from proposing his waste land scheme of 1847, under the combined influences of the Devon Commission Report and the propaganda of Mill and Thornton, but the criticism which he met in the House did deter him from going farther with it.[6] Mill afterwards accused Peel of having 'sneered down' the plan, and taxed him with inconsistency for having 'enfanté a scheme containing that and much more than was then proposed'

[1] Wellington to Clancarty, 16 July 1829, Despatches, vol. VI, p. 18.
[2] See above, p. 173. This brusque refusal to entertain any project for State reclamation of waste lands also contrasts noticeably with Wellington's earlier enthusiasm for a survey of bogs with a view to drainage, when, as Sir Arthur Wellesley, he was Chief Secretary for Ireland (see below p. 182). It serves to underline the distinction so frequently made by public men of the time between the State acting directly and 'aiding local efforts'. See the passage from J. P. Kennedy, quoted above, ch. V, p. 146.
[3] Sir Michael Hicks-Beach quoted a final figure of £17 per acre on reclamation, and a further cost of £8,000 for roads alone. Hansard, 3rd ser. vol. CCXXV, col. 1459 (14 July 1875).
[4] See Griffith to James Weale, 22 February 1834—No. 135 in Papers relating to Experimental Improvements, on the Crown lands at King William's Town, Co. Cork (1834 (173), vol. LI).
[5] J. Caird, Ireland and the Plantation Scheme (Edinburgh and London, 1850), p. 108.
[6] See above, p. 36. When Clarendon raised the question of a reclamation scheme again a year later, Russell replied: 'I am still of opinion that with a full Exchequer the experiment might be tried to the extent of half a million of money. But in this year the advances to individual landlords to reclaim and improve waste and to aggregate landlords for draining will exhaust all the spare cash that Charles Wood has got in his breeches pocket' (Russell to Clarendon, 15 January 1848, Clarendon Papers).

in the 1848 'Plantation Scheme'.[1] Here Mill's criticism fell wide of the mark, for Peel's scheme did not include any specific proposal for the reclamation of waste, but only 'encouragement to drainage'. Nor were any further proposals for Government-sponsored reclamation brought before the House between 1849 and 1870: a Bill somewhat similar to Russell's was brought in by an Irish member, J. G. McCarthy, in 1875, but was not supported by the Government and so came to nothing.[2]

Most advocates of land reclamation considered that it could only be undertaken on a large scale and would therefore require the backing of the State, but a few attempts were made to carry out projects through the agency of joint-stock companies or other associations. Of these the best known and most successful was the Irish Waste Land Improvement Society which was founded in 1836 by the Earl of Devon, with the support of Daniel O'Connell. The original sponsors of the Society intended that it should buy up tracts of waste land and lease them in small portions to tenants, assisting them to reclaim the land. Because of O'Connell's opposition to 'a body of English gentlemen' becoming absentee proprietors in Ireland, they were compelled to modify their plans and take lands on lease. The Society thus acquired four estates, amounting in all to some 16,000 acres, in Galway, Limerick and Sligo; they were leased for a term of ninety-nine years, with option to sell the lease, the landlord having first claim, at the end of twenty years.[3]

This condition handicapped the Society, since it could only afford to undertake improvements which would show a profit rent at the end of twenty years. Its difficulties were increased by the fact that it had necessarily to charge very low rents to reclaiming tenants during the first four years, at least, of their tenancy while the Society's Act of Incorporation[4] made no provision for any remission of local taxes, which were paid by the Society, during this period. Nor did owners of suitable tracts of waste land show any particular inclination to assist the venture by granting leases at low rents to the Society.

Consequently, although the Society did produce a substantial improvement in the condition of both the land and its tenants where it operated, it was never a financial success and therefore never contrived to expand the scope of its work to any substantial extent. Its managing director, Colonel Daniel Robinson, felt that 'with moderate support, the society

[1] John Stuart Mill to Harriet Taylor, 31 March 1849: printed in F. A. Hayek, *John Stuart Mill and Harriet Taylor* (London, 1951), p. 147.
[2] *Hansard*, 3rd ser. vol. ccxxv, col. 1459 (14 July 1875). Two other waste-lands Bills brought in in 1876 were also dropped, and one proposed by McCarthy in 1878, and including proposals for arterial drainage, likewise failed.
[3] Evidence of the Earl of Devon before the Select Committee on the Farmers' Estate Society (Ireland) Bill (1847–8 (535), vol. xvii).
[4] 6 and 7 Will. IV, c. 97.

might become essentially useful',[1] but its whole experience went to show that reclamation of waste could not be made a profitable commercial proposition, but must require some support from public funds. Public expenditure on land reclamation might have taken the form of assistance to private corporations like the Waste Land Improvement Society: the Devon Commission tended to favour this approach, which indeed would have been in accord with the familiar doctrine of 'aiding local effort', but it was never put into practice.

Yet while direct State reclamation of land never amounted to more than the one experiment of dubious value, and no specific support was given to private schemes, indirect assistance was nevertheless given on a considerable scale through legislation to promote drainage. As early as 1808, Wellesley, then Chief Secretary for Ireland, became impressed with the possibilities of bog drainage, and proposed to Liverpool the appointment of a Commission with power 'to survey the different bogs and ascertain their extent, the practicability of draining them and the expense of that operation'.[2] Such a Commission was set up in 1809 and surveyed over a million acres of bog land in the next five years. The Commission's reports were optimistic as to the possibility of draining and reclaiming bog land profitably, but no action was taken on them.[3] The major obstacles to the progress of drainage works in Ireland at this stage were the difficulty of obtaining the consent of all the proprietors to the works, and the costs of special local Acts. The need for a general drainage Act was frequently stressed, notably by the 1823 Committee on the Employment of the Poor,[4] but no measure reached the Statute Book until 1831, when 1 and 2 Will. IV, c. 57, which came to be generally known as 'More O'Ferrall's Act', was passed. This was merely a permissive Act, allowing individuals, with the consent of the Lord-Lieutenant, to form corporations for specific drainage projects, raising money by the issue of debentures. No works were ever completed under the powers given by this Act, and it became a dead letter.

A further recommendation for drainage works to be undertaken by the State itself came from A. H. Lynch's Committee on Public Works in 1835.[5] In 1836, as part of its comprehensive plan of improvement, the Whately Commission recommended that the Government should undertake the drainage of waste lands, and also that the 'Board of Improvement' which they proposed should have power to levy rates

[1] Evidence of Col. Robinson before the Devon Commission: *Minutes of Evidence*, pt. II, (1845 [616], vol. xxx), p. 6. The other facts cited above are taken from Robinson's evidence also.

[2] Undated memorandum, Wellesley to Liverpool, in Wellesley Letters 1807–9 and printed in Andrews, 'Some Precursors of Bord na Mona'—*Journal S.S.I.S.I.*, vol. xx (1953–4), p. 146.

[3] See *Reports of the Commissioners on Draining and Cultivating the Bogs of Ireland* (1810 (148), vol. IV); (1810 (365), vol. X); (1810–11 (96), vol. VI); (1813–14 (130, 131), vol. VI).

[4] *Report* (1823 (561), vol. VI), p. 11.

[5] *Second Report* (1835 (573), vol. X), especially pp. 26–7.

on proprietors for the drainage and fencing of lands in cultivation. Senior was prepared to approve of a measure for draining waste lands, but felt that the other proposal went too far; he also declined to share the regret which Whately and his colleagues expressed that More O'Ferrall's Act had proved a dead letter 'for one more capable of abuse I never saw'.[1]

The Melbourne administration evidently did not consider that drainage works should form any part of their plans for conciliating Ireland, for they took no action on any of these varied recommendations, and they did not support the Bill brought forward by Lynch 'to promote the Reclamation and Improvement of uncultivated Land in Ireland', which was confined to drainage in its proposed operation.[2]

But steps were taken at this time which had an important effect on the whole system of drainage legislation at a later stage. In 1835, provision was made for a complete survey of the Shannon, with a view to its improvement both as a navigation and for arterial drainage. At this time the Upper Shannon was under public control, the Lower Shannon in private hands. When it was decided to proceed with a comprehensive scheme of improvement, in 1839, the whole river was brought under the control of the Shannon Commission, and remained under that control until the works were completed in 1850, even though the Shannon Commission was formally absorbed into the enlarged Board of Works in 1846.[3]

The primary object of the improvements on the Shannon was to make it navigable throughout its great length—an object of considerable potential importance before the coming of railways, since it not only offered the benefits of cheap transport to the areas immediately adjoining the river, but also the possibility of completing a system of inland navigation serving most of Ireland, since the Shannon was connected by the Grand and Royal canals to Dublin and Leinster, and through the Ballinamore Canal to Lough Erne, which was linked by canals to Belfast, Newry and Coleraine. Drainage was a secondary, but important object since the alluvial lands on the banks of the Shannon, which were subject to frequent flooding, were capable of being converted into valuable meadows by effective draining.

The Shannon improvement project gave a new direction to the treatment of drainage in Ireland. In the early part of the nineteenth century drainage had been thought of principally as bog drainage, an essential step identified with reclamation. Now attention began to be devoted to the improvement of the main drainage of the country through its rivers, thus not merely improving adjoining lands subject to flooding, but facilitating the thorough

[1] *Letter from N. W. Senior, Esq., on Poor Laws, Ireland* (1837 [90], vol. LI), p. 8.
[2] Lynch, *Measures for Ireland*, pp. 27, 35, 112.
[3] By 9 and 10 Vic. c. 86. See *Report of the Committee appointed to inquire into the Board of Works, Ireland* (1878 [C. 2060], vol. XXIII), p. 37.

drainage of other areas already in cultivation.[1] This was the approach adopted in the first effective Drainage Act for Ireland to reach the Statute Book in 1842.[2] This Act was largely drafted by Sir John Burgoyne, Chairman of the Board of Works and the Shannon Commission, with the assistance of W. T. Mulvany, then one of the engineers of the Shannon improvements.[3] It provided that anyone interested in draining lands or clearing a river channel might apply to the Commissioners of Drainage to have the work surveyed, on his undertaking to bear the preliminary expenses himself if the work were not afterwards approved. After the survey had been completed and a report published, a meeting of interested parties was to be held; if those possessed of two-thirds of the lands affected consented to it, they could appeal to the Board of Works to carry out the drainage. The Board would then obtain the necessary funds, either from private sources or from the Treasury, and, on completion of the drainage, charge the several properties affected with the repayment of the loans in proportion to the benefit they would derive from it.

The Act was thus designed to aid rather than supplant private enterprise, the Government placing expert technical help at the disposal of proprietors, but leaving them to take the initiative, and relying on private finance as much as possible. The procedures under the Act were complex and slow-moving, and few applications for drainage under it had been received before the onset of the Famine. In the Famine years, drainage projects seemed well adapted to combine immediate employment of unskilled labour with ultimately useful results. Consequently the Board of Works prevailed on Sir Thomas Fremantle, Chief Secretary for Ireland in Peel's administration, to bring forward a Bill simplifying and shortening the procedure for undertaking drainage schemes. In the debates on the measure, some Irish proprietors expressed misgivings about the powers which it conferred on the Board of Works, arguing that the expense both of preliminary surveys and actual drainage tended to be excessive when undertaken by the Board.[4] Nevertheless in the circumstances of the time there was little real opposition to the Bill becoming law, and its operation was subsequently renewed.[5]

---

[1] Although the idea that thorough drainage and arterial drainage should be linked in a general scheme had not been applied in the nineteenth century, it was not a new one; the principle was in fact contained in an Act of 1715 (2 Geo. I, c. 12 (Ir.)), 'to encourage the Draining and Improving of the Bogs, and unprofitable Low Grounds, and for easing and dispatching the Inland Carriage, and Conveyance of goods, from one part to another within this Kingdom'. I am indebted to Mr John O'Loan, of the Department of Agriculture, Dublin, for drawing my attention to this Act.

[2] 5 and 6 Vic. c. 89.

[3] Evidence of Sir C. E. Trevelyan, *Minutes of Evidence before Select Committee on the Drainage of Lands (Ireland)* (1852–3) (10), vol. XXVI, p. 4.

[4] See *Hansard*, 3rd ser. vol. LXXXIII, cols. 223 *et seq*. (26 January 1846).

[5] The original Act was 9 Vic. c. 4, often referred to as 'the Summary Proceedings Act', extended and amended by 10 and 11 Vic. c. 79 (1847).

Under the new law, the applicant was not required to take responsibility for the whole expense of the preliminary survey, which itself was to be of a more summary character. The consent of only one-half of the proprietors affected was sufficient to allow the works to proceed, but if the expenditure subsequently came to more than £3 per acre, the renewed assent of the proprietors was necessary before any further expense could be incurred.

These simplified provisions gave a great fillip to drainage operations, which the landlords regarded as a profitable form of relief expenditure.[1] Unfortunately, after only two years it began to be evident that the speeding-up of the operations was not an unmixed success. In 1848, the Treasury grew concerned about the growing expense of surveys and estimates, and put a stop both to further preliminary proceedings and to action on works surveyed but not already begun. By 1850 it was clear that the cost of many of the schemes would be far in excess of the original estimates, and that the Board of Works and the landowners had very different ideas as to what constituted a proper drainage. The Board's engineers thought in terms of a complete drainage, making the lands affected suitable for tillage, while the proprietors asked for no more than would convert low-lying areas into usable pasture.[2] Early in 1852, a number of proprietors, mostly from the midlands of Ireland, began to bring pressure for a parliamentary inquiry into the conduct of the drainage works, which they alleged had been seriously mishandled by Mulvany, the Commissioner primarily responsible.[3]

On 3 May 1852, their spokesman, Lord Rosse, moved the appointment of a Committee of Inquiry in the Lords, and the Government agreed to this.[4] The Committee convicted the Board of Works of having acted irresponsibly in carrying on with drainage operations in excess of the estimates and not keeping the proprietors fully informed of the progress of the expenditure. They recommended that a Commission should be appointed to investigate the situation on the spot and decide what action should be taken towards the completion of works already begun and the conduct of further works.

The report led to Mulvany's resignation and some reorganisation inside the Board of Works.[5] Legislation was passed appointing a Special Commission whose members surveyed the works, and in most cases recom-

---

[1] 'The Drainage works are pressed on, with a view to the relief of the poor by employment upon the most profitable description of works'—Stickney to Leake, 22 May 1847—(Board of Works—Treasury correspondence, 2D. 51. 113. P.R.O.I.).

[2] See *Report of Select Committee of the House of Lords on Drainage of Lands (Ireland)* (1852–53 (10), vol. xxvi), p. v.

[3] See Mulvany to Larcom, 12 April 1852; Barry to Mulvany and reply, 12 April 1852 (Larcom Papers, National Library of Ireland MS. 7746).

[4] *Hansard*, 3rd ser. vol. cxxi, col. 88.

[5] Larcom Papers, National Library of Ireland MS. 7746. For Mulvany's later career as an industrialist in the Ruhr see Henderson, p. 136 above.

mended considerable remissions in the charges for drainage laid upon the lands. After this debacle, virtually no new drainage works were undertaken for a number of years; the apathy and suspicion of the proprietors contrasted with their early enthusiasm, the Treasury was naturally cautious about new advances, and money from private sources was not readily forthcoming.

Meanwhile, the process of improvement of the Shannon had come to an equally depressing stand. The works, formally completed in 1850, had from the outset been an avowed compromise between navigation and drainage; Trevelyan declared them 'the best compromise between the two that could have been effected',[1] but in fact drainage had been sacrificed to navigation, with the result that the water-level was kept too high and considerable stretches of land remained subject to flooding. This damage was not compensated for by any improvement in the navigation, since the traffic had fallen off greatly with the building of railways, and the vision of the Shannon as the core of an Irish system of inland waterways no longer had any practical importance. As a result of disagreements amongst the proprietors of lands bordering the Shannon as to the importance of lowering the level of the river, and the expense which they would be prepared to bear for that purpose, combined with a steadfast refusal by the Board of Works to accept responsibility for the state of the navigation, nothing was done in the ensuing twenty years to make the Shannon improvements effective, although nearly £300,000 had been spent on them.[2]

Hence for almost a decade the movement for arterial and thorough drainage seemed to have exhausted its impetus in Ireland, but the series of wet seasons in 1860–3 brought the question to the fore again. Once more drainage commended itself, on two grounds—first because of the flooding which the rains brought, but, secondly, because the distress produced by crop failures again created a need for employment on public works. For these reasons in 1862 Colonel Dickson, the member for Limerick, introduced a Bill designed to encourage proprietors to co-operate in undertaking arterial drainage, following a precedent set by an Act of 1861 relating to England.[3] The Bill passed the Commons, but reached the Lords too late for consideration before the end of the session. Reintroduced in 1863, it passed into law and became the foundation of a new code of Drainage Acts for Ireland.[4] Under this code, the Government no longer took responsibility for the execution of the drainage works,

---

[1] Evidence of Sir C. E. Trevelyan, *Minutes of Evidence* (1852–53 (10), vol. XXVI), p. 4.
[2] *Board of Works Committee Report* (1878 [C. 2060], vol. XXIII), pp. 38–9. *Forty-sixth Report of the Commissioners of Public Works, Ireland*, Appendix A. 7 (1878 [C. 2092], vol. XXIII), p. 42.   [3] 24 and 25 Vic. c. 133.
[4] The original Act was 26 and 27 Vic. c. 88 (1863); subsequent amending Acts were 27 and 28 Vic. c. 72 (1864), 28 and 29 Vic. c. 52 (1865), 32 and 33 Vic. c. 72 (1869) and 37 and 38 Vic. c. 32 (1874).

but stood ready to lend the necessary funds to proprietors. Any group of proprietors wishing to improve their lands by arterial drainage might send plans and estimates for the scheme to the Board of Works. The Board would then send an Inspector to hold a public inquiry on the spot; his report would be sent both to the Board and the proprietors. After this, if two-thirds of the proprietors gave their assent to the scheme, the Commissioners of Public Works would make a provisional Order (and subsequently obtain a confirming Act) constituting the area a drainage district. The proprietors, grouped into a Drainage Board, could then begin their works, borrowing the funds in instalments from the Board of Works; subsequent repayment would be by a rent charge on the lands, as under the Land Improvement Acts.

Although the Act of 1863 was praised at the time as introducing 'the self-reliant system' into Irish drainage schemes, it did not prove noticeably more successful than the Government-sponsored system which it superseded. After fifteen years of its operation some 33,000 acres had been improved by drainage as against 267,000 under the 'old code' dating from 1842.[1] A complete system of arterial drainage, linking in with and aiding thorough drainage of individual estates, was thus still far from achievement, and in the eighteen-seventies not a few Irish proprietors were inclined to feel that the system of State-conducted drainage had been abandoned without a fair trial because of its failure during the Famine years, and might be reverted to with advantage.[2]

The history of attempts to promote drainage and land reclamation in Ireland may appear as a chaotic sequence of ill-concerted measures, with official policy veering uncertainly between the extremes of doing nothing and doing everything. Yet the fact remains that considerable practical results were achieved. Of the 3,755,000 acres of waste land reported as improvable by Griffith in 1845 some 1,750,000 acres had been reclaimed by 1871, and some 300,000 acres had been improved by drainage between 1842 and 1878.[3]

From the available evidence it is not possible to determine exactly how much of this activity was the result of the facilities offered by the various Acts. Dr Connell has shown that considerable reclamation of land took place in the period from 1830 to 1845, mostly in the form of small patches brought into cultivation by tenants under pressure of necessity.[4] He

[1] *Board of Works Committee Report* (1878), pp. 29 and 33.
[2] See the debate on the motion for the second reading of J. G. MacCarthy's Waste Lands Reclamation Bill of 1878: *Hansard*, 3rd ser. vol. CCXXXVIII, cols. 1–29.
[3] The figure for waste land is based on the information given in Grimshaw, 'Notes on the Statistics of Waste Lands in Ireland', *Journal S.S.I.S.I.*, vol. VIII (1884), pp. 522–5; the figure for land drained is taken from the *Board of Works Committee Report*, as quoted above. Problems of definition make it impossible to ascertain how far the area drained and the area reclaimed according to these figures may have overlapped.
[4] Connell, 'The Colonization of Waste Land in Ireland, 1780–1845', *Econ. Hist. Rev.*, 2nd ser. vol. III, no. 1 (1950), pp. 44–71.

contends that 'it is most unlikely that there was as much reclamation in the five years after 1845 as in the preceding five' and is therefore inclined to attribute the bulk of the 1,271,751 acres which the Census returns show to have been reclaimed between 1841 and 1851 to tenant activity before the Famine rather than landlord response to the Drainage and Land Improvement Acts.[1] Tenant activity may well have been considerable, but on the other hand there is definite evidence that expenditure and employment on arterial drainage increased rapidly after the Summary Proceedings Act of 1846 came into force.[2] Nor did reclamation cease after the Famine; 828,000 acres were reclaimed between 1851 and 1861 and a further 277,000 between 1861 and 1871.[3] That there should be a slackening in pace through time is natural, as the most profitable land would tend to be first reclaimed.

As Hancock pointed out,[4] the period of most rapid emigration thus coincided with a period of considerable reclamation of waste. This was also a period when the area under crops did not alter significantly, but the area under grass increased by some 1,300,000 acres; it may therefore be presumed that most of the reclaimed land was devoted to pasture, for which it would have been primarily suited.[5]

This points to two conclusions: the first is that Government assistance towards land reclamation did not become effective until the problem which

[1] Loc. cit. p. 48.
[2] Total expenditure on drainage:

1845	1846	1847	1848	1849
£	£	£	£	£
19,634	98,870	289,483	209,504	228,163

Total employment, 'numbers equivalent to the labour of men for one day':

1845	1846	1847	1848	1849
146,856	901,766	3,463,593	2,231,965	3,148,056

Nineteenth Annual Report of the Commissioners of Public Works, Ireland (1851 [1414], vol. xxv).
The total area of land drained up to 1 January 1850 was 101,885 acres; this must be added to the figure of 74,000 acres which Dr Connell quotes from Professor O'Brien, Economic History of Ireland from the Union to the Famine (London, 1921). The latter is the figure for lands thorough-drained under the Land Improvement Act only. Professor O'Brien does notice the Arterial Drainage Act, but pronounces it 'to have been an undoubted failure' (p. 156). This is only true of the Act of 1842, and quite ignores the results of the 1846–7 Acts.
[3] See Grimshaw, loc. cit. pp. 523, 525. Grimshaw puts the area reclaimed between 1841 and 1851 at 1,073,652 acres, as against the Census figure of 1,271,751 acres, quoted by Hancock in the Memorandum cited below, and adopted by Dr Connell. The latter is obtained by direct subtraction of the 1851 Census figure for 'uncultivated land' from the 1841 figure; the former by taking the 1881 figure for total land area as fixed and deducting from it the figures of cultivated land given by the Census in 1841, and by the agricultural statistics in 1851. Since the basis of computation of the area of uncultivated land in the Census was altered between 1841 and 1851, Grimshaw's figures are followed here as more consistent for purposes of comparison.
[4] Memorandum on Waste Lands prepared by Hancock for the Chief Secretary, June 1864 (Larcom Papers, National Library of Ireland, MS. 7586).
[5] See Grimshaw, loc. cit. p. 525.

its advocates sought to solve by it—the pressure of population on resources—had been solved in another way by the Famine and its consequences. This is a familiar criticism,[1] but one which cannot be put forward without to some extent ignoring the second conclusion to which the facts point.

This is simply that, taken by itself, reclamation of waste could not have solved the Irish economic problem before 1846. The most probable use for the reclaimed land would have been as grassland, in which form it could have added but little to the subsistence and employment of the people. If this had been circumvented by a deliberate colonisation of reclaimed land, it could only have offered a very insecure livelihood to the tenants. Caird's comment[2] that the success of the experiment at King William's Town depended wholly on the potato must inevitably have been true of most other reclaimable areas; where the reclaimed land was low lying, the potato crop would also have been peculiarly vulnerable to disease, since the ground would tend to become waterlogged again in wet seasons. To allow, much less to encourage, land of the poorest quality to be colonised by an ever-growing population of small tenants, without security and dependent on a precarious potato crop, would have been to aggravate rather than alleviate Ireland's economic difficulties; even had the potato blight never come, the repeal of the Corn Laws, ultimately inevitable in the political circumstances of England, must have made it extremely difficult for the cottier to support himself and his family on a small patch of bad soil.[3]

IV

When the use of steam locomotives on railways had been shown to be a practical possibility, it was not long before the significance of the innovation for Ireland's economic future was being widely canvassed. As has been pointed out,[4] railways seemed to be an ideal example of a work which would afford much direct employment in the short run and indirectly open many new possibilities for investment and employment in the long run. Steamships and railways between them, it seemed, might alter the whole outlook for Ireland. Not only would Irish agricultural produce be more readily saleable in the British market, but many obstacles to the development of manufactures in Ireland might be reduced. The establishment of a packet station on the west coast of Ireland, linked by a railway line to Dublin, could greatly reduce the time required for the Atlantic crossing; this was a project strongly endorsed by Richard Cobden, who

[1] See O'Brien, *Economic History of Ireland from the Union to the Famine*, p. 156.
[2] See above, p. 180.
[3] See Senior, *Journals...Relating to Ireland*, vol. i, pp. 247–60. R. M. Fox, *Poor Laws in England and Ireland* (Dublin, 1849), makes skilful use of the Ricardian rent theory to show the dangers attending home colonisation in a free-trade economy.
[4] Above, p. 165.

argued 'that a traffic, of such magnitude as is here contemplated, would have the effect of imparting wealth and civilisation to the country through which it passed, all experience proves to be unquestionable'.[1] And Huskisson, it was said, had thought that such a development must make the south of Ireland a most important centre of the cotton manufacture.[2]

Not only capital investment, but expenditure of revenue, might follow from the opening up of the country by railways, tourists would be encouraged—Cobden thought that Ireland 'whose scenery is hardly rivalled in Europe, together with the frank and hilarious temperament of its people, could not fail to become popular and attractive with the English traveller'[3]—and absentees would find it easier to visit their estates more often.

After 1834, it was common knowledge that the successful introduction of the new Poor Law had been greatly aided by the increase of employment arising from railway building in England. Here was a lesson obviously applicable to Ireland, where the need of employment was so much greater. And if railway building could help to smooth the introduction of a Poor Law, so might it also help the transition from cottier to capitalist agriculture—giving immediate employment to those evicted from the land and ultimately giving them new occupations either in the industries or the improved agriculture produced under the stimulus of railways.[4]

All these advantages might be secured from a properly designed system of railways; but, in the abstract at least, a properly designed system of railways could be provided either by private or public enterprise. So, while the desirability of introducing railways into Ireland was never questioned, the problem of whether they should be provided by private capitalists or the State was for long the central issue in discussion of them.

On the one hand, all the standard classical arguments were in favour of private enterprise—the profit motive could be relied on to introduce an efficient system as rapidly as possible, while State intervention would paralyse initiative, delay progress and give opportunity for jobbery.[5] On the other, it was possible to argue generally that competition in railway

[1] [Cobden], *England, Ireland and America by a Manchester Manufacturer* (London, 1835), reprinted in *The Political Writings of Richard Cobden* (London and New York, 1867), vol. i, p. 89.
[2] *The Establishment of a General Packet Station, on the South-West Coast of Ireland, connected by Railways with Dublin and London, Considered* (London and Dublin, 1836), pp. 15–16.
[3] Cobden, *Political Writings*, vol. i, p. 84.
[4] *Second Report from the Railway Commissioners, Ireland* (1837–8 [145], vol. xxxv), pp. 83–93.
[5] For some contemporary statements of the case for private enterprise in Irish railways, see G. L. Smyth, *Railways and Public Works in Ireland* (London, 1839); H. Fairbairn, *Treatise on the Political Economy of Railroads* (London, 1836); T. Bermingham, *Report on the necessity of forming Railways throughout Ireland* (London, 1839). Bermingham subsequently changed his views, and produced *Statistical Evidence in Favour of State Railways in Ireland* (Dublin, 1841).

development must prove wasteful, while private monopoly could not be allowed to grow in an industry of such vital importance to the whole community. In the particular case of Ireland it could also be urged that while railways would be of great value to the country, there was little ready-made traffic for them. Hence private enterprise could expect profitable working in only a few areas, and would confine itself to these, leaving other districts excluded from the potential benefits of railway transport.[1]

At the outset, a number of projects for railways in Ireland were brought forward privately, with the Government playing a merely passive role. In 1825 a line from Sligo to Dundalk 'through the coal country' was projected, as well as one from Waterford to Limerick.[2] An Act sanctioning the latter was obtained in 1826, but the line was not actually open until 1854.[3] Ten years later, there were still only six miles of railway open for traffic in Ireland,[4] and though many competing projects were being urged on the attention of the public, none of them had passed beyond the planning stage. In 1836, the attention of Parliament as well as public was drawn to this unsatisfactory state of affairs by the occurrence of a peculiarly prolonged and costly struggle between the supporters of two alternative lines from Dublin to Drogheda.[5]

Before this, the attention of Thomas Drummond, the able Whig Under-Secretary for Ireland, had been drawn to the possibilities of railways as an ideal type of public works for Ireland. Drummond did not share the common faith of his day in the virtues of private enterprise, and when it seemed to be producing only confusion and litigation in the matter of Irish railways he persuaded Melbourne's administration to seek the appointment of a Commission 'to inquire and report upon the most advantageous lines of railways in Ireland' and secured his own appointment to it.[6] When Lansdowne moved for the Commission to be set up, he laid emphasis on the point that 'all that was proposed was, to give the public the benefit of the investigation of the Commissioners, and Government and Parliament were to remain unpledged'.[7] The Commission presented a preliminary report in March 1837, and a second and major

[1] See M. J. Quin, *A Letter to the House of Commons on Railways in Ireland* (London, 1839); H. E. Flynn, *An Appeal to the Wisdom, Justice and Mercy of the Imperial Parliament, in behalf of the Irish Peasantry, on the Subject of a National System of Railways in Ireland* (Dublin, 1839); J. Pim, *Irish Railways: A Letter to the Right Honourable Frederick Shaw* (London, 1839).   [2] Foster Papers, D.O.D. 562/CCCXXIX (P.R.O., N.I.).
[3] C. F. D. Marshall, *A History of British Railways down to the year 1830* (London, 1938), p. 137.
[4] This was the Dublin and Kingstown line, opened in 1834. J. C. Conroy (*History of Railways in Ireland* (London, 1928), p. 4) wrongly describes this as the first railway authorised for Ireland.
[5] See *Minutes of Evidence taken before the Committee on the Dublin and Drogheda Railway* (London, 1836).
[6] See J. F. McLennan, *Memoir of Thomas Drummond* (Edinburgh, 1867), p. 345.
[7] *Hansard*, 3rd. ser. vol. xxxv, col. 686 (1 August 1836).

one in July 1838;[1] during this period Drummond contrived to extend the scope of the investigation considerably, so that the final Report became a valuable survey of the whole Irish economy, and also to press his view that a general system of railways for Ireland should be executed by the State.

> It is a very common opinion [he wrote to Russell in March 1838], that the execution of such works should be left to individual enterprise. To say, that this should be a rule without exception, appears to be a delusion.... It is impossible to look at the magnificent district of country through which our lines to Cork, Limerick and Kilkenny run—it is impossible to think of its present state, its great capabilities, and its now imperfectly developed resources, without the ardent desire to see these lines executed as *National Works*.[2]

At this stage Drummond was endeavouring to persuade the Cabinet to adopt a scheme for diverting some 15 % of the receipts from Irish tithes towards payment of interest and principal on the funds borrowed for railway building. Some of the Cabinet, anxious to accompany the Poor Law Bill with some popular public works measure, were favourably disposed to Drummond's idea, but others held that it would be 'most injudicious' and would cost the Government much support in England; the more conservative view prevailed.[3]

Nevertheless, the recommendations of the Second Report of the Railway Commission were more favourable to State intervention and control than was common at that time. The Commissioners proposed the construction of two main-line networks—a Southern and a Northern line. 'If a body of capitalists be found to undertake either of these great works, as a whole, we presume that the general feeling of the Legislature and of the country, will be to leave the execution of it as little fettered as possible by restriction, to the management of private enterprise.'[4] That such a body of capitalists would be found, the Commissioners appeared to doubt; therefore, 'to avoid the evil of partial execution, and to accomplish so important a national object as that contemplated in the completion of the entire system', they advocated that the State should lend a considerable proportion of the requisite capital at low interest, taking a mortgage of the works, or else undertake the construction of either or both of the proposed networks, requiring the counties benefited to guarantee to meet any deficiency from presentments.[5]

---

[1] *First and Second Reports from the Railway Commissioners, Ireland* (1837 [75], vol. XXXIII; 1837–8 [145], vol. XXXV).

[2] Drummond to Russell, 20 March 1838 (Russell Papers, P.R.O. 30/22/3).

[3] See Mulgrave to Russell, 21 February 1838, and Cabinet memoranda, February–March 1838 (Russell Papers, P.R.O. 30/22/3).

[4] *Second Report*, pt. III, p. 94: 'Mr Drummond was much interested in this part, and weighed with extreme care and attention every sentence it contained'(McLennan, *Drummond*, p. 353).

[5] *Second Report*, pp. 94–5.

The Report met with a very mixed reception. It was widely favoured in Ireland and a considerable body of Irish peers petitioned the Crown in favour of its adoption.[1] On the other hand most of those who were interested in private railway schemes were seriously disappointed by the Report, and attacked it bitterly. Something of a 'railway mania' had been developing in Ireland in 1835–6, which the appointment of the Commission had checked. Railway promoters had had to suspend their projects pending the recommendations of the Commission, and now the insistence on a unified system finally dashed deferred hopes.

Opponents of the Commissioners' plan alleged that it was another instance of 'Castle jobbery' on a rather spectacular scale. Allegations were published, both in the Tory *Evening Mail* and the Radical *Northern Whig*, that the preliminary copies of the Second Report contained a recommendation that the execution of the proposed lines should be entrusted to a body of capitalists headed by Pierce Mahony, a well-known Irish supporter of the Whigs,[2] and that this indiscreet proposal had been hastily deleted from the copies printed for general circulation;[3] Drummond firmly denied this, but Spring Rice, when questioned about it in the House, had ultimately to make the embarrassed admission that such a passage had appeared in the proofs.[4]

This gave the opponents of the Report an opportunity to say that the Commissioners had been contemplating handing over Irish railway operations to a private monopoly of the worst type; but while this advantage was exploited to the full, it did not prevent the suggestion for public construction from being attacked with equal vigour. For this purpose 'the principles of political economy' were a useful weapon, frequently wielded. Thus G. L. Smyth, a vigorous critic of the whole system of public works in Ireland and promoter of the 'Suir and Shannon Junction Railway', declared that the Commissioners 'have obviously disregarded the lessons both of experience and political economy; and have rashly sought to force upon us a new theory, at variance, not only with their instructions, but with all that we have, in this country, been taught to think right, and when tried, have found to be correct'.[5]

---

[1] *Hansard*, 3rd ser. vol. XLV, col. 1062. McLennan (*Drummond*, p. 383) suggests that the enthusiasm of the great Irish proprietors for a comprehensive railway scheme was not unconnected with the passage of the Poor Law for Ireland.

[2] Mahony was a solicitor with considerable influence who often appeared in the background of Irish politics from 1830 to 1850. See Fitzpatrick, *Correspondence of Daniel O'Connell*, especially vol. II, p. 322.

[3] *Dublin Evening Mail*, 25 July, 1, 3, 13, 15 August 1838; *Northern Whig*, 19, 24, 31 July 1838. The *Whig*, which acted as spokesman for the promoters of the Ulster Railway, began by merely attacking Spring Rice for delaying publication of the Report, but later took up the charge against Drummond and Mahony.

[4] *Hansard*, 3rd ser. vol. XLIV, col. 978 (3 August 1838); *Dublin Evening Mail*, 15 August 1838.

[5] Smyth, *Railways and Public Works in Ireland*, p. 17; see also *A Letter to the Marquis of Lansdowne, on the Report of the Irish Railway Commissioners by a Shareholder in the Kilkenny Railway* (London, 1838).

Behind professions of disinterested desire to serve the best interests of the Irish people, most of the discussion can be seen to run along party lines. Macvey Napier apparently decided that support of the Whigs was more important than support of orthodox political economy, and obtained for the *Edinburgh Review* a highly favourable review of the report, written mainly by Marmion Savage, then an obscure Irish civil servant.[1] On the other hand, no hint of anything like Butt's liberal unorthodoxy was allowed to creep into the vituperative treatment which the Tory *Dublin University Magazine* meted out to the Commissioners.[2]

The Government was slow to take action on the Report; nearly nine months elapsed before Morpeth moved for the House to go into Committee on it.[3] He then explained that it was proposed to construct one line only, that from Dublin to Cork with a branch to Limerick, as a public work, it being thought 'that the Government should not monopolize the whole field at once...in order that the House might consider whether the whole plan should be eventually carried out, or whether private companies should be allowed to come in'.[4]

This modest proposal was strongly attacked by Peel as contrary to 'the great public principle of non-interference of government with private enterprise',[5] but Morpeth secured a majority of 44 for his motion. There was no great enthusiasm for it, however, and when, three weeks later, Fitzstephen French, an Irish supporter of the Whigs, brought forward a motion designed to commit Parliament to the undertaking of the whole system proposed by the Commissioners, the House was counted out.[6] At this stage of the session, the fate of the ministry was obviously in the balance, and Morpeth did not think fit to raise the controversial topic of Irish railways again.

'I much regret what you tell me of the abandonment of the railroad scheme', wrote Ebrington to Russell,[7] 'I am quite sure that the principle on which it was to have been carried into effect is that on which all such works ought to have been conducted...and that sooner or later the legislature will be obliged to place even those now existing in England under the direct control of the Government.'

An attempt to have the plans of the Railway Commission put into effect in a modified form was made in 1841 by Charles Vignoles, a leading engineer. Under his scheme, the necessary capital was to be raised

---

[1] *Edinburgh Rev.* vol. LXIX (April 1839). See Fetter, 'Economic Articles in the *Edinburgh Review*', *J.P.E.* vol. XLI (June 1953), p. 257. Savage later acquired a considerable reputation as a novelist.

[2] See 'Railways in Ireland', *Dublin University Magazine*, vol. XIII (January–June 1839). Butt had ceased to edit the magazine in 1838.

[3] *Hansard*, 3rd ser. vol. XLV, col. 1051 (1 March 1839).

[4] *Ibid.* col. 1077.   [5] *Ibid.* col. 1082.

[6] *Ibid.* vol. XLVI, cols. 1102–7 (21 March 1839).

[7] 26 June 1839 (Russell Papers, P.R.O. 30/22/3).

privately by debentures bearing a guaranteed interest of 4 %, any deficiency being made up by the counties concerned, which in turn would receive any excess of profits over 4 %; the lines were to be executed and managed by Commissioners, superintended by a Board of Control appointed by Parliament.[1] This scheme was taken up by the Government, and Morpeth introduced a Bill embodying its main points, but stated specifically that he did not intend to press it during that session.[2] After the return of the Tories in the general election of 1841, the plan was not heard of again.

In March 1842, Fitzstephen French attempted to introduce a motion committing the House to a public enterprise approach to Irish railways, but Eliot, the new Chief Secretary, laid down that 'the Government could not consent to any plan which would involve an expenditure of the public money'.[3]

Hence the construction of Irish railways was left to private enterprise, but progress continued to be extremely slow. The costs of surveying lines and obtaining private Acts of Parliament were considerable obstacles to Irish companies, which found difficulty in raising the necessary capital when British and even American lines offered better prospects to the investor; in 1845, at the first onset of famine, only seventy miles of railway were open for traffic in Ireland.[4] 'If your plan of the Government making the Railways had been carried out in 1838 in this country', the Duke of Leinster told Russell, 'the good they are now doing would be two-fold— but, like many other things now carried, put off until too late.'[5]

Faced with increasing difficulties as the Famine grew worse, the promoters of Irish railways began to appeal publicly for assistance from the Government. In fact there was provision for financial aid to railways from the Exchequer Loan Commissioners, and a number of Irish companies obtained help in this way, but the sum annually available for the purpose was limited, and the Treasury showed no anxiety to increase it.[6]

In October 1846, in fact, the possibility of giving loans to railway companies specifically as a means of providing employment was considered by the Treasury and rejected; a number of Grand Juries made presentments for executing railway earthworks in preference to roads, but

[1] *Railroad Monthly Journal* (June 1841).
[2] *Hansard*, 3rd ser. vol. LVIII, cols. 1347–50 (8 June 1841).
[3] *Ibid.* vol. LX, cols. 1400–29 (3 March 1842).
[4] Conroy, *History of Railways in Ireland*, p. 13. The panic which followed the collapse of the railway mania in England early in 1846 also served to hold up the construction of Irish lines; see *Annual Register* (1846), pp. 10, 53.
[5] Leinster to Russell, 22 October 1845 (Russell Papers, P.R.O. 30/22/4).
[6] In the period 1842–4, the Public Works Loan Commissioners had advanced £120,000 to Irish railways, and prior to this the Board of Public Works in Ireland had advanced £157,200. By March 1850 the total advanced by the Public Works Loan Commissioners had risen to £834,000—*A Return of all Monies lent to Railway Companies in Ireland* (1850 (159), vol. LI).
For the Treasury attitude, see Trevelyan to Chairman of Great Southern and Western Railways, 30 May 1846: Treasury Out-Letters, T. 14/30, f. 114.

these were disallowed.[1] In a letter to the Press in December 1846, Smith O'Brien protested against this course of action, and urged that 'if the intervention of the state in aid of such undertakings [as railways] be at any time justifiable, such is surely the case under the present circumstances of Ireland'.[2]

By this time the Government's programme of Irish measures was more or less settled[3] and plans for assistance to railways did not figure in it. Some two weeks after Russell had put forward the programme in the House, Lord George Bentinck, who had abandoned horse-racing to become the leader of the protectionists after Peel's decision to repeal the Corn Laws, came forward with a bold proposal to give employment in Ireland through railway development.

The essence of Bentinck's scheme was 'that for every £100 properly expended [by private investors] upon railways, £200 should be lent by Government, at the very lowest interest at which, on the credit of the Government, that amount can be raised'.[4] The total sum required to be raised by the Government Bentinck calculated at £16,000,000, to be lent at $3\frac{1}{2}$% repayable in a period of thirty years.[5] The scheme made a good impression on the House, and was naturally very favourably received in Ireland. In England, too, there was some appeal in the argument that if a considerable sum of public money must be spent on the relief of Irish distress it should be used for profitable rather than unprofitable purposes,[6] while the fact that Bentinck's Bill was endorsed by such authorities as Hudson 'the Railway King' and George Stephenson was not without effect.

Although Bentinck declared that he did not bring his plan forward 'either in hostility or in rivalry to Lord Russell', the Prime Minister did not hesitate to say that the Government would feel obliged to oppose the Bill on the second reading.[7] In fact, there were strong economic and political reasons which made it impossible for them to do otherwise. The period was one of increasing stringency in the money market and Government securities were weakening.[8] Wood, the hidebound and timid Chancellor of the Exchequer, always believed that he must follow the dictates of the market, rather than vice versa, and Russell tended to accept his views.[9] Consequently though the Irish executive looked favourably on

[1] Trevelyan to Nenagh Poor Law guardians, 10 October 1846; Trevelyan to Labouchere, 16 October 1846; T. 14/30, fos. 199, 202.
[2] *Nation*, 19 December 1846; *Freeman's Journal*, 23 December 1846.
[3] See above, p. 125.   [4] *Hansard*, 3rd ser. vol. LXXXIX, col. 780 (4 February 1847).
[5] *Ibid.* cols. 794, 801.   [6] *Annual Register* (1847), pp. 58–9.
[7] See B. Disraeli, *Lord George Bentinck: A Political Biography* (London, 1852), pp. 380–1.
[8] See D. Morier Evans, *The Commercial Crisis, 1847–48* (London, 1848), p. 57.
[9] These attitudes are very clearly shown in a correspondence on railway speculation which took place in August 1847 between Wood, Russell and Fitzwilliam. Russell was disturbed by the effect of railway calls on the money market, and wondered if some means of limiting borrowing for such purposes could be devised. Fitzwilliam had no doubt that

Bentinck's plan, or some variant of it, as a means of meeting the Famine crisis, to Wood and Russell it was simply a financial impossibility.[1]

Bentinck regarded his proposal as being a substitute for some of Russell's relief schemes, not an addition to them, but Russell and his ministers obviously could not accept this. Politically, they could not afford to let Bentinck's Bill pass, thereby admitting its superiority to their own previously announced programme. Russell, therefore, made it clear to his supporters that he would regard the vote on the second reading as one of confidence. The majority of the Irish members had been inclined to support Bentinck's Bill, but could not face the prospect of a possible return of the Tories to power, together with the breakdown of their traditional association with the Whigs. Many therefore voted with Russell, and the second reading was lost by 332 votes to 118.[2]

Lord George Bentinck had some compensation for this defeat when, in April 1847, Wood dropped the waste-lands proposal and replaced it with his scheme to advance £620,000 to three Irish railway companies.[3] This evidence of vacillation and timidity did not go unremarked;[4] in fact, after having repudiated the principle of aid to railway companies, the Government had indulged in the practice, but on a scale whose narrow limits contrasted contemptibly with the bold scope of Bentinck's proposals.

Nevertheless, even had Bentinck's Bill passed, it would not have been of great value as a measure of relief, though its ultimate consequences might have been better than those of the measures adopted. Bentinck quoted a figure of sixty men per mile, given him by George Stephenson, as the number who would be employed by railway construction, but this was highly optimistic; Isambard Brunel privately expressed his opinion that 'under any circumstances thirty to a mile is a full allowance'.[5] Even on the basis of the sixty-per-mile figure, the total number which Bentinck estimated his scheme would employ was 110,000, which has to be compared with the figure of 734,000 employed on relief schemes in March 1847. Drummond's idea of a railway system as giving 'a lift' to the Irish economy[6] was soundly conceived in 1838; by 1847 the Duke of Leinster's pessimism was justified, it was too late.

limitation of all capital issues which required parliamentary sanction was both possible and desirable. Wood, however, declared 'I don't see my way to fixing any amount of capital, which should be expended on railroads in, say, one year', and Russell apparently accepted his contention that a control over the market could not be enforced. See Wood to Russell, 20 August 1847; Fitzwilliam to Russell, 20 and 27 August 1847: P.R.O. 30/22/6.

[1] See Bessborough to Russell, 11 February 1847, and Russell's reply, 14 February 1847 (Russell Papers, P.R.O. 30/22/6).
[2] *Hansard*, 3rd ser. vol. xc, cols. 123–6. See Nowlan, 'The Political Background', *The Great Famine*, pp. 159–61; *Irish Railway Gazette*, 26 April 1847, vol. iii, p. 240.
[3] The companies were: the Great Southern and Western; the Waterford and Kilkenny; and the Dublin and Drogheda. See *Hansard*, 3rd ser. vol. xcii, cols. 207–99 (30 April 1847).
[4] See *Morning Chronicle*, 3 May 1847.
[5] Brunel to B. Hawes, 10 February 1847 (Russell Papers, P.R.O. 30/22/6).
[6] McLennan, *Drummond*, pp. 342–4.

After 1847, the railways of Ireland continued to be constructed by private enterprise, but not without considerable financial help from the State. In 1849, £500,000 was advanced to the Midland Great Western Company to complete its line, and by 1865 the total of Government advances to Irish railways had reached £2,364,000.[1] At this latter date, something more than 2000 miles of railway were open for traffic,[2] but while there was no real lack of facilities, the position was not satisfactory either to railway users or shareholders. While there were general complaints of high rates and fares, profits were low, net receipts yielding only $3\frac{1}{2}\%$ on the total sum invested.[3] This state of affairs was partly the inevitable outcome of the general poverty of the country, but also partly the result of the railways being operated by a large number of companies, whose management was not always the most efficient.[4]

In these circumstances, proposals for reform became frequent; amalgamation, subsidisation, and Government purchase all had their advocates. The question came into prominence from 1865 onwards, because in 1844 a Select Committee of the Commons, of which Gladstone was Chairman, had recommended that all railways thereafter authorised should be subject to State purchase, and this proposal was incorporated into the Railway Regulation Act of 1844.[5] Hence under this Act all railways authorised after 1844, which included the majority of Irish lines, were liable to be bought up by the State in or after 1865.

The exercise of this power was strongly urged by William Galt, who had been one of the few advocates of public operation of English railways in 1843.[6] Although public opinion was more favourably disposed to State intervention after the lapse of twenty-one years, the issue was not at this time a very live one in England. In Ireland, on the other hand, the problem was widely discussed; all parties agreed on the necessity of some measure of railway reform, the only difference being between those who advocated outright State purchase, and those who were prepared to accept a solution consisting of financial assistance to the railway companies given on condition of lowering fares and improving services.[7]

When the question was raised in Parliament in February 1865, Glad-

---

[1] *Report of the Royal Commission on Railways* (1867 [3844], vol. xxxviii), § 50.
[2] *Report of the Commissioners Appointed to Inspect the Accounts and Examine the Works of Railways in Ireland* (1867–8 [4018], vol. xxxii), p. 13.
[3] *Report of Royal Commission on Railways* (1867), § 79.
[4] In 1867 there were thirty-nine railway companies operating in Ireland, with a total of 333 directors. *Report...Railways in Ireland* (1867), pp. 30–31.
[5] 7 and 8 Vic. c. 85.
[6] See Galt's publications: *Railway Reform: Its Importance and Practicability Considered* (London, 1843) and the much larger work under the same title (London, 1865).
[7] See the series of papers in *Journal S.S.I.S.I.* vols. IV and V (1864–70) by S. M. Greer, Edward Gibson, J. J. Murphy, W. N. Hancock and Joseph T. Pim. All these are in some degree favourable to State intervention. Between 1865–70 all the leading Irish newspapers, from the *Nation* to the *Dublin Evening Mail*, were unanimous in stressing the need for railway reform.

stone indicated that it was not the intention of the Government forthwith to use the powers conferred by the Act of 1844, but that a Royal Commission would first be appointed to investigate the circumstances of railways throughout the United Kingdom.[1] Two months later, William Monsell, an influential Irish Liberal and one of the most tenacious advocates of State purchase of Irish railways, urged upon Gladstone that the problem of railways in Ireland was much simpler than the English problem, and might reasonably be first dealt with and disposed of by the Royal Commission. Gladstone accepted this, and went on to say that 'if it should be desired of the Imperial Parliament to confer a pecuniary boon on Ireland, there would probably be no mode in which that boon could be conferred so free from all taint of partiality, and at the same time so comprehensive and effective in its application, as some measure taken with the view to secure to her the benefits of cheap railway transit'.[2] From his statement it appeared that while he was not disposed to support State purchase, Gladstone favoured financial assistance to the railways, combined perhaps with a measure of amalgamation designed to secure operating economies and lower rates.

After this, hopes of reform ran high in Ireland, but while the Royal Commission proceeded to hear and publish an impressive volume of evidence on Irish railways, they decided to make no report until their investigation of English lines was completed.[3] In January 1866, Monsell was appointed to the Commission as its Irish member in place of Lord Donoughmore, who had resigned for health reasons, and this seemed a good augury for the supporters of State control. The Report of the Commission did not appear until May 1867; meanwhile the Conservatives, after taking office in June 1866, were compelled to carry through a temporary measure to tide some Irish railways over financial difficulties. By this, the Public Works Loans Commissioners were authorised to make loans up to a total of £500,000 on the security of debentures due or falling due: the difficult state of the money market at the time was the cause for this Act, under which less than £200,000 was actually advanced.[4]

When the Report of the Royal Commission ultimately appeared it proved that, while Sir Rowland Hill and Monsell had submitted minority reports in favour of State purchase, the majority Report was firmly opposed to its application either to Britain or Ireland.[5] Indeed in one respect the majority felt that State purchase in Ireland 'may be deemed more objectionable than in the case of the English railways, inasmuch as it is of more

---

[1] *Hansard*, 3rd ser. vol. CLXXVII, col. 235 (14 February 1865).
[2] *Ibid.* vol. CLXXVIII, col. 898 (7 April 1865).
[3] *Irish Times*, 23 November 1865.
[4] *Freeman's Journal*, 23 July 1866; *Dublin Evening Mail*, 18 March 1867; Conroy, *History of Railways in Ireland*, pp. 42–3.
[5] *Reports, Royal Commission on Railways* (1867 [3844], vol. XXXVIII).

importance not to discourage private enterprise and self-reliance in that country'.[1]

The Report was received with chagrin in Ireland, where it was already felt that the existence of the Commission had been used as an excuse for inaction.[2] A meeting of Irish peers and members of the House of Commons, held two weeks later, decided to approach the Government in favour of State purchase of railways;[3] a deputation was ultimately received by the Prime Minister, who admitted the importance of the question and agreed to refer it to a Committee of the Cabinet.[4]

The prospects for the State acquiring the Irish railways seemed at this time to be more favourable than under Russell's last administration. Lord Naas, the Chief Secretary, had publicly expressed agreement with Galt's views,[5] and was widely rumoured to be preparing a comprehensive measure.[6] He did in fact receive three confidential reports from Hancock at this time, favouring State purchase and indicating the lines of procedure for it,[7] but the ultimate decision of the Cabinet was to seek more information before introducing any legislation. Naas accordingly informed the House towards the end of the session that the Government intended to use powers given by the Act of 1844 to investigate the whole condition of Irish railways during the last three years.[8] This resulted in the appointment by the Treasury of a further Commission of investigation, which did not report until April 1868.[9] Of its first Report, *The Times* remarked: 'its immediate purport is not very decisive, but the information it contains is remarkable for its exactness.'[10] In fact, the Report contained no specific recommendations, but only the comment that reduced fares and consolidated management might greatly increase traffic and revenues 'but in the present state of their credit and finances, the Companies could not afford to run the risk of a period of diminished profit for the chance of any ultimate advantage'.[11]

The Treasury reaction to this was to direct a further inquiry into the financial consequences of lowering rates and fares and the possible savings resulting from concentration of management. The Irish members continued to press the Government for an immediate measure of purchase,

[1] *Royal Commission on Railways, Majority Report*, § 76. For another expression of the 'self reliance for Ireland' view on the railway question, see *Daily News*, 5 June 1865.
[2] See *Dublin Evening Mail* 17 April 1867.
[3] *Irish Times*, 23 May 1867.
[4] *Irish Times*, 21 June 1867.   [5] *Daily Express* (Dublin), 13 January 1866.
[6] *Freeman's Journal*, 13 and 20 May 1867.
[7] Hancock, *First, Second and Third Reports on a Plan for the State-Purchase of Railways in Ireland* (Dublin, 1867). The first Report was dated 27 April, the second 23 May, the third 15 August 1867; all are marked 'confidential'. Copies exist in the Larcom Papers (National Library of Ireland MSS. 7791).
[8] *Hansard*, 3rd ser. vol. CLXXXIX, col. 612 (1 August 1867).
[9] *Report of the Commissioners appointed to Inspect the Accounts and Examine the Works of Railways in Ireland* (1867–8 [4018], vol. XXXII).
[10] *The Times*, 3 June 1868.   [11] *Op. cit.* p. 18.

but none was introduced, and when the Treasury Commission reported again in December 1868 the Liberals were just taking office under Gladstone. Apart from the fact that Gladstone had never favoured State purchase, his conduct of the great measures for disestablishment and land reform left him no time to consider the comparatively minor problem of Irish railways. In April 1869, he did undertake that his Government would 'at the earliest period which it was in their power...give that careful consideration to the subject which its importance deserved',[1] but there he allowed the matter to rest.

The question continued to be agitated in Ireland, and, after receiving a deputation about it in December 1870, Chichester Fortescue found time to take the matter up with Gladstone. He complained that by recommending reductions in rates of the order of 50 % in their Second Report, the Treasury Commissioners had made it difficult to propose any moderate measure, but gave his opinion that most of those concerned in Ireland would be satisfied with any scheme which encouraged amalgamation and allowed gradual reduction of rates. 'But at all events I am sure you will agree with me that this question ought not to remain an open one much longer, but that soon after Parliament meets, the Government should either be prepared with a plan for dealing with it, as I hope may be the case, or else should announce decidedly that they mean to do nothing.'[2]

Gladstone decided in favour of the latter alternative; on 9 March 1871 he told a questioner that 'Her Majesty's Government had not prepared any measure for the purchase of Irish railways, nor was he sanguine that it would be in their power to make a proposal in any form on the subject this Session'.[3]

V

The policy pursued with regard to public works in Ireland over the half-century here examined could certainly not be described as inaction, but it would be equally difficult to characterise it as planning. W. O. Henderson has been somewhat over-generous in writing that 'the improvement of the Shannon navigation and the varied activities of the Public Works Commissioners [in Ireland] showed that English statesmen were no hidebound doctrinaires. Since a policy of *laissez-faire* was inappropriate when applied to Ireland a policy of capital investment was adopted.'[4]

That successive Governments did invest a large amount of capital in Ireland is manifest, but a consistent policy of investment did not really exist. If any general principle can be said to have motivated the various ministers who authorised public works for Ireland, it was the idea, here

[1] *Hansard*, 3rd ser. vol. cxcv, col. 1577 (26 April 1869).
[2] Chichester Fortescue to Gladstone, 13 December 1870, B.M. Add. MSS. 44122, f. 188.
[3] *Hansard*, 3rd ser. vol. cciv, col. 1675.
[4] W. O. Henderson, Review of Court's 'Concise Economic History of Britain from 1750 to Recent Times', *Kyklos*, vol. viii (1955), p. 441.

contended to have been respectably founded in classical theory, that if a basic equipment of public works were provided it would enable the economy to function of its own accord, lifting it into the stage where *laissez-faire* would become appropriate. But what the proper extent of the basic equipment would have to be was never clearly thought out. Would roads, bridges, and harbours be enough, combined with loans for approved purposes, leaving it to the initiative of private parties to take these up? Or was it necessary to go farther and positively undertake some large-scale schemes of development? While many, like Scrope, who had specifically studied Irish affairs, advocated the latter, the main body of classical doctrine sanctioned no more than the former. Ministers vacillated, and ultimately quailed at the prospect of proposing the heavy expenditures which special schemes must necessarily have involved.

This is not to deny that much was achieved by the patchwork of *ad hoc* measures which did reach the Statute Book: the Land Improvement Acts alone were a valuable aid to Irish economic improvement. Yet what was done certainly failed to produce the situation which the classical economists would have regarded as the desirable outcome—where further special public expenditure would be rendered unnecessary by the 'natural' forces of economic development taking over. The main reason for this is not hard to discover; it was perceived, though only partially, by Harriet Martineau when she wrote:

The impression which every day's observation strengthens in the traveller's mind is, that till the agriculture of Ireland is improved, little benefit can arise from the large grants which have been, and still are, made for public works. If public works which are designed to open up markets for produce should stimulate the people to the improvement of production, it will be a capital thing; but, till some evidence of this appears, there is something melancholy in the spectacle of a great apparatus which does not seem to be the result of any natural demand.[1]

Miss Martineau here came close to the heart of the matter: public works could be of little value unless they improved the basic industry of the country. Without security of tenure, however, opening markets gave the people no incentive to improve their agriculture. The absence of land reform, then, largely nullified the potential benefits from public works.

[1] H. Martineau, *Letters from Ireland* (Londo 1852), p. 17.

CHAPTER VII

EMIGRATION

I

THE various proposals made and policies adopted to aid Irish economic development through a growth of private or public investment have now been examined. It remains to consider the theoretical and practical aspects of the opposite approach—that of producing a more favourable relationship of capital to population by means of reducing population or checking its growth, through emigration primarily.

Many contemporary authorities regarded this approach as the most direct, and the most likely to be productive of improvement in the short run. To many, indeed, it appeared not so much as an alternative to other development policies as a condition precedent for their success.[1] Yet although belief in the desirability of emigration as a remedy for Ireland came to be very widespread, it did not find much favour with political economists in the early years of the nineteenth century. Thus, as has already been noticed,[2] Ricardo was decidedly of the opinion that reduction of population would not assist Ireland because 'productions would diminish in as great, or even in a greater, proportion'.[3] He agreed with Weyland's view that 'in the early stages of society when the population presses against food, no remedy would be afforded by lessening the number of the people, because the evil they then experience proceeds from the indolence and vice of the people and not in their inability to procure necessaries' but declared Weyland to be 'singularly inconsistent in denying the truth of this principle when applied to Ireland'.[4]

The more normal ground for scepticism about the value of emigration was the Malthusian idea that any 'vacuum' so created must inevitably be speedily filled by a fresh growth of population—McCulloch's statement of this position in 1822 is typical.[5] Malthus himself made no specific reference to emigration as a solution for Irish problems in the various editions of his *Essay on the Principle of Population*; apparently he saw no reason to make Ireland an exception when he stated his general view

---

[1] See, for example, the various works of Wheatley, Torrens and Wilmot Horton, to which specific references are made below; Monteagle to Clarendon, 21 October 1848 (Monteagle Papers, National Library of Ireland).

[2] Above, ch. IV, p. 86; ch. V, p. 134.

[3] *Principles*, p. 100.

[4] Ricardo to Trower, 15 July 1816. *Works and Correspondence*, vol. VII, p. 48. The reference is to John Weyland's *Principles of Population and Production* (London, 1816).

[5] Referred to above, ch. V, p. 134.

that emigration 'might appear, on a first view of the subject, an adequate remedy... but when we advert to experience and the actual state of the uncivilised parts of the globe, instead of anything like an adequate remedy, it will appear but a slight palliative'.[1] Nor was Malthus evidently much impressed with the need for emigration after his tour in Ireland in 1817;[2] but it is significant that when he was producing a new edition of his *Essay* in that same year he felt it necessary to add the passage which runs:

If, for instance, from a combination of external and internal causes, a very great stimulus should be given to the population of a country for ten or twelve years together, and it should then comparatively cease, it is clear that labour will continue flowing into the market with almost undiminished rapidity, while the means of employing and paying it have been essentially contracted. It is precisely under these circumstances that emigration is most useful as a temporary relief; and it is in these circumstances that Great Britain finds herself at present.[3]

By 1817 the distress resulting from the long and painful readjustment after the Napoleonic wars was becoming very conspicuous in Ireland as well as in Britain, and in the search for remedies emigration began to be looked on with more favour. Amongst its earliest advocates was Torrens, who in 1817 produced his *Paper on the Means of Reducing the Poors Rates*.[4] Torrens argued that 'when all the good and well-situated lands of a country have already been appropriated and occupied, it is found impossible to increase capital and subsistence as rapidly as the powers of procreation may multiply the people; and there is no possibility of obviating poverty and misery except by regulating population'.[5] Population might be kept within the limits of subsistence either by the prudential check or by 'a well regulated system of colonisation'. Whilst improved education and such institutions as savings banks might greatly strengthen the prudential check, their effect must necessarily be remote; the growth of pauperism compelled immediate action and, therefore, resort to colonisation. The benefits of such a policy would be political as well as economic, for colonisation 'acts as a safety-valve to the political machine, and allows the expanding vapour to escape, before it is heated to explosion'.[6]

While Torrens rested his case primarily on conditions in Britain, he used the evidence of rapid population growth in Ireland to strengthen it, and posed 'a momentous question.... When increasing capital and skill

---

[1] *Essay on Population* (1826 ed.), vol. II, p. 49.

[2] Unless the 'large manufacturing and commercial Towns' into which he thought 'a great part of this population should be swept from the soil' were to be towns outside Ireland—but this is not at all evident. Cf. above, ch. v, p. 136.

[3] *Essay on Population* (1826 ed.), vol. II, p. 62.

[4] *The Pamphleteer*, no. xx (September 1817), pp. 510–28. Torrens later claimed that in this paper 'the principle of self-supporting colonisation was for the first time propounded'—Torrens to Glenelg, 19 August 1836 (C.O. 384/39). The wording of the paper does not really bear out this claim.

[5] *The Pamphleteer*, loc. cit. p. 518.   [6] *Ibid.* p. 524.

enable the business of agriculture in Ireland to be performed by a smaller number of hands, how are those who must be thrown out of their customary employment to be provided for?' For a time at least, emigration must be the only possible answer, but in 1817 Torrens was prepared to admit that the question had not yet arisen; his arguments had 'confessedly, a reference to a period somewhat remote'.[1]

A distinctly less enthusiastic view of emigration was taken by James Mill when he wrote his well-known article 'Colony' for the Supplement to the *Encyclopaedia Britannica* in 1818. For any population transfer to be advantageous, Mill contended, the land in the region to be colonised must be capable of yielding a greater return to labour than the land in the home country, and the expense of removing the population must not be too great—otherwise the loss of capital from the home country might exceed any gain resulting from lowering population.[2]

These views, expressed by Mill in volume III of the *Supplement*, rather contrasted with those enunciated by David Buchanan in volume IV, under the head of 'Emigration'. Buchanan declared without hesitation that 'it is obvious, that, if there is too little either of subsistence or of employment, the emigration of those who require both to be employed and to be fed, will leave a greater supply for those who remain behind. Wherever there is a greater number of labourers than can be employed—where wages are consequently low, and general distress prevails, emigration is precisely the most effectual remedy for the evil.'[3]

A favourable opinion about the effects of emigration on the home country was also expressed by Whately, who specifically countered Mill's arguments about the possibility of loss of capital.[4] Emigration, he held, might sometimes 'be suggested by the wisest economy, even when the *immediate* support of the individuals in question might cost less at home: if, at a somewhat heavier expense, we have a fair prospect of getting rid of a permanent, and perhaps (as in the case of an increasing family) a growing burden....'.

As for the apprehensions of impoverishment to this country by the transfer of her capital to the other side of the Atlantic, we are convinced that they are altogether visionary. In the first place, we may be sure that whatever inducements we may hold out, few after all, will be found willing to carry their capital to Canada, who have a reasonable assurance of deriving from it the means of living in independence and prosperity at home; and those who have not such a prospect, are probably consulting the interest of their country, as well as their own, by emigrating.[5]

---

[1] *Ibid.* p. 527. The line of reasoning here is essentially the same as that used in *Substance of a Speech delivered by Colonel Torrens...15 Feb. 1827.* Cf. above, ch. v, p. 138.
[2] *Encyclopaedia Britannica: Supplement to the Fourth, Fifth and Sixth Editions,* vol. III, p. 262 (this volume appeared in February 1818).
[3] *Encyclopaedia Britannica Supplement,* vol. IV, p. 108 (published in December 1819).
[4] [Whately], 'Emigration to Canada', *Quarterly Rev.* vol. XXIII (July 1820), pp. 373–400.
[5] *Ibid.* p. 388.

Thus at the beginning of the eighteen-twenties there was some growth of feeling amongst economists in favour of emigration as a means of social improvement, but it could not be said to be either strong or universal. On the other hand some politicians were at this time beginning to take up the idea, and State-sponsored emigrations from Ireland were actually carried out in 1823 and 1825. Here policy moved rather apart from, or perhaps ahead of, current theory. The general trend of economic thought was moving in favour of commercial freedom and hence the removal of restrictions on emigration,[1] but there was as yet no strong body of economic opinion in favour of organised population transfers. The actions of those politicians who took up the idea were not primarily based on economic grounds, but they served to draw public attention to the possibilities of emigration and to stimulate economic thought on the subject.

In Ireland at this time the evidences of increasing population and increasing distress could no longer be ignored. The year 1822 was marked by a partial failure of the potato crop, leading to famine conditions in some districts; in the ensuing season there were bitter agrarian disturbances in the south, with the agitation mainly directed against tithes, though in many instances it was clear that the landlords were also the objects of resentment. The scarcity was met by private subscriptions and public works, while the Government sought to counter agitation by renewing the Insurrection Act, and subsequently by a measure of tithe reform.[2] But the landlords in the disturbed districts of the south were anxious for further measures, and in the spring of 1823 an opportunity of meeting their wishes to some extent presented itself to the ministry.

A certain Mr Ingram, who had emigrated to the Cape of Good Hope in 1819, returned to Britain at the end of 1822 with the object of organising a party of fifty people to be taken to the Cape at his expense to act as indentured servants. He approached the Government with a view to obtaining assistance to take out a larger number—an additional three hundred was suggested. Very soon after this a suggestion for an experiment in Government-sponsored emigration from the south of Ireland to Canada came from Sir John Beverley Robinson, Chief Justice of Upper Canada, and his brother Peter. Robert Wilmot Horton, then the Under-Secretary for the Colonies, was favourably disposed towards these schemes, which fitted in with his own general enthusiasm for emigration and colonial development; Peel and Goulburn, the Irish Chief Secretary, took up the proposals because they saw in them a means of meeting the Irish landlords' anxiety for action through the removal of some of the most turbulent elements in the population of Munster.

---

[1] See McCulloch's article 'Combination Laws—Restraints on Emigration', *Edinburgh Rev.* vol. xxxix (January 1824), pp. 315–45.

[2] *Annual Register* (1822), pp. (22) and (48).

For this purpose the main reliance was placed on the Robinson scheme for emigration to Canada, which was regarded as an experiment that might be repeated if successful and at the same time serve as an example to stimulate privately organised emigration. Under it, Peter Robinson was to go to Ireland to select 500 would-be emigrants: those chosen were to be conveyed from Cork to Quebec, and thence to Upper Canada, at the public expense: every adult male was to be given an order for 70 acres of land there and each individual supplied with provisions for one year.[1] Horton gave the details of the plan to a group of Irish peers and landlords at Goulburn's house, where 'it distinctly met with the approval and assent of the gentlemen to whom it was read'.[2]

So in May 1823 Peter Robinson went to Fermoy, in Co. Cork, to select the emigrants with the help of Lord Ennismore and other local proprietors.[3] Horton did not seek parliamentary approval for the scheme until 23 June, when he asked the Commons to agree to a vote of £15,000 towards the expenses of Robinson's undertaking. There was no real opposition to the request, but the attitude taken by Ricardo is noteworthy. In one of his last speeches in the Commons, he repeated his conviction that if security of property could be guaranteed in Ireland, abundant investment would soon follow; 'he should not, however, object to the present grant by way of experiment, and to show the people of Ireland that Parliament was anxious to afford them whatever assistance was possible'.[4]

There were some complaints of the inadequacy of the scheme to meet the evils existing in Ireland, to which Peel replied that 'the grant was not intended to do more than render emigration popular, by facilitating the removal of persons to the Colonies, and insuring the success of the enterprise. He thought it better to commence on a small scale, and thus form a basis for encouraging colonisation, which if found expedient, might afterwards be extended.'[5]

[1] Evidence of R. Wilmot Horton before the Select Committee on Employment of the Poor in Ireland: *Minutes of Evidence* (1823 (561), vol. vi), pp. 169–70.
For a full account of the emigrations organised by Robinson in 1823 and 1825, see H. I. Cowan, *British Emigration to British North America, 1783–1837* (Toronto, 1928), ch. v and W. F. Adams, *Ireland and Irish Emigration to the New World* (New Haven, 1932), ch. vi.
[2] Evidence of Horton, *loc. cit.* p. 170. See Goulburn to Wellesley, 21 May 1823 (B.M. Add. MSS. 37301).
[3] Evidence of Peter Robinson before the Select Committee of the House of Lords on Disturbances in Ireland, 1824: *Minutes of Evidence* (1825 (200), vol. vii), pp. 249–51.
While Robinson here stated that 'the measure was intended chiefly for the relief and comfort of the poorer classes', the private correspondence between Robinson, Ennismore and Horton, preserved in C.O. 384/12, shows clearly that the primary object was to get rid of 'troublesome characters'.
[4] *Morning Chronicle*, 24 June 1823. The report in the *Belfast News-Letter*, 1 July 1823, quotes Ricardo as having added that 'he could not consent to any large grants for the purpose hereafter'. There is no report of this debate in Hansard, nor is Ricardo's speech included by Mr Sraffa in vol. v of his edition of Ricardo's *Works*.
[5] *Morning Chronicle*, 24 June 1823.

The experiment proceeded, and in July, Robinson brought out a total of 568 Irish settlers to Canada at a cost of £22 per head. Both he and Horton declared the emigration to be a complete success, but reports of disturbances created by the settlers, and of numbers absconding from their holdings, provided ample material for critics of the scheme and sowed doubts among those less committed to it than Robinson and Horton.[1]

In the following year conditions in Ireland were somewhat improved, and Horton and his colleagues did not see fit to go ahead with any new scheme of emigration.[2] But in the evidence which he gave before the Select Committee on the State of Ireland in February 1825 Horton showed that he was still a strong believer in the value of emigration as a remedy for Ireland and declared that he saw 'no reason in principle why the emigration, which has been successfully carried into operation in the year 1823...may not be carried into effect with reference to any conceivable number of persons disposed to emigrate'.[3]

A second experiment, on a somewhat larger scale, was then being planned for the summer of 1825. In piloting his scheme through Parliament on this occasion Horton encountered decided opposition, based on reports of the bad behaviour of the emigrants of 1823 and the high cost of their removal and settlement. The funds which Horton sought were voted, but the temper of the House was against any further expenditure without investigation, and the Government thought it well to accede to requests for a committee on emigration.[4]

The emigration of 1825 followed the same lines as that of 1823; in April, Peter Robinson again went to the south of Ireland, this time to Mitchelstown. He found the people much more anxious to take advantage of the Government offer than in 1823; there were more than fifty thousand applicants for passages. Out of these he selected some two thousand, who were conveyed to Upper Canada at a slightly reduced cost—£21 per head.[5]

[1] See Evidence of Robinson before the Lords Committee on Disturbances in Ireland, 1824, *loc. cit.* pp. 249–61; evidence of Horton before the Select Committee of the House of Commons on the State of Ireland, 1825—reprinted as Appendix II to *First Report of the Emigration Committee* (1826 (404), vol. IV), p. 317.
For some account of the disturbances amongst the settlers of 1823, see J. B. Robinson to Horton 10 and 20 May 1824, C.O. 384/12; in the first of these letters, the Chief Justice of Upper Canada confessed to being 'something staggered in my opinion of Irish emigration'.
Historical judgments of the 1823 emigration have generally been unfavourable: see, for example, N. MacDonald, *Canada, 1763–1841—Immigration and Settlement* (London, 1939), pp. 256–7; Adams, *Ireland and Irish Emigration to the New World*, pp. 281–3.
[2] See Cowan, *British Emigration*, p. 107.
[3] Evidence of Horton, 23 February 1825, *loc. cit.* p. 322.
[4] *Hansard*, 2nd ser. vol. XII, cols. 1358–60 (15 April 1825); *Morning Chronicle*, 14 June 1825. The appointment of a Select Committee was deferred until the following session, as it was thought to be too late for it to complete any useful investigation in the session of 1825.
[5] Robinson to Horton, 31 May 1825 (C.O. 384/13). Evidence of Robinson before the Select Committee on Emigration, 10 May 1827: *Minutes of Evidence* (1827 (550), vol. V), p. 344.

The experiments of 1823 and 1825 did not have the effects which Horton and Peel had hoped to see. On the one hand, they did stimulate the desire to emigrate in Ireland, but led the people to look for a continuance of Government aid rather than to rely on voluntary efforts.[1] On the other, their heavy cost deterred Parliament and the Colonial Office from continuing the scheme and acted as an obstacle to future attempts to use emigration as a positive policy for Irish improvement.

But if the 'Canadian experiments' failed to set off a fresh tide of emigration, voluntary or otherwise, they certainly helped to set off a tide of discussion which flowed on for more than twenty years. In Parliament, in Horton's two Select Committees of 1826 and 1827, in pamphlets, newspapers and periodicals, the arguments for and against emigration were thrashed out at length, and most of the leading economists of the day were drawn into the controversy.

Emigration was not, either at this stage or later, a purely Irish question; it was one aspect of the whole 'condition-of-England question'. Nevertheless, most of the participants in the debate took it for granted that Ireland was the key factor in the problem. By the mid-eighteen-twenties Irish landlords were convinced that their only hope of salvation lay in removing the cottiers from the land and consolidating their holdings into large farms, and most economists were prepared to concede that this was the best, if not indeed the only possible line for economic advance in Ireland. With the passing of the Sub-letting Act in 1826, the policy received the formal endorsement of the legislature. It was clear that if it were to be carried into effect with any semblance of vigour, it must result in the eviction of large numbers of under-tenants, who could have but little prospect of finding alternative means of subsistence in Ireland.

The obvious, and almost the only, resource for such people was to migrate to Great Britain, and at this time that course had suddenly been made much easier for them by the opening of regular steam packet services between England and Ireland.[2] The prospect of a large-scale displacement of the Irish agricultural population, which had seemed 'somewhat remote' to Torrens in 1817 appeared uncomfortably imminent to many English writers in and after 1824. 'Is any one sanguine enough', asked Henry Booth, a philanthropic Liverpool merchant, 'to imagine that the independent character of the English labourer (too much an ideal

---

[1] The Colonial Office continued to receive applications for assistance to emigrate to North America from Ireland years after the schemes had been terminated. See, for example, applications filed in C.O. 384/16 (1827).
[2] The City of Dublin Steam Packet Company was founded in 1824 and was soon carrying deck passengers to Liverpool for 6d. per head. 'The Irish Channel became the centre of a competition so fierce that in 1825...the rival steamships between Belfast and Glasgow were carrying first-class passengers for 2s. a head and deck passengers for nothing at all'— Thornton, *British Shipping*, 2nd ed. (Cambridge, 1959), p. 12.

picture at the present moment) can be sustained amidst the debasing competition, resulting from the eternal influx of poverty and degradation in the never-ceasing importations of Irish peasantry?'[1] In 1826, William Ellis used the Ricardian wages and profits analysis to show that while a displacement of labour by machinery might ultimately benefit labourers as well as capitalists, the displacement of one grade of labour by a lower grade, such as he conceived the Irish to be, must be always injurious to the labourer, though it might increase the profits of the capitalist.[2]

Fears of the degradation of the English labourer to the Irish level, with the attendant dangers of increasing population and poor-rates, led, as has already been shown,[3] to some suggestions for the control of Irish migration but to more for the introduction of a Poor Law into Ireland. The former alternative was virtually a political impossibility if the Union was to be maintained,[4] and the latter was, to say the least, unpopular with Irish landlords. There remained a third possibility—to induce the Irish to emigrate to Canada or elsewhere instead of migrating to Britain. The advocates of emigration did not lose the opportunity of pointing out how a policy of colonisation could enable the Irish proprietors to achieve the desired clearance of their estates without imposing an intolerable burden of poor-rates either on their English neighbours or themselves.

One of the earliest and most optimistic advocates of the policy of speeding farm consolidation through emigration was Wheatley, who thought that 'by offering the labouring poor of Ireland more advantages to emigrate to Canada for good, than they could obtain by their temporary emigrations to England during harvest, the poor of England set free from the competition of the Irish, would be able to earn sufficient wages during summer to support themselves in winter without parish relief'; by a judicious extension of the emigration offer, then, to the English labourers the position might easily be reached where 'the poor rates would become extinct of themselves'.[5]

---

[1] Booth, *Condition of the Poor in Large Towns*, p. 45.
[2] 'There is a rate of wages below which not even an Irish labourer can be maintained. Laying aside all objections to the introduction of a poorer class of labourers on the ground of contamination, an influx of Irish labourers until that lowest rate was reached, might be a means of increasing the quantity of employment for the English, provided that employment were above the abilities of an Irish labourer. The introduction of horses and of Irish labourers would, if that were the case, be analogous, as to their effects upon the English labourers. But there is no such marked distinctions [*sic*] between English and Irish labourers. ...The general tendency of wages, therefore, would be to an equalisation between English and Irish.' [Wm. Ellis], 'Employment of Machinery', *Westminster Rev.* vol. v (January 1826), p. 121.   [3] Above, ch. IV, p. 103.
[4] That the Union must be maintained was invariably taken as axiomatic by the British politicians of the day, but not always by the economists. See [James Mill], 'State of the Nation', *Westminster Rev.* vol. VI (October 1826), p. 278; Ricardo to Maria Edgeworth, 26 May 1823: *Works and Correspondence*, vol. IX, p. 296.
[5] J. Wheatley, *A Letter to the Duke of Devonshire on the state of Ireland and the General Effects of Colonization* (Calcutta, 1824), p. 5.

Others were not always prepared to claim as much as this, but there were many who saw that if emigration and consolidation were put together each could strengthen the case for the other. The chief objection to consolidation was the probable burden of supporting the displaced tenants, but emigration could remove this: a strong objection to emigration was that the 'vacuum' would quickly be filled by a new growth of population, but this could be prevented by consolidation.

By the mid-twenties both McCulloch and Malthus had come to endorse this argument. Asked to suggest means of checking the excessive growth of population in Ireland, McCulloch replied: 'I should think that the abolition...of the practice of sub-letting without the consent of the landlord would, by lessening the facilities for obtaining small patches of land, have a tendency to diminish the ratio of the progress of population... and if you were to make a system of emigration carried on by government come in aid of those measures, it would also operate beneficially.'[1]

Malthus, when examined before the Emigration Committee, as to the desirability of the practice of consolidation, replied: 'I think it most particularly desirable, and that if Government ever makes a sacrifice in order to relieve a redundant population, it is at such a period that it is most called upon to do it; because the change cannot take place without depriving a number of persons of their means of living, and consequently if they are not removed by emigration, it cannot be done without producing most extreme distress.'[2]

Horton did not fail to make good use of these arguments in the reports of his two committees. In the first report, it was pointed out that the Sub-letting Act had 'met with the entire concurrence of both Houses of Parliament....But the House will not fail to remark, that all the advantages that may be derived from this Act will be diminished, if not rendered absolutely nugatory, unless a well-organised system of Emigration should be established, concurrently with the measure itself.'[3] And in the third report the ragged spectre of the 'potato-fed Irishman', which was still to haunt Carlyle a generation later,[4] was allowed to loom large:

The question of emigration, as connected with Ireland, has already been decided by the population itself; and that which remains for the legislature to decide is to

[1] Evidence of McCulloch before the Select Committee on the State of Ireland, 8 June 1825: *Minutes of Evidence*; (1825 (129)), vol. VIII, p. 817. And see his article 'Emigration' in the *Edinburgh Rev.* vol. XLV (December 1826), especially pp. 52 and 72—quoted above, p. 134.

[2] Evidence of Malthus before the Select Committee on Emigration, 5 May 1827: *Minutes of Evidence* (1826–7 (550), vol. V), p. 312. Adams states erroneously that Horton also called McCulloch before the Emigration Committee: *Irish Emigration*, p. 285.

[3] *Report from the Select Committee on Emigration from the United Kingdom* (1826 (404), vol. IV), p. 9.

[4] 'Not a wandering Irish lackall that comes over to us, to parade his rags and hunger, and sin and misery, but comes in all senses as an irrepressible missionary of the like to our people'—Carlyle, 'Ireland and the British Chief Governor', *Spectator*, 13 May 1848.

what points the emigration shall be directed, whether it shall be turned to the improvement of the North American colonies, or whether it shall be suffered and encouraged to take that which otherwise will be, and is, its inevitable course, to deluge Great Britain with poverty and wretchedness, and gradually but certainly to equalise the state of the English and Irish peasantry.... The question, whether an extensive plan of Emigration shall or shall not be adopted, appears to your Committee to resolve itself into the simple point, whether the wheat-fed population of Great Britain shall or shall not be supplanted by the potato-fed population of Ireland?[1]

It was natural that the advocates of State-aided emigration should thus attempt to prove that it was in the best interests of the English and Irish proprietors, who, after all, would have the deciding say in the passage of any measure through the legislature; but in so doing they laid themselves open to the charge of favouring the propertied classes whilst disregarding the feelings of the poor.[2] Although some statements of the case for emigration would certainly lend support to this opinion,[3] most of its advocates took care to point out that colonisation, properly organised, would be of real benefit not only to those who emigrated but also to those of the poorer classes who remained behind. Whilst the emigrants might be translated from a state of destitution or near-destitution to one of comfortable independence, the more favourable ratio of capital to population at home, which their removal would produce, would have the effect of raising wages and improving conditions for those remaining.[4]

On the other hand some critics argued that this very rise of wages might be detrimental to the long-term interests of Ireland. 'For if it were true that great things are to be expected from the introduction of foreign capital, to all such anticipations the answer is: the depreciation of wages is almost the *exclusive* inducement for its introduction.... In proportion then, as wages rise, the motive for its introduction diminishes.'[5] However, since the advocates of increased investment in Ireland did not rest their case on the persistence of lower wage-rates there, this was not a particularly important argument for the sponsors of emigration to meet. What was important for them to prove was that their plans would not deplete capital as much as population, since colonisation as Horton envisaged it did involve a cost, and a considerable one, to the mother country. The first answer to this was to say that all the sums advanced to aid emigration

---

[1] *Third Report* (1826–7 (550), vol. v), p. 7.

[2] For a strong statement of this view, see *No Emigration. The Testimony of Experience, before a Committee of Agriculturists and Manufacturers, on the Report of the Emigration Committee of the House of Commons: Sir John English in the Chair* (London, 1828).

[3] See Senior, *Remarks on Emigration* (London, 1831), p. 5.

[4] See Buchanan, *Encyclopaedia Britannica Supplement*, quoted above, p. 205.

[5] *Eclectic Rev.* n.s., vol. xxviii (1827), p. 240. The same point was later made, with more sophistication, by H. Merivale in his *Lectures on Colonisation and Colonies* (London, 1841), p. 152. Merivale there pointed out that emigration from Ireland would raise the rate of wages, but not immediately the productivity of labour.

could be recouped from the emigrants once they had established themselves;[1] but it was evident that no very certain method of doing this could easily be evolved. It was therefore necessary to prove that if some cost were incurred, it would be outweighed by the advantages of emigration. An answer must be given to such assertions as Hume's, that 'it never could answer for them to incur the expense of 100 l. for sending a poor man and his family from Ireland to the Canadas. Give the poor man the 100 l., and he would establish himself as comfortably in Ireland as anywhere else.'[2]

The first stage in the answer was really the point previously made by Whately in 1820—that the cost of emigration would be worth while if it ridded the country of a permanent and perhaps growing burden.[3] But for a complete answer it was necessary also to show that the funds used for emigration could not be invested to better advantage in schemes which would give employment at home. Here the main alternative was some scheme of public works, such as reclamation of waste lands.

Horton and his supporters were able to produce a number of arguments for the comparative ineffectiveness of such projects. First they contended that it was obviously preferable to employ capital in opening up the fertile lands of the colonies rather than in attempting to cultivate the poorest lands at home.[4] Not very consistently, Horton himself later argued that the production from reclaimed lands in Ireland coming on the English market must damage English landowners and farmers.[5] Secondly, it was argued that reclamation and other public works could only produce a temporary improvement in the condition of the labouring classes, which would ultimately stimulate a further increase in population.[6] This objection, however, could be overcome, 'if the poor who were selected for such employment were to be abstracted by colonisation when the public works were finished'.[7]

Such were the main arguments used in the debate which centred in and around the hearings of the Emigration Committees of 1826 and 1827. On the whole, its outcome was decidedly in favour of the introduction of some large-scale plan of emigration, primarily with reference to Ireland. The leading economists of the day had publicly given their endorsement to

[1] See *Third Report from Select Committee on Emigration*, p. 20.
[2] *Hansard*, 2nd ser. vol. XIV, col. 1364 (14 March 1826).
[3] See above, p. 205; also Senior, *Remarks on Emigration*, pp. 9–12.
[4] *Third Report from Select Committee on Emigration*, p. 40.
[5] Sir R. W. Horton, *Causes and Remedies of Pauperism*, series I (London, 1830), p. 53. For a statement of the obvious retort that cheap food from Canada would damage both the English and the Irish agricultural interests, see *Commentaries on National Policy, and Ireland* (1831), p. 234.
[6] '...Although the tenants that were at first employed might be tolerably well off, yet their children would greatly aggravate the evil intended to be remedied, and after a short time there would be a much greater redundancy of population than before.'—Evidence of Malthus before the Emigration Committee (1826–7 (550), vol. V), p. 321.
[7] Horton, *Causes and Remedies of Pauperism*, series IV (London, 1830), p. 65. The passage quoted formed part of a query addressed to Senior, who, in reply, concurred with Horton's view.

such a plan, and so had some of the principal Irish landlords. The main objection to it was the probable cost, but many of those who opposed State-aided emigration on this ground, such as Hume, did not object to emigration in principle, preferring only to see it carried on by private agencies. The most determined and constant opposition came from Sadler and Cobbett,[1] who vigorously championed the poor and their right to live and work at home rather than be thrust abroad. But their emotions did them greater credit than their use of reasoning, and their intemperate attacks were not likely to carry much weight with the groups whom Horton needed to influence in order to get his policy carried into effect. Yet just when circumstances seemed propitious for Horton's success, his influence in policy and theory alike suffered a serious reverse.

Horton had derived most support for his emigration schemes of 1823 and 1825 from Peel and Goulburn, but when Canning became Prime Minister in April 1827, Horton did not follow their example in resigning but remained a supporter of the ministry and was sworn of the Privy Council in May. At the end of June he brought forward the third report of his Emigration Committee 'distinctly recommending a pecuniary advance, in the nature of a loan, for the purpose of facilitating Emigration'. The proposal was for a loan of £1,140,000 to finance the removal of 95,000 people in three years; it was suggested that the process should begin with an advance of £240,000 in 1828–9.[2]

In the summer of 1827 Horton's prospects of securing a vote for his scheme in the next session appeared good. The fact that Huskisson had become Colonial Secretary when Goderich formed his short-lived ministry was in Horton's favour, for Huskisson was also a believer in systematic emigration. But when the Goderich ministry collapsed and Wellington and Peel came back to power in January 1828, Horton found himself out of office. He had identified himself with the Canningites, and while Wellington felt that the Canningite Huskisson was important enough to be retained, Horton was not.[3]

Huskisson remained friendly to Horton's ideas, but it was obvious that he could not commit the new ministry to adopt them.[4] In the event, Horton did not bring forward a motion on Irish emigration until 24 June, when he attempted to get the House to agree to adopt a measure early in 1829, without specifying the details of it. By this time, Huskisson had left the Government and Peel did not give Horton any encouragement.

[1] Sadler, *Ireland, its Evils and their Remedies*; *Cobbett's Weekly Political Register*, 26 April 1828, and vol. LXV *passim*.
[2] *Third Report*, p. 18.
[3] Adams, *Ireland and Irish Emigration*, p. 292; E. G. Jones, *Sir R. J. Wilmot Horton, Bart., Politician and Pamphleteer* (Unpublished thesis, University of Bristol, 1936), pp. 85–90.
[4] See his speech on Horton's motion for a Bill to enable English parishes to mortgage the poor-rates in aid of emigration—*Hansard*, 2nd ser. vol. XVIII, col. 1553 (17 April 1828).

Instead he pointed out what many considered the crucial objection to Horton's plan—that by a very large outlay it would remove only a very small fraction of the distressed population.[1] Peel's statement that 'he could not consent to the policy of laying out large sums of public money to encourage emigration', whilst stressing the desirability of aiding 'volunteer emigration', foreshadowed the form of many later official statements on the subject.

Horton continued to raise the question of emigration in the House in 1829 and 1830, but without ministerial support he was powerless to achieve anything.[2] He attempted to stimulate a wider interest in the subject by lecturing and writing, but in this field he was now faced with the competition of a better idea, more skilfully propagated. Edward Gibbon Wakefield's 'Letters from Sydney' had begun to appear in the *Morning Chronicle* in 1829, and already his schemes of 'systematic colonisation' were gaining a remarkable amount of attention and support.

II

At first, the leading economists of the day were sharply divided over the merits of Wakefield's proposals for financing emigration from the sale of colonial lands at a 'sufficient price'. The first step in Wakefield's campaign to gain support for his idea was the foundation of the National Colonisation Society, which he and Robert Gouger launched in May 1830.[3] Amongst the original members were John Stuart Mill, Charles Buller and Torrens. Wakefield's ideas were already accepted by a number of the philosophical radicals, even by the aged Bentham himself. On the other hand, they were vigorously opposed by Wilmot Horton, who, though he had joined the National Colonisation Society, objected to the whole principle of emigration financed from land sales. His own ideas were in turn the subject of attack from the Wakefield group, who constantly stressed the superiority of 'systematic colonisation' over 'mere emigration'.

When the aims of the National Colonisation Society were first published,[4] Horton persuaded James Mill, Malthus and Torrens to write criticisms of them, which he circulated. The main ground of their criticism was that the 'concentration', on which Wakefield so strongly insisted, would involve the cultivation of inferior soils, while good lands were still unused.

---

[1] *Hansard*, 2nd ser. vol. xix, col. 1515 (24 June 1828); Horton always met this criticism by saying that the removal of a fraction of the distressed population would allow the remainder to escape from distress.

[2] *Ibid.* vol. xxi, cols. 1720, 1740 (4 June 1829); vol. xxiii, col. 26 (9 March 1830).

[3] See R. C. Mills, *The Colonization of Australia (1829–42)* (London, 1915), ch. vi.

[4] In a pamphlet entitled *A Statement of the Principles and Objects of a Proposed National Society for the Cure and Prevention of Pauperism by Means of Systematic Colonisation* (London, 1830). See Mills, *Colonisation of Australia*, pp. 149–51.

In a pamphlet published over the name of Charles Tennant, M.P., one of his supporters,[1] Wakefield explained that this was not the case, the term concentration being used by him simply to imply an adequate combination of labour.

This explanation satisfied Torrens, who withdrew his objections and became one of the strongest exponents of the Wakefield scheme.[2] James Mill remained unconvinced, while Scrope also opposed Wakefield, but on different grounds. Looking primarily to the case of Canada, Scrope argued that fixing a high price on future land grants would simply prevent sales until all the 'vast tracts' already disposed of were fully settled; he therefore suggested a tax on labour as an alternative means of raising funds for emigration.[3] Senior had already given his support to Horton's schemes, and continued to do so.[4]

The hostility between Horton and Wakefield led to the dissolution of the National Colonisation Society at the end of 1830.[5] The whole episode attracted little public attention at the time, but it marked the beginning of a new period in the theory and policy of colonisation. Horton soon afterwards went to Ceylon as Governor, where he lamented that no ministry had ever taken his schemes seriously and complained that 'there is a *spell* and *curse* on my public career'.[6] Wakefield on the other hand continued to write and to organise and secured a steadily growing influence.

In the analysis of emigration problems, the principal advance which Wakefield and his followers were able to make over earlier thinkers was in showing how population transfers could be financed from land sales, thus eliminating the objection of cost to the mother country.[7] But as an additional counter to the argument that colonisation might reduce the resources of the home country, they developed the idea that not only population, but capital also, had reached the point of redundancy in Britain. Diverging from classical orthodoxy, they argued that accumula-

---

[1] C. Tennant, *A Letter to the Rt. Hon. Sir George Murray on Systematic Colonization* (London, 1830).

[2] Evidence of Torrens before the Select Committee on Disposal of Lands in the British Colonies, 30 June 1836: *Minutes of Evidence* (1836 (512), vol. XI), p. 135. See L. C. Robbins, *Robert Torrens and the Evolution of Classical Economics* (London, 1958), pp. 167–70.

[3] [Scrope], 'Causes and Remedies of Pauperism', *Quarterly Rev.* vol. XLIII (May 1830), p. 266. Scrope to Howick, 5 March 1831; Gouger to Scrope, 2 March 1831; Scrope to Gouger, 5 March 1831. (All in C.O. 384/28.)

[4] The pamphlet *Remarks on Emigration* (1831), written by Senior in collaboration with James Stephen, advocated colonisation according to Horton's principles. And see the correspondence between Senior and Horton reproduced in the latter's *Causes and Remedies of Pauperism*, series IV.

[5] See Pike, 'Wilmot Horton and the National Colonisation Society', *Historical Studies, Australia and New Zealand*, vol. VII, no. 26 (May 1956), pp. 205–10.

[6] Horton to Spring Rice, from Colombo, 5 November 1833 (Monteagle Papers, National Library of Ireland).

[7] See E. G. Wakefield, *A Letter from Sydney*, Appendix—Everyman edition (London, 1929), p. 101.

tion of capital would still continue after the rate of profits had reached a minimum. In this event, 'capital frequently increases without providing any more employment for labour....It follows, that capital, for which there is no employment at home, might be spent on emigration without diminishing employment for labour to the slightest extent.'[1]

This argument might be advanced plausibly enough for Great Britain, but it could hardly be said to apply to the United Kingdom. From Ireland there constantly came complaints of lack of capital; if it were redundant in England, why could the surplus not be diverted to Ireland and used to give employment at home, without asking the Irish people to emigrate? This point was specifically taken up on several occasions, not by Wakefield, but by Torrens, who argued that the first effect of using capital to improve agriculture in Ireland must be to reduce the numbers employed. Though ultimately these, and even more, people might be absorbed into manu-facturing employment 'Ireland, in advancing towards wealth and prosperity must necessarily pass through a period of the most aggravated and intoler-able distress', which could only be relieved by emigration.[2] In later years, as has been shown above,[3] Torrens came to doubt the possibility of absorbing the population displaced from agriculture into Irish industries, and this served to strengthen his conviction of the necessity for emigration. Yet, unlike many supporters of emigration, he was also prepared to advocate 'home colonisation' on waste lands.[4]

To Wakefield and most of his group, apart from Torrens, the Irish problem was of quite secondary importance, their main concern being with the development and administration of the British colonies. Yet in seeking to secure the acceptance of their schemes towards this end, they affected the policy of the Colonial Office towards emigration in a way which had considerable importance in relation to Irish affairs. Some account of the evolution of that general policy, and the influence of the Colonial Reformers upon it, is therefore necessary here.[5]

The first evidence of official acceptance of the Wakefield theory was Goderich's despatch to the Governor of New South Wales in February 1831, directing that unappropriated lands should only be disposed of by auction sale at a price of not less than five shillings per acre. The inspira-tion for this appears to have come from Howick, later the third Earl Grey, the first and probably the most important convert to Wakefield's doctrines amongst the politicians of the day. These 'Ripon Regulations', as they

[1] E. G. Wakefield, *England and America* (London, 1833), vol. II, pp. 99–100.
[2] Torrens, *Substance of Speech...on Emigration* (1827), p. 41.
[3] Ch. V, p. 139.
[4] See Torrens, *The Colonisation of South Australia* (London, 1835), pp. 229–49; *idem, Self-supporting Colonisation; Ireland Saved, without Cost to the Imperial Treasury* (London, 1847), p. 31.
[5] For a full account, see F. H. Hitchins, *The Colonial Land and Emigration Commission* (Philadelphia, 1931).

217

later came to be called,[1] did not embody the principle that all proceeds of land sales must be devoted to financing emigration, though a considerable proportion was so used.[2]

In February 1831, Howick brought forward a Bill to encourage pauper emigration from parishes in England, suggesting at the same time the desirability of its extension to Ireland.[3] This he conceded to be based on Wilmot Horton's ideas, but at the same time he added a proposal which owed more to Wakefield and Torrens—for establishing a commission with the responsibility of superintending emigration.

Howick's Bill lapsed owing to the dissolution of Parliament, but in June 1831, Goderich appointed a temporary commission 'to diffuse information on Emigration and to assist persons desirous to emigrate'. During their brief term of office, the Commissioners extended their functions to cover the financial assistance of emigration to New South Wales and Van Diemen's Land from the land revenues of those colonies; but in August 1832, the Commission was wound up, and its functions were transferred to the Colonial Office, which invoked the assistance of a voluntary charitable body known as the London Emigration Committee in the work of selecting emigrants who were to receive assisted passages financed from land sales.

Dissatisfied with the partial application of their principles in the case of the existing Australian colonies, the Colonial Reformers had now turned their attention to the formation of a wholly new one—South Australia. In 1834, the South Australia Act[4] became law and in May 1835 the South Australian Colonisation Commissioners were appointed, with Torrens as their Chairman.[5]

Meanwhile, the volume of private emigration, mostly Irish, was growing considerably, and complaints of the numerous frauds practised on the emigrants and the constant violation of the Passenger Act passed in 1828 for their protection, had forced the Colonial Office to undertake the appointment of emigration officers. These men, all half-pay naval officers, were assigned to the principal ports with loosely defined duties which included mainly the enforcement of the provisions of the Passenger Act and general assistance and protection to emigrants.[6]

In 1836, Wakefield and his associates contrived to secure the appointment of a Select Committee of the Commons to investigate the whole

[1] After Goderich's elevation to the Earldom of Ripon in 1833.
[2] See Mills, *Colonisation of Australia*, pp. 160, 170.
[3] *Hansard*, 3rd ser. vol. II, col. 875 (22 February 1831). Horton had brought in a Bill to enable parishes to mortgage their revenues to finance emigration in 1828 and again in 1830. See above, p. 214, note 4.
[4] 4 and 5 Will. IV, c. 95.
[5] See Mills, *Colonisation of Australia*, ch. VIII, for details of the negotiations.
[6] See O. McDonagh, 'Emigration and the State, 1833–55; An Essay in Administrative History', *Transactions of the Royal Historical Society*, 5th ser. vol. V (1955), pp. 133–60.

question of the disposal of colonial lands. Wakefield and Torrens were the principal witnesses, and most of the members of the Committee were favourably disposed towards their ideas. Not surprisingly, therefore, the report recommended the adoption of the main features of the Wakefield scheme, including the establishment of a Central Board in London, responsible not only for all arrangements in connection with the sale of colonial lands, but also for 'so directing the stream of Emigration, which may be expected to flow into the Colonies from the Mother Country, as to proportion, in each, the supply of labour to the demand'.[1]

At the end of 1836 the London Emigration Committee, which had been harshly criticised by Wakefield in his evidence before the Committee on Colonial Lands, resigned, and the Colonial Secretary decided to appoint one of his permanent officials, T. F. Elliot, to the newly created post of 'Agent-General for Emigration'. The Agent-General had the task of superintending emigration generally, and specifically of carrying on the existing schemes of State-aided emigration to Australia; in this latter connection, Elliot appointed officers in both England and Ireland to carry out the work of selecting emigrants who were [to receive Government passages.[2] Elliot's sphere of operations overlapped to some extent with that of the South Australian Colonisation Commissioners, and in 1839 James Stephen evolved a scheme for amalgamating the two offices, which he felt would produce some economies and at the same time 'go far to satisfy the demands of Mr Ward and his associates on this subject'.[3] Russell, who was then Stephen's chief at the Colonial Office, quickly adopted the suggestion, and in January 1840 appointed Torrens, Elliot and Edward Villiers to be the first Colonial Land and Emigration Commissioners.

The duties of the Commission included the collection and diffusion of information about the colonies, the sale of colonial lands, and the application of the proceeds to assist emigration. This system was carried on until 1856, when most of the Australian colonies took control of their own waste lands and began to appoint their own emigration agents; the Commission nevertheless continued in existence until 1872.[4]

By 1840, when the Colonial Land and Emigration Commission was established, the principles of Government policy with regard to emigration were firmly settled. In essence, they were two-fold: on the one hand, the Government was prepared to supply information and advice to the

[1] *Report from the Select Committee on Disposal of Lands in the British Colonies*, (1836 (512), vol. XI), p. iv.
[2] On the appointment of such officers in Ireland, see Elliot to Stephen, 18 and 19 July 1838—C.O. 386/43.
[3] Memorandum by Stephen, 10 December 1839, C.O. 13/15. Quoted in Mills, *Colonisation of Australia*, p. 304. H. G. Ward was the Radical Chairman of the 1836 Committee on Colonial Lands.
[4] Hitchins, *The Colonial Land and Emigration Commission*, p. 204.

voluntary emigrant, and protect him against some of the risks of his journey. On the other, a mechanism was provided whereby some portion of colonial land revenues was appropriated to assist emigration. Once these policies were determined and being administered by the Colonial Office, successive ministries, whether Whig or Tory, felt fully justified in withstanding any demands for a more vigorous system of State-aided colonisation which might involve the home Exchequer in increased expenditure.[1]

Hence after 1831 there was comparatively little chance of any grandiose scheme for aiding Ireland through planned emigration being officially adopted; but that did not prevent a great many schemes of the kind being put forward, although from the granting of Catholic Emancipation in 1829 until the enactment of the Irish Poor Law in 1838 the issue of emigration was more or less subsidiary to the problem of poor relief. Some of the opponents of a Poor Law for Ireland advocated a plan of emigration in the hope that it could render a compulsory provision for the poor unnecessary; some of the supporters of a Poor Law advocated emigration as a means of reducing the burden of a poor-rate and easing the process of its introduction.

Thus Spring Rice's Committee of 1830 on the Irish Poor, which seemed prepared to recommend every expedient in preference to compulsory relief, declared that 'Emigration, as a remedial measure, is more applicable to Ireland than to any other part of the Empire' and favoured the idea that labourers employed on public works should be encouraged to save a portion of their wages towards the cost of their emigration.[2] Similarly Senior in his *Letter to Lord Howick* of 1831 declared himself 'anxious that every experiment should be tried for the relief of Ireland' except assistance to the able-bodied poor; amongst the experiments he suggested was 'that public money should be advanced to facilitate emigration'.[3]

The views of Spring Rice and Senior differed much from those of G. C. Lewis, a confirmed believer in the value of the workhouse system; yet Lewis also wrote that 'the operation of a system of relief in facilitating the transition of cottier farmers into labourers ought at the same time to be assisted by COLONISATION, and this on as large a scale as the means of the country would permit'.[4]

There were, of course, those who at this period believed that the proper concomitant of, or even substitute for, a Poor Law in Ireland was a system of public works. Few, however, were prepared to assert that this could be carried to a point which would make emigration altogether

[1] See Hitchins, *ibid.* p. 57.
[2] *Fourth Report from Select Committee on the State of the Poor in Ireland* (1830 [667], vol. VII), pp. 49–50.
[3] P. 45.   [4] Lewis, *Local Disturbances in Ireland*, p. 332.

unnecessary. One exception was A. H. Lynch, who steadfastly opposed emigration plans and managed to get the Select Committee on Public Works, of which he was Chairman in 1835, to make a report declaring that 'it may be doubted whether the country does contain a sufficient quantity of labour to develop its resources; and while the Empire is loaded with taxation to defray the charges of its wars, it appears most politic to use its internal resources for improving the condition of its population, by which the revenue of the Exchequer must be increased, rather than encourage emigration, by which the Revenue would suffer diminution....'.[1]

More typical of the view adopted by advocates of development through public works was Drummond's comment in his Second Railway report: 'Emigration is another project to which there can be no objection, except that of its insufficiency as a remedy for so wide-spread and multitudinous evils.'...'It can only be resorted to as a secondary relief, effectual as far as it goes, and therefore deserving of attention and encouragement.'[2]

The appointment of Whately to the chairmanship of the Royal Commission on Irish Poor Laws in 1833 made some recommendation for the combination of emigration with poor relief probable, for Whately had been an early advocate of emigration[3] and his interest in the abolition of the system of convict transportation brought him into close contact with the Colonial Reformers.[4] When the report of the Commission was in preparation, Whately wrote to Torrens, 'inquiring in what way the principles of the South Australian colony might be applied so as to aid the introduction of poor laws into Ireland'.[5] Torrens replied optimistically that if the system were applied to the whole of Australia, funds might at once be raised for the transfer of 200,000 people there from Ireland. This influx would greatly increase the sales of land and hence the emigration fund—'thus there is a geometrical principle of progression in the system, which, under proper arrangements, might in a very short period indeed carry off the surplus population of Ireland'.[6]

This must have been encouraging to Whately, for a system of emigration formed the essence of his Commission's plan for the relief of the able-bodied. The recommendation made in the final report of the Commission was

that all poor persons, whose circumstances shall require it, shall be furnished with a free passage, and with the means of settling themselves in an approved British

[1] *Second Report from Select Committee on Public Works (Ireland)* (1835 (573), vol. xx), p. 25.
[2] *Second Report from the Railway Commissioners (Ireland)*, pt. III (1837–8 [145], vol. xxxv), p. 83.   [3] See above, p. 205.
[4] See Whately, *Life and Correspondence of Richard Whately*, vol. I, p. 388.
[5] Evidence of Torrens before the Select Committee on Disposal of Lands in the British Colonies, 30 June 1836: *Minutes of Evidence* (1836 (512), vol. XI), p. 135.
[6] *Ibid.*

Colony, to which convicts are not sent. We propose too, that the means of emigration shall be provided for the destitute of every class and description who are fit subjects for emigration; that depots shall be established, where all who desire to emigrate may be received in the way we shall mention; that those who are fit for emigration be there selected for the purpose, and that those who are not shall be provided for under the directions of the Poor Law Commissioners.'[1]

While the Commissioners envisaged that those who entered the depots should be maintained there out of the poor-rates, they recommended that one-half of the costs of their emigration should 'be borne by the general funds of the empire'. Taken with the suggestion that the pauper emigrants should be furnished with the means of settling themselves this was inevitably reminiscent of the costly schemes of Wilmot Horton, and there could be no hope of such proposals finding favour with the Whig Cabinet.

G. C. Lewis and Senior, the two critics to whom the Report was first referred, both fastened on the details of the emigration plan as objectionable, pointing out that it would be difficult to force those who entered the depots to emigrate, and that many could be expected to feign sickness or disability in order to be 'provided for under the directions of the Poor Law Commissioners', while others who would have emigrated voluntarily would go to the depots to get a free passage.[2] Nevertheless, Lewis and Senior both repeated their conviction that emigration from Ireland was desirable. Lewis held that it might be used in conjunction with the workhouse system, but stressed that it would have to be done on a large scale, and that it would be necessary to make certain that the colonies could absorb the settlers successfully.[3] Senior went so far as to 'rejoice that the Commissioners have boldly stated the necessity of emigration on a large scale' and to suggest that 'the question how the funds are to be provided, though certainly not of easy solution, will not present insurmountable difficulties', pointing out the possibilities of the Wakefield scheme in this respect.[4]

After this, when Russell despatched Nicholls to Ireland, he specifically listed 'the resource of Emigration' as one of the chief objects for Nicholls's attention.[5] Nicholls reported that 'Emigration not only may, but I believe

---

[1] *Third Report of Commissioners for Inquiring into the Condition of the Poorer Classes in Ireland* (1836 [43], vol. xxx), p. 27.

[2] *Remarks of G. C. Lewis, Esq., on Poor Laws, Ireland* (1837 [91], vol. LI), p. 17; *Letter from N. W. Senior, Esq., on Poor Laws, Ireland* (1837 [90], vol. LI), p. 9.

[3] Lewis, *op. cit.* p. 25.

[4] 'Many persons believe that a large fund may annually be provided by the sale of waste land in the colonies. If this is found to be true, that fund might be pledged for the purpose of raising a considerable sum, repayable by instalments, for effecting an extensive emigration, as rapidly as the means of absorption in the colonies and the United States will allow.' (p. 9). The wording of this passage suggests that Senior retained a certain scepticism about the operation of the Wakefield system, while the reference to the United States reveals that he had not studied its details too closely.

[5] Russell to Nicholls, 22 August 1836. (Printed with Nicholls's First Report (1837 [69], vol. LI.)

must, be had recourse to, as a present means of relief, whenever the population becomes excessive in any district, and no opening for migration can be found. The actual excess of population will be indicated by the pressure of able-bodied labourers upon the workhouse.' He went on to recommend that there should be express provision in the Act for the expense of pauper emigration to be divided equally between the Government and the Unions affected.[1]

In view of this, it is not surprising that Lansdowne and some other members of the Cabinet regarded some emigration scheme as still forming an important part of the Government plan as late as December 1836;[2] but Russell was not in favour of the Royal Commission's emigration plan or any other. On the Commission's plan, his final comment was: 'This was so insane, that it was necessary to devise something more rational'[3] and when he first brought forward the Irish Poor Law Bill it included no provision of any kind for assistance to emigration. Russell defended this on the ground that the colonies could not absorb a sudden influx of paupers, and that this type of immigrant was not wanted there. At the same time he repeated afresh the Government's willingness to facilitate those emigrants who could pay the cost of their own passage by extending the system of emigration agents in Ireland.[4]

The absence of any measure for promoting emigration was widely criticised in the ensuing debates, and many Irish members expressed the hope that such a measure might be included in supplementary legislation.[5] It was also, naturally, attacked by the Colonial Reformers, especially Torrens and H. G. Ward, both of whom held that the workhouse system could not operate in Ireland without the aid of extensive State-sponsored emigration.[6] This view was also supported by Scrope, who held that if the system were to work at all 'some means of an honest and industrious maintenance beyond the workhouse must be offered to the able-bodied. ...These means are open to you in the undertaking of public works on an extensive scale, and a well-devised system of emigration.'[7]

[1] *Report of Geo. Nicholls, Esq., on Poor Laws, Ireland* (1837 [69], vol. LI), § 117.
[2] See Lansdowne to Spring Rice, 15 December 1836, quoted above, ch. IV, p. 109.
[3] Memorandum by Russell, 21 November 1837, on a letter of protest against Nicholls sent by Whately to Senior (Monteagle Papers, National Library of Ireland). See above, ch. IV, p. 110.   [4] *Hansard*, 3rd ser. vol. XXXVI, cols. 474–6 (13 February 1837).
[5] *Ibid.* cols. 482 (Smith O'Brien), 485 (O'Connor), 491 (O'Connell); *Ibid.* vol. XXXVIII, cols. 1444 (Lansdowne), 1447 (Fitzgerald), 13 June 1837.
And see Memorandum of Matthew Barrington on the Bill, 28 April 1837—Monteagle Papers, National Library of Ireland. At this stage Morpeth would commit the Government to nothing more than a readiness 'to provide the fullest facilities to persons desirous of emigrating from Ireland to our colonies'. *Hansard*, 3rd ser. vol. XXXVIII, col. 403 (1 May 1837).
[6] See the passage from Torrens quoted above, ch. IV, p. 111; H. G. Ward, *The First Step to a Poor Law for Ireland* (London, 1837) *passim*.
[7] Scrope, *Remarks on the Government Irish Poor-Law Bill, in a Letter to Lord John Russell* (London, 1837), p. 20.

In his second report, Nicholls himself sided with those who had criticised the omission of any provision to aid emigration in the 1837 Bill and
specifically dealt with the suggestion that it would discourage voluntary
emigration. In reply, he used an argument frequently advanced by
advocates of Government emigration—that voluntary emigration tended
to take away the most industrious and provident, whereas under an
official scheme 'the emigrants would consist of persons possessing the
average qualifications of their class'.[1]

Faced with the frequently expressed desire of the Irish members for
emigration to be linked with the Poor Law scheme, and being furnished
with no arguments against it by Nicholls, Russell gave way and introduced into the second Bill a clause, similar to that in the English Act of
1834, empowering guardians, with the consent of the majority of rate-
payers, to apply a portion of the rate to assist emigration.[2] Most of the
Irish members condemned this as inadequate, and Russell did not pretend
that it was expected to produce any great volume of emigration.[3]

In the ensuing years, attempts to procure some more extensive measure
of official emigration as a relief to Ireland proved unavailing. On 2 June
1840, Smith O'Brien, who had shown a more active interest in colonisation than most Irish members,[4] drew attention to the contrast between the
distress and low wages prevalent in the United Kingdom, but especially
in Ireland, and the urgent demand for labour in the colonies, and moved
'that a free passage to those colonies which offer the greatest rewards to
industry should be provided by the State for such of the labouring classes
as are disposed to emigrate thither'.[5] Against this, Russell produced all
the arguments which were by then becoming standard—that the scheme
would add too much to public expenditure, that the colonies could not
absorb too large an immigration, that voluntary emigration would be
discouraged[6]—and Smith O'Brien withdrew his motion.

That change of Government meant no change of policy in this respect
was demonstrated at the opening of the session of 1842, when Stanley
firmly denied rumours which had been circulating, to the effect that the
Conservative Government were about to launch an extensive scheme of
assisted emigration.[7] Nor was he any more encouraging in the following
year, when Charles Buller brought forward his classic motion in favour of

[1] *Second Report of Geo. Nicholls, Esq., on Poor Laws, Ireland*, § 74; (1837–8 [104],
vol. xxxviii). For other statements of this argument see *Irish Railway Gazette*, vol. iii,
p. 352 (2 August 1847), and below, p. 229.
[2] *Hansard*, 3rd ser. vol. xxxix, col. 491 (1 December 1837); 1 and 2 Vic. c. 56, § 51.
[3] *Hansard*, 3rd ser. vol. xli, col. 378 (2 March 1838).
[4] He had been a founder member of the National Colonisation Society, and established
an emigration agency at Limerick in 1833. See O'Brien to Howick, 18 April 1833
(C.O. 384/33).
[5] *Hansard*, 3rd ser. vol. liv, col. 867.
[6] *Ibid.* cols. 885–91.
[7] *Ibid.* vol. lx, cols. 57 and 76 (3 and 4 February 1842).

systematic colonisation, than Russell had been to O'Brien in 1840.[1] Buller's motion was not specifically related to Irish conditions, but it drew from Sharman Crawford a sharp attack on emigration as a means of relieving Ireland, and a plea for the reclamation of waste lands there instead.

The whole question of emigration versus waste-land reclamation and other public works was again debated in 1844 and 1845 before the Devon Commission. Amongst other witnesses, Lord Devon and his colleagues heard a young Irishman who had recently been in Canada and was later to have much to do with the colonisation of New Zealand—John Robert Godley. Godley suggested that landlords might assist their poorer tenants to emigrate to Canada by forming an association to buy up a district there, and employing the emigrants on public works in it until they could purchase land for themselves. The improved land could then be profitably sold, and the process repeated on a new tract; but if the landlords were to do this, Godley thought, the Government would have to assist them to the extent of giving free passages to their emigrants.[2]

The Commission's conclusions were moderate and reasonable—'after considering the recommendations repeatedly made upon this subject, and the evidence of Mr Godley, in which the different views of this subject are well given, we desire to express our own conviction that a well organised system of emigration may be of very great service, as one amongst the measures which the situation of the occupiers of land in Ireland at present calls for. We cannot think that either emigration or the extension of public works, or the reclamation and improvement of land, can singly remove the existing evil.'[3]

Nevertheless, the Commissioners seemed to lean slightly in favour of a policy of land improvement as against emigration, and Stanley showed that he accepted this view when he brought in his Tenants' Compensation Bill of 1845; he then stated that 'as the means of proportioning the population of Ireland to its means of giving employment, emigration is not to be thought of for a moment'.[4]

Had it not been for the Famine, this might well have been the last that was to be heard of schemes for Government-assisted emigration to aid Ireland. Over the previous twenty years the volume of officially sponsored emigration had been very small, but the volume of voluntary emigration had increased greatly.

Between 1825 and 1845 the total number of Irish emigrants to North

[1] For the debate on Buller's motion, see *Hansard*, 3rd ser. vol. LXVIII, cols. 484–99 (6 April 1843).
[2] Evidence of Godley before the Devon Commission, 23 January 1845: *Minutes of Evidence*, pt. III (1845 [657], vol. XXI), p. 924.
[3] *Report of the Commissioners appointed to Inquire into the Occupation of Land in Ireland* (1845 [605], vol. XIX), p. 28.
[4] *Hansard*, 3rd ser. vol. LXXXI, col. 213 (9 June 1845).

America alone was some 875,000;[1] of these only the 2000 taken out by Peter Robinson in 1825 had been sent through Government action. The number of Irish given assisted passages to Australia in the first ten years after Elliot's appointment as Agent-General for Emigration was no more than 34,500,[2] so that Torrens's hopes that emigration financed from land sales might 'carry off the whole surplus population of Ireland' were very far from being realised.

The only other source of public funds to assist emigration was the poor-rate, but in Ireland this had proved even less effective than the framers of the 1838 Act had anticipated. As a result of an amendment introduced by the Duke of Wellington in the Lords, the costs of assisting emigration were chargeable on the electoral division, a smaller unit than the Poor Law union, and this made it impossible for the board of guardians of a union to raise funds for emigration by any general rate. The clause empowering the guardians to apply sums out of the poor-rates towards emigration of paupers therefore remained a dead letter until the original Act was amended in 1843;[3] but even when the legal impediments were removed, the Poor Law guardians did not make much use of their powers in this respect. Between 1843 and 1847 only 306 people had been assisted to emigrate under the provisions of the Irish Poor Law.[4]

In all the circumstances, then, there was a good deal of sense in the Colonial Office contention that the flow of privately financed emigrants was as large as the colonies could absorb without greatly increased expenditure, and that therefore while the Government might supervise the process, it had no grounds for attempting to force it forward.

III

It was not until the second failure of the potato crop, in 1846, that emigration as a mode of relief came to be seriously considered. Peel and his advisers in 1845–6 had never thought that the situation was one which could not be met by the well-tried expedients of relief works;

---

[1] Adams, pp. 413–14.

[2] The total number of persons who received assisted passages from the United Kingdom to Australia between 1837 and 1847 was 80,500. It was the practice of the Colonial Land and Emigration Commissioners to allot passages to the three parts of the Kingdom in proportion to their population; on this basis Ireland should have received three-tenths of the total, but the Commissioners stated in 1849 that in the preceding eight years they had allotted 8683 passages above the 'fair ratio' to Ireland, bringing her proportion up to almost three-sevenths. The figure given above has been arrived at, in the absence of direct figures for the whole period, by applying the three-sevenths proportion to the total figure of 80,500; it is thus, if anything, an over-estimate. See *Papers Relative to Emigration to the Australian Colonies* (1850 [1163], vol. XL), p. 216; *Seventh General Report, Colonial Land and Emigration Commission* (1847 [809], vol. XXXIII), p. 1; Hitchins, p. 205.

[3] 6 and 7 Vic. c. 92, § 18. See Nicholls, *History of the Irish Poor Law*, pp. 275, 288.

[4] See *Report from the Select Committee of the House of Lords on Colonisation from Ireland* (1847 (737), vol. VI), p. xi.

in any event, Peel was no longer much inclined to favour emigration schemes.[1]

Matters had taken on a different complexion in the autumn of 1846. The failure of the potato crop was complete; not only was it therefore obvious that the majority of the Irish people must soon be in the direst distress, it also seemed to most of those who thought at all about future policy that since the potato could no longer be depended upon, a fundamental reorganisation of Ireland's agriculture was necessary. Whatever might be hoped for in the long run, it was clear that in the short run the land, tilled for grain crops or used for stock-rearing, could not support so many people as it had done when used to grow potatoes. This pointed clearly to the conclusion that substantial emigration was inevitable; and the fact that Russell had appointed Earl Grey to be Colonial Secretary in his new Government gave grounds for hope that legislation to aid it might be forthcoming—for it was Grey who in 1831 had adopted Wakefield's ideas and who had maintained his belief in them ever since.

Monteagle, another consistent Whig believer in the merits of colonisation, approached Grey in October 1846, and put before him a scheme for State-aided emigration drawn up by Monteagle's son, Stephen Spring Rice, which included a revival of the suggestion made before the Irish Poor inquiry of 1830 that labourers on public works should be encouraged to save the means of paying for passages out of their wages.[2] Grey's reaction was cautious, to say the least; he argued that 'there is a danger if too much stress is laid upon emigration as the great means of relief, that the minds of all classes may be diverted from the necessity of a change in the present organisation of society, and that the opinion may be encouraged that it will do to allow things to go on as heretofore, merely relieving for the moment the pressure of population by removing a few thousands of those for whom no land can be at present obtained'. Nevertheless he declared himself 'far from being indifferent to emigration', and went on to sketch out a plan for sending groups of Irishmen, in charge of a priest or clergyman, to Canada or Australia; 'villages should be prepared for their reception in situations where there was a good demand for their labour'. The Government might undertake this, but Irish landlords would have to meet the cost of passages for the emigrants.[3]

Monteagle replied that he did not regard emigration as the single or even the principal remedy for Ireland's condition, but was anxious to see

---

[1] See his adverse comment on such schemes, *Hansard*, 3rd ser. vol. LXXXIX, col. 163 (20 January 1847); but that his opposition was not dogmatic is indicated by the letter quoted below, p. 231. Compare also McDonagh, 'Emigration during the Famine', *The Great Famine*, p. 342.

[2] Monteagle to Grey, 10 October 1846 (Monteagle Papers, National Library of Ireland). Rice suggested that wages on public works might be slightly raised to make the saving possible, so that in effect his plan was for assisted passages.

[3] Grey to Monteagle, 14 October 1846 (Monteagle Papers).

it used to supplement other measures, adding that he thought many landlords would be ready to meet the cost of passages for their tenants as Grey suggested.[1] Thus encouraged, Grey went on to develop the details of his scheme, assisted by Charles Buller.

At this stage, Russell was corresponding with Bessborough about the proposed extension of the Irish Poor Law and the measures which should be taken to supplement it,[2] but he was by no means committed to the view that aid to emigration must figure among them. 'I agree with you upon Emigration', he wrote to Bessborough, 'it could not possibly be carried to such an extent as to be really a relief to the peasantry.'[3] Within three weeks, however, he was writing to tell the Lord-Lieutenant that the Cabinet had agreed to include an emigration scheme amongst the Irish Bills to be brought forward at the beginning of the new session, and Bessborough seemed inclined to take a more favourable view of emigration himself.[4]

The scheme adopted was Grey and Buller's proposal for village settlements, which was to be tried out in Canada. Elgin, the new Governor-General, was despatched to Quebec on 31 December 1846, with instructions to recommend the scheme, but his Canadian advisers had no difficulty in producing criticisms which were decisive against it.[5] Apart from all other difficulties, the cost was expected to be prohibitive.[6] So it was that when Russell came before the Commons with his proposals for Ireland in January 1847, he took his stand firmly on the ground that the country was not over-populated, advocated measures for the development of its agriculture, and repeated all the standard arguments against Government encouragement to emigration—which Grey echoed in the Lords.[7]

Only after the Government had thus decided to leave Irish emigration to take care of itself, did public agitation for some scheme of systematic colonisation to relieve Ireland really get under way. The year 1847 produced a fresh crop of articles and pamphlets on the subject, mostly making use of well-worn arguments. Torrens found in the extension of the Irish Poor Law new grounds for arguing the necessity of a large measure of

[1] Monteagle to Grey, 22 October 1846 (Monteagle Papers).
[2] See above, ch. IV, p. 125.
[3] Russell to Bessborough, 26 November 1846 (Russell Papers, P.R.O. 30/22/5).
[4] Russell to Bessborough, 16 December 1846; Bessborough to Russell, 15 December 1846 (Russell Papers, loc. cit.).
[5] W. P. Morrell, British Colonial Policy in the Age of Peel and Russell (Oxford, 1930), pp. 429–31.
[6] 'I find the cost of settling immigrants in villages would be so enormous (the estimate I have had given to me is 48,000 l. for settling 500 families) that it would be practically impossible to attempt it'—Grey to Russell, 29 January 1847 (Russell Papers, P.R.O. 30/22/6). Opposition appears to have come not only from Canadian officials, but also from the Colonial Land and Emigration Commissioners—see memo of James Stephen, 31 July 1847 (C.O. 384/80).
[7] Hansard, 3rd ser. vol. LXXXIX, cols. 416–18, 447–9 (25 January 1847).

systematic colonisation, which might help in removing 'the predisposing cause of the misery of Ireland'—the cottier system.[1] Support for this proposal came from an Ulster landlord, Shafto Adair,[2] while Isaac Butt urged that although 'in this year, it is vain to look for any very extended system of colonisation from Ireland', the Government should realise that the need for emigration would be a continuing one, and make preparations in the colonies for the reception of as many Irish immigrants as possible in the following year.[3]

The most penetrating and original contribution came from Robert Murray, the general manager of Joplin's Provincial Bank of Ireland. Murray was the first to point out that the Famine had produced a readiness to emigrate in the great mass of the Irish people, and to show, from his inside knowledge of the banking system, how the voluntary movement was already being financed through bills of exchange for small sums sent home by emigrants—'from husband to wife, from father to child...from and to those united by all the ties of blood and friendship that bind us together on earth'.[4] To Murray, however, it did not seem that this excused the Government from aiding emigration, since he thought, as Nicholls had done ten years earlier, that in a voluntary movement 'the best go, the worst remain'.

Amongst those who were prepared not merely to write about the problem, but to do something positive as well, was J. R. Godley. In the early months of 1847, when he was working on the Landlords' Committee in Dublin, Godley evolved a plan for assisted emigration, not greatly dissimilar to Grey's, but worked out in more detail. He proposed the emigration to Canada, with State assistance, of as many as 1,500,000 Irish people, to be placed in settlements under the guidance of Roman Catholic clergy. The actual work of settlement was to be undertaken by an 'Irish Canada Company' which would receive £5 from the Imperial Government for each immigrant settled; the Government was also to contribute one-third of the cost of passage, obtaining the funds for this expenditure from a property-and-income tax levied on Ireland.[5]

Godley showed this plan to Stephen Spring Rice, who persuaded a number of Irish peers, including Clanricarde and Fitzwilliam, to endorse it;

[1] Torrens, *Self-supporting Colonisation: Ireland Saved Without Cost to the Treasury* (London, 1847).
[2] A. S. Adair, *The Winter of 1846–7 in Antrim: With Remarks on Out-door Relief and Colonisation* (London, 1847).
[3] Butt, 'The Famine in the Land', *Dublin University Magazine*, vol. xxix (1847), p. 535.
[4] Robert Murray, *Ireland: its Present Condition and Future Prospects; in a letter addressed to Sir Robert Peel* (Dublin, 1847).
[5] Godley, *To the Right Honourable Lord John Russell, First Lord of the Treasury, the Memorial of the Noblemen, Gentlemen and Landed Proprietors of Ireland*, 23 March 1847. Some printed copies of this memorial exist, but it is also reproduced in full as Appendix no. 25 to the First Report of the Lords Committee on Colonisation (1847 (737), vol. vi) and in K. N. Bell and W. P. Morrell, *Select Documents on British Colonial Policy 1830–1860* (Oxford, 1928).

Whately also gave his support, after consulting Senior.[1] In March 1847, the plan was made public in the form of a memorial to Russell. It was strongly endorsed by the *Spectator*, which, under the editorship of R. S. Rintoul, had always been the mouthpiece of Wakefield and the Colonial Reformers; but even the *Morning Chronicle*, which had been backing Mill's schemes for establishing peasant proprietors on Irish waste lands, was benevolent towards Godley: 'Turn cottiers into proprietors in Ireland, if possible, but it is better that they be proprietors in America, than cottiers, or even Dorsetshire Labourers, in Europe.'[2]

Peel showed himself more favourable to the plan than his earlier experience and statements might have suggested he would be, but Russell and Grey were hostile.[3] Godley's friend, Lord Lincoln, raised the matter in the Commons on 1 June, but before this there were ample reports from Canada that Godley's plan had been received with even more disfavour than Grey's a few months earlier.[4] Russell made good use of this information in replying to the debate, and Benjamin Hawes, then Under-Secretary for the Colonies, professed to be 'altogether staggered at the proposition that Ireland should be taxed to the amount of 9,000,000 l, to send away 2,000,000 of her able-bodied population.... If anything could remedy her evils, develop her resources, and induce the formation of her railways, it was surely capital, and yet the proposition was to take 9,000,000 l. of her capital, and 2,000,000 of the flower of her population away, by way of benefiting her!' Thus derided, the very general motion in favour of colonisation which Lincoln had put forward was allowed to pass, but Russell made it clear that the Cabinet had no intention of interpreting it in the positive way which Lincoln and Godley desired.[5]

Lincoln had asked for a Commission on colonisation—'a commission not for the postponement of a subject, but one formed with the full intention of action at as early a period as is possible or practicable'.[6] Russell would not agree to this, but a few days later Grey consented to a motion of Monteagle's for a Committee of the House of Lords on the same subject 'because he trusted the result of the inquiry would be to disabuse men's minds of a dangerous error, that to the greatest extent emigration could be made useful'.[7] The Committee devoted the remainder of the session to collecting a great volume of evidence on the subject, and

---

[1] Correspondence in Monteagle Papers, December 1846–March 1847.
[2] *Morning Chronicle*, 7 April 1847.
[3] C. E. Carrington, *John Robert Godley of Canterbury* (London, 1950), p. 38.
[4] Grey to Russell, 31 May 1847 (Russell Papers, P.R.O. 30/22/6). Godley's plan was also meeting with opposition from members of the Roman Catholic hierarchy in Ireland: see MacDonagh, 'The Irish Catholic Clergy and Emigration during the Great Famine', *Irish Historical Studies*, vol. v (1946–7), pp. 287–302.
[5] *Hansard*, 3rd ser. vol. xcii, cols. 1369–1450 (1 June 1847).
[6] *Ibid.* col. 1399.
[7] *Ibid.* vol. xciii, col. 108 (4 June 1847).

their report in some degree confirmed Grey's hopes, for although they declared the whole subject to be 'deserving the most serious reflection and the strictest examination' they declined to express 'any conclusive opinion of their own'[1]—nor did they express any in the following session, after hearing all the available evidence.[2]

So the parliamentary session of 1847 ended with a victory for the advocates of *laissez-faire* in emigration. Godley was frustrated and angered by his experience of official intractability;[3] looking back over his greater experience, Peel summed up the position by saying 'I have seen an irrational eagerness for emigration succeeded by an equally irrational prejudice against it. Departments of the Government are apt to be infected by opposite errors of this kind, and are sometimes unwilling to listen favourably to evidence at variance with the prevailing impression of the day.'[4]

When the full details of the panic emigration from Ireland in 1847 became known, Grey and his officials were able to make some claim that their inactive policy had been justified. Voluntary emigrants totalled 230,000, almost double the total for 1846, and there was abundant and horrifying evidence that resources both for their transport and their reception at their destinations had been strained to breaking point.[5] Resentment and fear of the consequences of a continued influx of paupers were widespread in the colonies, especially Canada, where the Imperial Government was ultimately forced to pay the heavy costs which the provinces had incurred for the relief of the flood of diseased and destitute immigrants.[6]

All the lessons of 1847 seemed to point to the need for an overhaul of the Passenger Acts, for a closer medical supervision of the emigrants and a closer check on the vessel in which they sailed, but not to any need to stimulate the flow of Irish emigration. Nevertheless the question of State aid to emigration was revived again in 1848; the continuing failure of the potato crop showed that the situation could not be met by a mere extension of the Poor Law, and there was a desire for measures which would be more rapid in their effects than land-improvement loans or the sale of incumbered estates, yet if possible equally permanent. Carlyle was giving vent to a fairly general sentiment when he declaimed that 'for Britain's sake itself, if Britain is to continue habitable much longer, Ireland must

[1] *Report from the Select Committee of the House of Lords on Colonisation from Ireland* (1847 (737), vol. VI), p. xvi.
[2] *First, Second and Third Reports from the same* (1847–8 (415, 593), vol. XVII; 1849 (86), vol. XI).
[3] See Godley, *Unemployed Labourers of the United Kingdom*, p. 28.
[4] Peel to Stephen Spring Rice, 15 August 1847 (Monteagle Papers).
[5] MacDonagh, 'Emigration During the Famine', *The Great Famine*, p. 322; Trevelyan, 'The Irish Crisis', *Edinburgh Rev.* pp. 294–7. Rintoul regarded Trevelyan's article as 'a semi-official manifesto against Irish emigration'—*Spectator*, 25 December 1847.
[6] MacDonagh, pp. 347 and 373.

actually attain remedial measures—and of a kind we have not been much used to, for two centuries back in this country'.[1]

Emigration seemed the only remaining possibility. Even such a staunch advocate of small farms and 'home colonisation' as Blacker had admitted that 'if we lose the potato crop, all the five and six acre men who depended entirely upon their small holdings must go'.[2] Only Poulett Scrope remained convinced that colonisation might be regarded as 'premature' and that development of waste lands could afford means of support adequate to the whole existing population of Ireland.[3]

As early as April 1848, Russell was writing to Clarendon that 'in some of the western parts emigration is the only remedy'[4] and as the summer wore on he was more and more influenced by Monteagle's arguments in its favour. Monteagle at this time was developing a plan whereby the expenses of emigration might be defrayed partly by Irish landowners and partly out of an annual vote of £180,000 then being made for the expenses of the Irish Constabulary. Prior to 1846 this sum had been charged on the Grand Jury rates, but it was then transferred to the Consolidated Fund.[5] Monteagle's proposal was that the expenses of the Constabulary should again be met from local rates, while a sum of £180,000 should be charged as an annuity on the Consolidated Fund for emigration purposes; he calculated that an immediate loan of £5,000,000 might be raised on the security of this.[6]

Russell, however, was at first disposed to work the emigration scheme into a larger plan. At the beginning of September 1848, he crossed to Ireland and had consultations with Clarendon, in the course of which they sketched out a scheme for applying part of the proceeds of a new tax on land and houses in Ireland to the endowment of the Roman Catholic clergy and using the balance as a basis for borrowing to finance emigration.[7] Redington, the Under-Secretary for Ireland, warned Russell that any proposal to levy taxes for the support of the Roman Catholic clergy would meet with serious opposition from the Presbyterians in Ulster, and the Cabinet was somewhat alarmed by the prospect of the disturbance it must create in England as well as in Ireland. Accordingly, Russell decided to concentrate on the emigration plan, which at first he thought might be combined with schemes for land improvement and railway development, all to be financed out of the proposed land tax or an exten-

[1] Carlyle, 'Ireland, and the British Chief Governor', *Spectator*, 13 May 1848.
[2] Evidence of William Blacker before the Lords Committee on Colonisation from Ireland, 23 June 1847: *Minutes of Evidence* (1847 (737), vol. VI), p. 249.
[3] G. P. Scrope, *Plea for the Rights of Industry in Ireland* (London, 1848), pp. 8–9.
[4] Russell to Clarendon, 21 April 1848 (Clarendon Papers).
[5] By 9 and 10 Vic. c. 97, § 2.
[6] 'Propositions to be considered by Committee on Colonisation from Ireland'—printed memo, dated July 1848, in Russell Papers (P.R.O. 30/22/7).
[7] Memorandum of Russell, 8 September 1848 (Clarendon Papers); Walpole, *Lord John Russell*, vol. II, p. 76.

sion of the income tax to Ireland. He explained to Monteagle that his objection to the latter's 'constabulary' plan was that certain counties would stand to benefit little from the emigration undertaken, and would therefore resent having the cost of the constabulary reimposed on them.[1] Monteagle, who was in London at the time, thought this a minor point, but was prepared to acquiesce in the larger plan. On his return to Ireland, he warned Russell that though he personally had been 'most reserved', Lord Devon and others in Dublin were already talking about the Government's proposal to finance emigration from a land tax.[2]

Unfortunately, Russell's proposals were still far from acceptance even in his own Cabinet, for they lacked the support of Grey and his brother-in-law, the parsimonious Charles Wood. Grey had already clashed with Monteagle on the subject of emigration in the Lords towards the end of the session and had then summed up his position by saying: 'My noble Friend thinks...that the State should carry out and settle emigrants upon the vacant land of our colonies; I on the other hand, am of the opinion that the State should only interfere to assist and direct the emigrant, leaving him to act for himself.'[3]

Grey, although he thus professed himself not interested in emigration schemes as a means of relieving Irish distress, was nevertheless much concerned with colonial development, and in this connection he was greatly enamoured of the project, first advocated by Durham, to construct a railway from Halifax to Quebec.[4] By November 1848, he had evolved a scheme requiring the Imperial Government to advance £5,000,000 for the construction of the line with Irish emigrant labour, securing the interest by an increase in the duty on colonial timber.[5] Grey found Wood at first surprisingly favourable to this idea, but Russell could hardly have been expected to endorse it. Apart from any desire he might naturally have to see his own scheme adopted, the man who had rejected Bentinck's proposal to build railways in Ireland in 1847 could scarcely have sponsored Grey's proposal to send the Irish to Canada to build them in 1848. To meet the expected opposition of Grey and his group, Russell narrowed his scheme down to one for emigration only, to be financed by a specific tax and administered in conjunction with the Poor Law.[6] Clarendon endorsed this plan, but remarked: 'the principal opponent of the scheme will, I fear, be Charles Wood'.[7]

So it proved. Russell was unable to secure Cabinet acceptance of his

---

[1] Russell to Monteagle, 12 November 1848 (Monteagle Papers).
[2] Monteagle to Russell, 26 November 1848 (Russell Papers).
[3] *Hansard*, 3rd ser. vol. CI, col. 40 (10 August 1848).
[4] See his comments on the plan in emigration debates—*Hansard*, 3rd ser. vol. XCIII, col. 115; vol. CI, col. 49 (4 June 1847 and 10 August 1848).
[5] Morrell, *Colonial Policy of Peel and Russell*, p. 437.
[6] Walpole, *Lord John Russell*, vol. II, p. 79.
[7] Clarendon to Russell, 17 December 1848 (Russell Papers, P.R.O. 30/22/7).

plan in the face of the concerted opposition of Grey, Wood and their relatives;[1] but Grey in his turn fared no better. In April 1849 he had to tell Elgin that the Halifax–Quebec railway plan would have to be shelved because of the exigencies of Imperial Government finance.[2] In fact, even had there been no difference of opinion between Russell and Grey, it seems highly improbable that they could have prevailed against the objection of cost, which had defeated every plan of assisted emigration since Wilmot Horton's day. At the very time when they were formulating their differing proposals, the Colonial Office received from one Sir Duncan McDougall 'a new plan for Systematic Colonisation'. In the time-honoured fashion of the Colonial Office, T. F. Elliot folded up the bottom right-hand corner of the letter and wrote his comments on it there: 'The worst of it is, that the result may be at once foretold, the experiment would succeed as to the prosperity of the settlers, but even if Sir D's estimate could be realised, would be too costly to be multiplied sufficiently for the wants of the country.'[3]

Even after the abandonment of Grey's and Russell's schemes, hopes of relieving Ireland by assisted emigration did not immediately fade. Monteagle and Clarendon continued to support the idea. When the Select Committee on the working of the Irish Poor Laws was appointed early in 1849, Clarendon told Russell 'I still hope that Emigration may be one of the subjects discussed in the Committee'.[4] So indeed it was, and after hearing much evidence on the subject, the Committee recommended that 'the means of facilitating Emigration under the provisions of the Poor Law should be increased'.[5]

The Poor Law Extension Act of 1847 had in fact slightly increased the powers of guardians, permitting them to assist the emigration of poor persons not in the workhouses.[6] The Commissioners of the Treasury were also authorised[7] to apply part of the proceeds of the rate-in-aid towards the emigration of the Irish poor. After consultation with the Poor Law Commissioners, however, they decided that 'having regard to the probable demands on that fund of a more pressing nature, My Lords do not feel that they should be justified in authorising any expenditure for this purpose at the present time'.[8]

A further increase in the powers of Poor Law guardians to assist

---

[1] Walpole, *Lord John Russell*, vol. II, p. 80. The Cabinet at this time included not only Grey's brother-in-law, Wood, but two of his cousins, Sir George Grey and Sir Francis Baring.

[2] Morrell, *Colonial Policy of Peel and Russell*, p. 438.

[3] Memorandum dated 19 October 1848 (C.O. 384/81).

[4] Clarendon to Russell, 6 February 1849 (Russell Papers, P.R.O. 30/22/7).

[5] *Twelfth Report from Select Committee on Poor Laws (Ireland)* (1849 [403], vol. xv), pt. II, p. iii.

[6] 10 and 11 Vic. c. 31, §§ 13–15.   [7] By 12 and 13 Vic. c. 24, § 3.

[8] Treasury Out-letters, 13 September 1849 (T. 14/31). Some expenditure for emigration from this source was allowed in later years.

emigration was actually authorised very soon after the Select Committee had reported in favour of it, the Irish Poor Law Further Amendment Act of 1849 giving power to raise loans for emigration purposes on the security of the rates.[1] This was a considerable advance over previous legislation, and caused a marked increase in the sums expended on emigration by Poor Law authorities, but at this time the pressure for immediate relief was so strong and the financial difficulties of many unions so severe that the use made of these powers was inevitably much less than it might have been in more normal conditions, and the numbers assisted to emigrate out of the poor-rates remained insignificant in comparison with the voluntary outflow.[2]

IV

After 1850, emigration ceased to be a matter of much public concern in Great Britain. The influence of Wakefield and the Colonial Reformers declined, while the increase of prosperity made the problem of providing relief for the poorer classes seem less urgent.[3]

From Ireland the exodus continued with almost undiminished force until 1852, then declined somewhat until 1859, the series of bad harvests which followed sending the numbers of emigrants up again.[4] Observers generally, and economists in particular, regarded the continuance of large-scale emigration as inevitable, and indeed as being the essential basis for the recovery of Ireland. As the years passed, statistics revealed a diminution in the numbers of very small agricultural holdings and a rise in the wages of agricultural labour, both of which were interpreted as signs of a more healthy development in the economic life of the country.[5]

On the other hand there were not a few who, from quite an early date, regarded the continuance of large-scale emigration from Ireland with

[1] 12 and 13 Vic. c. 104, § 26. See above, ch. IV, p. 129.
[2] See Nicholls, *Irish Poor Law*, pp. 369–70. The total number of persons assisted to emigrate by Poor Law guardians reached its highest level—4386—in 1852; the total Irish emigration in that year was 190,322.
[3] C. A. Bodelsen, *Studies in Mid-Victorian Imperialism* (Copenhagen, 1924), pp. 32–59; W. A. Carrothers, *Emigration from the British Isles* (London, 1929), pp. 207–24.
[4] The total number of emigrants was 190,322 in 1852 but had fallen to 64,337 in 1858; it rose to 80,599 in 1859 and to 117,229 in 1863 (I. Ferenczi, *International Migrations* (New York, 1929), vol. I, p. 730).
[5] The number of holdings of under 1 acre had declined from 134,000 in 1841 to 42,000 in 1861, and the number of holdings between 1 acre and 5 acres in size had fallen from 310,000 to 85,000 in the same period. See Harkness, 'Irish Emigration', in Ferenczi, *International Migrations*, vol. II, p. 268. In 1855 the Poor Law Commissioners stated that 'wages of 1s. per day are given, where formerly the rate was 4d., 6d. or 8d.'; Longfield estimated in 1861 that agricultural wages had risen between 1844 and 1856 by amounts varying from 25 % to 80 %, 'the greatest increase having taken place in those districts where the greatest wretchedness previously prevailed', and that between 1856 and 1861 a further general increase of 10 % occurred. See *Eighth Annual Report of Poor Law Commissioners (Ireland)* (1855), p. 15; Longfield, 'Address on Social Economy', *Transactions of the National Association for Promotion of Social Science* (1861), p. 109.

regret and alarm, and regarded it as symptomatic of the failure of the Government to produce any policy enabling the Irish people to earn their subsistence at home. The most frequent and vehement statements of this point of view are to be found in the *Nation* newspaper, which persistently maintained that continued emigration was a direct consequence of 'the peasant exterminating and farm consolidating policy of Irish landlordism'.[1] In this it was supported by the more moderate *Freeman's Journal*.[2]

The agricultural depression of 1859–63 added strength to such ideas, which then found more reasoned expression in the papers of D. C. Heron, the originator of the 'Irish prosperity debate' of 1862–4.[3] From Irish papers and journals the debate, in which one group viewed emigration as the primary indication of a long and dangerous decline, while the other continued to regard it as a symptom of healthy recovery and progress, found its way into the columns of *The Times* and the *Economist*.[4] There, as might be expected, the ideas of the anti-emigration party met with little sympathy. 'We can understand', the *Economist* commented editorially, 'that an Irish patriotic poet, whose fancy is stronger than his reason, should lament over shiploads of Celts leaving their native land. But that men who know...that every emigrant who leaves those shores improves both his own position, and that of those who remain behind...should whine over the exodus, appears to us simply either silly or immoral.'

By this time, however, it was not merely those whose 'fancy was stronger than their reason' who found something disquieting in the Irish exodus, and were inclined to see the cause of it in the land system. Although Merivale could still say in 1861—'with regard to emigration, I am not indeed aware that any writers, whose views are at all worth examining, regard it as economically mischievous',[5] this was even then no longer strictly true. Already in 1857 John Stuart Mill had written: 'When the inhabitants of a country quit the country *en masse*, because its Government will not make it a fit place for them to live in, the Government is judged and condemned. It is the duty of Parliament to reform the landed tenure of Ireland.'[6]

Some ten years later Cliffe Leslie treated the subject in more detail, but arrived at a similar conclusion.[7] Leslie pointed out that much of the rise in wages since 1850 was due to the rise in world prices consequent on

[1] *The Nation*, 19 March 1859; cf. also the issue for 16 October 1858.
[2] See *Freeman's Journal*, 13 July 1860.
[3] R. M. Heron, 'Historical Statistics of Ireland'; and 'Ireland in 1864'; *Journal S.S.I.S.I.*, vol. III, p. 235; vol. IV, p. 105. See above, ch. II, pp. 47–48.
[4] *The Times*, 5 October, 21 and 30 November 1863; *The Economist*, 6 June and 21 November 1863 (vol. XXI, pp. 620–1, 1290–1).
[5] Merivale, *Lectures on Colonisation and Colonies* (1861 edition), p. 136.
[6] Mill, *Principles*, 4th ed. (London, 1857), vol. I, p. 398.
[7] Cliffe Leslie, 'Political Economy and Emigration', *Fraser's Magazine*, May 1868. (Reprinted in *Land Systems and Industrial Economy* (London, 1870), pp. 85–116); 'Emigration, Land and Wages', *The Economist*, 2 May 1868, vol. XXVI, pp. 497–9.

the gold discoveries and was not a rise in real wages. He attacked the view that wage increases could be regarded as a natural result of a more favourable relationship of population to capital, arguing that 'there are no funds necessarily destined to employment as wages; and coincidently with a vast emigration there may be, as its very result, or as the result of a common cause, a substitution of pasture for tillage, and a withdrawal of capital from farming, with a diminished demand for labour in consequence'. The common cause of these developments Leslie believed to be 'legal impediments to the prosperity of the island'—primarily defects in the law of landed property, which, he contended, not merely inhibited agriculture, but manufactures as well.[1]

All such assertions were naturally strenuously countered by spokesmen of the landed interest. In a series of letters to *The Times* in 1867,[2] Lord Dufferin endeavoured to prove, with the aid of statistics, that Ireland was still over-populated and could not reach a healthy economic state until emigration had continued to the point where small-holdings would disappear and all farms be consolidated into units of efficient size. For this argument, Lord Dufferin incurred, though probably without ever knowing it, the stinging censure of Karl Marx. In the first volume of *Capital* Marx also employed statistics of Irish progress, but to prove that since the Famine 'concomitantly with the decline of population, there has been an increase in rents and farming profits, although the farming profits have not risen so rapidly as the rents'. Marx, like Leslie, argued that emigration had been accompanied by falling real wages, a symptom of 'relative surplus population' created by farm consolidation and conversion of tillage into pasture. But while Marx thus also traced a connection between emigration and the land system, he naturally did not see the remedy in any piecemeal reform of the latter; he had already stated his view on this in 1853: 'The modern changes in the art of production... have expropriated...the Irish cottier and tenant...they will expropriate in due time the landlord....'[3]

While some economists who had come to believe that status might be a better basis for Irish land tenures than contract had also accepted the corollary that emigration was a symptom of insecurity of tenure, by no means all of those who looked on it as being natural and necessary could be dismissed as biased by vested interests, or unthinking advocates of *laissez-faire*. Thus M. J. Barry, who had been active both in the Repeal and Young Ireland movements, declared himself satisfied, as a result of

---

[1] *Land Systems and Industrial Economy*, pp. 87, 99. For another treatment of the relation between emigration and insecurity of tenure, see I. Butt, *The Irish People and the Irish Land* (Dublin, 1867).
[2] Afterwards published in book form as *Irish Emigration and the Tenure of Land in Ireland*, already quoted.
[3] Marx, *Capital*, vol. I, pt. 7, ch. XXIII, § 5 F; and 'Forced Emigration', *New York Daily Tribune*, 22 March 1853 (reprinted in Marx–Engels, *On Britain* (Moscow, 1953), pp. 372–6).

his own investigations, 'that the emigration going on is a healthy symptom, that its continuance is necessary, and that it is desirable, whether as regards the emigrant, Ireland, or the Empire generally'.[1] On the narrower issue of the relation between emigration and the land laws, Longfield, who was not merely immensely experienced in the working of those laws but also favourable to the tenants' case, stated firmly: 'I do not think that the emigration is much caused by the landlord and tenant question.'[2]

It has already been suggested here[3] that the debates on the economic condition of Ireland in the eighteen-sixties were carried on to some extent at cross purposes, since the nationalists regarded the maintenance of the existing population on the land as the touchstone of prosperity, while their opponents envisaged progress primarily in terms of increased real product. These different approaches necessarily involved a fundamental divergence of opinion as to the size of the optimum population for Ireland, and it is impossible to say that either was 'right' or 'wrong', independently of the viewpoint which they adopted.

Although the theory that emigration had become excessive had no direct influence on policy, it may be said to have had an indirect one, in so far as it formed part of the case for land reform. In this respect subsequent experience undoubtedly proved that the diagnosis which saw emigration as a consequence of insecurity of tenure was incorrect, or at least incomplete. However necessary reform of the land system may have been in other respects, it did not prove to be a preventive for emigration.

---

[1] M. J. Barry, *Irish Emigration Considered* (Cork, 1863), p. 3. For another opinion favourable to emigration at this period, see Senior, *Journals...Relating to Ireland*, vol. II, p. 267.

[2] Evidence of M. Longfield before the Select Committee on the Tenure and Improvement of Land (Ireland) Act, 15 May 1865: *Minutes of Evidence* (1865 (402), vol. XI), p. 5.

[3] Above, ch. II, p. 48.

CHAPTER VIII

CONCLUSION

I

IT would be wrong to describe the Irish question of the nineteenth century as wholly, or perhaps even primarily, economic, and nineteenth-century writers did not generally look upon it exclusively in that light. Yet it was commonly recognised, certainly after 1829, that the political and social discontents of Ireland had deep economic roots, and therefore that any settlement of Irish problems would necessarily involve considerable economic changes and reforms. The evidence of the preceding chapters shows that the political economists of the time, of all shades of opinion, did not fail to recognise and discuss the problem. In this chapter a general assessment of the ideas of the economists and their influence will be given, and some answers to the questions posed at the outset[1] indicated.

In most of the economists' discussions on Ireland certain assumptions were generally, though not invariably, made. These were that the political union of Great Britain and Ireland was desirable and would be maintained, and that a substantial increase in the real product, and real income per head, of Ireland should be the fundamental aim of economic policy.[2] Making these assumptions and using their stock of theoretical tools, most of the classical economists put forward their ideas of appropriate policies for economic development in Ireland. They were not deterred from this by the fact that their system included such concepts as the tendency for population to outrun subsistence, the tendency of profits to decline, and the stationary state; for acceptance of these as theoretical possibilities did not imply that they could not be evaded or postponed by appropriate policies. In the case of Ireland they recognised that there were serious obstacles to economic development, but never conceived that it was impossible.

Up to 1845 at least, the various comments of the economists can fairly be said to sum together into a commonly accepted diagnosis and treatment programme for the Irish situation. The diagnosis ran essentially in terms of comparison of the rates of growth of population and capital, and the treatment amounted to a deliberate policy of raising aggregate real income through replacement of the semi-subsistence agriculture of

---

[1] Above, ch. I, pp. 3, 13.
[2] Most writings of English economists in this period take these points for granted, but that does not mean that they were not prepared to contemplate other possibilities: see above, pp. 86 and 210.

239

Ireland with a system of capitalist leasehold cultivation, transmuting as many of the displaced cottiers and small tenants as that system might require into agricultural wage-labourers, and absorbing the remainder into alternative employments where possible, otherwise removing them through emigration.

When stated and looked at as a whole, this plan of treatment seems commendably straightforward and logically consistent. It cannot be characterised as merely a policy of *laissez-faire*, although if that term be interpreted in its positive sense as the removal of barriers to the operation of market forces much of the proposed programme would come under that head. But it would have involved rather more than this; where necessary, as perhaps in the field of public works, the State would have to intervene positively to create the conditions where free enterprise could work effectively. On the face of things too, this programme cannot be criticised as irrelevant to the situation created by the Act of Union; for although the political economists rarely gave explicit consideration to the problems created by the union of two economies so widely differing in character and development as Britain and Ireland, there was implicit in most of their writing on this subject the view that the only correct procedure was to assimilate the two by raising the less-developed economy towards the level of the more-developed one. This, they believed, could be achieved through the changes outlined above.

A plan of economic development, however, requires to be not merely consistent in itself, but consistent with and appropriate to the circumstances of the area to which it is intended to apply. Judged by this standard, the prescriptions of the economists appear much less satisfactory. Not only were there great obstacles to their application, but even if these had been overcome, it is very doubtful if the policies recommended would have achieved the desired result. In theory, it would seem eminently reasonable to propose a reform of the landlord and tenant relationship, but in doing so most writers fell into the easy trap of treating 'landlords' and 'tenants' as abstractions, not as people. Ireland before the Famine possessed many kinds of landlords and many kinds of tenants, but the majority of the landlords were either careless of their obligations as proprietors, or so handicapped by incumbrances and settlements as to be unable to discharge those obligations. Equally, the majority of tenants were poor, ignorant, and suspicious. The standard economic prescription of the day required these men and women to be transmuted into responsible, active and affluent proprietors on the one hand, thrifty and intelligent yeomen, or sober and industrious labourers on the other. That this would necessarily have been a long process is only too obvious, but even in the long run its achievement would depend on the simultaneous realisation of a number of unlikely possibilities.

If the landlords were to attract substantial tenants, they would have had to offer them farms well equipped and in good heart. Even had they been able to rid themselves of their existing tenantry without cost or trouble, most Irish landlords would not have been able to make the investment necessary to create good farms. This obstacle, though more serious than many reformers recognised, would not have been insuperable. The Government could step in with loans to solvent proprietors and aid the insolvent to dispose of their properties—as eventually it did through the Land Improvement and Incumbered Estates Acts. But, as experience showed, few could be persuaded to assume the arduous role of the responsible, investing landlord without proof of the existence of well-doing and well-disposed tenants. To find such tenants would inevitably have been a matter of the greatest difficulty. Some existing Irish small farmers might have been found both willing and able to undertake the running of a large farm, if they could have overcome their suspicion of the landlord and their fear of their less fortunate fellows—but the available evidence does not suggest that there would have been many with the requisite capital and skill. Nor were there any substantial economic advantages to tempt an English or Scottish farmer to take the lease of an Irish farm and endure the social disadvantages of settling in a depressed and alien community.

If the right type of landlords and tenants could somehow have been found to set up a heavily capitalised agriculture in Ireland this might well have increased the volume and value of the total produce, but it does not necessarily follow that the mass of the existing population would have profited to any great extent in its distribution. Over much of Ireland, the climate and soil are such as to make rich natural pasture, but not to favour grain crops. Hence the larger and wealthier Irish farmers, even in the early nineteenth century, always tended to prefer grazing to tillage,[1] and any substantial tenant would have been wise to do so, more especially after the repeal of the Corn Laws. Hence it did not follow that increase of capital would necessarily mean increase of employment; in fact, the reverse was much more likely. Despite their general inclination to think of an increase of capital as an increase of the wages-fund, most of the classical economists recognised this, though few perhaps so clearly as Torrens.[2] Even so, they tended generally to under-estimate the size of the agricultural population which must be displaced if their schemes were adopted, and to assume all too readily that it could be absorbed into non-agricultural employment or removed by emigration, without considering the incidental hardships. In fact, the orthodox economists, and more especially their popularisers in this period, generally took it as axiomatic that increase of capital must be to the general good, and so tended to gloss over the disturbances which its introduction might create in a given

[1] See E. R. R. Green, 'Agriculture', *The Great Famine*, p. 104.
[2] See above, p. 139.

region. Here their approach contrasts interestingly with that of Karl Marx, who, concerned always to bring out the contradictory results of capital accumulation, did not fail to note how capital in Ireland had been devoted mainly to livestock production, and to stress the consequent rural depopulation as contributing to the reserve army of labour.[1]

If the economists tended to under-estimate the strictly economic difficulties which their proposals would have encountered, they took even less account of the social problems involved. In particular, they generally took no account at all of the attitudes of the Irish people towards land. Thus, they were always prepared to assume that the cottiers and small tenants would accept the status of wage-labourers if it offered a better subsistence; this ignored the vital fact that the Irish tenants believed themselves to have a just claim to occupation of the soil, and had no desire to give it up and become labourers, however comfortable. Nor did the economists generally understand, or pay sufficient attention to, the bitter religious differences which so often poisoned social relationships in Ireland, and caused free institutions which worked successfully in Britain to become perverted in their operation in Ireland. Quite rightly they stressed the importance of security as a condition precedent for economic progress, but failed to go deeply enough into the question of what the necessary conditions were for the genuine attainment of security in Ireland. Hence they failed to appreciate that there could never be more than an uneasy calm in Ireland so long as there existed a land system and a Church establishment which affronted the sense of equity and the conscience of the majority of the people.

Thus, while the classical economists did recognise that the differing economic development of Great Britain and Ireland created a problem, they failed to make any deep examination of the nature and causes of the difference. To them it seemed that the solution of the problem lay in remodelling the Irish economy along the lines of the English one, which they certainly tended to regard as a norm. If this should involve relying on State intervention, then they were prepared to recommend it, but where market forces could be relied on they would have preferred to use them, and to try to create a situation in which they could be used. The majority of writers undoubtedly regarded the doctrines which had first been developed from English models as having general validity, and were thus led to give advice on policy which was to a large extent inappropriate to Ireland's condition and requirements.[2]

[1] Marx, *Capital*, vol. I, pt. VII, ch. XXIII (Everyman edition: vol. II, pp. 780–1).
[2] See the present author's article, 'The Classical Economists and the Irish Problem', *Oxford Economic Papers*, vol. V, no. I (March 1953), pp. 39–40.

II

In these circumstances, it is remarkable not how little, but how much, of the economists' proposals was translated, or attempted to be translated, into actual policy. Over the period here examined economic policy in Ireland may appear as a tangled, drab skein of shifts and expedients, but up to Gladstone's time there is a central thread running through it—the settlement of landlord-tenant relationships on a contract basis, and the creation of conditions suitable to farming on the English model. But it seems fair to say that legislators adopted this approach not so much because it embodied the advice of the economists, as because it accorded with the ideas and wishes of the landowning classes, then still dominant in both Houses of Parliament. It may appear strange that the proposals of the economists accorded so well with the interests of the landlords, when traditionally the economists have been depicted as the champions of the urban middle class against the old landed aristocracy; but it should be remembered that the economists' quarrel was not with the landlords as landlords, but as protectionists. Tories and the older Whigs might look askance at political economy with its Radical associations, but in regard to the fundamentals of Irish policy its recommendations accorded with their own preconceptions. Measures such as the Sub-letting Act of 1826 were not passed because political economists suggested them, but the fact that they were endorsed by the economists gave added assurance of rightness to the sponsors of such legislation, and helped to disarm potential opponents. Here economic theory did not create policy, but came in support of it. This is not to say that the economists acted, wittingly or otherwise, as the mere hired lackeys of the ruling classes; on the contrary, because their theories led them independently to propose a line of action which fitted in with the landowners' inclinations, their influence was the more significant.

Although doctrine and policy broadly chimed together over much of this period, policy by no means incorporated all that theory suggested. In the theoretical model of land reform and economic development, the displaced tenants must either find employment at home through the spontaneous growth of private investment or public works, or be assisted to emigrate and find employment in the colonies. No consistent line of policy was ever adopted and maintained in this regard. Cabinets inherited the problem from each other; if it did not seem pressing, they allowed matters to drift on; when it became pressing they adopted the expedient which seemed most hopeful in the immediate circumstances. It was almost inevitable, under the prevailing conditions of political organisation, that no attempt should be made to analyse the problem in detail, to decide how much might be achieved by public works, how much by private enterprise, how much by emigration, and then proceed to act accordingly for a sustained period. So various ministries are to be found now convinced that the key to the problems lies in a Poor Law which will compel the rate-payers to give employment, now seized with a belief that emigration is the only hope, now hopeful of the effects of a large dose of public works as sedative or stimulant, perhaps both. In most instances, the policy presented to Parliament was not put forward with any real conviction that it would contribute to the ultimate solution of the Irish problem, but had been cast in that form because it seemed the only acceptable compromise likely to pass in the current political or financial conditions.[1]

The results of the erratic mixture of intervention and non-intervention which ensued were far from impressive. They are certainly not deserving of unqualified condemnation, for in detail a number of quite valuable reforms and advances were achieved; but, in general, they did not touch the core of the problem. So far from setting Ireland on the desired path of sound economic development, they allowed her to stagger on into the catastrophe of the Famine.

It can be argued that the economists had no responsibility for this; policy may have coincided roughly with the lines which they indicated, but only a part of what they proposed was ever carried into effect, and that part tardily. All this is true, but the economists cannot be completely absolved, for they contributed to the making of the climate of public opinion as well as to the making of Irish policy directly. Whatever qualifications and reservations there may have been in the works of the leading economists, there can be no doubt that the message which reached the public, through the medium of popular works, newspapers and reviews, exhorted them to believe in the virtues of free trade and *laissez-faire*. By the eighteen-forties, practically all public men were imbued with the belief that market forces should not be tampered with, that self-reliance must not be weakened or local efforts superseded by the activities of the Government. Along with this went the conviction that public expenditure must be kept to a minimum if the nation was to be kept in economic health. These maxims were inappropriate to Ireland, and most economists recognised this when their attention was specifically directed to the problem, but nevertheless public opinion and parliamentary action on Irish matters was strongly influenced by such maxims. Positive action, especially if it seemed likely to have budgetary consequences, was frequently inhibited by reference to 'the principles of sound political economy'.

Considering the very indifferent results achieved by economic policy in Ireland from 1817 to 1845 the amount of rethinking of the problem which was done by economists and politicians appears remarkably slight. Even

[1] Russell's choice between land improvement and emigration schemes in 1847 is a typical example of this: see above, p. 228.

after the Famine had occurred it was not generally felt that any fundamentally new approach to the Irish situation was required. Contemporary opinion tended to look on the Famine as a natural calamity which had brought about the final collapse of the old order and opened up a new prospect for establishing Irish prosperity—but still on the basis of a contract relationship between landlord and tenant. Although this general policy had been in use for twenty years the tendency was to ascribe its failure not to any inherent defect in the prescribed policy, but rather to its not having been pushed far enough. But the work of such writers as J. S. Mill, Thornton, and Cairnes shows that the economists were not unwilling to revise their ideas and suggest a new approach to the problem. These writers still used the fundamental apparatus of classical economics, but combined with it a greater use of institutional material and comparative methods. They no longer assumed English conditions to be a norm, but drew widely on Continental examples, which they recognised as being often of more direct relevance to Ireland's position. The theoretical problems involved in this do not seem to have troubled Mill or Cairnes greatly; they did not, for example, consider the analytical implications of such policies as fixing rents by valuation. In the matter of policy, on the other hand, their escape from the 'high *priori*' dogmatism of their predecessors enabled them to produce proposals better adapted to the circumstances of the case they were considering.

Even with the influence of such a widely known and respected figure as Mill, it took some considerable time for the ideas of this group to have any marked effect on public opinion. After some twenty years, they were only being translated into policy in a limited form against the still vigorous opposition of adherents of the 'old political economy'. The parliamentary history of the late 'sixties affords the remarkable spectacle of J. S. Mill, whose *Principles* are now thought of as the final synthesis of classical economics, fighting against the implications of the stereotype of political economy which had taken root in the popular mind.

III

At the distance of a century it is not difficult to see that both the orientation of economic thought and the circumstances of policy-making in the period here covered were such as to militate against a successful diagnosis and treatment of Ireland's economic condition. Professor Myrdal has pointed out that the Benthamites, whose influence dominated English economic thinking at the opening of this period, 'were radical in all respects, except in their views on property....Their reform interest extended to almost every social sphere. Property alone was sacrosanct.'[1]

[1] G. Myrdal, *The Political Element in the Development of Economic Theory* (London, 1953), p. 118.

Such a combination of attitudes was peculiarly unfortunate when applied to the Irish problem, whose solution primarily called for radical thinking on the issue of property relations. Without this, advocacy of radical reforms in other respects was often more calculated to harm than to help the cause of Irish improvement.

John Stuart Mill and other economists of his generation were prepared to take a radical attitude towards property, but their ideas made slow progress against the older doctrine, which had gained wide public acceptance and still accorded with the preconceptions of a majority of British politicians. Before these new ideas could reach the stage of influencing policy decisively, the majority of the Irish people had grown weary of the consequences of the old ones. They could no longer be satisfied by concessions which would have been welcomed as a boon a generation earlier; the Irish question was entering on a new phase.

If the trend of ideas was ill-suited to the framing of a constructive Irish economic policy, political conditions were even less favourable to its implementation. The combination of a united legislature and a divided executive which was created by the Act of Union was peculiarly unfortunate in this respect. Reports of debates in Parliament and discussions in Select Committees and Commissions afford frequent evidence of the ambivalent attitude towards Ireland adopted by many ministers. At one time they would stress the fundamental unity of Britain and Ireland and 'the impossibility of treating Limerick differently from Lancashire'; at another they would speak of Ireland as a separate country requiring separate legislation. If Britain and Ireland were to be regarded as separate islands, linked by a merely nominal Union, then a case could be made for social experiments in Ireland that would not be applied to Britain—but a case could also be made for leaving Ireland to work out her own salvation, without troubling the British taxpayer. If Britain and Ireland were to be regarded as truly united in every respect then it could be said that privileges and responsibilities should be equally shared, but it could also be said that nothing must be done for Ireland which would constitute a dangerous precedent for Britain.

The consequences of this ambiguous situation were sometimes to Ireland's advantage, but sometimes to her disadvantage too. So, for example, Ireland could be provided with a Board of Works which did many things that no public agency would do in England, but the political unity of the two countries was a serious obstacle to the development of a separate code of land law in Ireland. Under the Union, too, it was possible for the New Poor Law to be applied to Ireland in all its rigour, but also possible to insist that Irish property alone must support Irish poverty. It would be impossible to draw up any objective balance sheet to determine whether Ireland gained or lost economically from the Union; but, without attempting this, it can be said that the Union made it very difficult for any consistent and special treatment of Ireland's economic problems to be carried out.

In the united Parliament, the majority of members were comparatively ill-informed about Irish affairs and had but little interest in them, while the time available for discussion of those affairs was necessarily limited. At the same time the superficial similarity in many respects between Irish and British customs and institutions made it natural for many to assume that what was good for Britain must also be good for Ireland. Ireland might well have fared better at the hands of British legislators had she differed more markedly from Britain, or been geographically more remote.[1] From this point of view, it was a dubious gain to Ireland to participate in the representative institutions of the United Kingdom. Sir James Sinclair once suggested that Ireland's difficulties could only be tackled by 'a *Board of Able Men*, exclusively appointed for the management of that single object, and who have nothing else to divert their attention',[2] and Ireland might certainly have fared better under some arrangement of this kind.

To a great many Irishmen of the day, of course, it seemed abundantly obvious that the solution was to give back to Ireland the management of her own affairs. It does not come within the province of historical scholarship to speculate on what might have been: yet any consideration of the difficulties which the Act of Union created for the framing of Irish economic policy so inevitably suggests the question, what would have been the consequences if it had been repealed, that some comment on this seems necessary.

Repeal of the Union would not in itself have solved Ireland's economic problems. Some nationalists were disposed to imagine that it would have, but the more sober amongst them argued instead that it would make a rational solution of those problems easier. There is force in this argument: had Repeal come in O'Connell's day, the landlord interest in a restored Irish Parliament might have been strong enough, but even so it seems unlikely that it would have taken twenty-five years to get a measure of tenant compensation on to the Statute Book. Nor does it seem reasonable to think that an Irish Parliament and ministry could have adopted the attitudes towards food purchase and distribution during the Famine which were in fact taken up in Westminster and Whitehall.

Nevertheless, to produce even a passable solution for Ireland's

---

[1] 'Englishmen are not always incapable of shaking off insular prejudices, and governing another country according to its wants, and not according to English habits and notions. It is what they have had to do in India; and those Englishmen who know something of India are even now those who understand Ireland best.... But, by a fortunate accident, the business of ruling India in the name of England did not rest with the Houses of Parliament or the offices at Westminster; it devolved on men who passed their lives in India, and made Indian interests their professional occupation.' (Mill, *England and Ireland*, p. 22.)

[2] Sinclair to Wilmot Horton, 22 October 1827 (C.O. 384/17.)

economic problems in the pre-Famine period would have been a formidable task under any political and administrative arrangement. Since the nationalists of the time were never called to take on the task, they could paint Utopian pictures of an Ireland in which a population of ten or fifteen millions would be comfortably supported from a combination of small-scale agriculture with manufactures of a rather nebulous form and organisation. On an appraisal of the facts it appears that to make this situation a reality would have been a virtual impossibility. It has already been pointed out[1] that reclamation of waste lands could not have afforded a reasonable subsistence for even the existing population; some measure of emigration would therefore seem to have been inevitable. It might then have been possible to create a stable agriculture based on peasant proprietorship, and to employ the remainder of the population in trades associated with agriculture; but it deserves to be emphasised that to achieve even this would have been no simple matter. The nationalists tended always to believe that an indefinite amount of industrial expansion might be stimulated through protection, but all experience showed that the only industries capable of absorbing a significant amount of the working population and at the same time affording a reasonable return were those which could compete in export markets. In general these were the industries most difficult to establish and develop in Ireland.

Again, in regard to agriculture, while examples from Ulster and further afield showed that small farms could be highly efficient, it does not follow that the mere enactment of fixity of tenure or some system of occupying ownership would have made Irish farming highly productive. Advocates of such schemes were fond of quoting the phrase 'the magic of property turns sand into gold', but to make the poor soils of western Ireland yield more than a scanty subsistence must necessarily have required not only years of hard work on the part of the cultivator, but also the dissemination of improved techniques, and some system of State aid to enable him to build up the equipment of his farm. In this respect concern with the problems of land tenure tended to prevent consideration of the problems of land use to a striking extent in nineteenth-century Ireland. Writers sympathetic to the tenants were always inclined to attribute all their faults to the manifest injustices under which they suffered and to gloss over the fact that many of them had a fair share of stupidity and cupidity, which no land reform would necessarily have altered.

While, therefore, the policy actually pursued in Ireland over the period here examined may merit ample criticism, it deserves to be pointed out that while it would have been possible to design and carry out a better policy, it could never have been easy.

[1] Above, ch. VI, p. 189.

BIBLIOGRAPHY

I. MANUSCRIPTS

IRELAND

(*a*) *Dublin*

National Library of Ireland
Butt Papers
O'Neill Daunt Papers
Drummond Papers
Gavan Duffy Papers
Larcom Papers
Monteagle Papers
Public Record Office of Ireland
Board of Works Papers
Railway Commission Records

(*b*) *Belfast*

Public Record Office of Northern Ireland
Anglesey Papers
Dufferin Papers
Foster Papers
Massereene Papers

ENGLAND

(*a*) London

British Museum
Aberdeen Papers (Add. MSS. nos. 43190, 43207, 43208)
Broughton Papers (Add. MSS. no. 36467)
Croker Papers (Add. MSS. nos. 41124–41128)
Gladstone Papers (Add. MSS. nos. 44112–44123, 44758)
Peel Papers (Add. MSS. nos. 40181–40614)
Wellesley Papers (Add. MSS. nos. 37298–37307 and 38103)

Public Record Office
Russell Papers
Colonial Office Papers (C.O. 324, 384 and 386)
Home Office Papers (H.O. 100)
Treasury Out-letters (T. 14 and T. 28)

University College, London
Chadwick Papers

(*b*) Oxford
Bodleian Library
Clarendon Papers

UNITED STATES OF AMERICA

(*a*) New York City
Columbia University
Scrapbooks of Francis Place (Seligman Collection)

BIBLIOGRAPHY

(b) Cambridge, Mass.
Kress Library, Harvard School of Business
Letters of Wellesley, Sir Robert Peel, Henry Hunt, Francis Horner, and George
Pryme

(c) Princeton, New Jersey
Princeton University Library
Blessington Collection (A.M. 12757)
T. Crofton Croker Collection (A.M. 12719)
Fonblanque Collection (A.M. 13115)
Letters of John Bright (A.M. 9553–7)
Letters of John Stuart Mill

(d) New Haven, Connecticut
Yale University Library
John Stuart Mill Collection
James M. Osborn Collection (Peel Correspondence)
Manuscripts of Thomas Carlyle: 'The Rakes of Mallow'; 'Notes on Sir Robert
Peel'; 'The English Talent for Governing'; Draft of *Latter-day Pamphlets*.
Letters of John Bright, Harriet Martineau, Robert Owen, T. Spring Rice,
J-B. Say, T. Perronet Thompson

II. PRINTED ORIGINAL SOURCES

(I) DIARIES, COLLECTIONS OF LETTERS AND PAPERS

Bright, John. *The Diaries of John Bright*, edited by R. A. J. Walling (London, 1930).
Broughton, Lord (John Cam Hobhouse). *Recollections of a Long Life. With Additional Extracts from His Private Diaries*, edited by Lady Dorchester (6 vols. London, 1909–11).
Burgoyne, [Sir] John F. *Life and Correspondence of Field Marshal Sir John Burgoyne* (2 vols. London, 1873).
Clarendon, George Wm. Frederick, fourth Earl of. *Life and Letters*..., edited by Sir Herbert Maxwell (2 vols. London, 1913).
Cloncurry, Valentine, Lord. *Personal Recollections of the Life and Times of*...*with Extracts from the Correspondence* (Dublin, 1849).
Creevey, Thomas. *The Creevey Papers*, edited by Sir Herbert Maxwell (2 vols. London, 1903).
Croker, J. W. *Correspondence and Diaries*..., edited by L. J. Jennings (3 vols. London, 1885).
Daunt, W. J. O'Neill. *A Life Spent for Ireland. Being Selections from the Journals of* ...*edited by his daughter* (London, 1896).
Duffy, [Sir] Charles Gavan. *My Life in Two Hemispheres* (London, 1903).
Ellenborough, Edward Law, Earl of. *A Political Diary, 1828–30*, edited by R. C. Abbot, Lord Colchester (2 vols. London, 1881).
Graham, Sir James. *Life and Letters of Sir James Graham, Second Baronet of Netherby, 1792–1861*, edited by C. S. Parker (2 vols. London, 1903).
Gregory, Augusta, Lady, (ed.). *Mr Gregory's Letter-box, 1813–30* (London, 1898).
Gregory, Sir Wm. H. *An Autobiography*, edited by Lady Gregory (London, 1894).
Greville, Charles Cavendish Fulke. *The Greville Memoirs. A Journal of the Reigns of King George IV and King William IV*, edited by Henry Reeve (3 vols. London, 1874).

BIBLIOGRAPHY

Greville, Charles Cavendish Fulke. *The Greville Memoirs. Second and third parts. A Journal of the Reign of Queen Victoria, from 1837 to 1860* (5 vols. London, 1885–1887).

Liverpool, Robert Banks, second Earl of. *Life and Administration*, compiled from original documents by C. D. Yonge (3 vols. London, 1868).

Mill, John Stuart. *Autobiography* (London, 1873).

—— *The Letters of John Stuart Mill*, edited by H. S. R. Elliot (2 vols. London, 1910).

—— *John Stuart Mill and Harriet Taylor: their Correspondence and Subsequent Marriage*, by F. A. Hayek (London, 1951).

Morris, Wm. O'Connor. *Memories and Thoughts of a Life* (London, 1895).

Napier, Macvey. *Selections from the Correspondence...*, edited by his son, Macvey Napier (London, 1879).

O'Connell, Daniel. *Correspondence of Daniel O'Connell*, edited by W. J. Fitzpatrick (2 vols. London, 1888).

O'Connell, John. *Recollections and Experiences during a Parliamentary Career from 1833 to 1848* (2 vols. London, 1849).

Peel, [Sir] Robert. *Sir Robert Peel from his Private Papers*, edited by C. S. Parker (3 vols. London, 1891–9).

Russell, Lord John. *The Early Correspondence of Lord John Russell, 1805–1840* (2 vols. edited by Rollo Russell, London, 1913).

—— *The Later Correspondence of Lord John Russell* (2 vols. edited by G. P. Gooch, London, 1925).

—— *Recollections and Suggestions, 1813–1873* (London, 1875).

Sadler, M. J. *Memoirs of the Life and Writings of Michael Thomas Sadler, Esq., M.P., F.R.S.* (London, 1842).

Wellington, Arthur Wellesley, first Duke of. *Despatches, Correspondence and Memoranda, 1819–32*, edited by his son, the second Duke (8 vols. London, 1867–80).

Whately, Richard. *Life and Correspondence of Richard Whately, D.D.*, by E. Jane Whately (2 vols. London, 1866).

(II) PARLIAMENTARY DEBATES

Cobbett's Parliamentary Debates from the Year 1803 to the Present Time (1820) (London, 1806–20).

The Parliamentary Debates Published under the Superintendence of T. C. Hansard, new series (London, 1820–30).

J. H. Barrow (ed.). *The Mirror of Parliament* (London, 1828–39).

Hansard, *Parliamentary Debates*, Third Series (London, 1831–70).

(III) PARLIAMENTARY PAPERS

1810 (365), X; 1810–11 (96), VI; 1813–14 (130, 131), VI. *Reports of the Commissioners on the Practicability of Draining and Cultivating the Bogs of Ireland*.

1814–15 (283), VI. *Report from the Select Committee on Grand Jury Presentments of Ireland*.

1816 (374, 375), IX. *Reports from the Select Committee on Grand Jury Presentments of Ireland*.

1819 (314), VIII; 1819 (409), VIII. *First and Second Reports from the Select Committee on the State of Disease, and Condition of the Labouring Poor in Ireland*.

1819 (378), VIII. *Report from the Select Committee on Grand Jury Presentments of Ireland*.

BIBLIOGRAPHY

1821 (32), XI. *First Report of the Commissioners of Irish Fisheries, Appointed under 59 Geo. III, c. 109.*

1821 (432), X. *Ninth Report of the Commissioners for Roads and Bridges in Scotland.*

1822 (353), VII; 1822 (413), VII; 1822 (451), VII. *Reports from the Select Committee on Grand Jury Presentments.*

1822 (560), VII. *Report from the Select Committee on the Laws which Regulate the Linen Trade of Ireland.*

1823 (249), X. *Copies of the Reports made to the Irish Government by the Civil Engineers Employed During the Late Scarcity, in Superintending the Public Works; and an Account of the Appropriation of the Sums Expended to Find Employment for the Irish Poor, During the Last Year.*

1823 (561), VI. *Report from the Select Committee on the Employment of the Poor in Ireland.*

1825 (129), VIII. *Reports from the Select Committee on the State of Ireland.*

1825 (181, 521), IX. *Minutes of Evidence* before the same.

1825 (200), VII. *Report and Minutes of Evidence from the Select Committee on Disturbances in Ireland.*

1825 (411, 463), V. *Report from the Select Committee on the Linen Trade of Ireland.*

1826 (40), V. *Report from the Select Committee of the House of Lords, Appointed to Inquire into the State of Ireland.*

1826 (102), XI. *Roads and Bridges, Ireland. First Report of Commissioners under 6 Geo. IV, c. 101.*

1826 (404), IV; 1826–7 (88, 237, 550), V. *Reports from the Select Committee on Emigration from the United Kingdom.*

1826–7 (555), III. *Report from the Select Committee on Proceedings for Regulating Grand Jury Presentments of Ireland.*

1829 (342), IV. *Report from the Select Committee on the Irish Miscellaneous Estimates.*

1830 (589, 654, 655, 667), VII. *Reports from the Select Committee on the State of the Poor in Ireland.*

1831–2 (177, 508), XXI. *Reports from the Select Committee on Tithes in Ireland.*

1831–2 (271, 663), XXII. *Reports from the Lords' Committee on Tithes in Ireland.*

1831–2 (327), XXIII. *First Report of the Commissioners upon the State of the Several Roads and Bridges Placed under their Care by 1 and 2 Will. IV, c. 33, Pursuant to 6 Geo. IV, c. 101.*

1831–2 (355, 418), XLV. *Papers Relating to Proposed Experimental Improvements on the Lands of Pobble O'Keefe.*

1831–2 (677), XVI. *Report from the Select Committee on the State of Ireland.*

1831–2 (724), XXXII. *Reports from the Commissioners for Emigration to the Colonial Secretary.*

1834 (173), LI. *Papers Respecting Experimental Improvements on the Crown Lands at King William's Town, in the Barony of Duhallow, in the County of Cork; and to New Lines of Public Roads Constructing in the Counties of Cork and Kerry.*

1834 (532), XVII. *Report from the Select Committee on the State of the River Shannon and the Best Means of Improving the Same.*

1835 (329), XX. *First Report from the Select Committee on Advances made by the Commissioners of Public Works (Ireland).*

1835 (573), XX. *Second Report* from the same, with *Minutes of Evidence.*

BIBLIOGRAPHY

1835 (369), XXXII. *First Report of H.M. Commission of Inquiry into the Condition of the Poorer Classes in Ireland.*
Appendices A–H to the above:
1835 (369), XXXII, Part II; 1836 [35], XXX; 1836 [36], XXXI, [37], XXXII, [38], XXXIII [39–42], XXXIV.
1837 [68], XXXI. *Second Report.*
1836 [43], XXX. *Third Report.*
1837 [90], LI. *Letter from N. W. Senior, Esq., to His Majesty's Principal Secretary of State for the Home Department, on the Third Report.*
1837 [91], LI. *Remarks of G. C. Lewis, Esq., On Poor Laws, Ireland.*
1837 [77, 82], XXII. *First and Second Reports of H.M. Commissioners of Inquiry into the Irish Fisheries.*
1837 [69], LI; 1837–8 [104, 126], XXXVIII. *First, Second and Third Reports of George Nicholls, Esq., on Poor Laws, Ireland.*
1837 [75], XXXIII; 1837–8 [145], XXXV. *First and Second Reports of the Commissioners Appointed to Consider and Recommend a General System of Railways for Ireland.*
1837–8 (677), XVII. *Report of the Select Committee on Pawnbroking in Ireland.*
1845 (119, 119–II), XXXIX; (154, 154–II), XXXIX. *Reports of the Railways Department of the Board of Trade on Schemes for Extending Railway Communication in Ireland.*
1845 [605], XIX; 1845 [606], XIX, [616], XX, [657], XXI, [672] and [673], XXII. *Report from H.M. Commissioners of Inquiry into the State of the Law and Practice in Respect to the Occupation of Land in Ireland.*
Minutes of Evidence taken before the same, with Appendices and Index.
1846 (694), XI. *Report from the Select Committee of the House of Lords on the Laws Relating to the Destitute Poor and the Operation of Medical Charities in Ireland, with the Minutes of Evidence.*
1846 [735], XXXVII. *Correspondence Explanatory of the Measures Adopted by H.M. Government for the Relief of Distress Arising from Failure of the Potato Crop in Ireland.*
1847 (193), LIV. *Emigration of Destitute Irish into Liverpool. Correspondence with Secretary of State.*
1847 (718), LIV. *An Account (since the Union) of All Sums of Money Advanced on Loan for Public Works or Other Purposes.*
1847 (737), VI. *Report and Minutes of Evidence from the Select Committee of the House of Lords on Colonization from Ireland.*
1847 [761], LI, [796], LII. *Correspondence Relating to the Measures Adopted for the Relief of Distress in Ireland.* Commissariat Series, Parts I and II.
1847 [764], L, [797] LII. *Correspondence Relating to the Relief of Distress in Ireland.* Board of Works Series, Parts I and II.
1847–8 (415), (593), XVII; 1849 (86), XI. *First, Second and Third Reports from the Select Committee of the House of Lords on Colonization from Ireland; with the Minutes of Evidence.*
1847–8 (535), XVII. *Report from the Select Committee on the Farmers' Estate Society (Ireland) Bill.*
1847–8 (693), XVII; 1849 (21), XIV. *Report and Minutes of Evidence from the Select Committee on Savings Banks (Ireland).*
1849 (593), XXXVIII; 1850 [1163], XL; 1851 [347, 347–II], XL; 1852 [1489], XXXIV. *Papers Relative to Emigration to the Australian Colonies.*
1849 (58), XV, Part I; (356), XV, Part II. *Reports and Minutes of Evidence from the Select Committee on Poor Laws (Ireland).*

BIBLIOGRAPHY

1849 (192), XVI. *Reports and Minutes of Evidence from the Select Committee of the House of Lords on the Irish Poor Law.*

1850 (159), LI. *A Return of all Monies Lent to Railway Companies in Ireland.*

1850 [1268], XXV. *Report from the Commissioners for Sale of Incumbered Estates in Ireland.*

1852 (HL. 123), XVII. *Copies or Extracts of Communications between the Secretary of State for the Home Department, the Lord-Lieutenant of Ireland, the Poor Law Commissioners (Ireland) or any other Person, in the Years 1846–47, Respecting the Means of Affording Temporary Relief in Ireland, by Employment on Public Works or Otherwise.*

1852–3 (10), XXVI. *Report and Minutes of Evidence from the Select Committee of the House of Lords on the Drainage of Lands (Ireland).*

1852–3 (726), XCIV. *Roman and Foreign Law Considered with Reference to the Relations of Landlord and Tenant in Ireland—Communicated by the Secretary for Ireland to the Members of the Committee on Irish Land Bills.*

1852–3 [1641], XLI. *Report from H.M. Commissioners of Inquiry on Arterial Drainage, Ireland.*

1854–5 (259), VII. *Report from the Select Committee on Loan Fund Societies (Ireland).*

1854–5 [1938], XIX. *Report from H.M. Commissioners of Inquiry into the Operation of the Incumbered Estates Court in Ireland.*

1861 (408), X. *Report from the Select Committee on the Relief of the Poor in Ireland.*

1862 (399), XVI. *Special Report from the Select Committee on the Debentures on Land (Ireland) Bill.*

1865 (402), XI. *Report and Minutes of Evidence from the Select Committee on the Tenure and Improvement of Land (Ireland) Act.*

1867 [3844], XXXVIII. *Report and Minutes of Evidence from H.M. Commission of Inquiry into the Railways of Great Britain and Ireland.*

1867 (518), XIV; 1867–8 (HL. 129), XXX. *Reports and Minutes of Evidence from the Select Committee of the House of Lords on the Tenure (Ireland) Bill.*

1867–8 [4018], XXXII. *First Report of the Commissioners Appointed to Inspect the Accounts and Examine the Works of Railways in Ireland.*

1868–9 [4086], XVII. *Second Report* of the same.

1870 [C. 31], XIV. *Relations between Landlord and Tenant in Respect of Improvements in Farms. Poor Law Inspectors' Reports.*

1870 [C. 35], XIV. *Agricultural Labourers' (Ireland) Wages: Poor Law Inspectors' Reports.*

1876 (412), LXXX. *Return of Owners of Land (Ireland).*

1878 [C. 2060], XXIII. *Report and Minutes of Evidence from the Committee Appointed by the Treasury to Examine the Constitution and Duties of the Board of Works, Ireland.*

1887 [C. 5038], XXV; 1888 [C. 5264], XLVIII. *First and Second Reports and Minutes of Evidence from H.M. Commissioners of Inquiry into Public Works in Relation to Industrial Development in Ireland.*

1895 [C. 7851], LXXV. *Tithe Rentcharge in Ireland: Memorandum Prepared by Treasury.*

Series of Annual Reports:
Reports of the Commissioners of Public Works in Ireland
commencing at 1833 (75), XVII.

Reports of the Poor Law Commissioners (Ireland)
commencing at 1847–8 [963], XXXIII.
Reports of the Colonial Land and Emigration Commissioners
commencing at 1842 (567), XXV.

(IV) NEWSPAPERS, PERIODICALS, AND PERIODIC RECORDS

British

Blackwood's Magazine
City Magazine
Cobbett's Weekly Political Register
Contemporary Review
Eclectic Review
Economist
Edinburgh Review
Examiner
Fortnightly Review
Fraser's Magazine
Morning Chronicle
North British Review
Quarterly Review
Railroad Monthly Journal
Spectator
The Times
Westminster Review
The Annual Register, being a Review of the History, Politics, and Literature of the Year...(London, 1817–70)

Irish

Ballyshannon Herald
Belfast News-Letter
Daily Express (Dublin)
Dublin Evening Mail
Dublin Evening Post
Dublin University Magazine
Freeman's Journal
Irishman
Irish People
Irish Quarterly Review
Irish Railway Gazette
Irish Times
Nation
Newry Magazine
Northern Whig
Saunders' News-Letter
Tipperary Vindicator
Thom's Irish Almanac and Official Directory (Dublin, 1844–70)

(V) OTHER CONTEMPORARY WORKS

Adair, A. S., Baron Waveney. *The Winter of 1846–7 in Antrim, with Remarks on Out-door Relief and Colonization* (London, 3rd ed. 1847).
Adair, R., Baron Waveney. *Ireland and her Servile War* (London, 1866).
Adams, G. *Observations on the Present State of Ireland; to which is Added, a Hint to the Land Owners of Great Britain* (Ross, 1831).
Adams, Capt. *Causes of the Wretched Condition of the Irish Peasantry, with a Sketch of a Plan for Restoring them to Habits of Industry and Good Order, in Lieu of a Poor Rate* (London, 1833).
Alcock, T. *The Tenure of Land in Ireland Considered* (London, 1848).
Alexander, J. *A Letter to Sir R. A. Ferguson, Bt., M.P., on the Relative Rights of Landlord and Tenant, Proposing an Adjustment of their Interests on the Basis of Certain Principles Already Recognised in India, and Held to be Applicable to the Present Condition of Ireland* (London, 1848).
Alison, A. *England in 1815 and 1845; and the Monetary Famine of 1847: or, a Sufficient and a Contracted Currency* (London, 1847).
—— *The Principles of Population, and their connection with Human Happiness* (2 vols. Edinburgh, 1840).
Alison, W. P. *Observations on the Famine of 1846–7, in the Highlands of Scotland and in Ireland* (Edinburgh, 1847).

255

BIBLIOGRAPHY

Allen, W. *Colonies at Home; or, the Means for Rendering the Industrious Labourer Independent of Parish Relief; and for Providing for the Poor Population of Ireland, by the Cultivation of the Soil* (4th ed. Lindfield, Sussex, 1827).

Allingham, W. *Laurence Bloomfield in Ireland: A Modern Poem* (London, 1864).

Alvanley, W. A., Baron. *The State of Ireland Considered* (London, 1841).

Andrew, [Sir] W. P. *Indian Railways; as Connected with the Power and Stability of the British Empire in the East...by an Old Indian Postmaster* (London, 1846).

Anketel, W. R. *The Effects of Absenteeism Briefly Considered* (London, 1843).

Anonymous. *Abstract of the Final Report of the Commissioners of Irish Poor Inquiry; with Remarks thereon, and upon the Measures now before Parliament for the Relief of the Destitute Poor in Ireland* (London, 1837).

—— *Address to the Irish and their Descendants in the United States and the British Provinces, October 1848.* By 'Hibernicus' (Columbia, S.C., 1848).

—— *An Antidote to Revolution; or a Practical Comment on the Creation of Privilege for Quadrating the Principles of Consumption with Production, and thereby Creating Stimulus for the Unlimited Production of National Wealth...By Eight-Seven* (Dublin, 1830).

—— *An Appeal to the King, on the Present State of Ireland* (London, 1822).

—— *Brief Observations on the Proposed Measure for Promoting the Employment of the Labouring Classes in Ireland, and Suggestions for Rendering the Plan Available to the Encouragement of the Irish Fisheries.* By an Officer of the Late Board of Irish Fisheries (Cork, 1831).

—— *A Call upon the People of Great Britain and Ireland, for Immediate Attention to the State of their Public Affairs, Debts and Taxes* (London, 1828).

—— *Commentaries on National Policy, and Ireland* (Dublin, 1831).

—— *Conciliatory Observations to the People of Ireland on the Union.* By an Irishman (Dublin, n.d. 1810?).

—— *The Constitutional Rights of Landlords; the Evils Springing from the Abuse of them in Ireland; and the Origin and Effects of Banks, of Funds, and of Corn Laws, considered* (Dublin, 1844).

—— *Coup d'œil historique et statistique sur l'état passé et présent de l'Irlande.* By C-H. M. D. C. (Paris, 1828).

—— *A Cry to Ireland and the Empire (Against the Repeal of the Union, and in Favour of a Legal Provision for the Irish Poor).* By an Irishman (London, 1833).

—— *Dangers from the Policy of England in the Depression of Ireland* (London, 1810).

—— *Direct Communication between Dublin and London via Portdynllaen in 12 hours.* (London, 1836).

—— *An Essay on the Subject of a Repeal of the Union, between Great Britain and Ireland.* By J.M. (Dublin, 1831).

—— *Essays on the Population of Ireland, and the Characters of the Irish.* By a Member of the Last Irish Parliament (London, 1803).

—— *The Establishment of a General Packet Station, on the South-West Coast of Ireland, Connected by Railways with Dublin and London, Considered* (London and Dublin, 1836).

—— *The Famine as Yet in its Infancy; or, 1847 Compared with the Prospects of 1848, 1849, etc. Addressed to Everybody.* (London, n.d. 1847?).

—— *A Few Remarks on the Present State of Ireland, Sufficient to Set Others Thinking* (London, 1833).

256

BIBLIOGRAPHY

Anonymous. *A Few Words on the Promoting and Encouraging of Free Emigration to the West India Colonies. Addressed to the Right Honourable Lord John Russell* (Liverpool, 1840).
—— *Fixity of Tenure. A Dialogue.* By an Irish Landlord (London, 1870).
—— *Foreshadowings. A Proposal for the Settlement of the Irish Land Question. Addressed to the Tenant Farmers.* By 'Ignotus' (Dublin, 1870).
—— *Has Ireland Gained or Lost by the Union with Great Britain?* (London, 1831).
—— *Hints to Philanthropists: or, a Collective View of Practical Means of Improving the Condition of the Poor, and Labouring Classes of Society* (Dublin, 1825).
—— *How is Ireland to be Governed?* (London, 1844).
—— *Important Suggestions in Relation to the Irish Poor Law, Designed to Ameliorate the condition of the Labouring Class*....By A Gentleman of Lincoln's Inn (postscript signed M.D.), (Dublin, n.d. 1842?).
—— *Influence of the Public Debt, over the Prosperity of the Country.* By M.B. (London, 1834).
—— *An Inquiry, but not a Parliamentary Inquiry, into the Past and Present Abuses of the Irish Revenue, and into the Plunder of the Irish Patronage* (Dublin, 1824).
—— *Ireland as it is, and as it might be: being Three Letters on the Land Question.* By A Scot (Dundee, 1879).
—— *Ireland: her Evils and Remedies* (London, 1841).
—— *Ireland under Lord de Grey* (Dublin, 1844).
—— *Ireland's Miseries: Their Cause. From* The Plough, the Loom and the Anvil, *for September 1852* (New York, 1852).
—— *Irish Church. A Letter to the Right Honourable Lord Holland, or a Reply to the 'Parliamentary Talk' of a Disciple of Selden.* By a Pupil of Canning (London, 1836).
—— *The Irish Difficulty.* By an Irish Peer (Dublin, 1867).
—— *The Irish Landlord and his Accusers.* By 'Political Economy'. (Dublin, 1882).
—— *Irish Landlords as they are, and the Poor Law Bill Accompanied as it Ought to Be;...With a Few Words on Landowners and Slaveowners, Waste Lands and Weighty Debts* (Dublin, 1838).
—— *Irish Poor. A Word for Mr Nicholls.* By a Looker-on (London, 1837).
—— *The Irish Poor Law Bill. Two Letters to Daniel O'Connell, Esq., M.P., in Reply to his Letters to his Constituents on the Irish Poor-Law Bill. Reprinted from 'The Courier',* with notes (London, 1838).
—— *Irish Poor Law: Past, Present and Future* (London, 1849).
—— *Irish Railways and the Board of Trade, Considered in a Letter to the Right Honourable Lord Brougham* (signed 'Locomotive'), (Dublin, 1845).
—— *Irish Railways. Should Government Purchase the Irish Railways? A Question for the Shareholders and the Public* (Dublin, 1867).
—— *Justice to Ireland. Addressed to the Marquis of Chandos.* By Amicus Hiberniae (London, 1837).
—— *The Land Question in Ireland, Viewed from an Indian Stand-Point* (Dublin, 1870).
—— *Letter from an Irish Beneficed Clergyman, Concerning Tithes* (London, 1822).
—— *Letter to an English Member of Parliament, upon the Subject of the Present State of Ireland.* By an Irish Country Gentleman (Dublin, 1843).
—— *A Letter to the Earl of Mulgrave, Lord Lieutenant of Ireland.* By a Dissatisfied Country Gentleman (Dublin, 1836).

BIBLIOGRAPHY

Anonymous. *A Letter to the Marquis of Lansdowne, on the Report of the Irish Railway Commissioners.* By A Shareholder in the Kilkenny Railway (London, 1838).

—— *Letter to the People, on the Protestant Established Church, and the Irish Tithe Question.* By a Late Member of Parliament (London, 1835).

—— *A Letter to the Right Honourable Lord Stanley.* By the Younger Brother of a Dissatisfied Country Gentleman (Dublin, 1836).

—— *A Letter to the Right Honourable Mr Lamb, Containing a Few Practical Hints for the Improvement of Ireland.* By a Landowner (3rd ed. Dublin, 1828).

—— *A Letter to the Right Honourable The Earl of Darnley, on the Introduction of a Labour Rate, for the Employment of the Poor in Ireland* (signed 'A Well-Wisher to Ireland'), (Dublin, 1831).

—— *A Letter to the Right Honourable the Lord Mayor of the City of Dublin, Proposing an Wholesome and Improved System of Poor-Laws for Ireland.* By 'Patricious' (Dublin, 1830).

—— *Letter to the Right Honourable W. C. Plunkett, Attorney-general for Ireland, by an Irish Landlord, on the Subject of Tithes* (London, 1822).

—— *A Letter to William Sharman Crawford on the Condition of Ireland by T.D.D.* (n.p., 1844).

—— *Letters Addressed to the Marquis Wellesley on the Means of Ameliorating the Condition of the Irish Peasantry.* By 'Clericus' (Cork, 1823).

—— *Letters from an Irish Landlord and Others on the Internal Situation of Ireland; Published in the Sun Newspaper. With the Editor's Remarks* (Bristol, 1822).

—— *Letters of Lælius on Various Topics Connected with the Present Situation of Ireland, as Published in the Carlow Morning Post, in the years 1822 and 1823* (Carlow, n.d.).

—— *Letters on Emigration, Containing a Few Remarks on the Benefits, Likely to be Derived by the Adoption of a National System of Emigration.* By C.H. (London, 1841).

—— *Letters on Ireland: to Refute Mr George Barnes's Statistical Account, etc.* By a Citizen of Waterford (Waterford, 1813).

—— *Letters on the State of Ireland.* By a Landed Proprietor (London, 1847).

—— *Letters to an Editor on the Land Question. No. 1. January 1866.* By W.T.W. (London, 1866).

—— *Letters to a Friend in England, on the Actual State of Ireland* (London, 1828).

—— *Letters to an Irish Radical, upon the Subject of his Projected Change of the British Constitution, etc.* By a Saxon (London, 1836).

—— *The Measures Which can Alone Ameliorate Effectually the Condition of the Irish People* (London, 1847).

—— *No Emigration. The Testimony of Experience...* (London, 1828).

—— *Notes Relative to the Condition of the Irish Peasantry, Especially in the Province of Ulster. Addressed to Lord Viscount Melbourne.* By an Ulster Landlord (London, 1831).

—— *Observations on Ireland.* By an Irishman (Kilkenny, 1820).

—— *Observations on the Exchange Between London and Dublin.* By a Merchant of Dublin (Dublin, 1804).

—— *Observations on the Habits of the Labouring Classes in Ireland, Suggested by Mr G. C. Lewis' Report on the State of the Irish Poor in Great Britain* (Dublin, 1836).

258

BIBLIOGRAPHY

Anonymous. *On Contracts between Landlord and Tenant in Ireland.* By A Leinster Agent. (Dublin, 1865).

—— *One More Specific for Ireland.* By R.T.H. (London, 1825).

—— *Past and Proposed Legislation on the Presentment of Public Money by Grand Jury Presentments for Public Works in Ireland* (Dublin, 1857).

—— *A Political Poor Relation.* Preface signed 'R.W.E.L.' (London, 1863).

—— *Poor Laws in Ireland. A Letter to Lord Viscount Cole, and Mervyn Archdall, Esq., Representatives in Parliament of the County of Fermanagh.* By J—I—, Esq. (Dublin, 1838).

—— *A Practical Plan for Alleviating the Distresses of the Poor of Ireland.* By 'Howard' (Dublin, 1826).

—— *Practicability of a Legislative Measure for Harmonizing the Conflicting Interests of Agriculture and Manufactures.* By Eight-Seven (Dublin, 1830).

—— *Prospectus of a Joint-Stock Company for the Improvement of Ireland* (London, 1834).

—— *Prosperity of the Labourer the Foundation of Universal Prosperity.* By Eight-Seven (Dublin, 1827).

—— *Remarks on the Consumption of Public Wealth by the Clergy of every Christian Nation, and Particularly by the Established Church in England and Wales, and Ireland* (London, 1822).

—— *Remarks on Observations on the Necessity of a Legal Provision for the Irish Poor, etc. by John Douglas Esq., with an Epitome of the Poor-Laws of England, and proving their superiority over those of Scotland. Illustrated by Contrasted Cases in both Countries.* By T.B. (Edinburgh, 1828).

—— *Repeal of the Legislative Union of Great Britain and Ireland considered* (London, 1831).

—— *A Repeal of the Union the Ruin of Ireland.* By R.B.G. (Dublin, 1831).

—— *Repeal, or No Repeal. Repeal of the Union with Ireland Considered in its Practical Bearings* (2nd ed. London, 1834).

—— *The Repealers* (Dublin, n.d. 1831?).

—— *A Review of the 'Past and Present Policy of England towards Ireland', extracted from the 'Morning Chronicle' of May 13th, 1845* (London, 1845).

—— *The Saying of Sir Robert Peel, 'My Chief Difficulty is Ireland', Considered. In a Letter to the Right Honourable Baronet, by a Clergyman of the Archdiocese of Canterbury* (London, 1841).

—— *Sketches of the Merino Factory, Descriptive of its Origin and Progress* (Dublin, 1818).

—— *A Short Inquiry into the Causes of the Present Distresses of the Irish Traders* (Dublin, 1810).

—— *Short Statement Relative to the Bishops Court in Ireland, and the Conduct of Tithe Proctors in that Country* (London, 1824).

—— *Some Notices Touching the Present State of Ireland.* By C.C.C. (London, 1831).

—— *Some of the Difficulties of Ireland, in the Way of an Improving Government, Stated. In a Letter to Sir R. Peel, Bart.* By a Clergyman of the Archdiocese of Canterbury (London, 1843).

—— *Some Suggestions for a Public Measure to Promote Emigration* (Dublin, 1848).

—— *The South of Ireland and her Poor* (London, 1843).

—— *State of Ireland Considered, with an Enquiry into the History and Operation of Tithe; 2nd ed. with an Appendix, containing the Rev. Mr Howlett's Plan of Commutation, and a Proposition for taxing Absentees* (Dublin, 1810).

17-2

BIBLIOGRAPHY

Anonymous. *The State of the Poor of Ireland Briefly Considered and Agricultural Education Recommended, to Remedy Redundant Population and to Promote National Improvement* (Dublin, 1820).

—— *Strictures on the Proposed Poor Law for Ireland, as recommended in the Report of George Nicholls, Esq.* (London, 1837).

—— *Suggestions for Giving Employment to the Labouring Classes, through the Medium of the Landholder* (Dublin, 1824).

—— *Suggestions for the Improvement of Ireland by the Author of 'Civil Disabilities on Account of Religion, Considered with Reference to the Christian Dispensation, History and Policy'* (London, 1824).

—— *Thoughts on Ireland* (London, 1847).

—— *Thoughts on Repeal and Separation. By a Repealer, not a Separatist* (n.p., 1833).

—— *Thoughts on the Proposed Introduction of Poor Laws into Ireland* (London, 1837).

—— *Three Months in Ireland: by an English Protestant* (London, 1827).

—— *Timely Hints, Addressed to the Landlords and Tenantry of England, Scotland and Ireland...by their Country Cousins* (London, 1843).

—— *Turnips, Sheep, Wool and Prosperity: versus Flax, Potatoes, Mud Hovels, and Poverty*, by an Irish Landlord (Bristol, 1824).

—— *Travellers' New Guide Through Ireland* (London, 1819).

—— *The United Kingdom Tributary to France: the Real Cause of the Distresses of the Country Demonstrated in a Letter to the Right Honourable the Earl of Liverpool* (London, 1820).

—— *A View of the State of Pauperism in Ireland; its Evils and its Remedies* (London, 1836).

Armagh. *Words of Wisdom, Addressed to the Working Classes....To which are Subjoined the Laws of the First Armagh Co-operative Society* (Armagh, 1830).

Atherton, H. *An Acre of Land in his Native Parish the Right of Every British Subject, ...with Remarks on the State of the Country in General and Ireland in Particular* (Battle, n.d., signed 'July 15th', 1869?).

—— *Remarks on the Condition of Ireland* (n.p., 1873).

Atkinson, A. *Ireland Exhibited to England, in a Political and Moral Survey of her Population, etc....* (2 vols. London, 1823).

—— *Ireland in the Nineteenth Century* (London, 1833).

Atkinson, W. *The Reason for Protecting Home Trade, or, the Principle of Free Trade Refuted* (London, 1833).

—— *The State of the Science of Political Economy Investigated* (London, 1838).

—— *Principles of Political Economy; or, the Laws of the Formation of National Wealth* (London, 1840).

Bagenal, P. H. *A Compendium of the Acts Referring to Loans, as Obtained through the Board of Works (Ireland)*, (Dublin, 1875).

Bain, D. *Ireland, its Wants and Capabilities* (London, 1836).

Baines, T. *The Agricultural Resources of Great Britain, Ireland, and the Colonies, Considered, in Connection with the Rise in the Price of Corn and the Alarming Condition of the Irish People* (Liverpool, 1847).

Balch, W. S. *Ireland, as I saw it: the Character, Condition and Prospects of the People* (New York, 1850).

Ball, J. *What is to be Done for Ireland?* (London, 1849).

Barkley, J. T. *Report on Purchase and Occupation of Landed Property in Connaught* (London, 1850).

BIBLIOGRAPHY

Barrington, [Sir] M. *On a Western Packet Station at Limerick, and a Railroad between that City and Dublin* (Limerick? 1836).
—— *Letter of Sir Matthew Barrington, Bart. to the Right Honourable Sir Robert Peel, Bart.* (n.p.; dated Dublin October 28, 1844).
Barry, M. J. *Ireland, as She was, as She is, and as She Shall Be* (Dublin, 1845).
—— *Irish Emigration Considered* (Cork, 1863).
Barton, E. *Recent Scenes and Occurrences in Ireland* (London, 1823).
Battersby, W. J. *The Fall and Rise of Ireland, or the Repealer's Manual* (2nd ed. Dublin, 1834).
Baxter, R. *The Irish Tenant-Right Question Examined* (London, 1869).
Beare, J. *Improvement of Ireland: a Letter to the King on the Practical Improvement of Ireland* (London, 1827).
de Beaumont, G. *Ireland, Social, Political and Religious*, ed. W. Cooke Taylor (London, 1839).
Begbie, M. B. *Partnership 'en Commandite' or Partnership with Limited Liabilities* (London, 1848).
Begg, J. D. D. *Pauperism and the Poor Laws* (Edinburgh, 1849).
Bennett, W. *Narrative of a Journey of Six Weeks in Ireland* (London and Dublin, 1847).
Bergin, T. F. *The Atmospheric Railway* (Dublin, 1843).
Bermingham, T. *Additional Statements on the Subject of the River Shannon to the Reports Published in 1831* (London, 1834).
—— *The Social State of Great Britain and Ireland Considered with Regard to the Labouring Population, etc. etc.* (London, 1835).
—— *First Report and Proceedings of the General Railway Committee, Appointed at a Public Meeting Held at the Commercial Buildings on Friday, the 22nd Day of November, 1838* (Dublin, 1838).
—— *Report of the Proceedings at Two Public Meetings, Held at the Thatched House Tavern, on the 13th and 20th of April, 1839, for the Purpose of Taking into consideration the Necessity of Forming Railways Throughout Ireland* (London, 1839).
—— *A Letter to the Right Honourable Lord Viscount Morpeth* (London, 1839).
—— *Irish Railways. A Full and Interesting Report of the Public Proceedings on this Important Question* (London, 1839).
—— *Statistical Evidence in Favour of State Railways in Ireland* (Dublin, 1841).
—— *Letter Addressed to the Right Honourable Lord John Russell, containing Facts Illustrative of the Good Effects from the Just and Considerate Discharge of the Duties of a Resident Landlord in Ireland, etc.* (2nd ed. London, 1846).
Bernard, J., M.D. *Thoughts on Emigration, as Connected with Ireland, in a Series of Letters* (Dublin, 1840).
Bicheno, J. E. *Ireland and its Economy* (London, 1830).
Bish, T. *A Plea for Ireland: Submitting the Outline of a Proposition for Holding the Court and Parliament, at Occasional Intervals, in Dublin* (London, n.d.,—1834).
Black Book. *The Black Book; or, Corruption Unmasked* (London, 1828).
Blacker, W. *The Claims of the Landed Interests to Legislative Protection Considered* (London, 1836).
—— *Prize Essay....on the Management of Landed Property in Ireland* (Dublin, 1837).
—— *An Essay on the Best Mode of Improving the Condition of the Labouring Classes of Ireland* (London, 1846).

Blacker, W. *Review of Charles Shaw Lefevre, Esq.'s Letter to his Constituents, as Chairman of the Select Committee appointed to inquire into the Present State of Agriculture* (London, 1837).

Blayney, Major-General Lord. *Sequel to a Narrative of a Forced Journey through Spain and France, as a Prisoner of War, in 1810 to 1813; Including Observations on the Present State of Ireland, etc. etc.* (vol. III, London, 1816).

Blessington, C. J. Gardiner, Earl of. *A Letter to his Excellency the Marquis of Wellesley, on the State of Ireland. By a Representative Peer* (London, 1822).

Boase, H. *A Letter to the Right Honourable Lord King in Defence of the Conduct of the Directors of the Banks of England and Ireland* (London, 1804).

Bodington, G. *On the Deep-seated Causes of Irish Adversity, and the Appropriate Remedial Measures* (London and Dublin, 1850).

Booth, H. *Thoughts on the Condition of the Poor, in Large Towns, Especially with Reference to Liverpool* (Liverpool, 1824).

—— *The Question of the Poor Laws Considered....* (Liverpool, 1818).

Borrett, W. P. *Three Letters upon a Poor Law and Public Medical Relief for Ireland, to Daniel O'Connell, Esq., M.P.* (London, 1838).

Brabazon, W. *The Deep Sea and Coast Fisheries of Ireland, with Suggestions for the Working of a Fishing Company* (Dublin, 1848).

Bridges, W. *Ireland and America. Railway Colonization and a Colonization Currency. Reprinted from the 'Monthly Railway Record'* (London, 1847).

—— *Three Practical Suggestions for the Reorganisation of Ireland* (London, 1849).

Bright, J. *Speeches on Questions of Public Policy.* Ed. J. E. Thorold Rogers (2 vols. London, 1868).

Broadhurst, J. *Letter to Lord Melbourne on the Irish Church and Irish Tithes* (London, 1835).

—— *Political Economy* (London, 1842).

Bromwell, W. J. *History of Immigration to the United States* (New York, 1856).

Brooke, W. G. (ed.). *The Landlord and Tenant (Ireland) Act, 1870, with Introduction, Notes, Explanations and an Index* (Dublin, 1870).

Brown, H. *Irish Wants and Practical Remedies; an Investigation as to the Applicability of a Government System of Railways in Ireland* (London, 1848).

Browne, D. *Letter to the Marquis of Wellesley on the present state of Ireland* (London, 1822).

Browne, J. W. *Ireland in 1847: its Present State and Future Prospects. An Appeal to the British Public for the Promotion of Domestic Industry in Ireland* (London, n.d. 1847?).

Browning, G. *The Domestic and Financial Condition of Great Britain* (London, 1834).

Bruce, W. *Poor Rates the Panacea for Ireland* (Bristol, 1828).

Bryan, J. B. *A Practical View of Ireland, from the Period of the Union* (Dublin, 1831).

Buchanan, A. C. *Emigration Practically Considered; in a Letter to the Right Honourable R. Wilmot Horton, M.P.* (London, 1828).

—— *Outline of a Practical Plan for the Immediate, Effective and Economical Relief of the Starving and Destitute Poor of Ireland* (Brighton, preface dated 12 February 1837).

Buchanan, G. C. *Ireland as she Ought to Be* (Dublin, 1825).

Buckingham, J. S. *National Evils and Practical Remedies* (London, n.d. 1847–8?).

[Buckingham, ——.] *Remarks on the Present State of the United Kingdom.... Demonstratively Proving the cause of Irish Prostration, and recommending a Cure.* By A Manufacturer (Sheffield, 1833).

Buret, E. *De la Misère des Classes Laborieuses en Angleterre et en France* (Paris, 1840).

Burgess, H. *A Letter to the Right Honourable George Canning...With a Postscript on the Tendency of the Wages of Labour in England and Ireland to Become Equal, and the Consequences Resulting Therefrom Exemplified* (London, 1826).

Burgoyne, Sir John Fox, Bt. *Ireland in 1831. Letters on the State of Ireland* (London, 1831).

Burness, W. *Essay on the Elements of British Industry: Comprising Remarks on the Cause of our Present Depressed State....English, Scotch and Irish: Together with Suggestions for its Removal* (London, 1848).

Burritt, E. *A Journal of a Visit of Three Days to Skibbereen, and its Neighbourhood* (London and Birmingham, 1847).

Butler-Johnstone, H. A. *Ireland. Letters Reprinted from the 'Morning Post', and Dedicated with the Utmost Respect to the Right Honourable W. E. Gladstone, M.P.* (London, 1868).

Butt, I. *The Poor-Law Bill for Ireland Examined, its Provisions, and the Report of Mr Nicholls Contrasted with the Facts Proved by the Poor Inquiry Commission* (London, 1837).

—— *Protection to Home Industry: Some Cases of its Advantages Considered* (Dublin, 1846).

—— *The Transfer of Land, by Means of a Judicial Assurance: its Practicability and Advantages Considered* (Dublin, 1857).

—— *Land Tenure in Ireland; a Plea for the Celtic Race* (Dublin, 1866).

—— *Fixity of Tenure; Heads of a Suggested Legislative Enactment; with an Introduction and Notes* (Dublin, 1866).

—— *The Irish Querist: A Series of Questions Proposed for the Consideration of all who Desire to Solve the Problem of Ireland's Social Condition* (Dublin, 1867).

—— *The Irish People and the Irish Land: A Letter to Lord Lifford* (Dublin, 1867).

[Byles, [Sir] John Barnard.] *Sophisms of Free-Trade and Popular Political Economy Examined.* By a Barrister (1st ed. London, 1849).

Byrne, S. (Rev). *Irish Emigration to the United States; what it has been and what it is* (New York, 1873).

Caird, J. *Ireland and the Plantation Scheme; or, the West of Ireland as a Field for Investment* (Edinburgh and London, 1850).

—— *The Irish Land Question* (London, 1869).

Cairnes, J. E. *Political Economy as a Branch of General Education: Being an Inaugural Lecture Delivered in Queen's College, Galway, in Michaelmas Term, 1859* (London, 1860).

—— *Essays in Political Economy, Theoretical and Applied* (London, 1873).

—— *Some Leading Principles of Political Economy, Newly Expounded* (London, 1874).

Campbell, [Sir] G. *The Irish Land* (London, 1869).

—— *The Progress of the Land Bill* (London, 1870).

Cannon, W. J. *Outline of a Plan for the Relief and Improvement of Ireland* (London, 1849).

BIBLIOGRAPHY

Carey, M. *Emigration from Ireland, and Immigration into the United States* (Philadelphia, 18 July 1828).

—— *View of the Very Great Natural Advantages of Ireland; and of the Cruel Policies Pursued for Centuries Towards that Island* (Philadelphia, 1823).

Carlow College Magazine. *The Irish Land Bill in Committee. A Plea for the Ulster Custom, and Valuation Rents* (April, 1870).

Carlyle, T. *Latter-day Pamphlets* (London, 1855).

—— *Reminiscences of my Irish Journey in 1849* (London, 1882).

[Carmalt, W. (Rev.)] *A Defence of the English Poor Laws, with Remarks on the Applicability of the System to Ireland.* By a Select Vestryman of the Parish of Putney (London, 1831).

Chadwick, E. *The Comparative Results of the Chief Principles of the Poor-Law Administration in England and Ireland, as Compared with that of Scotland* (London, 1864).

Chaine, W. *A Letter to the Most Noble the Marquis of Downshire, in Reply to the Letter of Robert Williamson, Esq., of Lambeg House, on the Proposed Repeal of the Transit Duty on Foreign Linens* (Belfast, 1817).

Chichester, Edward. *Oppressions and Cruelties of Irish Revenue Officers* (Dublin, 1818).

Clapperton, J. *Instructions for small farmers of Ireland, on the Cropping and Culture of their Farms* (London, 1847).

Clarke, H. *Theory of investment in railway companies. First published in the fourth volume of the Railway Register* (London, 1846).

—— *Physical economy. A preliminary enquiry into the physical laws governing the periods of famines and panics* (n.p., 1847).

Clarke, Rev. Dr. *The Case of Ireland, setting forth Various Difficulties experienced in its Commercial Intercourse with Great Britain, Since the Union* (London, 1802).

Clements, Lord. *The Present Poverty of Ireland convertible into the Means of her Improvement, under a well-administered Poor Law* (London, 1838).

[Cloncurry, Lord.] *Suggestions on the Necessity, and on the best mode of levying assessments for local purposes in Ireland* (Dublin, 1831).

Cloncurry, Lord. *Letter from the Right Honourable Lord Cloncurry, to the Most Noble the Marquis of Downshire, on the conduct of the Kildare-Street Education Society, and the Employment of the Poor* (Dublin, 1826).

—— *The Design of a Law, for promoting the Pacification of Ireland* (Dublin, 1834).

Cobbett, W. *The Emigrants' Guide* (London, 1829).

—— *Cobbett's Manchester Lectures, in support of his 14 Reform Propositions...to which is subjoined a Letter to Mr O'Connell, on his Speech made in Dublin, on the 4th of January, 1832, against the Proposition for the establishing of Poor Laws in Ireland* (London, 1832).

—— *Three Lectures on the Political State of Ireland, delivered in Fishamble-Street Theatre, Dublin* (Dublin, 1834).

Cochrane, G. *On the Employment of the Poor in Great Britain and Ireland* (London, 1845).

Coffey, A. *Observations on the Rev. Edward Chichester's Pamphlet, entitled Oppressions and Cruelties of Irish Revenue Officers* (London, 1818).

Collins, R., M.D. *A Proposal to the Right Honourable Earl Grey to Establish a Charge upon Estates, as in Drainage, etc., to Enable Landlords to Promote Emigration, as the only Means of Preserving the Lives of One Million of our Fellow Creatures* (Dublin, 1847).

264

BIBLIOGRAPHY

Colquhoun, J. C. *Ireland: the Policy of Reducing the Established Church, and Paying the Roman Catholic Priests* (Glasgow, 1836).

[Colquhoun, P.] *Considerations on the Means of Affording Profitable Employment to the Redundant Population of Great Britain and Ireland, through the Medium of an Improved and Correct System of Colonization in the British Territories in Southern Africa* (London, 1818).

Congreve, R. *Ireland* (London, 1868).

Conner, W. *The Speech of William Conner, Esq., against Rack-rents, etc.* (Dublin, 1832).

—— *The True Political Economy of Ireland; or, Rack-rent the one Great Cause of all her Evils, with its Remedy* (Dublin, 1835).

—— *The Axe Laid to the Root of Irish Oppression; and a Sure and Speedy Remedy for the Evils of Ireland* (Dublin, 1840).

—— *The Prosecuted Speech: Delivered at Mountmellick in Proposing a Petition to Parliament in Favour of a Valuation and Perpetuity of his Farm to the Tenant* (Dublin, 1842).

—— *A Letter to the Right Honourable the Earl of Devon, Chairman of the Land Commission, on the Rackrent System of Ireland* (Dublin, 1843).

—— *Two Letters to the Editor of The Times, on the Rackrent Oppression of Ireland* (Dublin, 1846).

Connery, J. *An Essay on Charitable Economy, upon the Loan Bank System, Called on the Continent 'Mont de Piété'* (Dublin, 1836).

—— *The Reformer; or, an Infallible Remedy to Prevent Pauperism and Periodical Returns of Famine* (Cork, 1831).

Cooke, S. *Explanation of the Payment of First Fruits by the...Beneficed Clergy... of Ireland* (London, 1830).

Cooke, [Sir] W. F. *Telegraphic Railways; or, The single way Recommended by Safety, Economy and Efficiency...* (London, 1842).

Copley, J. S. [Baron Lyndhurst]. *Administration of the Affairs of Great Britain, Ireland, and their Dependencies, at the Commencement of the Year 1823* (4th ed. London, 1823).

[Corrie, J., F.R.S.] *Remarks on the Bill for the More Effectual Relief of the Destitute Poor in Ireland* by Philo-Hibernus (London, 1837).

Coulter, H. *The West of Ireland: its Existing Condition and Prospects* (Dublin, 1862).

Crawford, G. and Dix, E. S. *The Drainage Acts of Ireland, with a Commentary, Digest, Appendix of Forms, and Index* (Dublin, 1846).

Crawford, W. S. *Defence of the Small Farmers of Ireland* (Belfast, 1839).

[Croker, J. W.] *A Sketch of the State of Ireland, Past and Present* (Dublin, 1808).

Cropper, J. *Present State of Ireland: with a Plan for Improving the Condition of the People* (Liverpool, 1825).

Crory, W. G. *A Treatise on Industrial Resources in Ireland* (Dublin, 1860).

—— *The Commercial Importance of Ireland's Industrial Resources* (London, 1865).

Cullen, M. *A Letter to James Grattan, Esq., M.P., in which the Subject of Poor Laws being Introduced in Ireland, is Considered* (Dublin, 1824).

Cunningham, H. S. *Is Good News from Ireland True?* (London, 1864).

[Dalton, G.] *The English Press on the Irish Question, with an Irishman's View of it.* By Philo-Celt (Dublin, 1864).

D'Alton, J. *The History of Tithes, Church Lands and other Ecclesiastical Benefices* (Dublin, 1832).

265

Davis, G. E. *A Letter Addressed to the Commissioners of Irish Railways, on Transatlantic Steam Navigation* (Dublin, 1839).

Dawson, J. *Canal Extensions in Ireland, Recommended to the Imperial Legislature* (Dublin, 1819).

Dennehy, C. *Letters on the Banking Systems and Industrial Resources of Ireland, Taxation of Ireland, etc. etc.* (Dublin, 1875).

Desmond, D. *Project for the Reclamation of One Million Acres of Waste Lands, in Ireland, By Colonies of her Present Surplus and Unemployed Population* (Dublin, 1847).

De Vere, A. *English Misrule and Irish Misdeeds* (London, 1848).

Devyr, T. A. *Our Natural Rights* (Belfast, 1836—republished in New York, 1882).

Dewar, D. *Observations on the Character, Customs and Superstitions of the Irish; and on Some of the Causes which have Retarded the Moral and Political Improvement of Ireland* (London, 1812).

Dill, E. M. *The Mystery Solved: or, Ireland's Miseries: the Grand Cause and Cure* (Edinburgh and New York, 1854).

Doran, L. *Five Letters on the Irish Railways, Projected in 1844, and to be Produced to Parliament in 1845* (London, 1845).

Douglas, J. *Observations on the Necessity of a Legal Provision for the Irish Poor* (London, 1828).

—— *Life and Property in Ireland Assured by Employment of the Destitute Poor in the Waste Lands* (London? 1849).

[Doyle, J. W.] *Letters on the State of Ireland; Addressed by J.K.L. to a Friend in England* (Dublin, 1825).

Doyle, J. W. *Letter to Thomas Spring Rice, Esq., M.P., on the Establishment of a Legal Provision for the Irish Poor, and on the Nature and Destination of Church Property* (Dublin, 1831).

[——] *The Church of Ireland: a Dialogue between a Bishop and a Judge, on Tithes* (Dublin, 1831).

Doyle, W. *Considerations Vitally Connected with the Present State of Ireland* (Scarborough, 1824).

[Drummond, H., ed. and tr.] *On the Condition of the Agricultural Classes of Great Britain and Ireland, with Extracts from the Parliamentary Reports and Evidence, from 1833 to 1840 and Remarks by the French Editor, published at Vienna. Vol. I: State of Ireland* (2 vols., n.p., 1842).

Dufferin, Frederick, Marquis of. *Contributions to an Inquiry into the State of Ireland* (London, 1866).

—— *Mr Mill's Plan for the Pacification of Ireland Examined* (London, 1868).

—— *The Case of the Irish Tenant, as Stated 16 years ago, in a speech delivered in the House of Lords, February 28, 1854* (London, 1870).

—— *Irish Emigration and the Tenure of Land in Ireland* (London, 1867).

Dutens, J. M. *Mémoires sur les travaux publics de l'Angleterre* (Paris, 1819).

Edmonstone, Sir Archibald, Bt. *Some Remarks on the State of the Established Church in Ireland* (Glasgow, 1836).

Elmore, J. R. *Letters to the Earl of Darnley on the State of Ireland, in Advocacy of Free Trade* (London, 1828).

[Elrington, T.] *An Inquiry whether the Disturbances in Ireland have Originated in Tithes, or can be Suppressed by a Commutation of Them. By S.N.* (London, 1823).

BIBLIOGRAPHY

Ensor, G. *Observations on Present State of Ireland* (Dublin, 1814).
—— *An Inquiry Concerning the Population of Nations: Containing a Refutation of Mr Malthus's* Essay on Population (London, 1818).
—— *Addresses to the People of Ireland on the Degradation and Misery of their Country* (Dublin, 1823).
—— *The Poor and their Relief* (London, 1823).
—— *Anti-Union: Ireland as she ought to be* (Newry, 1831).
Entwistle, W. *Government Railways* (London, 1847).
Evans, E. *State and Prospects of Ireland* (Liverpool, 1846).
Evans, G. H. *Remarks on the Policy of Introducing the System of Poor Rates into Ireland* (London, 1829).
Fairbairn, H. *A Treatise on the Political Economy of Railroads* (London, 1836).
Ferguson, W. D. and Vance, A. *The Tenure and Improvement of Land in Ireland* (Dublin, 1851).
Firth, W. The Case of Ireland set at Rest. *The Pamphleteer*, vol. xxv, no. XLIX (London, 1825).
Fisher, J. *How Ireland may be Saved* (London, 1863).
—— *The Case of Ireland; an Examination of the Treaty of Union... Together with some Letters on the Excessive Taxation of Ireland* (London, 1863).
—— *History of Landholding in Ireland* (London, 1877).
Fitzgerald, J. E. *Irish Migration: a Letter to W. Monsell* (London, 1848).
Fitzgerald, P. *The Story of the Incumbered Estates Court. From 'All the Year Round'* (London, 1862).
Fitzgerald, Lord William. *Some Suggestions for the Better Government of Ireland, Addressed to the Marquis of Kildare* (London, 1846).
Fitzgibbon, G. *Ireland in 1868, the Battle-field for English Party Strife* (London, 1868).
—— *The Land Difficulty of Ireland, with an Effort to Solve it* (London, 1869).
Fitzwilliam, C. W., third Earl. *Letter to the Right Honourable John Sargeaunt, Rector of Stanwick, Northamptonshire* (London, 1848).
Fletcher, J. Judge Fletcher's Charge to the Grand Jury of the County of Wexford, Delivered at the Summer Assizes, July, 1814, and Containing a Comprehensive and Important View of the State of Ireland. *The Pamphleteer*, vol. IV, no. 8 (London, 1814).
Flood, H. *Poor Laws. Arguments Against a Provision for Paupers, if it be Parochial or Perpetual* (Dublin, 1830).
Flynn, H. E. *An Appeal to the Wisdom, Justice and Mercy of the Imperial Parliament, in behalf of the Irish Peasantry, on the Subject of a National System of Railways in Ireland* (Dublin, 1839).
Fontaine, J. *The Philosophy of Trade and Manufactures; and its Application to the Relative Situation of England and Ireland* (London, 1825).
Forbes, [Sir] John. *Memorandums Made in Ireland* (2 vols. London, 1853).
Foster, J. L. *An Essay on the Principle of Commercial Exchanges and more Particularly of the Exchange between Great Britain and Ireland* (London, 1804).
Fox, R. M. *Poor Laws in England and Ireland* (Dublin, 1849).
Fox, W. J. *Lectures Addressed Chiefly to the Working Classes* (2 vols. London, 1845).
Fraser, R. *Gleanings in Ireland, Particularly Respecting its Agriculture, Mines and Fisheries* (London, 1802).
—— *Sketches and Essays on the Present State of Ireland* (Dublin, 1822).

French, F. *The Question are the Government Entitled to the Support of the Irish Liberal Members at the Present Crisis? Considered in Relation to the Past and with Reference to the Future* (London, 1839).

Friends Relief Committee. *Transactions during the Famine in Ireland 1846–7* (Dublin, 1852).

Gale, P. *A Letter to the Commissioners of Railway Enquiry in Ireland* (Dublin, 1837).

[Galt, W.]. *Railway Reform; its Expediency and Practicability Considered* (London, 1843).

—— *Railway Reform: its Importance and Practicability Considered as Affecting the Nation, the Shareholders and the Government* (London, 1865).

Gardiner, H. *Absenteeism Considered; with some Remarks on a Part of Mr McCulloch's Evidence. The Pamphleteer*, vol. XXVII, no. LIII (London, 1826).

—— *Essays on Currency and Absenteeism* (London, 1827).

Godkin, J. *The Rights of Ireland* (Dublin, 1845).

—— *The Land War in Ireland* (London, 1870).

Godley, J. R. *Observations on an Irish Poor-Law. Addressed to the Committee of Landed Proprietors, Assembled in Dublin, January, 1847* (Dublin, 1847).

—— *To the Right Honourable Lord John Russell, First Lord of the Treasury, etc., etc.* (London, n.d. 1847?).

—— *An Answer to the Question what is to be Done with the Unemployed Labourers of the United Kingdom?* (London, 1847).

Gordon, A. J. *Emigration and its Evils; Contrasted with the Great and Incalculable Benefits which would arise from the Cultivation of the Waste Lands of our Colonies, and the Importation of the Corn and other Produce into the Mother Country. Addressed to the National Emigration Society* (London, 1830).

Gordon, R. *A Review of the Trade of Banking in England and Ireland* (Dublin, 1836).

Gore, M. *A Free Trade in Corn, Considered, in its Influence on Ireland, and our Foreign Policy* (London, 1834).

—— *Suggestions for the Amelioration of the Present Condition of Ireland* (London, 1847).

—— *Thoughts on the Present State of Ireland* (London, 1848).

Grattan, R. *Observations on the Causes and Prevention of Fever and Pauperism in Ireland* (Dublin, 1826).

Gray, S. *The Happiness of States* (London, 1819).

[Graydon, W.] *Reflections on the State of Ireland, in the 19th Century* (London, 1822).

[——] *Relief for Ireland, Prompt and Permanent, Suggested in a Letter to the Right Honourable Lord John Russell. By Agricola* (London, 1847).

Greenhow, C. H. *An Exposition of the Danger and Deficiencies of the Present Mode of Railway Construction, with Suggestions for its Improvement* (London, 1846).

Greer, A. *Erin Be-Whigged; or, Ireland as it has been Made by the Whig-Manchester Politicians* (Cork, 1867).

Grey, Henry George Gordon, 3rd Earl. *The Colonial Policy of Lord John Russell's Administration* (2 vols. London, 1853).

Grierson, G. A. *The Circumstances of Ireland Considered with Reference to the Question of Poor Laws* (London, 1830).

Griffin, D. *Enquiry into the Mortality Occurring Among the Poor of the City of Limerick* (n.p., n.d., c. 1840).

BIBLIOGRAPHY

Griffith, R. *Practical Domestic Politics; being a Comparative and Prospective Sketch of the Agriculture and Population of Great Britain and Ireland; including some suggestions on the Practicability and Expediency of Draining and Cultivating the Bogs of Ireland* (London, 1819).

Hale, E. E. *Letters on Irish Emigration* (Boston, 1852).

[Haliday, C.] *Necessity of Combining a Law of Settlement with Local Assessment in the Proposed Bill for the Relief of the Poor of Ireland* (Dublin, 1838).

Hall, G. W. *The Connexion between Landlord and Tenant, and Tenant and Labourer, in the Cultivation of the British Soil; their Rights, their Duties and their Interests.* Parts I and II (London, 1841).

Hamilton, J. *A Word from an Irish Landowner to his Brethren of the United Kingdom* (Dublin, 1847).

Hamilton, W. T. *The Irish Land Bills of the Late Government Considered* (Dublin, 1853).

Hancock, W. N. *The Tenant-Right of Ulster, Considered Economically* (Dublin, 1845).

—— *Three Lectures on the Question: Should the Principles of Political Economy be Disregarded at the Present Crisis?* (Dublin, 1847).

—— *Impediments to the Prosperity of Ireland* (London, 1850).

—— *Statistics Respecting Sales of Incumbered Estates in Ireland* (Dublin, 1850).

—— *Is there Really a Want of Capital in Ireland? Transactions of the Dublin Statistical Society,* vol. II (3rd and 4th sessions, 1849–51).

—— *Report on the Supposed Progressive Decline of Irish Prosperity* (Dublin, 1863).

—— The Workhouse as a Mode of Relief for Widows and Orphans. *J.D.S.S.* vol. I, p. 91.

—— *Report on the Landlord and Tenant Question in Ireland from 1860 till 1866; with an Appendix, Containing a Report on the Question from 1835 till 1859* (Dublin, 1866).

—— *First and Second Reports on a Plan for the State Purchase of Railways in Ireland* (Dublin, 1867 ('Confidential')).

—— *Third Report on a Plan for the State Purchase of Railways in Ireland* (Dublin, 1867 ('Confidential')).

[Hartnett, J. W. N.] *Excursions from Bandon, in the South of Ireland.* By a Plain Englishman (London, 1825).

Haughton, S. *A Sketch of the History of French Railways; With Suggestions in Favour of Thorough Railway Reform at Home* (Dublin, 1867).

Helferrich, A. *Skizzen und Erzählungen aus Irland* (Berlin, 1858).

Hemans, G. W. *On the Railway System in Ireland, the Government Aid Afforded, and the Nature and Results of County Guarantees.* (Excerpt—*Minutes of Proceedings of the Institution of Civil Engineers,* vol. XVIII, Session 1858-9), (London, 1859).

Henchy, J. *Ireland: its Past and Present Condition* (Dublin, 1865).

Heron, R. M. *Industry for Ireland founded upon a system of local superintendence* (London 184–?; 2nd ed. 1870).

[Hewitt, J.] *Ireland, Her Church and Her People.* By a Tory (London, 1841).

[Hickey, W.] *An Address to the Landlords of Ireland on Subjects Connected with the Melioration of the Lower Classes.* By Martin Doyle (Dublin, 1831).

[——] *Hints on Emigration to Upper Canada.* By Martin Doyle (Dublin, 1831).

BIBLIOGRAPHY

[Hickey, W.] *Common Sense for Common People, or Illustrations of Popular Proverbs, Designed for the use of the Peasantry of Ireland.* By Martin Doyle (Dublin, 1835).

[——] *A Cyclopaedia of Practical Husbandry and Rural Affairs in General* (Dublin, 1839).

[——] *Hints Addressed to the Small Holders and Peasantry of Ireland.* By Martin Doyle (Dublin, 1839).

Hillary, [Sir] Augustus W. *A Letter to the Right Honourable Lord John Russell Suggesting a Plan for the Adjustment of the Relation between Landlord and Tenant in Ireland* (London, 1849).

—— *A Sketch of Ireland in 1824:* the Sources of her Evils Considered, and their Remedies Suggested. *The Pamphleteer,* vol. xxv, no. xlix (London, 1825).

Hoare, E. N. *Letters on Subjects Connected with Ireland, Addressed to an English Clergyman* (Dublin, 1839).

Holmes, R. *The Case of Ireland Stated.* (5th ed. corrected, Dublin, 1847).

Hopkins, T. *Economical Inquiries Relative to the Laws which Regulate Rent, Profits, Wages, and the Value of Money* (London, 1822).

—— *On Rent of Land, and its Influence on Subsistence and Population: with Observations on the Operating Causes of the Condition of the Labouring Classes in Various Countries* (London, 1828).

Hore, H. F. *Inquiry into the Legislation, Control, and Improvement of the Salmon and Sea Fisheries of Ireland* (Dublin, 1850).

Horton, [Sir] R. W. *The Causes and Remedies of Pauperism in the United Kingdom Considered: Introductory Series. Being a Defence of the Principles and Conduct of the Emigration Committee against the Charges of Mr Sadler* (London, 1830).

—— *An Enquiry into the Causes and Remedies of Pauperism,* 2nd–4th series (2 vols. London, 1830).

—— *Lectures on Statistics and Political Economy, as Affecting the Condition of the Operative and Labouring Classes. Delivered at the London Mechanics Institution, in 1830 and 1831* (London, 1832).

—— *Ireland and Canada; Supported by Local Evidence* (London, 1839).

Howard, J. E. *The Island of Saints: Ireland in 1855* (London, 1855).

Hughes, J. *A Lecture on the Antecedent Causes of the Irish Famine in 1847* (New York, 1847).

Hume, A. *Results of the Irish Census of 1861* (London, 1864).

Hutchinson, G. L. *Plan for Equalisation of Poor Rates Throughout United Kingdom* (n.p., 1846).

Hutton, H. D. *Land-transfer and Land-securities in Ireland under the Provisions of the Act of 1865* (Dublin, 1866).

—— 'The Stein-Hardenberg Land Legislation; its Basis, Development and Results' and 'A Plan for the Gradual Creation of a Farmer Proprietary in Ireland'. *Transactions of the National Association for the Promotion of Social Science,* Belfast Meeting, 1867 (London, 1868).

—— *Proposals for the Gradual Creation of a Farmer Proprietary in Ireland* (London, 1868).

Inglis, H. D. *Ireland in 1834: A Journey Throughout Ireland, During the Spring, Summer and Autumn of 1834* (2 vols. London, 1835).

[——] *Switzerland, the South of France and the Pyrenees in 1830,* by Derwent Conway (London, 1831).

Ireland and India. *Ireland and Western India: A Parallel: A Reprint from the 'Times of India', January 1868* (London, 1868).

Irish Peasantry Society. *On the Employment of the Peasantry in Ireland. From the Irish Peasantry Society* (London, 1825).

Irvine, W. *What they are Doing in Ireland. Three Sketches* (Manchester, 1859).

Jackson, R. *Hand Book of Irish Railway Reform: Containing Copy of Memorial Addressed to the Lords Commissioners of H.M. Treasury by the People of Ireland* (Dublin, 1866).

Jackson, W. H. R. *An Address to the Honourable the Members of the House of Commons, on the Landlord and Tenant Question* (Cork, 1848).

Jennings, F. M. *Present and Future of Ireland as the Cattle Farm of England* (Dublin, 1865).

―― *An Inquiry into the Causes of the Poverty and Discontent of Ireland, with Suggestions for their Removal* (Dublin, 1866).

Jephson, H. L. *Notes on Irish Questions* (Dublin, 1870).

Johnson, P. *A Letter upon the Deficiency of the Revenue, and the Present State of Ireland, Addressed to Lord John Russell, by an Official Assignee* (London, 1849).

Jones, R. (Rev.) *An Essay on the Distribution of Wealth and on the Sources of Taxation: Part I, Rent* (London, 1831).

―― *A Few Remarks on the Proposed Commutation of Tithe, with Suggestions of Some Additional Facilities* (London, 1833).

―― *Literary Remains, Consisting of Lectures and Tracts on Political Economy*, ed. by Rev. William Whewell (London, 1859).

Jones, W. B. *Twenty-five Years' Work in Ireland* (n.p.; dated January 1, 1865).

Joynt, W. L. *Suggestions for the Amendment of the Arterial Drainage Laws of Ireland* (Dublin, 1865).

Kane, [Sir] R. *The Industrial Resources of Ireland* (2nd. ed. Dublin, 1845).

Kay, J. P. *The Moral and Physical Condition of the Working Classes employed in the Cotton Manufacture in Manchester* (London, 1832).

Kay, J. *Free Trade in Land. Ed. by his Widow, with Preface by the Right Honourable John Bright, M.P.* (London, 1879.)

Kearney, R. *Letter to the Lords Commissioners of H.M. Treasury and a Letter to Sir F. Burdett* (Banagher, 1818).

Keating, Rev. M. I. *A Letter to Wilmot Horton, Esq., M.P., on Emigration from Ireland* (Limerick, n.d. 1828?).

Kendall, E. A. *Letters to a Friend, on the State of Ireland* (3 vols. London, 1826).

Kennedy, J. P. *Instruct; Employ: Don't Hang Them: or, Ireland Tranquilized without Soldiers, and Enriched without English Capital* (London, 1835).

―― *Analysis of Projects Proposed for the Relief of the Poor of Ireland* (London, 1837).

Keshan, D. *Ireland, an Inquiry into the Social Condition of the Country, with Suggestions for its Improvement* (London, 1853).

Kilkenny. *Association for Promoting the Employment of the Poor...in the County of Kilkenny and Adjoining Counties. Report Presented at the First Annual Stated Meeting* (Dublin, 1818).

Kinahan, D. *An Outline of a Plan for Employing, Relieving, and Educating the Poor of Ireland* (Dublin, 1831).

King, Hon. J. *Letter to the Right Honourable Lord Cranworth, on the Practical Injustice and Impolicy of the Proceedings under the Irish Encumbered Estates Acts* (Cork, 1855).

BIBLIOGRAPHY

King, P., seventh Baron. *Thoughts on the Effects of the Bank Restrictions* (2nd ed. London, 1804).

Knight, P. *Erris in the 'Irish Highlands' and the 'Atlantic Railway'*...(Dublin, 1836).

Laing, S. *Notes of a Traveller on the Social and Political State of France, Prussia, etc.* (London, 1842.)

—— *Observations on the Social and Political State of the European People in 1848 and 1849; being the Second Series of the Notes of a Traveller* (London, 1850).

Lambert, J. *The 'Land Question' Solved: being Part of a Plan for Making Ireland a Rich and Prosperous Country* (Dublin, 1869).

Lascelles, R. *The Ultimate Remedy for Ireland* (London, 1831).

Lasteyrie, Jules de. L'Irlande depuis la dernière famine. *Revue des deux mondes*, vol. VII (August 1853).

Lauderdale, James, eighth Earl of. *Thoughts on the Alarming State of the Circulation, and on the Means of Redressing the Pecuniary Grievances in Ireland* (Edinburgh, 1805).

Lavelle, P. *The Irish Landlord since the Revolution, with Notices of Ancient and Modern Land Tenures in Various Countries* (Dublin, 1870).

Lavergne, L. de. *The Rural Economy of England, Scotland and Ireland* (Edinburgh, 1845).

Lawless, J. *A Short Address to the Tradesmen of Dublin, on the Proceedings of the Crown Prosecution, against the Friends of the Repeal of the Legislative Union* (Dublin, 1830).

Lawson, J. A. *Five Lectures on Political Economy, Delivered before the University of Dublin in Michaelmas Term, 1843* (London, 1844).

Lequesne, C. *Ireland and the Channel Islands; or, a Remedy for Ireland* (London, 1848).

Leslie, T. E. C. *Land Systems and Industrial Economy of England, Ireland and Continental Countries* (London, 1870).

—— *Essays in Political and Moral Philosophy* (Dublin, 1879).

Lever, C. *Davenport Dunn: A Man of Our Day* (2 vols. London, 1859).

Levinge, W. *The Landlord and Tenant Question (Ireland), Proposed Measures on Tenants Improvements, Emblements and Away-going Crops, with Introductory Remarks* (Dublin, 1858).

—— *Reasons for Extending the Land Improvement Act, to Improve the Irish Labourers' Dwellings* (Dublin, 1859).

—— *The Agricultural Statistics of Ireland (1860) Considered* (Dublin, 1860).

Lewis, G. C. *On Local Disturbances in Ireland, and on the Irish Church Question* (London, 1836).

Lifford, J. H., Viscount. *Thoughts on the Present State of Ireland* (London, 1849).

—— *'Who is Blacker?'—Speech of Sir Robert Peel, February 24, 1865* (Dublin, 1865).

—— *A Plea for Irish Landlords. A Letter to Isaac Butt, Esq.* (Dublin, 1867.)

Light, A. W. *A Plan for the Amelioration of the Condition of the Poor of the United Kingdom (more particularly Ireland)* (London, 1830).

Lindsay, H. L. *The Present State of the Irish Grand Jury Law Considered, as it respects the Promotion and Execution of Public Works, and an Improved Plan of Jurisprudence Recommended* (Armagh, 1837).

272

Lloyd, W. F. *Two Lectures on the Checks to Population* (Oxford, 1833).
—— *Four Lectures on Poor Laws* (n.p., 1834).
—— *Two Lectures on the Justice of the Poor Laws and one on Rent* (n.p., 1837).
[Locke, J.] *Ireland. Observations on the People, the Land and the Law, in 1851; with Special Reference to the Policy, Practice and Results of the Incumbered Estates Court* (Dublin, 1852).
Locke, J. *On Irish Emigration, with Especial Reference to the Working of the Incumbered Estates Commission* (London, 1853).
—— [*Additional Observations*] *On the Valuation and Purchase of Land in Ireland. Read before the Statistical Society of London, 15th November 1852* (London, 1853).
—— *Ireland's Recovery; or, Excessive Emigration and its Reparative Agencies in Ireland* (London, 1854).
—— *The Land Question: Expediency of Facilitating the Sale and Transfer of Land in Great Britain* (Belfast, n.d.—1858?).
London Tavern Committee. *Report of the Committee for the Relief of the Distressed Districts in Ireland, Appointed at a General Meeting held at the City of London Tavern, on the 7th of May 1822* (London, 1823).
Longfield, M. *Four Lectures on Poor Laws* (Dublin, 1834).
—— *Three Lectures on Commerce and One on Absenteeism* (Dublin, 1835).
—— *The Longfield Scheme of Parliamentary Tenant-Right* (n.p., 1870).
—— 'Tenure of Land in Ireland': Essay no. 1 in the Cobden Club volume *Systems of Land Tenure* (London, 1870).
—— Land Tenure in Ireland. *The Fortnightly Review* no. CLXIV, August 1, 1880 (New Series).
Loudon, C. *Solution du Problème de la Population et de la Subsistance, soumise à un Médecin dans une Série de Lettres* (Paris, 1842).
Loudon, Mrs. *Philanthropic Economy; or, the Philosophy of Happiness, Practically Applied to the Social, Political and Commercial Relations of Great Britain* (London, 1835).
[Lovett, W.] *The Radical Reformers of England, Scotland, and Wales to the Irish People* (London, 1838).
—— *A Letter to Daniel O'Connell, Esq., in Reply to the Calumnies he put Forth in the Corn Exchange, August 8, in Answer to the Address of the National Association to the People of Ireland* (London, 1843).
[Low, D.] *Remarks on Certain Modern Theories Respecting Rents and Prices* (Edinburgh, 1827).
Lynch, A. H. *Measures to be Adopted for the Employment of the Labouring Classes in Ireland* (London, 1839).
—— *An Address to the Electors of Galway, on the Poor-Law Bill for Ireland* (London, 1838).
Maberly, Mrs K. C. *Present State of Ireland and its Remedy* (London, 1847).
MacArthur, J. *Statistics, etc., of the Operations of the Irish Incumbered Estates Commission, with Opinions of the Press* (Dublin, 1854).
MacCalmont, R. *Letter to the Right Honourable Lord John Russell, on Communication with Ireland* (London, 1850).
MacCarthy, J. G. *Irish Land Questions, Plainly Stated and Answered* (London, 1870).
McCombie, W. *The Irish Land Question Practically Considered* (Aberdeen, 1869).
M'Convery, J. *A Letter on Tenant-Right (Second Letter) by Mr James M'Convery, late Editor and Proprietor of 'The Vindicator'* (Belfast, 1855).

273

BIBLIOGRAPHY

M'Cormac, H. *An Appeal in Behalf of the Poor* (Belfast, 1830).
—— *A Plan for the Relief of the Unemployed Poor* (Belfast, 1830).
—— *On the Best Means of Improving the Moral and Physical Condition of the Working Classes* (London, 1830).
McCullagh, W. T. *Letter to the Representative Peers of Ireland, on the Ministerial Measure of Irish Poor Laws* (Dublin, 1838).
McCulloch, J. R. *An Essay on the Circumstances which Determine the Rate of Wages, and the Condition of the Labouring Classes* (Edinburgh, 1826).
—— *Principles of Political Economy: with a Sketch of the Rise and Progress of the Science* (2nd ed. London, 1830).
—— *The Literature of Political Economy* (London, 1845).
—— *A Descriptive and Statistical Account of the British Empire* (2 vols. 3rd ed., London, 1847).
—— *A Treatise on the Succession to Property vacant by Death: Including Inquiries into the Influence of Primogeniture, Entails, Compulsory Partition...over the Public Interest* (London, 1848).
—— *Treatises and Essays* (2nd ed. Edinburgh, 1859).
—— *A Catalogue of Books, the Property of a Political Economist; with Critical and Bibliographical Notices* (London, 1862).
[MacDonnell, E.] *Practical Views on the Present Condition and Permanent Improvement of Ireland.* By Hibernicus (Dublin, 1823).
—— *Irish Sufferers, and Anti-Irish Philosophers, their Pledges and Performances* (London, n.d. 1847?).
MacDonnell, J. *Survey of Political Economy* (Edinburgh, 1871).
MacDougall, A. *A Treatise on Irish Fisheries* (Belfast, 1819).
MacLagan, P. *Land Culture and Land Tenure in Ireland: the Results of Observations during a Recent Tour in Ireland* (Edinburgh and London, 1869).
Macnaghten, [Sir] F. W. *Some Observations upon the Present State of Ireland* (London, 1837).
—— *Poor Laws—Ireland. Observations upon the Report of George Nicholls, Esq.* (2nd ed. London, 1838).
MacNevin, R. C. *The Practice of the Landed Estates Court in Ireland* (3rd ed. Dublin, 1859).
Madden, D. O. *Ireland and its Rulers Since 1829* (London, 1843).
[Madden, S. (Rev.)] *Reflections and Resolutions Proper for the Gentlemen of Ireland* (Dublin, 1738).
Maguire, J. F. *The Industrial Movement in Ireland, as Illustrated by the National Exhibition of 1852* (Cork, 1853).
Mahony, P. *Letters from Mr Mahony to the Right Honourable E. J. Littleton, M.P. and Chief Secretary for Ireland, on the Irish Tithe or Land Tax Bill* (London, 1834).
[Maley, A. J.] *Observations upon the Policy and Provisions of the Act for Facilitating the Sale of Incumbered Estates, Considered with Reference to their Supposed Economic Effects upon the Condition of Ireland.* By A.J.M. (Dublin, 1852).
[——] *Observations upon the Inutility of Exterminating the Resident Landlords of Ireland, by Act of Parliament, or Otherwise; and some Suggestions for their Self-Preservation.* By A.J.M. (Dublin, 1849).
Mallet, C. F. *Mallets Bericht uber die atmosphärische eisenbahn von Dublin nach Dalken in Irland* (Darmstadt, 1844).

Malthus, T. R. *An Essay on the Principle of Population* (1st ed. London, 1798; 6th ed. London, 1826).

— *Principles of Political Economy, Considered with a View to their Practical Application* (London, 1820).

Martin, H. M. *La Question Irlandaise* (Paris, 1860).

Martin, J. *Observations on the Evils and Difficulties of the Present System of Poor Laws in Ireland; with Suggestions for Removing or Obviating Them Considered* (Dublin, 1849).

Martin, R. M. *Ireland as it Was, Is and Ought to be* (London, 1832).

— *Society in America* (2nd ed. London, 1837).

— *Poor Laws for Ireland, a Measure of Justice to England* (London, 1833).

— *Ireland Before and After the Union with Great Britain* (London and Dublin, 1843).

— *Railways—Past, Present and Prospective* (London, 1849).

Martineau, H. *Ireland—a Tale* (London, 1832).

— *Society in America* (2nd ed., London, 1837).

— *Letters from Ireland* (London, 1852).

Marx, K. *Capital* (Everyman edition, 2 vols. London and New York, 1930), ch. XXIII, Part VII, Section F: 'Ireland'.

— and Engels, F. *On Britain* (Moscow, 1953). (Includes Engels, *Condition of the Working Class in England in 1844.*)

Mason, W. S. *A Statistical Account, or Parochial Survey of Ireland, drawn up from the Communications of the Clergy* (3 vols. Dublin, 1814–19).

— *Bibliotheca Hibernicana: or a Descriptive Catalogue of a Select Irish Library, Collected for the Right Honourable Robert Peel* (Dublin, 1823).

Maunsell, H. *The Only Safe Poor Law Experiment for Ireland. A Letter to the Right Honourable Lord Viscount Morpeth* (Dublin, 1838).

Meekins, R. *Plan for the Removal of Pauperism, Agrarian Disturbances, and the Poor's Rate in Ireland* (Dublin, 1847).

Meekins, T. C. M. *Report to the Attorney-General for Ireland (Right Honourable Joseph Napier, M.P.) on Compensation to the Tenant for Improvements* (London, 1852).

Merivale, H. *Five Lectures on the Principles of a Legislative Provision for the Poor in Ireland* (London, 1838).

— *Lectures on Colonization and Colonies.* Vol. I (London, 1841; 2nd ed. 1861).

Meyler, A. *Irish Tranquillity under Mr O'Connell, My Lord Mulgrave, and the Romish Priesthood* (Dublin, 1838).

Miles, P. *The Social, Political and Commercial Advantages of Direct Steam Communication and Rapid Postal Intercourse between Europe and America, via Galway, Ireland* (London, 1859).

Mill, J. *Elements of Political Economy* (London, 1821).

Mill, J. and J. S. *James and John Stuart Mill on Education.* Edited by F. A. Cavenagh (Cambridge, 1931).

Mill, J. S. *Principles of Political Economy, with Some of their Applications to Social Philosophy.* (1st ed. London, 1848; 4th ed. London, 1857. Edited, with an introduction, by W. J. Ashley, London, 1909.)

— *Essays on some Unsettled Questions of Political Economy* (London, 1844).

[—] *Memorandum of the Improvements in the Administration of India, During the Last Thirty Years* (London, 1858).

Mill, J. S. *Dissertations and Discussions, Political, Philosophical and Historical* (Vols. 1–4. London, 1859–75).
—— *England and Ireland* (London, 1868).
—— *Chapters and Speeches on the Irish Land Question* (London, 1870).
—— Notes on N. W. Senior's *Political Economy* (edited by F. A. Hayek). *Economica*, new series, vol. XII, no. 47 (August 1945).
Mills, A. *Systematic Colonization* (London, 1847).
Molinari, M-G. de. *Entretiens sur Les Lois Économiques et Défense de la Propriété* (Paris, 1849).
Monsell, W. *On Some of the Impediments to Irish Manufacturing Industry* (Dublin, 1865).
Monteath, R. *A New and Easy System of Draining and Reclaiming the Bogs and Marshes of Ireland: with Plans for Improving Waste Lands in General* (Edinburgh and London, 1829).
Moore, A. *A Compendium of the Irish Poor Law* (Dublin, 1846).
Moorsom, C. R. *Observations Tending to Shew the Advantage of Railways in Ireland being Undertaken by Government, Instead of Being Left to 'Private Enterprise'* (Birmingham, 1840).
Morgan, Lady S. *Absenteeism* (London, 1825).
Mornington, W. W., 4th Earl. *The Irish Question Considered in its Integrity.* By Viscount Wellesley (Brussels, 1844).
Morris, P. *Six Letters Intended to Prove that the Repeal of the Act of Union, and the Establishment of a Local Legislature in Ireland, are Necessary to Cement the Connection with Great Britain: and Containing a Short View of the Trade, Manufactures and Agriculture of Ireland. Addressed to the Right Honourable Sir J. Newport, Bt., M.P.* (Waterford, 1831).
Morris, W. O'C. *Letters on the Land Question of Ireland* (London, 1870).
Mosse, R. B. *Ireland, its State, its Evils, and its Remedies* (London, 1849).
Mudge, R. Z. *Observations on Railways, with Reference to Utility, Profit, and the Obvious Necessity for a National System* (London, 1837).
Muggeridge, R. M. *Notes on the Irish Difficulty: With Remedial Suggestions* (Dublin, 1849).
Mullins, B. *Observations upon the Irish Grand Jury System* (Dublin, 1831).
Mulock, T. *Disenthralment of Incurably-Involved Irish Estates* (Edinburgh, 1849).
Mure, W. *The Commercial Policy of Pitt and Peel 1785–1846* (London, 1847).
Murphy, J. N. *Ireland: Industrial, Political and Social* (London, 1870).
Murray, J. F. *Ireland Contrasted with Scotland* (Belfast, 1832).
—— *Repeal No Remedy; or, the Union with Ireland Completed: Addressed at this Crisis to Every Englishman* (London, 1834).
Naper, J. L. W. *A Plan of a Labour Rate, Submitted to the Consideration of the Right Honourable Sir Henry Hardinge* (Dublin, 1830).
—— *Suggestions for the More Scientific and General Employment of Agricultural Labourers, Together with a Plan which would enable the Landlords of Ireland to Afford them Suitable Houses and Gardens with Applotments at a Fair Rent, being Observations on Chapter X of Dr Kane's 'Industrial Resources of Ireland'* (Dublin and London, 1844).
Napier, Sir C. J. *An Essay on the Present State of Ireland, Showing the Chief Cause of, and the Remedy for, the Existing Distresses in that Country. Dedicated to the Irish Absentee Landed Proprietors, as Proving that, Although their Absence*

is Injurious to Ireland, it is not the Primary Cause of the Sufferings Endured by the Irish People (London, 1839).

Nevile, C. (Rev.). *Justice and Expediency of Tenant-right Legislation Considered, in a Letter to Philip Pusey, Esq.* (London, 1848).

Newenham, T. *View of the Natural, Political and Commercial Circumstances of Ireland* (n.p., 1809).

[Nicholls, G.] *Eight Letters on the Management of our Poor, and the General Administration of the Poor Laws.* By an Overseer (Newark, 1822).

Nicholls, [Sir] G. *A History of the Irish Poor-Law* (London, 1856).

Nolan, G. *Practical Observations upon the Projected Alterations of the Law for Regulating the Import of Corn into the United Kingdom of Great Britain and Ireland* (London, 1828).

Norreys, Sir D. J. *Letter to Lord Clarendon on the Better Organisation of Ireland, for Local and General Government* (London, 1849).

[O'Beirne, T. L.] *Letter from an Irish Dignitary to an English Clergyman on the Subject of Tithes in Ireland, with the Addition of some Observations and Notes* (Dublin, 1822).

O'Brien, W. S. *Plan for the Relief of the Poor in Ireland; with Observations on the English and Scotch Poor Laws: Addressed to the Landed Proprietors of Ireland* (London, 1830).

O'Connell, D. *Observations on Corn Laws, on Political Pravity and Ingratitude, and on Clerical and Personal Slander, in the Shape of a Meek and Modest Reply to the Second Letter of the Earl of Shrewsbury to Ambrose Lisle Phillipps, Esq.* (Dublin, 1842).

O'Connell, J. *An Argument for Ireland* (Dublin, 1844). With 7 Appendices, including no. 4 'The Commercial Injustices' and no. 6 'The Taxation Injustice' (often printed separately, and some before *An Argument for Ireland* appeared).

O'Connor, A. *State of Ireland* (London, 1843). Reprint by Feargus O'Connor of a Tract by his Uncle, one of the United Irishmen in 1798.

O'Connor, F. *The Remedy for National Poverty and National Ruin; or the only Safe way of Repealing the Corn Laws by Enabling each Working Family to Produce a 'Big Loaf' and a 'Cheap Loaf' for Themselves, at home. Addressed to the Landlords of Ireland* (Leeds, 1841).

Oddy, J. J. *European Commerce, Shewing New and Secure Channels of Trade with the Continent of Europe* (London, 1805).

O'Driscol, J. *Views of Ireland, Moral, Political and Religious* (2 vols. London, 1823).

[O'Driscol, J.] *Letter to the Honourable J. Abercrombie, M.P. on the new Irish Tithe Bill* (Dublin, 1824).

O'Flynn, J. *Extracts from a Pamphlet on the Present State of the Irish Poor, to which is Added the Means of Profitable Employment for the Whole Population, Both of England and Ireland* (London, 1836).

Ogilby, W. *Irish Railways: Their Present Depression and Future Prospects of Amelioration* (Dublin, 1868).

O'Hanlon, W. M. (Rev.). *Walks Among the Poor of Belfast, and Suggestions for their Improvement* (Belfast, 1853).

O'Kelly, P. *Advice and Guide to Emigrants, Going to the United States of America* (Dublin, 1834).

O'Malley, T. (Rev.). *An Idea of a Poor Law for Ireland* (London, 1837).

277

BIBLIOGRAPHY

[O'Malley, T. (Rev.)] *A Word or Two on the Irish Poor Relief Bill, and Mr Nicholls' Report; or, a Postscript to the Rev. Mr O'Malley's 'Idea of a Poor Law for Ireland'* (London, 1837).

O'Rourke, D. *A Voice from Ireland upon Matters of Present Concern. Addressed to Legislators and Ministers of State* (London, 1837).

[Osborne, R. B.] *Plan, or Proposed System, by which above One Hundred and Fifty Thousand Poor in Ireland may not only be Supported, but Lodged in Comfort, and Made useful Members of Society; Promote the National Peace and Prosperity of the Kingdom, without any Additional Taxation* (Wexford, 1831).

Osborne, S. G. (Hon. and Rev.) *Gleanings in the West of Ireland* (London, 1850).

O'Sullivan, J. B. *A Letter Addressed to the Right Honourable W. Wellesley Pole, M.P. Comprising, among other Interesting Particulars, an Account of a Most Extraordinary Agricultural Meeting that Took Place in Ireland, at which Upwards of 850 Ploughs were seen in Motion at the same time, in one field, belonging to an Individual* (London, 1818).

O'Sullivan, M. (Rev.) *Captain Rock Detected* (London, 1824).

—— *Case of the Protestants of Ireland, Stated in Addresses Delivered at Meetings in Dublin, Liverpool, Bristol and Bath, in the year 1834* (London, 1836).

[Owen, R.] *A Report of the British and Foreign Philanthropic Society, with other Statements and Calculations, Explanatory of Mr Owen's Plan for the Relief of Ireland, and of the Poor and Working Classes Generally in all other Countries* (Dublin, 1823).

Owen, R. *Report of the Proceedings at the Several Public Meetings, held in Dublin, by Robert Owen, Esq., on the 18th March, 12th April, 19th April and 3rd May* (Dublin, 1823).

—— *Statements Showing the Power that Ireland Possesses to Create Wealth Beyond the Most Ample Supply of the Wants of its Inhabitants* (Pub. separately, London, 1823).

—— *Communism (Primitive Christianity advocated)*, (Dublin, 1823).

—— *Volume of Newspaper Reports on the Owenite Movement in Ireland* (1823–4). Kress Library, Harvard.

Owen-Madden, D. *The Castle and the Country* (Dublin, 1850).

Page, F. *Observations on the State of the Indigent Poor in Ireland* (London, 1830).

Parker, W. *Observations on the Intended Amendment of the Irish Grand Jury Laws.* (Cork, 1816).

—— *A Plan for the General Improvement of the State of the Poor of Ireland* (Cork, 1816).

—— *A Plea for the Poor and Industrious. Part the First, The Necessity of a National Provision for the Poor in Ireland; Deduced from the Argument of the Right Reverend R. Woodward, Late Lord Bishop of Cloyne: And from the Present Deplorable State of the Lower Orders* (Cork, 1819).

Parker, W. D'E. *The Irish Poor Law is a National Grievance: with suggestions for its Amendment* (Cork, 1868).

Parnell, [Sir] H. *Observations upon the State of Currency in Ireland, and upon the Course of Exchange between Dublin and London* (London, 1804).

—— *The Principles of Currency and Exchange Illustrated by Observations upon the State of the Currency of Ireland* (London, 1805).

—— *Observations on the Irish Butter Acts* (London, 1825).

278

[Parnell, W.] *An Enquiry into the Causes of Popular Discontents in Ireland. By an Irish Country Gentleman* (London, 1805).
Patterson, R. H. *The State, the Poor and the Country, Including Suggestions on the Irish Question* (Edinburgh and London, 1870).
Payne, D. B. *Exposition of Irish Exchange* (Wells, 1806).
Pearson, C. *Ireland and Canada....Plan of the Colonial Association for the profitable Employment of Capital, in planting British colonies in H.M.'s North American Provinces, by means of a Systematic Emigration from the United Kingdom, of Persons of all Classes and Conditions* (London, 1839).
Peel, Sir R. *Memoirs by the Right Honourable Sir Robert Peel, Bt., M.P.* (2 vols. London, 1857).
Pemberton, B. *An Address to the Nobility, Gentry and Mercantile Classes, on the Extension of Railway Communication to the West of Ireland* (Dublin, 1841).
Perraud, A. *Ireland in 1862. Translated from the French* (Dublin, 1863). (1864 edition has the title *Ireland under English Rule*.)
Pettman, W. R. A. *An Essay on Political Economy; shewing in what way Fluctuations in the Price of Corn may be Prevented....Part I* (London, 1828).
—— *An Essay on Political Economy; shewing the Means by which the Distresses of the Labouring Poor may be Relieved....Part II* (London, 1828).
—— *Resources of the United Kingdom* (London, 1830).
Petrie, F. *The Irish Poor-Law Rating as it Affects Tithe Rent Charge Property* (3rd ed. London and Dublin, 1867).
Pichot, A. *L'Irlande et le Pays de Galles* (Paris, 1850).
Piesse, C. *Sketch of the Loan Fund System in Ireland* (Dublin, 1841).
Pim, J., jr. *Irish Railways. A Letter to the Right Honourable Frederick Shaw* (London, 1839).
—— *Irish Railways. The Atmospheric Railway. A Letter to the Right Honourable Lord Viscount Morpeth* (London, 1841).
[Pim, J.] *Observations on the Evils Resulting to Ireland from the Insecurity of Title and the Existing Laws of Real Property, with some Suggestions Towards a Remedy* (Dublin, 1847).
Pim, J. *The Condition and Prospects of Ireland* (Dublin, 1848).
—— *The Land Question in Ireland; Suggestions for its Solution by the Application of Mercantile Principles to Dealing with Land* (Dublin, 1867).
Place, F. *Illustrations and Proofs of the Principle of Population* (London, 1822).
Porter, J. G. V. *Some Agricultural and Political Irish Questions Calmly Discussed* (London, 1843).
—— *Ireland....A Federal (the only fair) Union between Great Britain and Ireland Inevitable, and Most Desirable for Both Islands* (London, 5th ed. n.d., 1844?).
Pratt, J. T. *The History of Savings Banks in England, Wales and Ireland* (London, 1830).
Price, J. *A Proposed System of Minor Railways, Specially Adapted for Ireland* (Dublin, privately printed, 1865).
[Prior, T.] *A List of the Absentees of Ireland* (Dublin, 1729).
Purdon, R. E. C. *Observations on the Introduction of the Poor Laws into Ireland* (Bristol, n.d. 183–?).
Quin, M. J. *A Letter to the House of Commons, on Railways in Ireland* (London, 1839).
Ramsay, G. *A Proposal for the Restoration of the Irish Parliament* (Dublin, 1845).
Raumer, F. von. *England in 1835*. Translated by H. E. Lloyd (3 vols. London, 1836).

Reformed Presbyterian Church. *The Signs of the Times: in which the Evils and Dangers of the Present System of Tithes and Regium Donum are Exposed....* by the Eastern Presbytery of the Reformed Presbyterian Church in Ireland (2nd ed. Belfast, 1835).

Reid, T. *Travels in Ireland in the Year 1822, Exhibiting Brief Sketches of the Moral, Physical and Political State of the Country: with Reflections on the Best Means of Improving its Condition* (London, 1823).

Revans, J. *Evils of the State of Ireland: their Causes and their Remedy—A Poor Law* (London, n.d., 1835?).

Revue des deux mondes. French Thoughts on Irish Evils; Translated from the *Revue des deux mondes* with Notes by a Son of the Soil (London, 1868).

Ricardo, D. *Works and Correspondence.* Edited by P. Sraffa with the Collaboration of M. H. Dobb (10 vols. Cambridge, 1951–5).

Rice, S. S. *Letter to C. E. Trevelyan on 'The Irish Crisis'* ('Not printed for circulation'; dated January 26, 1848, n.p.).

Rice, T. S. (Lord Monteagle). *An Inquiry into the Effects of the Irish Grand Jury Laws* (London, 1815).

[——] *Considerations on the Present State of Ireland and on the Best Means of Improving the Condition of its Inhabitants.* By an Irishman (London, 1822).

Richardson, W. *Simple Measures, by which the Recurrence of Famines may be Prevented, and the Pressure of the Poor Laws Greatly Abated, by a Slight and Partial Change in our Common Agricultural Practices* (London, 1816).

Rickards, Sir G. K. *Population and Capital* (London, 1854).

Ritchie, L. *A Bystander's View of the Irish Poor Law Question* (London, 1837).

[Robertson, F. W.] *The Irish Difficulty.* By an Englishman (London, 1848).

Robinson, H. *Union in Ireland.* By an Irish Landlord (Dublin, 1847).

Roden, R. J., Earl of. *Observations on Lord Alvanley's Pamphlet on the State of Ireland* (London, 1841).

[Rogers, E.] *An Essay on Some General Principles of Political Economy, on Taxes upon Raw Produce, and on Commutation of Tithes.* By a Fellow of Gonville and Caius College, Cambridge (London, 1822).

Rogers, J. W. *Plan for Road and Steam Communication* (Dublin, 1841).

—— *The Potato Truck System of Ireland the Main Cause of her Periodical Famines and of the Non-Payment of her Rents* (London, 1847).

—— *An Appeal for the Irish Peasantry* (London, 1847).

—— *Employment of the Irish Peasantry the Best Means to Prevent the Drain of Gold from England. Originally Published in 'The Mark Lane Express'* (London, 1847).

—— *Facts for the Kind-Hearted of England, as to the Wretchedness of the Irish Peasantry, and the Means for their Regeneration* (London, 1847).

Rolph, T. *Emigration and Colonization* (London, 1844).

Rooke, J. *An Inquiry into the Principles of National Wealth, Illustrated by the Political Economy of the British Empire* (Edinburgh, 1824).

Rosse, L. P., Earl of. *A Few Words on the Relation of Landlord and Tenant in Ireland and other Parts of the United Kingdom* (London, 1866).

[Rowan, A. B. (Rev.)] *What's to be Done? or, A Collection of the Various Suggestions for Amending the Poor Law, with Observations* (Tralee, 1849).

Rowecroft, C. *Currency and Railways* (London,? 1845).

Russell, R. *Ulster Tenant-Right for Ireland* (Edinburgh, 1870).

Ryan, P. B. *Provision for the Poor in Ireland, without any Additional Taxation, on the Principles of the Musical Charitable Loan Society* (2nd ed. Dublin, 1838).

Ryan, R. (Rev.). *An Essay upon the Following Subject of Inquiry, 'What are the Best Means of Rendering the National Sources of Wealth Possessed by Ireland Effectual for the Employment of the Population?' Proposed by the Royal Irish Academy 1822* (London, 1824).

—— *Practical Remedies for the Practical Evils of Ireland* (Dublin, 1828).

Sadler, M. T. *Ireland, its Evils and their Remedies* (London, 1828).

—— *The Law of Population: A Treatise, in Six Books; in Disproof of the Super-fecundity of Human Beings, and Developing the Real Principle of their increase* (2 vols. London, 1830).

—— *A Refutation of an Article in the* Edinburgh Review *(no.* CII) *entitled 'Sadler's Law of Population, and Disproof of Human Superfecundity'* (London, 1830).

Samuelson, B. *Studies of the Land and Tenantry of Ireland* (London, 1870).

Sargant, W. L. *Essays of a Birmingham Manufacturer*, vol. I, no. II: *Ireland and the Tenure of Land* (3 vols. London, 1869).

Saumarez, R. *A Letter on the Evil Effects of Absenteeism; being an Answer to Hastings Elwin, Esq.* (Bath, 1829).

Say, J-B. *A Treatise of Political Economy.* Translated from the 4th Edition of the French by C. R. Prinsep (London, 1821).

—— *Cours complet d'économie politique pratique* (7th ed. Brussels, 1844).

[Scanlan, J. T. and Dunne, P. W.] *Ireland's Contribution (?) to Free Trade* (Irish Labour League for Protection to American Industry, Chicago, 1871).

[Scrope, G. P.] *A Letter to the Agriculturists of England on the Expediency of Extending the Poor Laws to Ireland.* By a Landowner (London, 1830).

Scrope, G. P. *Common Cause of Landlord, Tenant and Labourer* (London, 1830).

—— *Principles of Political Economy, Deduced from the Natural Laws of Social Welfare, and Applied to the Present State of Great Britain* (London, 1833).

—— *Plan of a Poor Law for Ireland, with a Review of the Arguments for and against it* (London, 1833).

—— *Friendly Advice to the Peasantry of Ireland* (Dublin, 1834).

—— *Remarks on the Government Irish Poor-Law Bill, in a Letter to Lord John Russell* (London, 1837).

—— *How is Ireland to be Governed? A Question Addressed to the New Admin-istration of Lord Melbourne in 1834, with a Postscript, in which the same Question is Addressed to the Administration of Sir Robert Peel in 1846* (London, 1846).

—— *Letters to the Right Honourable Lord John Russell, on the Expediency of Enlarging the Irish Poor-Law to the Full Extent of the Poor-Law of England* (London, 1846).

—— *A Letter to the Landed Proprietors of Ireland, on the Means of meeting the Present Crisis, by Measures of a Permanent Character* (London, 1847).

—— *Extracts of Evidence... on the Subject of Waste Lands Reclamation; with a Prefatory Letter to the Right Honourable Lord John Russell* (London, 1847).

—— *Reply to the Speech of the Archbishop of Dublin, against the Poor Relief (Ireland) Bill* (London, 1847).

—— *Letters to Lord John Russell, M.P. etc., on the Further Measures Required for the Social Amelioration of Ireland. From G. Poulett Scrope, M.P.* (London, 1847).

—— *Remarks on the Irish Poor Relief Bill* (London, 1847).

Scrope, G. P. *The Rights of Industry, or the Social Problem of the Day, as exemplified in France, Ireland and Britain* (London, 1848).

—— *A Plea for the Rights of Industry in Ireland* (London, 1848).

—— *The Irish Relief Measures, Past and Future* (London, 1848).

—— *Notes of a Tour in England, Scotland and Ireland* (London, 1849).

—— *The Irish Difficulty: and How it Must be Met* (London, 1849).

—— *Draft Report on the Kilrush Union, with Prefatory Remarks* (London, 1850).

Scully, V. *Irish Land Question, with Practical Plans for an Improved Land Tenure and a New Land System* (Dublin, 1851).

Seebohm, F. The Land Question, *Fortnightly Review*, new series, vol. VI (1869), pp. 626–40.

—— The Historical Claims of Tenant-Right, *Nineteenth Century*, vol. IX (1881), pp. 19–36.

Senior, N. W. *Two Lectures on Population, to which is Added a Correspondence Between the Author and the Rev. T. R. Malthus* (London, 1829).

—— *A Letter to Lord Howick, on a Legal Provision for the Irish Poor* (2nd ed. London, 1831).

[——] *Remarks on Emigration, with the Draft of a Bill* (London, 1831).

—— *An Outline of the Science of Political Economy* (for the Encyclopaedia Metropolitana, 1836), (Library of Economics ed. London, 1938).

—— *Journals, Conversations and Essays Relating to Ireland* (2 vols. London, 1868).

Seymour, W. D. *How to Employ Capital in the West of Ireland* (London, 1851).

Shackleton, E. *Proposal of a Public Provision for the Poor of Ireland* (Dublin, 1824).

Sheahan, T. '*Articles' of Irish Manufacture; or, Portions of Cork History* (Cork, 1833).

Shee, W. *Papers, Letters, and Speeches in the House of Commons, on the Irish Land Question, with a Summary of its Parliamentary History, from the General Election of 1852, to the Close of the Session of 1863* (London, 1863).

Shelley, P. B. *Address to the Irish People* (Dublin, 1812). Reprinted by the Shelley Society, 1890, ed. by T. J. Wise, with an Introduction by T. W. Rolleston (London, 1890).

Shiel, [Sir] J. *French Thoughts on Irish Evils* (London, 1868).

Shrewsbury, J. Talbot, Earl of. *Thoughts on the Poor-Relief Bill for Ireland; together with Reflections on her Miseries, their Causes and their Remedies* (London, 1847).

Shuldham, W. L. *Remarks on the Small Loan-Fund System, Addressed to the Duke of Wellington* (London, 1839).

Simpson, J. H. *An Englishman's Testimony to the Urgent Necessity for a Tenant Right Bill for Ireland, after a Residence of Three Years in that Country* (London, 1856).

Simpson, W. W. *A Letter to his Excellency the Earl De Grey, Lord Lieutenant of Ireland, on the Ameliorated Condition of that Country* (London, 1842).

—— *A Defence of the Landlords of Ireland, with Remarks on the Relation between Landlord and Tenant* (London, 1844).

Slaney, R. A. *An Essay on the Employment of the Poor* (London, 1819).

[Sleeman, [Sir] W. H.] *On Taxes, or Public Revenue, the Ultimate Incidence of their Payment, their Disbursement and the Seats of their Consumption.* By an Officer in the Military and Civil Service of the Honourable East India Company (London, 1829).

Sleeman, [Sir] W. H. *Analysis and Review of the Peculiar Doctrines of the Ricardo, or New School of Political Economy* (Serampore, 1837).

Smiles, S. *History of Ireland and the Irish People under the Government of England* (London, 1844).

BIBLIOGRAPHY

Smith, A. *An Inquiry into the Nature and Causes of the Wealth of Nations* (edited by Edwin Cannan, 2 vols. London, 1904).

Smith, H. *A Lecture on the Capability of Great Britain and Ireland to Give Employment, and Provide a Sufficient Maintenance for the Whole Population, with some Introductory Remarks on the Science of Political Economy* (Southampton, 1846).

Smith O'Brien, W. *Reproductive Employment; a Series of Letters to the Landed Proprietors of Ireland; with a Preliminary Letter to Lord John Russell* (Dublin, 1847).

—— *Plan for the Relief of the Poor in Ireland* (London, 1830).

Smyth, A. *Outlines of a New Theory of Political Economy* (Cork, 1828).

Smyth, G. L. *Aids to the Irish Poor Law in the Reclamation of Irish Waste Lands* (London, 1838).

—— *Railways and Public Works in Ireland* (London, 1839).

—— *Banking in Ireland, Remarks upon the Renewal of the Charter of the Bank of Ireland* (London, 1840).

—— *Ireland: Historical and Statistical* (3 vols. London, 1844–9).

Smyth, J. *Observations on the Poor Laws, as Regards their Introduction into Ireland, the Mendicity Institutions Established in that Country, and the Drainage of the Wet Lands and Bogs* (Dublin, 1830).

Society for the Improvement of Ireland. *Statement of the Proceedings of the Society for the Year 1828. With an Appendix Containing its Rules and Regulations, Names of Members and other Illustrative Documents* (Dublin, 1828).

—— *Report of the Committee...as adopted at the Public Meeting of the Citizens of Dublin...held 21st May, 1846* (Dublin, 1846).

Somers, R. *Letters from the Highlands, or the Famine of 1847* (London, 1848).

'Spectator', The. *Supplement for the Week Ending 3 April 1847: A Plan of Colonisation for Ireland* (London, 1847).

Spencer, Rev. T. *Evils of Undue Legislative Interference* (London, 1848).

Sproule, J. *Facts and Observations on the Irish Land Question; also, Observations on the New Irish Land Bill* (Dublin, 1870).

Stanley, W. *Commentaries on Ireland* (The Cloncurry Prize Essays), (Dublin, 1833).

—— *Facts on Ireland* (Dublin, 1832).

—— *Remarks on the Government Measure for establishing Poor-Laws in Ireland* (London, 1837).

Stanton, H. B. *Sketches of Reforms and Reformers, of Great Britain and Ireland* (New York, 1849).

Stapleton, A. G. *The Real Monster Evil of Ireland. Sequel to the Real Monster Evil of Ireland* (London, 1843).

Stark, A. G. *The South of Ireland in 1850; being the Journal of a Tour in Leinster and Munster* (Dublin, 1850).

[Starkey, D. P.] *Ireland. The Political Tracts of Menenius, 1848* (2nd ed. Dublin, 1849).

Staunton, M. *Reasons for a Repeal of the Legislative Union between Great Britain and Ireland* (Dublin, 1845).

[——] *Tracts on Ireland, Political and Statistical* (Dublin, 1824).

Stephenson, Sir R. M. *Report upon the Practicability and Advantages of the Introduction of Railways into British India* (London, 1844).

Steven, R. *Remarks on the Present State of Ireland, with Hints for Ameliorating the Condition of the Irish Peasantry* (London, 1822).

Stewart, J. V. *A Letter to the Earl of Clarendon, on the Subject of Poor Laws, with an Appendix* (Letterkenny, 1849).

BIBLIOGRAPHY

Stoddart, G. H. (Rev.). *The True Cure for Ireland, the Development of her Industry* (London, 1847).

Stoney, B. B. *On the Land Question in Ireland* (Dublin, 1869).

Stourton, W. seventeenth Baron. *A Third Letter to the Right Honourable the Earl of Liverpool, in which the Justice, Policy, and Necessity of Legislative Relief to the Agricultural Distresses of the Country are Considered* (London, 1821).

—— *A Letter to the Right Honourable George Canning, on the Nature of Absenteeism and its Influence on the State of Ireland, in Reply to an Article of the Edinburgh Review (November 1825)*, (London, 1827).

—— *Some Remarks on the Social Relations of Great Britain and Ireland at the Present Day* (London, 1844).

Strickland, G. (later Cholmley). *A Discourse on the Poor Laws of England and Scotland, on the State of the Poor of Ireland, and on Emigration* (London, 1827).

Sturch, W. *Grievances of Ireland, their Causes and their Remedies, in a Letter to Sir Francis Burdett* (London, 1826).

Swift, J. *The Truth of Some Maxims in State and Government Examined with Reference to Ireland* (London, 1765).

Sylas, S. (pseud.?). *A Letter to the People of Great Britain and Ireland, in which the Flagrant Falsehoods and Malignant Aspersions contained in a Letter from a Conservative Whig to Lord Melbourne, on the administration of Lord Mulgrave in Ireland, are analysed and refuted by Mr Sylvester Sylas* (London, n.d.).

[Symes, —.] *The Absentee; or, a Brief Examination into the Habits and Condition of the People of Ireland.* By an Officer of the Customs of Ireland (London, 1820).

Templar, A. *Six Weeks in Ireland* (London, 1862).

Tennant, C. *A Letter to the Right Honourable Sir George Murray on Systematic Colonization* (London, 1830).

[Thom, W.] *Plan for the Improvement of the Condition of the People of Ireland* (Dublin, 1824).

Thompson, H. S. *Ireland in 1839 and 1869* (London, 1870).

Thornton, W. T. *Over-population, and its Remedy* (London, 1846).

—— *A Plea for Peasant Proprietors, with the Outlines of a Plan for their Establishment in Ireland* (London, 1848).

Torrens, R. A Paper on the Means of Reducing the Poors Rates, and of Affording Effectual and Permanent Relief to the Labouring Classes. (London, 1817—*The Pamphleteer*, no. xx, September 1817, pp. 510–28).

—— *An Essay on the Production of Wealth* (London, 1821).

—— *Substance of a Speech Delivered by Colonel Torrens, in the House of Commons, 15 February 1827, on the Motion of Sir Robert Wilmot Horton, Bart., for the Re-appointment of a Select Committee on Emigration from the United Kingdom* (2nd ed. London, n.d.).

—— *The Colonisation of South Australia* (London, 1835).

—— *A Letter to the Right Honourable Lord John Russell, on the Ministerial Measure for Establishing Poor Laws in Ireland* (London, 1837).

—— *Emigration from Ireland to South Australia.* (London printed, 1839: 'Obtained Gratis from John Bernard, Esq., M.D., 47 Lower Mount Street, Dublin, Secretary to the Irish South Australian Association.')

—— *The Budget. No. V. A Letter to the Right Honourable Lord Eliot on Colonisation, Considered as a Means of Removing the Causes of Irish Misery; and of Preventing the Wages of Labour in England from being Permanently Forced Down, by Irish Immigration, to the Starvation Level* (London, 1842)).

BIBLIOGRAPHY

Torrens, R. *Systematic Colonisation. Ireland Saved, without Cost to the Imperial Treasury.* (2nd ed. to which is prefixed *An Introductory Letter to Earl Grey, on the Results of the Emigration Branch of the South Australian Experiment* (London, 1849)).

Trench, W. S. *Realities of Irish Life* (London, 1870).

Trenor, K. *A Letter to the Right Honourable Robert Peel, in Answer to a Letter on the Comparative Operation of the Corn Laws and Public Taxation as Causes of the Depression of Trade* (London, 1820).

—— *An Inquiry into the Political Economy of the Irish Peasantry, as Connected with the Commissariat Resources of Ireland* (London, 1822).

—— *A Letter to John Charles Herries, Esq., M.P., upon the Cause of Famine in the South and West of Ireland, and the Decline of the Irish Export Trade to the British Colonies and Foreign Countries, as Connected with the Commissariat Resources of Ireland* (Dublin, 1824).

Trevelyan, C. E. *The Irish Crisis* (London, 1848).

Trimmer, J. K. *A Brief Inquiry into the Present State of Agriculture in the Southern Part of Ireland* (London, 1809).

—— *Further Observations on the Present State of Agriculture, and Condition of the Lower Classes of the People, in the Southern Parts of Ireland* (London, 1812).

Tuckett, J. D. *A History of the Past and Present State of the Labouring Population* (2 vols. London, 1846).

Tuke, J. H. *A Visit to Connaught in the Autumn of 1847* (London, 1847).

Twiss, T. *On Certain Tests of a Thriving Population* (London, 1845).

Tylden, Sir J. *On Irish Poor Laws. Addressed to Lord Viscount Morpeth* (Sittingbourne, 1837).

Venedey, J. *Ireland and the Irish During the Repeal Year, 1843.* Translated by W. B. McCabe (Dublin, 1844).

[Wade, J.] *The Extraordinary Black-Book...a Complete View of the Expenditure, Patronage, Influence and Abuses of the Government, in Church, State, Law and Representation* (London, 1831).

—— *History of the Working Classes* (London, 1835).

Wakefield, E. *An Account of Ireland, Statistical and Political* (2 vols. London, 1812).

Wakefield, E. G. *A Letter from Sydney, the Principal Town of Australasia* (London, 1829; reprinted, with an introduction by R. C. Mills, 1929).

—— *England and America* (New York, 1834).

—— *A View of The Art of Colonization* (London, 1849).

Waller, [Sir] C. T. *A Plan for the Relief of the Poor in Ireland* (Bath, n.d.—1826 or 1827).

Walsh, [Sir] J. *Poor Laws in Ireland, Considered in their Probable Effects upon the Capital, the Prosperity, and the Progressive Improvement of that Country* (London, 1831).

Ward, H. G. *The First Step to a Poor Law for Ireland* (London, 1837).

Ward, J. *How to Reconstruct the Industrial Condition of Ireland* (London, 1845).

—— *Remedies for Ireland. A Letter to the Right Honourable Lord Monteagle, on the Fallacy of the Proposed Poor Law, Emigration, and Reclamation of Waste Lands, as Remedies: being a Postscript to 'How to Reconstruct the Industrial Resources of Ireland'* (London, 1847).

Wason, R. *Letter to the Right Honourable Lord John Russell, M.P. etc., Suggesting that the Mode Adopted for the Reclamation of Waste Land at Corwar, Should be Pursued in Ireland* (Edinburgh, 1847).

Wason, R. *A Letter to J. Bright, Esq., M.P. on the Remedies he Proposed for the Relief of Ireland: with a Suggestion for the Introduction of Capital into that Country.* (Ayr, 1850).

Watts, J. *The Facts and Fictions of Political Economists* (Manchester, 1842).

Weale, J. *Ensamples of Railway Making...submitted, with Practical Illustrations, to the Civil Engineer and the British and Irish public* (London, 1843).

Webster, W. B. *Ireland Considered as a Field for Investment or Residence* (London, 1852).

Wellwood, S. *A Letter to Feargus O'Connor, Esq., Against his Plan of Dividing the Land, and in Favour of the Association of Property, Skill and Labour* (London, 1842).

West, J. *Report of the Mansion-House Relief Committee, Appointed at a Public Meeting, Held on 25 September 1829, at the Royal Exchange, for the Relief of the Distressed Manufacturers of the City of Dublin and its Vicinity, the Right Honourable Jacob West, Lord Mayor, Chairman* (Dublin, 1830).

Wexford and Valentia Railway Company: *Evidence and Opinions on the Harbour of Valentia as to its Fitness for a Western Packet Station* (London, 1847).

Weyland, J. *The Principles of Population and Production* (London, 1816).

Wheatley, J. *A Letter to the Duke of Devonshire on the State of Ireland and the General Effects of Colonization* (Calcutta, 1824).

Whishaw, F. *The Railways of Great Britain and Ireland* (London, 1840).

White, G. P. *Letter to the Right Honourable Lord John Russell, on the Expediency of Promoting Railways in Ireland* (London, 1849).

—— *Three Suggestions for the Investment of Capital* (London, 1851).

Whitmore, W. W. *Letter to Lord John Russell on Railways* (London, 1847).

[Whyte, R.] *The Ocean Plague; or, a Voyage to Quebec in an Irish Emigrant Vessel.* By a Cabin Passenger (Boston, 1848).

[Wiggins, J.]. *Letter to the Absentee Landlords of the South of Ireland* (London, 1822).

—— *Hints to Irish Landlords, on the Best Means of Obtaining and Increasing their Rents* (London, 1824).

—— *The 'Monster' Misery of Ireland; a Practical Treatise on the Relation of Landlord and Tenant* (London, 1844).

[——] *Poor Laws, Beneficial to Landed Property in Ireland, Deduced from their Effects in England.* By a Land Agent, of Thirty Years Experience in Both Countries (London, 1833).

[Wilcocks, J. B.] *Emigration, its Necessity and Advantages* (2nd ed. enlarged, Exeter, 1841).

Williams, C. W. *Observations on an Important Feature in the State of Ireland and the Want of Employment of its Population* (London, 1831).

Williamson, R. *Letter to the Most Noble the Marquis of Downshire, on the Proposed Repeal of the Transit Duty on Foreign Linens* (Belfast, 1817).

[Wilson, J.] *Mordecai Mullion: Some Illustrations of Mr McCulloch's 'Principles of Political Economy'* (Edinburgh, 1826).

Woods, J. *Notes on Some of the Schools for the Labouring Classes in Ireland* (Lewes, 1841).

Woollett, G. *A Remedy against False Alarms of Famine and Real Scarcity* (London, 1847).

Young, G. F. *Free Trade Fallacies Refuted; in a Series of Letters to the Editor of the* Morning Herald (London, 1852).

III. SECONDARY SOURCES

Adams, W. F. *Ireland and Irish Emigration to the New World* (New Haven, 1932).

Arnold, Matthew. *Irish Essays and Others* (London, 1882).

Aschrott, P. F. *The English Poor Law System, Past and Present* (translated by H. Preston-Thomas: London, 1888).

Aspinall, A. *Politics and the Press, 1780–1850* (London, 1949).

Auchmuty, D. *Irish Education: A Historical Survey* (Dublin and London, 1937).

Baran, P. A. On the Political Economy of Backwardness. *Manchester School*, vol. xx, no. 1 (January 1952), pp. 66–84.

Bell, K. N. and Morrell, W. P. *Select Documents on British Colonial Policy, 1830–1860* (Oxford, 1928).

Bodelsen, C. A. *Studies in Mid-Victorian Imperialism* (Copenhagen, 1924).

Bowle, J. *Politics and Opinion in the Nineteenth Century* (London, 1954).

Bowley, M. *Nassau Senior and Classical Economics* (London, 1937).

Brebner, J. B. *Laissez-faire* and State Intervention in 19th century Britain—'The Tasks of Economic History'. *J. Economic History*, supplement, viii, 1948, pp. 59–73.

Brightfield, M. F. *John Wilson Croker* (Berkeley, California, 1940).

Broderick, J. *The Holy See and the Irish Movement for the Repeal of the Union with England* (Rome, 1951).

Burke, J. F. *Outlines of the Industrial History of Ireland* (Dublin, 1920).

Burn, W. L. Free Trade in Land: an Aspect of the Irish Question. *Trans. Royal Historical Society*, 4th series, vol. xxxi (1949), p. 61.

Carrington, C. E. *John Robert Godley of Canterbury* (London, 1950).

Carrothers, W. A. *Emigration from the British Isles, with Special Reference to the Development of the Overseas Dominions* (London, 1929).

Chaytor, D. G. *The Law and Practice Relating to the Variation of Tithe Rent Charge in Ireland* (Dublin, 1897).

Checkland, S. G. The Propagation of Ricardian Economics in England. *Economica*, n.s. vol. xvi (February 1949), pp. 40–52.

Clancy, J. J. The Castle System. No. 5 in *Essays and Speeches on the Irish Question* (London, 1886).

Connell, K. H. *The Population of Ireland, 1780–1845* (Oxford, 1950).

—— Land and Population in Ireland 1780–1845. *Economic History Rev.* 2nd series, vol. ii, no. 3 (1950), pp. 278–89.

—— The Colonization of Waste Land in Ireland, 1780–1845. *Economic History Rev.* 2nd series, vol. iii, no. 1 (1950), pp. 44–71.

Conroy, J. C. *History of Railways in Ireland* (London, 1928).

Corry, B. A. The Theory of the Economic Effects of Government Expenditure in English Classical Political Economy. *Economica*, n.s. vol. xxv, no. 97 (February 1958), pp. 34–48.

Cowan, H. I. *British Emigration to British North America, 1783–1837* (Toronto, 1928).

Craig, E. T. *Co-operative Farming: Irish Land and Labour Question, Illustrated in the History of Ralahine, and Co-operative Farming* (London and Manchester, 1893).

Cusack, M. F. *The Case of Ireland Stated: A Plea for My People and My Race* (Dublin, 1880).

Dardis, P. G. *The Occupation of Land in Ireland in the first half of the Nineteenth Century* (Dublin and London, 1920).

Daunt, W. J. O'Neill. *Personal Recollections of O'Connell* (2 vols. London, 1850).

BIBLIOGRAPHY

Daunt, W. J. O'Neill. *Essays on Ireland* (Dublin, 1886).
—— *Eighty-five years of Irish History, 1800–1885* (London, 1888).
Dicey, A. V. *Law and Public Opinion in England* (London, 1914).
Dillon, M. *The History and Development of Banking in Ireland from the Earliest Times to the Present Day* (London and Dublin, 1889).
Disraeli, B. *Lord George Bentinck: a Political Biography* (London, 1848).
Duffy, [Sir] C. G. *The League of North and South: an Episode in Irish History, 1850–1854* (London, 1886).
—— *Young Ireland: a Fragment of Irish History. 1840–1850* (London, 1880).
—— *Four Years of Irish History, 1845–1849. A sequel to* Young Ireland (London, 1883).
—— *Thomas Davis, The Memoirs of an Irish Patriot 1840–1846* (London, 1890).
—— *Conversations with Carlyle* (London, 1892).
Dunning, W. A. Irish Land Legislation Since 1845. *Political Science Quarterly*, vol. VII, nos. 1–3 (1892), article I: pp. 57–79; article II: pp. 500–21.
Dunraven, Lord. *The Finances of Ireland before the Union and After* (London, 1912).
Edwards, R. D. and Williams, T. D. *The Great Famine: Studies in Irish History, 1845–52* (Dublin, 1956).
Erickson, A. B. *The Public Career of Sir James Graham* (London, 1952).
Evans, A. L. *The Disestablishment of the Church of Ireland in 1869* (Lancaster, Pa., 1929).
Eversley, C. Shaw-Lefevre, Viscount. *Peel and O'Connell* (London, 1887).
—— *Gladstone and Ireland. The Irish Policy of Parliament from 1850–1894* (London, 1912).
Ewald, A. C. *The Life of Sir Joseph Napier, Bart., ex-Lord Chancellor of Ireland, from his Private Correspondence* (London, 1887).
Farrer, J. A. The Failure of Free Contract in Ireland. *Contemporary Rev.* (February 1881), pp. 25–30.
Ferenczi, I. *International Migrations* (2 vols. New York, 1929–31).
Fetter, F. W. The Authorship of Economic Articles in the *Edinburgh Review* 1802–47. *J. Political Economy*, vol. LXI (1953), pp. 232–259.
—— *The Irish Pound, 1797–1826. A Reprint of the Report of the Committee of 1804 of the British House of Commons on the Condition of the Irish Currency. With Selections from the Minutes of Evidence presented to the Committee and an Introduction* (London, 1955).
Finer, S. E. *Life and Times of Sir Edwin Chadwick* (London, 1952).
Fitzpatrick, W. J. *Life and Times of Rev. Dr Doyle* (Dublin, 1861).
—— *Memoirs of Richard Whately, Archbishop of Dublin. With a Glance at his Contemporaries and Times* (London, 1864).
Fox, R. W. *Marx, Engels, and Lenin on Ireland* (New York, 1940).
Fox-Bourne, H. R. *English Newspapers: Chapters in the History of Journalism* (2 vols. London, 1887).
Freeman, T. W. *Ireland; its Physical, Historical, Social and Economic Geography* (London, 1950).
—— *Pre-Famine Ireland; a Study in Historical Geography* (Manchester, 1957).
Froude, J. A. *The English in Ireland in the Eighteenth Century* (3 vols., London, 1872–4).
Fry, Sir E. *Memoir of James Hack Tuke* (London, 1899).
Gill, C. *The Rise of the Irish Linen Industry* (Oxford, 1925).
Glasgow, M. *The Scotch-Irish in Northern Ireland and the American Colonies* (New York, 1936).

BIBLIOGRAPHY

Glass, D. V. (ed.). *Introduction to Malthus* (London, 1953).

Goodrich, C. National Planning of Internal Improvements. *Political Science Quarterly*, vol. LXIII, no. 1 (March 1948), pp. 16–44.

Gower, L. C. B. *The Principles of Modern Company Law* (London, 1954).

Graham, W. *Tory Criticism in the Quarterly Review* (New York, 1921).

—— *English Literary Periodicals* (New York, 1930).

Green, E. R. R. *The Lagan Valley, 1800-50: a Local History of the Industrial Revolution* (London, 1949).

Grey, H. G. G., 3rd Earl. *Ireland; the Causes of its Present Condition, and the Measures Proposed for its Improvement* (London, 1888).

Halévy, E. *The Growth of Philosophic Radicalism* (translated by M. Morris, London, 1928).

—— *A History of the English People in the Nineteenth Century*, translated by E. I. Watkin (5 vols. London, 1949–51).

Hall, F. G. *The Bank of Ireland, 1783–1946* (Dublin and Oxford, 1949).

Hammond, J. L. *Gladstone and the Irish Nation* (London, 1938).

Handley, J. E. *The Irish in Scotland, 1798–1845* (Cork, 1945).

—— *The Irish in Modern Scotland* (Cork, 1947).

Hansen, M. L. *The Atlantic Migration, 1607–1860* (Cambridge, Mass., 1941).

Harlow, V. and Madden, F. *British Colonial Developments, 1774–1834: Select Documents* (Oxford, 1953).

Hartz, L. *Economic Policy and Democratic Thought: Pennsylvania, 1776–1860* (Cambridge, Mass., 1950).

Henderson, W. O. W. T. Mulvany: an Irish Pioneer in the Ruhr. *Great Britain and Industrial Europe, 1750–1870* (Liverpool, 1954), pp. 179–93.

Hertz, G. B. *The Manchester Politician 1750–1912* (London, 1912).

Hervé, E. *La Crise Irlandaise depuis la Fin du dix-huitième siècle jusqu'à nos jours* (Paris, 1885).

Hicks, J. R. *The Social Framework* (Oxford, 1942).

Hitchins, F. H. *The Colonial Land and Emigration Commission* (Philadelphia, 1931).

Hooker, E. R. *Readjustments of Agricultural Tenure in Ireland* (Chapel Hill, N.C., 1938).

Horne, H. O. *A History of Savings Banks* (London, 1947).

Hutt, W. H. *Economists and the Public* (London, 1936).

Inglis, B. *The Freedom of the Press in Ireland, 1784–1841* (London, 1954).

Jephson, H. L. Irish Absenteeism. *Nineteenth Century*, vol. VII (January 1880), pp. 871–83.

Joehr, W. A. and Singer, H. W. *The Role of the Economist as Official Adviser* (London, 1955).

Johnson, H. G. The Taxonomic Approach to Economic Policy. *Economic J.* vol. LXI, no. 244 (December 1951).

Johnson, S. C. *A History of Emigration from the United Kingdom to North America, 1763–1912* (London, 1913).

Jones, W. B. *The Life's Work in Ireland of a Landlord Who Tried to Do his Duty* (London, 1880).

Kennedy, B. A. *William Sharman Crawford, 1780–1861* (Unpublished D. Litt. Thesis, Queen's University, Belfast, 1953).

Kennedy, T. *A History of the Irish Protest against Over-Taxation, from 1853 to 1897* (Dublin, 1897).

Knorr, K. E. *History of British Colonial Theories, 1570–1850* (Toronto, 1944).

Large, D. The House of Lords and Ireland in the age of Peel, 1832–50. *Irish Historical Studies*, vol. IX, no. 36 (September 1955), pp. 367–99.

Leadam, I. S. *Coercive Measures in Ireland, 1830–1880* (London, 1881).

Lever, T. *Life and Times of Sir Robert Peel* (London, 1942).

Locker-Lampson, G. L. T. *A Consideration of the State of Ireland in the Nineteenth Century* (London, 1907).

Lucas, C. P. (ed.). *Lord Durham's Report on the Affairs of British North America* (Oxford, 1912).

Lyall, [Sir] A. *Life of Lord Dufferin* (London, 1906).

McCarthy, J. *Ireland's Cause in England's Parliament* (Boston, 1888).

McCullagh, W. T. *Memoirs of the Right Honourable Richard Lalor Sheil* (2 vols. London, 1855).

—— *Memoirs of . . . William, Second Viscount Melbourne* (2 vols. London, 1878).

MacDonagh, M. *Bishop Doyle, 'J.K.L.'; a Biographical and Historical Study* (London, 1896).

MacDonagh, O. The Irish Catholic Clergy and Emigration During the Great Famine. *Irish Historical Studies*, vol. V (1946–7), pp. 287–302.

—— The Regulation of the Emigrant Traffic from the United Kingdom, 1842–55. *Irish Historical Studies*, vol. IX (1954), pp. 162–89.

—— Emigration and the State, 1833–55: An Essay in Administrative History. *Trans. Royal Historical Society*, 5th series, vol. V (1955), pp. 133–60.

MacDonald, N. *Canada, 1763–1841—Immigration and Settlement* (London, 1939).

McDowell, R. B. *Public Opinion and Government Policy in Ireland, 1801–1846* (London, 1952).

McGrath, K. Writers in *The Nation*, 1842–45. *Irish Historical Studies*, vol. VI (1948–9), pp. 189–223.

MacGregor, D. H. *Economic Thought and Policy* (London, 1949).

Mackay, C. *Forty Years Recollections, 1830–70* (2 vols. London, 1877).

McKinley, E. W. *The Theory of Economic Development in the English Classical School* (Unpublished Ph.D. Thesis, University of California, 1954).

—— The Problem of 'Underdevelopment' in the English Classical School. *Quarterly J. Economics*, vol. LXIX, no. 2 (May 1955), pp. 235–52.

McLennan, J. F. *A Memoir of Thomas Drummond* (Edinburgh, 1867).

Magnus, [Sir] P. *Gladstone: A Biography* (London, 1954).

Mansergh, N. *Ireland in the Age of Reform and Revolution* (London, 1940).

Marshall, C. F. D. *A History of British Railways down to the year 1830* (London, 1938).

Mason, W. E. *The Classical Theory of Adjustment to Unilateral Capital Transfers* (Ph.D. Thesis, Princeton University, 1952; University Microfilms, Ann Arbor, Michigan: no. 5155).

—— Some Neglected Contributions to the Theory of International Transfers. *J. Political Economy*, vol. LXIII (1955), pp. 529–35.

—— The Stereotypes of Classical Transfer Theory. *J. Political Economy*, vol. LXIV (1956), pp. 492–506.

Meek, R. L. Physiocracy and Classicism in Britain. *Economic J.* vol. LXI, no. 241, (March 1951), pp. 26–47.

—— Physiocracy and the Early Theories of Under-Consumption. *Economica*, new series vol. XVIII, no. 71 (August 1951), pp. 229–69.

Mills, R. C. *The Colonization of Australia* (1829–42), (London, 1915).

Montgomery, W. E. *The History of Land Tenure in Ireland* (Cambridge, 1889).

BIBLIOGRAPHY

Monypenny, W. F. and Buckle, G. E. *The Life of Benjamin Disraeli, Earl of Beaconsfield* (6 vols. London, 1910–20).

Morgan, W. H. *Some Aspects of Thomas Carlyle's Reaction upon Political Economy* (Unpublished Dissertation for M.A., University of Chicago, 1915).

Morley, John, 1st Viscount. *Life of Richard Cobden* (2 vols. London, 1881).

—— *Life of William Ewart Gladstone* (3 vols. London, 1903).

Morrell, W. P. *British Colonial Policy in the Age of Peel and Russell* (Oxford, 1930).

Morris, W. O'C. *Land System of Ireland* (Dublin, 1888).

Myrdal, G. *The Political Element in the Development of Economic Theory*. Translated by P. Streeten (London, 1953).

Neff, E. *Carlyle and Mill: An Introduction to Victorian Thought* (New York, 1926).

Nesbitt, G. L. *Benthamite Reviewing: The First Twelve Years of the* Westminster Review *1824–36* (New York, 1934).

Nurkse, R. *Problems of Capital Formation in Underdeveloped Countries* (Oxford, 1953).

O'Brien, G. *An Economic History of Ireland from the Union to the Famine* (London, 1921).

—— *William Conner. Studies,* vol. XII (June 1923), pp. 279–89.

O'Brien, R. B. *The Irish Land Question and English Public Opinion* (Dublin and London, 1880).

—— *Parliamentary History of the Irish Land Question* (London, 1880).

—— *Fifty Years of Concessions to Ireland* (2 vols. London, 1883).

—— *Thomas Drummond, Under-Secretary in Ireland, 1835–40: Life and Letters* (London, 1889).

—— *Dublin Castle and the Irish People* (London, 1909).

—— *John Bright: A Monograph* (London, 1910).

O'Connor, [Sir] J. *A History of Ireland, 1798–1924* (2 vols. London, 1925).

O'Donovan, J. *Economic History of Live Stock in Ireland* (Cork, 1940).

O'Faolain, S. *King of the Beggars, a life of Daniel O'Connell* (London, 1938).

O'Mahony, C. *The Viceroys of Ireland* (London, 1912).

O'Neill, T. P. *The great Irish Famine, 1845–52. Irish Ecclesiastical Record,* vol. LXIX (November 1947), pp. 945–56.

—— *The Economic and Political Ideas of James Fintan Lalor. Irish Ecclesiastical Record,* vol. LXXIV (1950), pp. 398–409.

—— *Food problems in the Great Famine. J. Royal Society of Antiquaries of Ireland* vol. LXXXII (1952), pp. 99–108.

—— *The Irish Land Question 1830–50. Studies,* vol. XLIV (1955), pp. 325–36.

Opie, R. *A Neglected English Economist: George Poulett Scrope. Quarterly J. Economics,* vol. XLIV (1930), pp. 101–37.

O'Rourke, J. *History of the Great Irish Famine of 1847, with notices of earlier Irish famines* (Dublin, 1875).

Oser, J. *Must Men Starve? The Malthusian Controversy* (London, 1956).

Packe, M. *John Stuart Mill* (London, 1954).

Palmer, N. D. *The Irish Land League Crisis* (New Haven, 1940).

Penrose, E. F. *Malthus and the Underdeveloped Areas. Economic J.* vol. LXVII, no. 266 (June 1957), pp. 219–39.

Phillips, W. A. (ed.). *History of the Church of Ireland* (3 vols. London, 1933).

Polanyi, K. *Origins of Our Time, the Great Transformation* (London, 1945).

Political Economy Club. *Centenary Volume, with Proceedings, 1821–1920* (London, 1921).

Pomfret, J. E. *The Struggle for Land in Ireland, 1800–1932* (Princeton, 1930).

BIBLIOGRAPHY

Pressensé, F. de. *L'Irlande et l'Angleterre depuis l'acte d'union jusqu'à nos jours, 1800–88* (Paris, 1889).

Primm, J. N. *Economic Policy in the Development of a Western State—Missouri 1820–60* (Cambridge, Mass., 1954).

Ratzlaff, C. J. Economic Control in the Nineteenth Century, in *Planned Society, Yesterday, To-day and To-morrow*, edited by Findlay Mackenzie (New York, 1937).

Reynolds, J.A. *The Catholic Emancipation Crisis in Ireland 1823–29* (New Haven, 1954).

Richey, A. G. *The Irish Land Laws* (London, 1880).

Robbins, L. C. *The Theory of Economic Policy in English Classical Political Economy* (London, 1952).

—— *Robert Torrens and the Evolution of Classical Economics* (London, 1958).

Ryan, W. P. *Irish Labour Movement from the 'Twenties to our Own Day* (Dublin, 1919).

Samuelson, P. A. The Transfer Problem and Transport Costs, II: Analysis of the Effects of Trade Impediments. *Economic J.* vol. LXIV, no. 254 (June, 1954), pp. 264–89.

Schlatter, R. *Private Property; the History of an Idea* (New Brunswick, N. J., 1951).

Schumpeter, J. A. *History of Economic Analysis* (New York and London, 1954).

Seligman, E. R. A. On Some Neglected British Economists. *Economic J.* vol. XIII (1903), pp. 335–63, 511–35.

Shepperson, W. S. *British Emigration to North America* (Oxford, 1956).

Sherlock, P. T. *The Case of Ireland Stated Historically* (Chicago, 1880).

Shine, H. and Chadwick, H. *The Quarterly Review under Gifford. Identification of Contributors 1809–1824* (Chapel Hill, N.C., 1949).

Smith, K. *The Malthusian Controversy* (London, 1951).

Stettner, W. F. *Nineteenth-Century Public Debt Theories in Great Britain and Germany, and their Relevance for Modern Analysis* (Ph.D. Thesis, Harvard, 1943).

Sullivan, A. M. *New Ireland: Political Sketches and Personal Reminiscences of Thirty Years of Irish Public Life* (2nd ed. London, 1877).

Thorner, D. *Investment in Empire, British Railway and Steam Shipping Enterprise in India, 1825–49* (Philadelphia, 1950).

Thornton, R. H. *British Shipping* (2nd ed. Cambridge, 1959).

Times, The. *The History of* The Times (5 vols. London, 1935–52).

Tinbergen, J. *On the Theory of Economic Policy* (Amsterdam, 1952).

Trevelyan, G. M. *The Life of John Bright* (London, 1913).

Tyszynski, H. Economic Theory as a Guide to Policy. *Economic J.* vol. LXV, no. 258 (June, 1955), pp. 195–215.

Viner, J. *Studies in the Theory of International Trade* (New York and London, 1938).

Walker, E. R. *From Economic Theory to Policy* (Chicago, 1943).

Walpole, K. A. The Humanitarian Movement of the Early Nineteenth Century to Remedy Abuses on Emigrant Vessels to America. *Trans. Royal Historical Society*, 4th series vol. XIV (1931), pp. 197–284.

Walpole, S. *A History of England from the Conclusion of the Great War in 1815* (3 vols. London, 1878–80).

—— *Life of Lord John Russell* (2 vols. London, 1889).

Webb, S. and B. *English Poor Law History* (3 vols. London, 1927–9).

White, T. de V. *The Road of Excess* (Life of Isaac Butt), (Dublin, 1945).

Woodward, E. L. *The Age of Reform, 1815–1870* (Oxford, 1938).

INDEX

Aberdeen, 4th Earl of, 43
Absenteeism, 72–85 *passim*
    effects on demand for labour, 74–9; on
    balance of payments, 79–81, 141
    social consequences of, 82–4
Absentee taxes, 83–4, 163
Adair, A. Shafto, 229
Agrarian outrages, 6
    as means of enforcing tenants' rights, 23
    as affecting investment in land, 136,
    157
Agricultural and Commercial Bank, 150
Agricultural labourers, 8
    wages of, 9, 235, 237
    conversion of small tenants into, 240,
    242
Agriculture
    inadequate capitalisation of Irish, 156
    numbers dependent on, in Ireland, vi; in
    1841, 3
Allowance system
    of poor relief, 90, 91, 99, 101, 103
Althorp, Viscount, 106
Anglesey, 1st Marquess of, 9, 100, 101, 106,
    149, 164, 167
Anglesey, 7th Marquess of, xiv
Argyll, 8th Duke of, 64, 67
Australia, 221, 226, 227

Bank Act, of 1844, 151
Bank of Ireland, 149, 150, 151
Bankers (Ireland) Act, 1845, 151
Banking in Ireland, 149
    joint-stock banks, 150, 151
    contemporary criticism of, 151–2
Banking and Currency controversy, 150
Barry, M. J., 237
Beare, J., 142
Beaumont, Gustave de, 30
Belfast, industrial development in, 4, 9, 156,
    157
Belgium, small farms in, 30
Bentham, Jeremy, viii, 15, 16, 98, 215
Bentinck, Lord George, and Irish railways,
    196–7, 233
Bessborough, 4th Earl of, 9, 115, 116, 118,
    124, 126, 228
Bianconi, Charles, 156
Bicheno, J. E., 94
Black, John, 104, 106
Blacker, W., 29, 32, 232
Board of Works, Ireland, 57, 117, 148, 173–
    4, 176, 177–8, 183, 184, 185, 187, 201,
    246

Bogs, survey of Irish, 1809–14, 182
    drainage and reclamation of
    see Drainage of lands
Booth, Henry, 209
Bounties to aid industry, 145, 146
Bright, John, 33, 34, 39, 41, 57, 58, 61, 62,
    64, 67
Broadhurst, J., 79
Brunel, Isambard K., 197
Bryan, J. B., 21, 95
Buchanan, David, 205
Buller, Charles, 215, 224–5, 228
Burgoyne, J. F., 175, 184
Burn, W. L., xiii
Butler-Johnstone, H. A., 60
Butt, Isaac, 51, 52, 53, 66, 70, 81, 110, 118,
    130, 141, 175, 194, 229
Byles, Sir J. B., 141

Caird, Sir James, 177, 180, 189
Cairnes, J. E., 16, 54, 58, 70, 245
Campbell, Sir George, 55, 56, 69
Canada, 205, 206, 207, 208, 210, 213, 216,
    225, 227, 228, 229, 231
Canals, 159, 161, 165, 171, 183, 186
Canning, George, 214
Capital
    alleged drain of, from Ireland under Act
    of Union, 140
    and population, 86, 134, 212, 216–17, 239
    importation of, 137
    lack of, in Ireland, 134, 217
Cardwell, Edward, 45, 46, 64, 132, 133
'Cardwell's Act', 1860, 45, 50, 64
Carlyle, J., 32, 42, 44, 211, 231
Catholic emancipation, 106, 147, 148, 170,
    173, 220
Central Loan Fund Board, 154
Chadwick, Edwin, 104, 111, 112
Chalmers, Thomas, 93, 94
Chancery, Court of, 33, 37
Charitable Loan Funds, 153
    abuses of, 154
Church of Ireland
    disestablishment of: proposed, 57, 62,
    147; Act of 1869, 11, 201
    lands of, 61
    Temporalities Act, 1833, 148
Clancarty, 2nd Earl of, 179
Clanricarde, 1st Marquess of, 59, 60, 118, 229
Clarendon, 4th Earl of, 37, 38, 64, 126, 127,
    153 n., 232, 233, 234
Clarendon, 7th Earl of, xiv
Cloncurry, 2nd Baron, 100

293

Coats, A. W., xiii
Cobbett, William, 103, 214
Cobden, Richard, viii, 33, 189
Coercion Acts, 12
Cole, Arthur H., xiii
Colonial Office, 209, 217, 218, 220, 226, 234
Colonial Land and Emigration Commission, 219, 228 n.
Colonisation, 204, 207, 212, 230, 234
  Wakefield system of, 215–18, 222
Commissioners
  for the Relief of Trade and Manufactures, 150, 171
  of Woods and Forests, 180
Comte, Auguste, 57
Conacre system, 8
Connell, K. H., 187–8
Conner, William, 24, 29
Cork, city, 157, 192, 206
Corn Laws, 33, 196
  effects of repeal on Irish tenant-farmers, 48, 143, 189, 241
  and famine of 1846, 113
Cottier system
  abolition of: facilitated by railway construction, 190; and by emigration, 220, 229
  as obstacle to economic development, 87, 88
Cottiers, 7, 8, 23, 31, 37, 45, 104, 129, 137, 189, 209, 242
County cess, 168, 169, 170, 175
Crawford, W. Sharman, 27, 28, 29, 36, 38, 43, 46, 62, 101, 225
Currency, Irish, 149

Dargan, William, 156
Davis, Thomas, 140, 144
Deasy, Rickard, 45
'Deasy's Act', 1860, 46
'Decline of Irish Prosperity', Debate of 1862–4, 47–8, 236
Delane, J. T., 65
Devon, 11th Earl of, 165, 181, 233
Devon Commission on Occupation of Land in Ireland, 27–8, 61, 63, 64, 179 n., 180, 182, 225
Devonshire, 6th Duke of, 147
Dickson, S. A., 186
Disraeli, Benjamin, 61, 68
Donoughmore, 4th Earl of, 199
Downing, W. McCarthy, 66
Doyle, J. W. ('J. K. L.'), 94, 95, 97, 99, 101
Drainage of lands, 125, 166, 180, 182–9
Drogheda, Co. Louth, 191
Drummond, Thomas, 112, 148, 191, 193, 197, 221
Dublin, city, 9, 153, 157
Dublin Evening Mail, 193, 198 n.

Dublin University Magazine, 194
Dufferin and Ava, 1st Marquess of, 50, 52, 65, 237
Duffy, Charles Gavan, 41, 42
Dundalk, Co. Louth, 191
Durham, 1st Earl of, 233

Ebrington, Baron, 194
Economist, The, 54, 236
Edinburgh Review, The, 74, 75, 123, 130
Education
  as check to population, 204
  and economic development, 147
  National Board of, 148
Elgin, 8th Earl of, 228, 234
Eliot, Lord, afterwards 3rd Earl of St Germans, 195
Ellenborough, 1st Earl of, 172
Elliot, T. F., 219, 226, 234
Ellis, William, 210
Emigration, vi, vii, 3, 11, 23, 44, 51, 77, 92, 98, 107, 109, 124, 125, 129, 130, 131, 134, 138, 178, 203–38 passim, 240, 241, 243, 244, 248
  Select Committees on, 1826–7, 209, 211, 213, 214
Emigration Agents, 218, 223
Employment of the poor in Ireland, Select Committee of House of Commons on, 91, 145
Encyclopaedia Britannica, 205
Ennismore, Baron, 207
Exchequer Loan Commissioners, 195

Famine
  of 1817, 10, 89
  of 1822, 10, 113, 206
  of 1846–9, 3, 10, 28, 32, 34, 44, 45, 113–31 passim, 154, 175, 176, 184, 189, 195, 225, 244, 245, 247
  and emigration, 226–35
Farms
  consolidation of, 20–1, 23, 28, 45, 87–8, 98, 134 n., 145, 209, 210–11, 236, 241
  large and small, economic effects of, 19, 29, 145, 248
Fawcett, Henry, 55
Fenian Movement, 11, 49, 50, 51, 52
Fermoy, Co. Cork, 207
Fetter, F. W., xiii
Fisheries, Irish, 171, 174
Fitzgerald, Maurice, 173
Fitzgibbon, G., 63
Fitzwilliam, 3rd Earl of, 196 n., 229
Fixity of tenure, 26, 29, 42, 43, 49, 51, 52, 53, 56, 57, 58, 63, 65, 68, 248
  see also Tenant-right
Fortescue, Chichester, 50, 51, 52, 60, 61, 63, 64, 65, 66, 67, 201

Fortnightly Review, The, 54
Forty-shilling freeholders, 20
Foster, John, 170 n.
Foster, John Leslie, 73, 74, 178
Freehold Land Society, 41
Freeman's Journal, The, 52, 53, 68, 236
Free Trade in Land, 33–4, 37
  and occupying ownership, 39, 42, 58, 65
Free Trade, 244
  and food supplies, 1846–7, 117–18, 130
Fremantle, Sir Thomas, 184
French, Fitzstephen, 194, 195

Galt, William, 198, 200
Gardiner, Henry, 80
Gladstone, W. E., 2, 11, 53, 58, 61, 62, 63, 64, 65, 66, 67, 68, 69, 167, 198, 201, 243
Goderich, Viscount, afterwards Earl of Ripon, 214, 217, 218
Godley, J. R., 122, 123, 225, 229, 230, 231
'Gombeen men', 153
Goodrich, Carter, 161
Goold, G. J., 47
Gouger, Robert, 215
Goulburn, H., 150, 172, 173, 206, 207, 214
Graham, Sir James, 39, 113
Grand Jury System
  reform of, 148
  in relation to public works, 168–70, 175–6
Granville, 2nd Earl of, 64
Gray, Sir Alexander, 1
Gray, Sir John, 52, 53, 56, 66, 68
Green, E. R. R., xiii
Gregory, William, 125
Greville, F. S., 43
Grey, Sir George, 115
Grey, 2nd Earl, 9, 148, 180
Grey, 3rd Earl, *see* Howick
Griffith, Richard, 177, 179 n., 180, 187

Halévy, E., 40, 98
Hancock, John, 64, 176
Hancock, W. Neilson, 34, 46, 47, 48, 50, 63, 64, 65, 122, 131, 132, 133, 153, 188, 200
Hansard's Parliamentary Debates, 1, 14, 134, 139
Hatherley, Baron, 66
Hawes, Benjamin, 230
Henderson, W. O., 201
Heron, D. C., 47, 236
Hill, Sir Rowland, 199
Holland, 3rd Baron, 164
Hopkins, Thomas, 17
Howick, Viscount, afterwards 3rd Earl Grey, 217, 218, 227, 228, 229, 230, 231, 233, 234

Hudson, George, 196
Hume, David, 79
Hume, Joseph, viii, 146, 213, 214
Huskisson, William, 190, 214
Hutton, H. D., 57, 58, 62

Incumbered estates
  Act of 1848, 37
  Act of 1849, 11, 38–40, 156, 177, 241
  Court, 48, 130
  proposals for legislation, 1846–7, 35, 36, 121, 125, 126, 231
India, viii, 3
  land systems of, 55, 56
Industrial development in Ireland, 156–7
Industrial Revolution, 158
'Infant Industry' argument, 140
Inglis, H. D., 4, 30, 135 n., 157
Ingram, J. K., 131, 133
Ingram, Mr, 206
Inland navigation
  Directors of, 171
  see also Canals
Investment of capital in Ireland, 52, 135–6, 155–6
  by Irishmen outside Ireland, 136
  and level of wages, 212
  and volume of employment, 217, 241
Irishman, The, 49
Irish People, The, 49
Irish Poor Law Further Amendment Act, 1849, 129, 235
'Irish property must support Irish poverty', 102, 119, 246
Irish Reproductive Loan Fund, 153, 154
Irish Waste Land Improvement Society, 181, 182
Isles, K. S., xiii

Jevons, W. S., 2
Joplin, Thomas, 150, 229

Kane, Sir R., 141
Kennedy, J. P., 146 n.
Keogh, William, 41 n., 43
Keynes, J. M., Baron, 71
Kilkenny, city, 192
Killarney, Co. Kerry, 153
King, 1st Baron, 73

Labouchere, Henry, 116
'Labouchere Letter', the, 116
Labour-rates, 100, 101, 106
Labour-rate Act of 1846, 114
Laing, Samuel, 22, 30
Lalor, James Fintan, 24, 41
Land Act, Irish, 1870, 2, 11, 69, 71, 201
Land Improvement Acts, 126, 156, 176–7, 187, 202, 241

Land reform
and economic development, vi, 145, 158, 240, 248
and emigration, 237–8
English landlords' attitude to Irish, vii
and public works, 202
Land tenure
by contract, 40, 46, 55, 56, 59, 69, 71, 243
and investment in agriculture, 136
by status, 24, 55, 57, 66, 69, 71, 242
Landed Estates Court, 57
Landlords
absentee, 10, 56, 58; as proportion of all, 72
classical economists' view of Irish, 22, 240
financial weakness of many Irish, 32, 129
general character of Irish, vi
numbers of, in Ireland, 5 n.
Lansdowne, 3rd Marquess of, 109, 116, 191, 223
Larcom, Thomas A., 44, 48, 49, 177
Lavergne, Leonce de, 85
Lawson, J. A., 79
Leinster, 4th Duke of, 195, 197
Leslie, T. E. Cliffe, 236, 237
Lewis, G. C., 105, 108, 109, 112, 123, 220, 222
Lewis, J. Frankland, 108
Liberals, Irish, 50, 52
Lifford, 4th Viscount, 52
Limerick, 1st Earl of, 99
Limerick, city, 157, 191, 192
Limerick Declaration of 1868, 70
Limited partnerships, 155
Lincoln, Earl of, 35, 230
Linen Board, 145, 146
Linen industry
in Ireland, 145
Select Committee on, 1825, 146
Locke, John, 98
London Emigration Committee, 218, 219
London Tavern Committee of 1822, 113, 153
Longfield, M., 49, 50, 68, 77, 78, 80, 81, 151, 238
Lowe, Robert, 60, 64, 65, 67
Lynch, A. H., 174, 182, 183, 221

McCarthy, J. G., 181
McCulloch, J. R., 28, 74, 75, 78, 79, 80, 81, 82, 83, 84, 85, 97, 103, 104, 111, 134, 137, 138, 147, 159, 160, 203, 211
MacDonnell, Randal, 47
McDougall, Sir Duncan, 234
MacGregor, D. H., 1
M'Knight, James, 42
Madden, Samuel, 72
Magistracy, reform of Irish, 147, 148
Maguire, J. F., 45, 49, 50, 60, 62
Mahony, Pierce, 193
Malcolmson, William, 156

Mallet, J. L., 104
Malthus, T. R., vii, 21, 86, 87, 90, 92, 96, 98, 103, 136, 137, 138, 140, 144, 162, 163, 203, 204, 211, 215
Manning, Henry, Cardinal, 69
Manufactures
conditions for growth of, in Ireland, 137, 248
English competition in, 139
Young Irelanders' attitude to, and handicrafts, 144
Marnell, John, 41
Martineau, Harriet, 160, 202
Marx, Karl, 237, 242
Mason, W. E., xiii, 79, 80, 81
Meek, R. L., 79
Melbourne, 2nd Viscount, 106, 110 n.
Merivale, H., 18, 105, 236
Middle class in Ireland, v, 52, 135
Migration
of Irish labourers to England, vi, 8, 90, 102, 106, 209–10
suggestions for control of, 103, 210
Mill, James, 95 n., 103, 159, 205, 215, 216
Mill, John Stuart, viii, 13 n., 16, 30–1, 34, 36, 41, 42, 51, 53, 56, 57, 60, 61, 62, 70, 80, 81, 86, 104, 136, 158, 161, 166, 178, 180, 215, 230, 236, 245, 246
Mitchelstown, Co. Cork, 208
Monck, 4th Viscount, 66
Money market, crises: of 1847, 37, 122; of 1866, 199
Monsell, William, 199
Morgan, Sydney, Lady, 72
Moriarty, David, bishop of Kerry, 53
Morley, 1st Viscount, 64, 67
Morning Chronicle, The, 22, 30, 36, 39, 75, 80, 104, 215, 230
Morpeth, Viscount, 107, 148, 194, 195
Morris, W. O'C., 65
Morrison, Walter, 68
Mulvany, W. T., 184, 185
Murray, Robert, 229
Musgrave, Sir Richard, 101, 107
Myrdal, G., 245

Naas, Lord, afterwards 6th Earl of Mayo, 58, 61, 62, 200
Napier, Macvey, 194
Napier, Thomas, 43
Nation, The, 51, 140, 198 n., 236
National Association of Ireland (1864), 49
National Colonisation Society, 215, 216
National Debt Commissioners, 153
New South Wales, 217, 218
New Zealand, 225
Nicholls, Sir George, 19, 108, 109, 110, 112, 123, 131, 222, 224, 229
Nimmo, Alexander, 172

North, Lord, 84
North British Review, The, 118
Northern Whig, The, 193
Nurkse, R., 137 n.

O'Beirne, J. L., 60
O'Brien, George, 188 n.
O'Brien, Richard B., dean of Limerick, 53, 70
O'Brien, R. Barry, 40
O'Brien, William Smith, 101, 106, 107, 196, 224, 225
O'Connell, Daniel, 4, 26, 100, 102, 164, 181, 247
O'Connor, Sir James, 44
O'Donoghue, The, 50
O'Hagan, Thomas, 53, 68
O'Loan, John, 184 n.
O'Loghlen, Sir Colman, 59, 60
O'Neill, T. P., xiii
Ordnance Survey of Ireland, 170
Outdoor relief, 111, 120, 123, 124, 125, 126, 127, 131, 132, 133
Owen, Robert, 25

Paley, William, 98
Palmer, Sir Roundell, 69
Palmerston, Viscount, 49
Parnell, Sir Henry, 73, 74
Passenger Acts, 218, 231
Peasant proprietorship, 30, 53, 57, 63, 67, 70, 144, 230, 248
Peel, Sir Robert, 2nd Baronet, 27, 28, 36, 113, 114, 117, 139, 146, 149, 151, 165, 167, 173, 178, 180, 184, 194, 196, 206, 207, 209, 214, 215, 226, 227, 230, 231
and the 'Plantation Scheme', 38, 181
Peel, Sir Robert, 3rd Baronet, 50, 133
Penal Laws, 135
Pettman, W. R. A., 77, 78, 163-4
Petty, Sir William, 72, 169
Pichot, Amédée, 25
Pim, Jonathan, 33, 34, 52, 60
Political Economy Club, 92
Poor Law Amendment Act (English), 1834, 104, 107, 109, 122, 190, 224
Poor Law Commission
English, 108, 122
Irish, 127, 131, 132, 133
Poor Law Extension Act (Ireland), 1847, 125, 129, 234
Poor Laws, v, vi, 86-133 passim
as correlative of farm consolidation, 21, 23
and emigration, 210, 220, 223
proposed for Ireland, 12, 244, 246
and public works, 173, 177
Scotch, 124
Poor-rates, 10, 91, 119
as absentee tax, 83

effect on landowners, 1849, 130
responsibility for, in Ireland, vi, 127
use to assist emigration, 226, 234-5
Poor Relief Act (Ireland), 1838, 111, 129, 131, 192, 220
Population
excess, and Irish poverty, vii, 86
growth in Ireland before 1846, 3
Malthusian theory of, 93, 95, 134, 203
Sadler's 'law' of, 96
Porter, G. R., 153 n.
Post Office, vii
Post Office Savings Bank, 153
Potato-truck system, 7, 10, 88, 135
Presbyterians, 157, 232
Prior, Thomas, 72
Private enterprise, vii, 134-58 passim, 243
versus public in railway building, 190-5 passim
Property, private
Benthamite attitude to, 245-6
Irish tenants' view of, in land, 24-5
justification of, 15-16
and rights of poor, 97-8
Protection
to Irish agriculture, 142-3
and landlord interest, 144
as means of stimulating employment in Ireland, 139, 141, 145, 156
and nationalism, 140
and redistribution of income, 142
Provincial Bank of Ireland, 150, 229
Prussia
land-system of, 30, 55
Stein-Hardenberg reforms in, 57
Public debt and public works, 163-4
Public works, 12, 98, 105, 107, 112, 113, 114, 121, 130, 148, 159-202 passim, 206, 213, 220, 225, 240, 243, 244
Public Works Loans Commissioners, 199
Pusey, Philip, 37

Quakers and land reform in Ireland, 33
'Quarter-Acre Clause', 10 n., 35, 125, 129, 133
Quarterly Review, The, 83
Quebec, 207, 228
Quebec-Halifax railway, 233

Railways, vi, 12, 36, 156, 161, 165, 177, 183, 186, 189-201 passim, 232
as famine relief works, 113, 195-7
financial aid to Irish, 195, 198, 199
State purchase of, 198-201
Ralahine, Co. Clare
Owenite community at, 25
Rate-in-aid, 1849, 128
Raumer, Friedrich von, 30, 57
Redington, Thomas, 115, 232

Religion, and economic development, 157
Rent, Ricardian theory of, 15–17
  and Irish cottier system, 18, 54
Rents, 9
  by valuation, 24, 31, 42, 52, 54, 56, 58, 63
  compulsory settlement of, 66, 69
Repeal Movement, 26, 27, 70, 140, 237, 247
Revans, John, 23
Ricardo, D., 2, 15, 18, 19, 21, 22, 28, 54, 86, 87, 91, 134, 136, 137, 144, 159, 166, 203, 207
Rice, Stephen Spring, 227, 229
Rice, T. Spring (later Lord Monteagle), 83, 98, 99, 100, 103, 105, 109, 113, 115, 116, 123, 169, 173, 178, 180, 193, 220, 227, 230, 232, 233, 234
Rintoul, R. S., 230
Roads, 159, 161, 165, 167, 174, 177
Robbins, Lionel, Baron, 1
Robinson, Daniel, 181
Robinson, Sir John Beverley, 206, 208 n.
Robinson, Peter, 206, 207, 208
Rockingham, 2nd Marquess of, 84
Rogers, Jasper W., 121
Rogers, J. E. Thorold, 56
Roman Catholics, 52, 135, 157
Roman Catholic clergy, endowment of, 232
Rooke, J., 142–3, 161
Rosse, 3rd Earl of, 185
Routh, Sir Randolph, 118
Royal Mint, vii
Russia, viii
Russell, Lord John, 34, 35, 37, 38, 39, 40, 41, 107, 108, 109, 112, 115, 117, 118, 124, 125, 128, 131, 153, 167, 176, 178, 180, 192, 194, 195, 196, 197, 200, 219, 222, 223, 224, 225, 228, 230, 232, 233, 234

Sadleir, John, 41, 43
Sadler, M. T., 95–6, 97, 98, 106, 214
Samuelson, P. A., 81
Saurin, J., 171
Savage, Marmion W., 194
Savings banks, 152–3, 204
Say, J.-B., 87 n., 160
Scotland, 116, 131
  public works in, 172
Scrope, G. Poulett, 22, 27, 30, 36, 42, 76, 93, 96, 98, 101, 107, 120, 121, 122, 130, 166, 178, 179, 202, 216, 223, 232
Security
  interpretation of the term by classical economists, 147, 242
  of property as condition for investment, 136, 147, 157–8
Seebohm, F., 29, 56
Seligman, E. R. A., 142
Senior, Edward, 156

Senior, N. W., 21, 23, 31–2, 76, 77, 82, 92, 93, 94, 98, 102, 108, 121, 122, 123, 126, 129, 130, 136, 141, 147, 148, 155, 156, 161, 220, 222, 230
Shannon navigation, 175, 183, 186, 201
Shee, William, 43
Sidmouth, Viscount, 84
Sinclair, Sir James, 247
Sismondi, J. C. L. Simonde de, 30, 163
Sleeman, Sir W., 162–3
Sligo, Co. Sligo, 191
Smith, Adam, 60, 159, 160
Smyth, G. L., 193
Somerville, Sir William, 38, 42, 177
South Australia, 218, 221
South Australian Colonisation Commissioners, 219
Specie movements, 73, 79
Spectator, The, 36, 67, 230
Sraffa, P., 207 n.
Stanley, E. G., afterwards 14th Earl of Derby, 28, 43, 59, 148, 173, 175, 224, 225
Statistical and Social Inquiry Society of Ireland, 47
Stephen, James, 216 n., 219
Stephenson, George, 196, 197
Stourton, Baron, 77, 79
Stuart, Villiers, 105
Sub-letting, 5, 6, 211
  Act, 1826, 6, 20, 209, 211, 243
Sullivan, A. M., 42
Sullivan, Sir Edward, 63, 64
Swift, Jonathan, 72
Switzerland, small farms in, 30

Tariffs
  under Act of Union, 136, 138
  between Britain and Ireland, 141
  removal of, 140
Taxation of Ireland, 128, 148 n.
Tenant compensation
  for disturbance, 38, 63–7, 68
  for improvements, 26, 33, 42, 45, 49
Tenant-compensation Bills
  W. S. Crawford's, **1835–36**, 27; **1843**, 27, 28
  Lord Stanley's, **1845**, 28, 225
  Lord Lincoln's, **1846**, 35
  Ministerial controversy on, 1847, 37
  Somerville's, **1848**, 38; **1850**, 40, 42
  Tenant League Bill, **1852**, 43
  Napier's Bill, **1852**, 43, 65
  Cardwell's Bill, **1860**, 45
  Irish Liberals Bill, **1866**, 50
  Chichester Fortescue's Bill, **1866**, 50, 52, 63
  Lord Naas's Bill, **1867**, 58–9
  Lord Naas's proposed Bill, **1868**, 61, 62
  Jonathan Pim's Bill, **1868**, 52, 60

INDEX

Tenant League (1852), 42, 43
  split in, 43–4
  Irish (1869), 53
Tenant-right, 26, 29, 34, 35, 40, 45, 49, 54,
  66, 67
  see also Ulster
Tenant-right, 'parliamentary', 68
Tennant, Charles, 216
Terms of trade, and absentee remittances,
  80, 81
Thornton, W. T., 4, 30–1, 34, 41, 166, 178,
  180, 245
Times, The, 44, 45, 49, 65, 68, 200, 236, 237
Tithes, 9, 22, 147, 192
Tooke, T., 104
Torrens, R., 18, 19, 21, 29, 54, 77, 83, 93, 98,
  104, 111, 138, 139, 204, 209, 215, 216,
  217, 218, 219, 221, 223, 226, 228, 241
Tralee, Co. Kerry, 153
Treasury, The, 114, 116, 119, 127, 154, 178,
  180, 185, 186, 195, 200
Trenor, K., 143
Trevelyan, C. E., 115, 116, 126, 129, 177, 178,
  186
Trower, H., 18, 136
Twisleton, E. T. B., 123

Ulster, 3, 9, 42, 128, 146, 232
  comparative prosperity of, 4
  industrial development in, 157–8
  tenant-right of, 5, 6–7, 35, 38, 42, 46, 63,
  64, 65, 66, 67
Under-consumption, theories of, 162
Unemployment amongst Irish agricultural
  labourers, 88
Unilateral transfers
  classical doctrine of, 73, 79
  demand shifts and, 80, 81
Union, Act of, 1800, 2, 70, 72, 84, 89, 103,
  210, 239, 240, 246, 247
United States of America, 114, 222 n.
  Congress of, 160
  internal improvements in, 161
Unproductive consumption, 78

Valuation of lands, 170, 175

Van Diemen's Land, 218
Vesey-Fitzgerald, W., 170
Vignoles, Charles, 194
Villiers, Edward, 219
Viner, Jacob, xiii, 79

Wages-fund doctrine, 13, 76, 87, 102
Wakefield, Edward, 17
Wakefield, Edward Gibbon, 215, 216, 217,
  218, 219, 230, 235
Walsh, Sir John, 101, 104
Ward, H. G., 219, 223
Waste lands
  Bill for State reclamation of, 1847, 36,
  125, 126, 180, 197
  experimental reclamation of Crown lands
  in Co. Cork, 180, 189
  extent of land reclaimed, 188
  reclamation, 120, 164, 178–82, 213, 225,
  248
  settlement on, 30–1
Waterford, 191
Wellington, 1st Duke of, 111, 172, 173, 179,
  180, 182, 214, 226
Westminster Review, The, 82
Weyland, John, 203
Whately, Richard, archbishop of Dublin,
  107, 108, 109, 110, 161, 205, 213, 221,
  230
Wheatley, John, 210
Whitworth, Viscount, 84
Wilberforce, William, 116
Williams, C. W., 165
Wilmot Horton, Sir R. J., 17, 206, 207, 208,
  209, 211, 213, 214, 215, 218, 222, 234
Wood, Charles, 36, 37, 39, 115, 116, 126,
  153 n., 166, 196, 197, 233, 234
Wood, Matthew, 155
Woodward, R., bishop of Cloyne, 89, 98
Workhouse system, 92, 107, 108, 109, 112,
  125
  enforcement of in Ireland, 131–2
Workhouses, numbers in Irish, 1848, 126,
  127

Young Ireland, 140, 143, 237